T0202834

Communications
in Computer and Information Science 1578

More information about this series at https://link.springer.com/bookseries/7899

Kazuhiko Sumi · In Seop Na ·
Naoshi Kaneko (Eds.)

Frontiers of Computer Vision

28th International Workshop, IW-FCV 2022
Hiroshima, Japan, February 21–22, 2022
Revised Selected Papers

 Springer

Editors
Kazuhiko Sumi 🆔
Aoyama Gakuin University
Kanagawa, Japan

In Seop Na 🆔
Chosun University
Gwangju, Korea (Republic of)

Naoshi Kaneko 🆔
Aoyama Gakuin University
Kanagawa, Japan

ISSN 1865-0929   ISSN 1865-0937 (electronic)
Communications in Computer and Information Science
ISBN 978-3-031-06380-0   ISBN 978-3-031-06381-7 (eBook)
https://doi.org/10.1007/978-3-031-06381-7

This Springer imprint is published by the registered company Springer Nature Switzerland AG
The registered company address is: Gewerbestrasse 11, 6330 Cham, Switzerland

Preface

It is our great pleasure to present the proceedings of the International Workshop on Frontiers of Computer Vision (IW-FCV 2022), held online during February 21–22, 2022.

IW-FCV started as the Japan-Korea Joint Workshop on Computer Vision (FCV 1995), held for the first time in Daejon, South Korea. The workshop alternated between South Korea and Japan, annually, and it was hosted by Japan in 2022. Although the workshop is hosted by a different country each year, the basic policy has been decided by the Steering Committee in order to ensure continuous operation. This year, we first planned to accommodate the workshop at Hiroshima University. However, due to continuing threat of COVID-19 infection, the workshop unfortunately had to be held online. Despite these difficult circumstances, we received 63 submissions from authors in 11 countries. Each paper was reviewed by three Program Committee members in a single-blind manner. Following the workshop presentations, 24 high-quality full papers were selected for publication in these post-workshop proceedings. The acceptance ratio was about 38.1%.

We would like to thank each member of the committee for their great efforts in planning and operating this workshop. We also thank the General Chairs, the Secretaries, and the Finance Chair for their work in organizing this workshop. We thank the Local Arrangement Chairs for online workshop management through the use of Zoom and Slack. We thank the Program Committee, the Secretary, and the Publication Chair for their excellent programs and booklets. We thank the following sponsors for their support: the Symposium on Sensing via Image Information (SSII), the Technical Committee on Industrial Application of Image Processing (IAIP) of the Japan Society for Precision Engineering (JSPE), Hiroshima University, and the Higashihiroshima City Academic Promotion Subsidy. Finally, we thank the continuous support of the Institute of Electrical Engineers of Japan as organizers.

March 2022

Kazuhiko Sumi
In Seop Na
Naoshi Kaneko

Organization

General Chairs

Takio Kurita   Hiroshima University, Japan
Soon Ki Jung   Kyungpook National University, South Korea
Akinori Hidaka (Secretary)   Tokyo Denki University, Japan
Muthu Subash Kavitha (Secretary) Nagasaki University, Japan

Program Chairs

Kazuhiko Sumi   Aoyama Gakuin University, Japan
In Seop Na   Chosun University, South Korea
Naoshi Kaneko (Secretary) Aoyama Gakuin University, Japan

Local Arrangement Chairs

Junichi Miyao   Hiroshima University, Japan
Hiroaki Aizawa   Hiroshima University, Japan

Publication Chair

Junichiro Hayashi   Kagawa University, Japan

Financial Chair

Hiroyuki Ukida   Tokushima University, Japan

Web Chair

Takayuki Fujiwara   Hokkaido Information University, Japan

Steering Committee

Yoshimitsu Aoki   Keio University, Japan
Hiroyasu Koshimizu   Chukyo University and YYC Soultion, Japan
Takio Kurita   Hiroshima University, Japan
Chikahito Nakajima   CRIEPI, Japan
Makoto Niwakawa   Meidensha, Japan
Rin-ichiro Taniguchi Kyushu University, Japan

Kazuhiko Yamamoto	Gifu University, Japan
Jun-ichiro Hayashi	Kagawa University, Japan
Kazuhiko Sumi	Aoyama Gakuin University, Japan
Kanghyun Jo	University of Ulsan, South Korea
Soon Ki Jung	Kyungpook National University, South Korea
Chilwoo Lee	Chonnam National University, South Korea
Weon Geun Oh	ETRI, South Korea
Jong-Il Park	Hanyang University, South Korea
In Seop Na	Chosun University, South Korea
Hieyong Jeong	Chonnam National University, South Korea

Program Committee

Hiroaki Aizawa	Hiroshima University, Japan
Shuichi Akizuki	Chukyo University, Japan
Kaushik Deb	Chittagong University of Engineering & Technology, Bangladesh
Takayuki Fujiwara	Hokkaido Information University, Japan
Hironobu Fujiyoshi	Chubu University, Japan
Hitoshi Habe	Kinki University, Japan
Jun-ichiro Hayashi	Kagawa University, Japan
Akinori Hidaka	Tokyo Denki University, Japan
Van-Dung Hoang	Ho Chi Minh City University of Technology and Education, Vietnam
Maiya Hori	Kyushu University, Japan
Md Zahidul Islam	Islamic University, Bangladesh
Masakazu Iwamura	Osaka Prefecture University, Japan
Soon Ki Jung	Kyungpook National University, South Korea
Naoshi Kaneko	Aoyama Gakuin University, Japan
Yasutomo Kawanishi	Nagoya University, Japan
Jaeil Kim	Kyungpook National University, South Korea
Soo-Hyung Kim	Chonnam National University, South Korea
Wonjun Kim	Konkuk University, South Korea
Go Koutaki	Kumamoto University, Japan
Yoshinori Kuno	Saitama University, Japan
Takio Kurita	Hiroshima University, Japan
My-Ha Le	Ho Chi Minh City University of Technical Education, Vietnam
Chul Lee	Dongguk University, South Korea
Jae-Ho Lee	ETRI, South Korea
Tsubasa Minematsu	Kyushu University, Japan
Junichi Miyao	Hiroshima University, Japan
Jonathan Mojoo	Hiroshima University, Japan

Muthu Subash Kavitha	Nagasaki University, Japan
Masashi Nishiyama	Tottori University, Japan
Hidehiro Ohki	Oita University, Japan
Wataru Ohyama	Saitama Institute of Technology, Japan
Takahiro Okabe	Kyushu Institute of Technology, Japan
Kaushik Roy	West Bengal State University, India
Hideo Saito	Keio University, Japan
Atsushi Shimada	Kyushu University, Japan
Kazuhiko Sumi	Aoyama Gakuin University, Japan
Toru Tamaki	Nagoya Institute of Technology, Japan
Hiroshi Tanaka	Fujitsu Limited, Japan
Kenji Terada	Tokushima University, Japan
Kengo Terasawa	Future University Hakodate, Japan
Diego Thomas	Kyushu University, Japan
Hiroyuki Ukida	Tokushima University, Japan
Wahyono	University of Ulsan, South Korea
Kwanghee Won	South Dakota State University, USA
Takayoshi Yamashita	Chubu University, Japan
Keiji Yanai	University of Electro-Communications, Japan

Co-sponsors

Symposium on Sensing via Image Information (SSII)
Technical Committee on Industrial Application of Image Processing (IAIP), Japan
Society for Precision Engineering (JSPE)
Hiroshima University
Higashihiroshima City

Contents

Camera, 3D, and Imaging

6D Pose Estimation of Transparent Objects Using Synthetic Data

Munkhtulga Byambaa[1,2](✉) [ID], Gou Koutaki[1] [ID], and Lodoiravsal Choimaa[2] [ID]

[1] Department of Computer Science and Electrical Engineering,
Kumamoto University, Kumamoto 860-8555, Japan
{munkhtulga,koutaki}@navi.cs.kumamoto-u.ac.jp
[2] Machine Intelligence Laboratory, National University of Mongolia,
Ulaanbaatar 14201, Mongolia
lodoiravsal@num.edu.mn

Abstract. Transparent objects are one of the most common objects in everyday life. The poses of these objects must be estimated to pick and manipulate such objects. However, recognizing and estimating the poses of transparent objects is still a challenging task in robot vision, even after the emergence of 3D sensors. It is difficult to detect transparent objects because of the absorption and refraction of light, and the appearance of transparent objects can vary in different backgrounds. In this work, we propose a simple yet effective method for transparent object pose estimation, in which we address the problem using a synthetic dataset to train a deep neural network and estimate the pose of known transparent objects. After creating a synthetic dataset for transparent objects, we used a one-shot deep neural network to estimate the 6D pose of a known object. To the best of our knowledge, this is the first time synthetic data have been used for transparent object pose estimation. We conducted experiments on 3D printed transparent objects in a real environment as well as in a simulation environment. The results show that the proposed method can successfully estimate the pose of a transparent object even though it is only trained using synthetic data.

Keywords: Pose estimation · Transparent object · Synthetic data

1 Introduction

With the rapid development of automation, numerous fields use robots for hard and repetitive tasks, which range from service robots in home environments to industrial robots in assembly lines. In particular, bin and shelf picking are gaining attention for their possible applications. Recognition and pose estimation are needed for pick-and-place robots. Recently, numerous studies and datasets have focused on 6D pose estimation. Some methods use traditional feature point matching between 3D models and images [1–3]. Other methods that use deep neural networks have also been applied [4–6]. However, many of them did not consider transparent objects.

K. Sumi et al. (Eds.): IW-FCV 2022, CCIS 1578, pp. 3–17, 2022.
https://doi.org/10.1007/978-3-031-06381-7_1

Transparent objects are one of the most common objects in everyday life at home or in the industry. However, recognizing and estimating the pose of transparent objects is still a challenging task in robot vision, even after the emergence of 3D sensors. It is difficult to detect transparent objects because the appearance of transparent objects can vary under different backgrounds. We can use modern 3D sensors (Kinect, Asus Xtion, or RealSense), which provide RGB and depth information simultaneously; however, they cannot capture reliable depth data of the surfaces of transparent objects. Most 3D sensors rely on a clearly detectable pattern of light reflected by the object's surface. Consequently, these sensors do not capture a good depth map of transparent, refractive, and specular surfaces.

Synthetic data can be very useful in addressing certain problems in 6D pose estimation. In 3D object detection and pose estimation, a dataset is crucial, and it is difficult to label real images manually. In contrast to 2D object detection, in which bounding boxes are relatively easy to annotate, 3D object detection requires labeled data that are nearly impossible to manually generate. Acquiring ground-truth data is time-consuming and error-prone. The time-consuming nature of the task makes it difficult to generate training data with sufficient variation. Thus, we cannot generate large datasets required for training deep neural networks. As an alternative, synthetic data can be used for training deep neural networks because unlimited amount of annotated data are generated. Specifically, we use a combination of domain randomized (DR) data and photorealistic data to take advantage of the strengths of both [6]. Thus, we can eliminate the problem of the reality gap, which occurs when networks trained with synthetic data underperform when exposed to real data.

Munkhtulga et al. [25] proposed a method to use a synthetic dataset for transparent object pose estimation. After creating a dataset, a deep neural network was trained. The results have shown that synthetic data can be alternative in transparent object pose estimation. However, the experiments were only performed in simulation.

The main contributions of this work are:

- We proposed method for 6D pose estimation of transparent objects using synthetic data to replace unreliable depth images captured by 3D sensors. To our knowledge, this is the first time synthetic data have been used for transparent object 6D pose estimation.
- We experimentally validated the performance of the method for real-world applications by implementing the method for detection of a 3D printed transparent object.

The remainder of this paper is organized as follows. Section 2 provides a review of previous works on 6D object pose estimation for transparent objects and the usage of synthetic data for training deep neural networks. In Sect. 3, a detailed description of the proposed method is provided, explaining the network and synthetic datasets. Section 4 presents the results of our method on synthetic data in simulations and real transparent objects, providing settings and details. Section 5 summarizes the theories and algorithms developed in this study, followed by a brief discussion of potential future work.

2   Related Works

2.1   Transparent Object Recognition and Pose Estimation

In [8], RGB-D images and IR images were used to localize and detect transparent objects. In the detection task, RealSense was employed to retrieve the transparent candidates from the depth image, and the corresponding candidates in the RGB and IR images were then separately extracted. They then used SIFT features to recognize the transparent features from the candidates. In the location process, they obtained a new group of RGB images and IR images by adjusting the camera orientation to make its optical axis perpendicular to the normal direction of the plane on which the object is placed. The object contours in the RGB and IR images were then extracted. The three-dimensional object was finally reconstructed using stereo matching of the two contours, and the current pose information of the object was calculated.

Three-dimensional point clouds have been successfully used for object recognition and pose estimation. However, modern 3D sensors (structured light, ToF, stereo cameras, or laser scanners) cannot reliably estimate the depth and produce point clouds for transparent and specular objects; therefore, these algorithms cannot be applied. To solve these problems, [21] divided the problem into segmentation, pose estimation, and recognition tasks. Then, unknown transparent objects were segmented from a single image of the Kinect sensor by exploiting its failures on specular surfaces. Next, 3D models of objects created at the training stage were fitted to the extracted edges. Finally, a cost function value was used to decide the instance of the object and determine its 6DOF pose relative to the robot.

In [23], the authors proposed a deep learning approach for accurately estimating the 3D geometry of transparent objects from a single RGB-D image for robotic manipulation. Given a single RGB-D image of transparent objects, ClearGrasp uses deep convolutional networks to infer surface normals, masks of transparent surfaces, and occlusion boundaries. It then uses these outputs to refine the initial depth estimates for all transparent surfaces in the scene. They also provided large-scale synthetic datasets and real-world test benchmarks with 286 RGBD images of transparent objects and their ground truth geometries.

Liu et al. [24] addressed two problems: first, they established an easy method for capturing and labeling 3D keypoints on desktop objects with an RGB camera; second, they developed a deep neural network called KeyPose that learns to accurately predict object poses using 3D keypoints from stereo input and works even for transparent objects. To evaluate the performance of their method, they created a dataset of 15 clear objects in five classes, with 48K 3D-keypoint-labeled images.

2.2   Synthetic Data for Training

Given the significant need for massive amounts of annotated training data, recently, the research trend has shifted to providing synthetic datasets for training [9,12,13]. Most of these datasets are photorealistic; thus, creating a dataset requires significant 3D modeling skills. To solve this challenge, domain randomization [14,15] was proposed as a reasonable alternative that forces the network to learn to focus on essential features of the data by randomizing the training input in non-realistic ways. While domain randomization has shown promising results for several tasks, it is yet to produce state-of-the-art results compared with real-world data. In [14,16], for example, the authors concluded that fine-tuning using real data was necessary for domain randomization to compete with real data. Tremblay et al. [6] proved that domain randomization alone is not sufficient for the network to fully understand a scene, given its non-realism and lack of context. Thus, their approach of using photorealistic data to complement domain randomization is an effective solution for this problem.

Hinterstoißer et al. [20] used synthetic data generated by adding Gaussian noise to the object of interest and Gaussian blurring of the object edges before composing a background image. The resulting synthetic data were used to train the later layers of a neural network while freezing the early layers pretrained on real data (e.g., ImageNet).

In [18], photorealistic synthetic data were used to train a car detector that was tested on the KITTI dataset. As an alternative to high-fidelity synthetic images, domain randomization was introduced by [14], who proposed to close the reality gap by generating synthetic data with sufficient variation so that the network views real-world data as just another variation. Using DR, they trained a neural network to estimate the 3D world position of various shape-based objects with respect to a robotic arm fixed to a table. This introduction of DR was inspired by the earlier work of [15], who trained a quadcopter to fly indoors using only synthetic images. The Flying Chairs [9] and FlyingThings3D [19] datasets for optical flow and scene flow algorithms can be considered as different versions of domain randomization.

2.3 Object 6D Pose Estimation

In this work [4], PoseCNN was introduced, a CNN for 6D object pose estimation. PoseCNN estimates the 3D translation of an object by localizing its center in the image and predicting its distance from the camera. The 3D rotation of the object is estimated by regressing to a quaternion representation. They also introduced a novel loss function that enables PoseCNN to handle symmetric objects. Experiments were conducted on YCB-Video dataset and the OccludedLINEMOD dataset to show that PoseCNN is highly robust to occlusions, provides accurate pose estimation using only RGB image as input and is able to handle symmetric objects. When using depth data as a addition to refine the poses, this approach achieves state-of-the-art results on the OccludedLINEMOD dataset.

DenseFusion [5] proposed, a generic framework for estimating 6D pose of a set of known objects from RGB-D images. DenseFusion is a heterogeneous architecture that processes the two data sources individually and uses a novel dense fusion network to extract pixel-wise dense feature embedding, from which the pose is estimated. Furthermore, they integrated an end-to-end iterative pose refinement procedure that further improves the pose estimation while achieving near real-time inference. The experiments show that their method outperforms state-of-the-art approaches in two datasets, YCB-Video and LineMOD.

3 Proposed Pose Estimation of Transparent Objects

We propose a simple yet effective method for transparent object pose estimation, which we address using a synthetic dataset to train deep neural networks and estimate the pose of known transparent objects. A deep neural network estimates the belief maps of the 2D keypoints of all objects in the image coordinate system. Second, peaks from these belief maps are fed to a standard perspective-n-point (PnP) algorithm [22] to estimate the 6D pose of each object instance. In this section, we describe these steps along with our proposed method for using synthetic data for transparent objects.

3.1 Data Generation

Generating effective data for the network is crucial in the case of fully synthetic datasets. We used a combination of non-photorealistic DR data and photorealistic data to leverage the strengths of both. As shown in previous research [6], these two types of data complement one another, yielding results that are much better than those achieved by either alone. Synthetic data have an additional advantage in that synthetic data avoid overfitting to the distribution of a particular dataset, thus producing a network that is robust to lighting changes, camera variations, and backgrounds. Because our future goal is robotic manipulation of the objects whose 6-DoF pose has been estimated, we chose objects that are easy to pick up by a robot, common on an assembly line, easy to grasp, and transparent. Owing to the lack of research interest in transparent object pose estimation, a standard dataset similar to the LineMOD or YCB-Video does not yet exist. Therefore, we deliberately chose three objects that are fully customizable in the scope of shape and size for convenience. We used a 3D printed object because we wanted to make the transparent object exactly the same as the 3D model. Thus, we printed transparent objects using a clear resin on an SLA printer. The objects were 3-way tubes, bottles, and T-joints, as shown in Fig. 1.

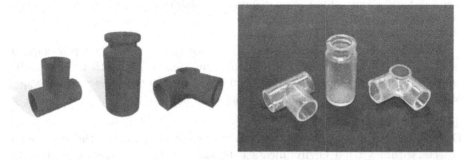

Fig. 1. Objects used for dataset generation and its 3D model. **Left:** textured 3D object models rendered by CG which we used in our dataset generation. **Right:** actual transparent objects used in the experiments.

Both DR and photorealistic data were created by placing transparent object models in different virtual environments. All data were generated by a custom plugin developed by NVIDIA for Unreal Engine 4 (UE4) called NDDS [10]. By leveraging asynchronous, multithreaded sequential frame grabbing, the plugin generates data at a rate of 50–100 Hz, which is significantly faster than either the default UE4 screenshot function or the publicly available Sim4CV tool [11]. Figure 2 highlights examples of images generated using a custom plugin, illustrating the diversity and variety of both DR and photorealistic data.

Fig. 2. DR and photorealistic datasets used for training. **Top:** photorealistic images for dataset generation. Photorealistic data were generated by placing foreground objects in 3D background scenes with physical constraints. Backgrounds were chosen from standard UE4 virtual environments for high-fidelity modeling and quality, as well as for a variety of indoor and outdoor scenes. (From left: Industry, Forest, and Temple). **Bottom:** DR images. Images were generated by randomly varying distractors, overlaid textures, backgrounds, object poses, lighting, and noise.

As mentioned before, modern sensors cannot capture reliable depth maps of transparent objects. However, in a virtual environment, a depth image can be obtained because transparent objects can be handled in the same way as opaque objects. The synthetic depth image is shown in Fig. 3.

Domain Randomization. DR images were created by placing the foreground objects within virtual environments comprising various distractor objects in front of a random background. Images were generated by randomly varying distractors, overlaid textures, backgrounds, object poses, lighting, and noise. More specifically, the following aspects of the scene were randomized, similar to [16]:

RGB image   Depth image

Fig. 3. Synthetic images captured in custom plugin for Unreal Engine 4 called NDDS. As you can see, in a virtual environment, we can obtain a depth map similar to an opaque object, which is crucial for successful pose estimation.

number and types of distractors, selected from a set of 3D models (cones, pyramids, spheres, cylinders, partial toroids, arrows, etc.); texture of the object of interest, as well as of the distractors (solid, striped); solid colored background, photograph (from a subset of 10,000 images from the COCO dataset [17]), or a procedurally generated background image with a random multicolored grid pattern; 3D poses of objects and distractors, sampled uniformly; directional lights with random orientation, color, and intensity; and visibility of distractors.

Photorealistic Images. Photorealistic data were generated by placing foreground objects in 3D background scenes with physical constraints similar to [10]. Backgrounds were chosen from standard UE4 virtual environments, such as an industry, sun temple, and forest. These environments were chosen for their high-fidelity modeling and quality, as well as for various indoor and outdoor scenes. For this dataset, we included the same three objects. For each environment, we manually selected five specific locations covering a variety of terrain and lighting conditions (e.g., on a barrel in an industry workshop, next to a rock, and above a grassy field). Together, these yielded 15 different locations comprising various 3D backgrounds, lighting conditions, and shadows. For each run, some of the object models were placed at random positions and orientations within a vertical cylinder. The vertical cylinder was placed at a fixed point with a radius of 5 cm and a height of 10 cm. The initial positions of the objects were sampled within this volume to avoid initial penetration. The objects were then allowed to fall under the force of gravity, as well as to collide with one another and with the surfaces in the scene. When the objects fell, the virtual camera system was rapidly teleported to random azimuths, elevations, and distances with respect to the fixation point to collect data. The azimuths ranged from −120° to +120° (to avoid collision with the wall, when present), elevation ranged from

5° to 85°, and the distance ranged from 0.5 m to 1.5 m. The dataset (consisting of 18,000 unique frames) was divided into two parts:

- Mixed objects. The first part of the dataset was generated in the same manner, except for the number of uniformly sampled objects. By sampling the objects with replacement, we allow multiple instances of the same category in an image, unlike many previous datasets. For each location, we generated 900 images, yielding 13,500 frames.
- Single objects. The second part of the dataset was generated by dropping each object model in isolation ∼ five times at each of the 15 locations. For each run, ∼20 image frames were generated by taking screenshots at a rate 10 Hz while the object fell for ∼2 s. Therefore, this part of the dataset comprised 1500 (100 × 15) unique images for three objects, thus totaling 4,500 frames.

Details of the combined datasets are shown in Table 1.

Table 1. Statistics of our dataset.

Types	DR	Photorealistic	
		Mixed	Single
Number of frames	18,000	13,500	4,500
Number of objects	3	3	1
Number of locations	N/A	15	15
Resolution	640 × 480		
Total number of frames	36,000		

3.2 Network Architecture

In this study, we adopted the method proposed in [6]. Their one-shot fully convolutional deep neural network detects keypoints using a multistage architecture (see Fig. 4). The feedforward network takes an RGB image of size $w \times h \times 3$ as the input (in our experiments, $w = 640$, $h = 480$.) and branches to produce two different outputs: belief maps and vector fields. There are nine belief maps, one for each of the projected eight vertices of the 3D bounding boxes, and one for the centroids. There are eight vector fields that indicate the direction from each of the eight vertices to the corresponding centroid, similar to [4], to enable the detection of multiple instances of the same type of object. The network operates in stages, with each stage considering not only the image features but also the outputs of the immediately preceding stage. Image features are computed by the first ten layers from VGG-19 [7] (pretrained on ImageNet), followed by two 3×3 convolution layers to reduce the feature dimensions from 512 to 256 and from 256 to 128. These 128-dimensional features are fed into the first stage comprising three $3 \times 3 \times 128$ layers and one $1 \times 1 \times 512$ layer, followed by either a $1 \times 1 \times 9$ (belief maps) or a $1 \times 1 \times 16$ (vector fields) layer. The remaining five stages are identical to the first stage, except that they receive a 153-dimensional input $(128+16+9 = 153)$, consisting of five $7 \times 7 \times 128$ layers and one $1 \times 1 \times 128$ layer before the $1 \times 1 \times 9$ or $1 \times 1 \times 16$ layer. All stages are of size $w/8$ and $h/8$, with ReLU activation functions interleaved throughout.

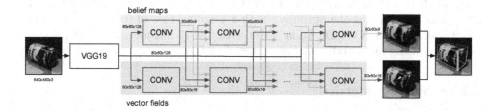

Fig. 4. The deep object pose estimation (DOPE) network architecture [6].

3.3 Detection and Pose Estimation

After the network has processed an image, the individual objects must be extracted from the belief maps. This approach [6] relies on a simple post-processing step that searches for local peaks in the belief maps above a threshold, followed by a greedy assignment algorithm that associates the projected vertices with the detected centroids. For each vertex, the latter step compares the vector field evaluated at the vertex with the direction from the vertex to each centroid, assigning the vertex to the closest centroid within an angular threshold of the vector. Once the vertices of each object instance have been determined, a PnP algorithm is used to retrieve the pose of the object. This step uses the detected projected vertices of the bounding box, camera intrinsics, and object dimensions to recover the final translation and rotation of the object with respect to the camera. All detected projected vertices are used as long as at least the minimum number (four) are detected.

4 Experimental Results

4.1 Setting and Dataset

We used an 18k photorealistic image and an 18k DR image, which has multiple instances of the same object for training. For data augmentation, the Gaussian noise ($\sigma = 2{:}0$), random contrast ($\sigma = 0{:}2$), and random brightness ($\sigma = 0{:}2$) were added.

To avoid the vanishing gradient problem with the network, a loss was computed at the output of each stage, using the L_2 loss for the belief maps and vector fields. The L_2 loss function was used to minimize the error, which is the sum of all squared differences between the true value and the predicted value.

$$L_2 = \sum_n^{i=1} \left(y_{true} - y_{predicted}\right)^2 \tag{1}$$

The network was implemented using the PyTorch v1.0. The VGG-19 feature extractions were obtained from publicly available trained weights in torchvision open models. The networks were trained for 60 epochs, with a batch size of 32. Adam was used as the optimizer with a learning rate of 0.001. The system was trained on an NVIDIA Tesla V100 with 16GB memory, and testing was performed using an NVIDIA GeForce 1080 Ti 8 GB.

4.2   Evaluation Metrics

We adopted the average distance (ADD) metric [4,6] for evaluation, which is the average Euclidean distance of all model points between the ground truth pose and estimated pose. The model points are eight vertices of the bounding boxes.

$$ADD = \frac{1}{m} \sum_{i \in M} \|q_i - p_i\| \tag{2}$$

where M denotes the set of model points, q_i is ground truth pose, p_i is estimated pose and m is the number of points.

4.3   Results of Synthetic Image

For the simulation experiment, we created a test dataset that has 70–120 images for each object, similar to the photorealistic dataset. The results are presented in Table 2. From these results, we can prove our hypothesis that synthetic data can be used for transparent object pose estimation. We conducted experiments on only photorealistic images because of the realistic looking environment.

Example can be seen from Fig. 5.

Table 2. Average error of pose estimation (Simulation).

Object	Pose estimation error (pixel)
3-way tube	21.4
Bottle	27.6
T-joint	27.4
Average	25.5

4.4   Results of Real Image

For the real object experiment, we used a 3D printed object because we wanted to make the transparent object exactly the same as the 3D model. Transparent objects were printed using a clear resin on an SLA printer. The objects were placed on the table. The table had a marker attached to it. The objects were used to estimate the ground truth pose. Approximately 300 images with a resolution of 640×480 were captured (70–120 images per object). The results are presented in Table 3.

Table 3. Average error of the pose estimation (3D printed objects).

Previous method [21]		Proposed method	
Object	Mean translation error (cm)	Object	Mean translation error (cm)
Bank	0.3	3-way tube	0.521
Bottle	1.2	Bottle	0.591
Bucket	0.5	T-joint	0.385
Glass	0.4	N/A	N/A
Average	0.7		0.499

The proposed method outperforms the existing method for transparent object pose estimation by 0.2 cm. Poses were estimated with an accuracy of several millimeters. Ground truth data can have a systematic error of approximately 0.4 cm owing to the approximate measurement of the distance to a test object. We compared our results with those of this method [21]. As mentioned previously, there is no standard dataset for transparent object pose estimation. Even though the object is different, we can approximate how the previous method and proposed method relate. The pose estimation results show that our proposed method, which is trained on only synthetic data, can be applied to bin-picking or robotic grasping. The reason for the higher translation error of the bottle is its symmetry and shape. Examples of transparent object pose estimations are shown in Fig. 6. We can see that the proposed method performs considerably well.

Input

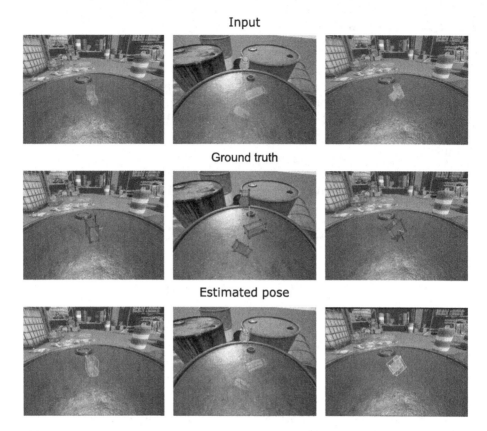

Ground truth

Estimated pose

Fig. 5. Results of the simulation experiment of pose estimation of a transparent object. **Left column** is a 3-way tube. **Middle column** is a bottle, and the **right column** is a T-joint. **Top row**: test images. **Middle row**: ground truth, which was annotated on NDDS. **Bottom row**: our method was trained on 36k photorealistic and DR data.

4.5   Discussion and Limitation

The pose estimation results show that our proposed method, which is trained on only synthetic data, can be applied to bin-picking or robotic grasping. First, we proved our hypothesis that synthetic data can be used for transparent object pose estimation by training a deep neural network with synthetic data only. Synthetic data can solve the numerous problems that are encountered when using real images for training. For example, unlimited ground truth data with an acceptable error, customizable background, and lighting can be generated relatively easily. However, synthetic data have one problem, i.e., the reality gap. The reality gap can be dealt with using a combination of domain randomization and photorealistic datasets similar to previous research. We employed our method on 3D printed transparent objects. As mentioned previously, there is a lack of a standard test dataset. In this study, we conducted experiments on a few objects that we voluntarily chose. For our ground truth, we manually labeled the real

Input

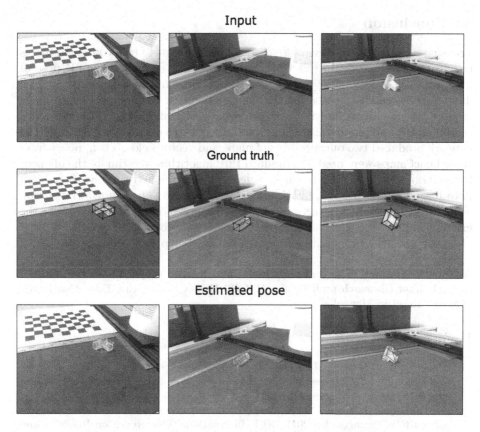

Ground truth

Estimated pose

Fig. 6. Experimental results of pose estimation of a transparent object. **Left column** is a 3-way tube. **Middle column** is a bottle, and the **right column** is a T-joint. **Top row**: test images. **Middle row**: ground truth, which was manually drawn. **Bottom row**: our method was trained on 36k photorealistic and DR data.

image. Thus, the ground truth had a systematic error of approximately 4 mm because of the approximate measurement of the distance to the test object. For evaluation metrics, we adopted the same method (ADD) as that used in previous studies. Our next work should be directed at increasing the number of objects, adopting additional evaluation metrics, and comparing our method with opaque 6D pose estimation methods. The limitation of our method is that it is not effective against reflective or symmetric objects. In addition, our methods cannot handle overlapping transparent objects. These challenges should be the main direction for transparent object recognition and pose estimation. In future work, we plan to use the estimated pose for a random bin-picking system.

5   Conclusion

Transparent objects are inevitable when robots attempt to pick common objects in houses or industries. In this work, we successfully estimated the 6D pose of a transparent object using a deep neural network trained solely on synthetic data. We showed that synthetic data can be a solution to unreliable depth maps of transparent objects and the lack of pre-labeled training data. We created a combined DR and photorealistic dataset and fed it to a deep neural network. The network produced two outputs—belief maps and vector fields. Then, peaks from these belief maps were used for standard PnP algorithm to estimate the 6D pose for each object. To the best of our knowledge, this is the first time synthetic data have been used for transparent object pose estimation. The average translation error is 0.49 cm, which is acceptable. The proposed method outperforms the existing method for transparent object pose estimation by 0.2 cm. The results also show that the proposed method can be used for picking and grasping.

Acknowledgement. The authors are thankful for the support from the MJEED research grant (Research profile code: J14C16) Higher Engineering Education Development Project in Mongolia.

References

1. Chen, Y., Sun, G., Lin, H., Chen, S.: Random bin picking with multi-view image acquisition and CAD-based pose estimation. In: 2018 IEEE International Conference on Systems, pp. 2218–2223 (2018)
2. He, R., Rojas, J., Guan, Y.: A 3D object detection and pose estimation pipeline using RGB-D images. In: 2017 IEEE International Conference on Robotics and Biomimetics (ROBIO), pp. 1527–1532 (2017)
3. Wu, C., Jiang, S., Song, K.: CAD-based pose estimation for random bin-picking of multiple objects using a RGB-D camera. In: 2015 15th International Conference on Control Automation and Systems (ICCAS), pp. 1645–1649 (2015)
4. Xiang, Y., Schmidt, T., Narayanan, V., Fox, D.: PoseCNN: A Convolutional Neural Network for 6D Object Pose Estimation in Cluttered Scenes. c (RSS) (2018)
5. Wang, C., et al.: DenseFusion: 6D object pose estimation by iterative dense fusion. In: Computer Vision and Pattern Recognition (CVPR), pp. 3343–3352 (2019)
6. Tremblay, J., To, T., Sundaralingam, B., Xiang, Y., Fox, D., Birchfield, S.: Deep object pose estimation for semantic robotic grasping of household objects. In: Conference on Robot Learning (CoRL), pp. 306–316 (2018)
7. Simonyan, K., Zisserman, A.: Very deep convolutional networks for large-scale image recognition. In: International Conference on Learning Representations (2015)
8. Guo-Hua, C., Jun-Yi, W., Ai-Jun, Z.: Transparent object detection and location based on RGB-D camera. J. Phys. Conf. Ser. (JPCS) **1183**, 012011 (2019)
9. Dosovitskiy, A., et al.: FlowNet: learning optical flow with convolutional networks. In: 2015 IEEE International Conference on Computer Vision (ICCV), pp. 2758–2766 (2015)
10. Tremblay, J., To, T., Birchfield, S.: Falling things: a synthetic dataset for 3D object detection and pose estimation. In: 2018 IEEE/CVF Conference on Computer Vision and Pattern Recognition Workshops (CVPRW), pp. 2119–21193 (2018)

11. Müller, M., Casser, V., Lahoud, J., Smith, N., Ghanem, B.: Sim4CV: a photo-realistic simulator for computer vision applications. Int. J. Comput. Vis. **126**, 902–919 (2018)
12. McCormac, J., Handa, A., Leutenegger, S., Davison, A.J.: SceneNet RGB-D: 5M photorealistic images of synthetic indoor trajectories with ground truth. In: Proceedings of the IEEE International Conference on Computer Vision (ICCV), pp. 2678–2687 (2016)
13. Ros, G., Sellart, L., Materzynska, J., Vázquez, D., López, A.: The SYNTHIA dataset: a large collection of synthetic images for semantic segmentation of urban scenes. In: 2016 IEEE Conference on Computer Vision and Pattern Recognition (CVPR), pp. 3234–3243 (2016)
14. Tobin, J., Fong, R., Ray, A., Schneider, J., Zaremba, W., Abbeel, P.: Domain randomization for transferring deep neural networks from simulation to the real world. In: 2017 IEEE/RSJ International Conference on Intelligent Robots and Systems (IROS), pp. 23–30 (2017)
15. Sadeghi, F., Levine, S.: CAD2RL: Real Single-Image Flight without a Single Real Image. CoRR (2016)
16. Tremblay, J., et al.: Training deep networks with synthetic data: bridging the reality gap by domain randomization. In: 2018 IEEE/CVF Conference on Computer Vision and Pattern Recognition Workshops (CVPRW), pp. 1082–10828 (2018)
17. Lin, T.-Y., et al.: Microsoft COCO: common objects in context. In: Fleet, D., Pajdla, T., Schiele, B., Tuytelaars, T. (eds.) ECCV 2014. LNCS, vol. 8693, pp. 740–755. Springer, Cham (2014). https://doi.org/10.1007/978-3-319-10602-1_48
18. Johnson-Roberson, M., Barto, C., Mehta, R., Sridhar, S., Rosaen, K., Vasudevan, R.: Driving in the matrix: can virtual worlds replace human-generated annotations for real world tasks? In: 2017 IEEE International Conference on Robotics and Automation (ICRA), pp. 746–753 (2017)
19. Mayer, N., et al.: A large dataset to train convolutional networks for disparity, optical flow, and scene flow estimation. In: 2016 IEEE Conference on Computer Vision and Pattern Recognition (CVPR), pp. 4040–4048 (2016)
20. Hinterstoisser, S., Lepetit, V., Wohlhart, P., Konolige, K.: On pre-trained image features and synthetic images for deep learning. In: Leal-Taixé, L., Roth, S. (eds.) ECCV 2018. LNCS, vol. 11129, pp. 682–697. Springer, Cham (2019). https://doi.org/10.1007/978-3-030-11009-3_42
21. Lysenkov, I., Rabaud, V.: Pose estimation of rigid transparent objects in transparent clutter. In: 2013 IEEE International Conference on Robotics and Automation, pp. 162–169 (2013)
22. Moreno-Noguer, F., Lepetit, V., Fua, P.: Accurate non-iterative O(n) solution to the PnP problem. In: 2007 IEEE 11th International Conference on Computer Vision, pp. 1–8 (2007)
23. Sajjan, S., et al.: Clear grasp: 3D shape estimation of transparent objects for manipulation. In: 2020 IEEE International Conference on Robotics and Automation (ICRA), pp. 3634–3642 (2020)
24. Liu, X., Jonschkowski, R., Angelova, A., Konolige, K.: KeyPose: multi-view 3D labeling and keypoint estimation for transparent objects. In: 2020 IEEE/CVF Conference on Computer Vision and Pattern Recognition (CVPR), pp. 11599–11607 (2020)
25. Byambaa, M., Choimaa, L., Koutaki, G.: 6D pose estimation of transparent object from single RGB image. In: The 25th Conference of FRUCT Association, pp. 444–447 (2019)

Color Exaggeration for Dichromats Using Weighted Edge

Daisuke Miyazaki[1]([✉])[iD] and Harumichi Morimoto[1,2P]

[1] Hiroshima City University, Hiroshima 731-3194, Japan
`miyazaki@hiroshima-cu.ac.jp`
[2] Hitachi Solutions West Japan, Ltd., Hiroshima, Japan
`http://www.info.hiroshima-cu.ac.jp/∼miyazaki/`

Abstract. Dichromats recognize colors using two out of three cone cells; L, M, and S. To extend the ability of dichromats to recognize the color difference, we propose a method to expand the color difference when observed by dichromats. We analyze the color between the neighboring pixels not in intensity space but chromaticity space and form a Poisson equation. In addition, we use the sigmoid function to weigh the edge of a color image. The color difference can be adequately tuned manually by the weight parameter so that the dichromats can obtain the image that they want where the visibility of the color is enhanced.

Keywords: Color blindness · Color vision deficiency · Dichromat · Recoloring · Edge exaggeration

1 Introduction

Red, green, and blue colors are detected by three kinds of cone cells embedded in the retina. Dichromats use two of them to recognize colors. In this paper, we propose a method to enhance the visibility of dichromats.

Enhancing the visibility of color image for dichromats is an important research field [1, 2, 4, 6–12, 14–17, 19–26, 28–31].

Unlike these methods, our method analyzes not in color space but image space (*i.e.*, pixel coordinates) (Fig. 1). We formulate the Poisson equation so that the relative color difference between neighboring pixels will be preserved. Some methods [5, 18, 27] also solve the Poisson equation to enhance the visibility of dichromats. These methods [5, 27] form the Poisson equation in RGB intensity space, while our method forms in xy-chromaticity space. As a result, our method exaggerates the color difference between neighboring pixels. One of the existing methods [18] also forms the Poisson equation in xy-choromaticity space, however, our method can exaggerate the color difference by changing the parameter of the exaggeration weight.

Section 2 explains the basic theory, and Sect. 3 shows our method. We show some results in Sect. 4. Section 5 concludes our paper, and we also discuss the disadvantage of our method.

K. Sumi et al. (Eds.): IW-FCV 2022, CCIS 1578, pp. 18–33, 2022.
https://doi.org/10.1007/978-3-031-06381-7_2

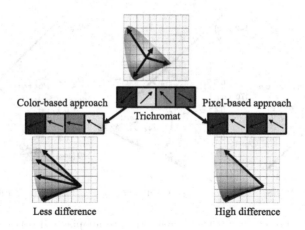

Fig. 1. Schematic explanation of color-based approach and pixel-based approach.

2 Hue for Dichromats

The color value which dichromats perceive can be calculated as follows. RGB value is first converted to CIE-XYZ value, and after that, it is converted to LMS value. LMS represents the sensitivity of cone cells. The procedures to calculate the LMS values of dichromats are shown in some pieces of literature such as Judd [13] and Brettel et al. [3]. In this paper, we follow Judd [13]. The conversion formula for protanopia is shown below.

$$\begin{pmatrix} L_p \\ M_p \\ S_p \end{pmatrix} = \begin{pmatrix} 0.0 & 2.02 & -2.52 \\ 0.0 & 1.0 & 0.0 \\ 0.0 & 0.0 & 1.0 \end{pmatrix} \begin{pmatrix} L \\ M \\ S \end{pmatrix}. \tag{1}$$

And, the conversion formula for deuteranopia is shown below.

$$\begin{pmatrix} L_d \\ M_d \\ S_d \end{pmatrix} = \begin{pmatrix} 1.0 & 0.0 & 0.0 \\ 0.49 & 0.0 & 1.25 \\ 0.0 & 0.0 & 1.0 \end{pmatrix} \begin{pmatrix} L \\ M \\ S \end{pmatrix}. \tag{2}$$

In xy-diagram calculated from CIE-XYZ value, the white color is placed in $(x, y) = (0.33, 0.33)$ for trichromats. First, the hue α of trichromats is defined as an angle defined in xy-plane (Fig. 2 (a)). The trichromatic hue α is defined as an angle around the white point $(x, y) = (0.33, 0.33)$. 0° of α is defined, for example, as the direction of $-45°$. The hue angle α of a certain color (x, y) is calculated as follows.

$$\alpha = \frac{\pi}{4} + \tan^{-1} \frac{y - 0.33}{x - 0.33}. \tag{3}$$

The hue β of dichromats (Fig. 2 (b)–(c)) has strong relation with the L*a*b* hue of trichromats [19]. Following Judd [13], the white point of protanopia is $(x, y) = (0.747, 0.253)$ and that of deuteranopia is $(x, y) = (1.000, 0.000)$.

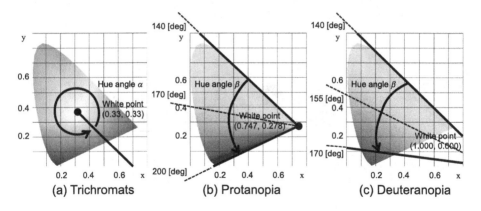

Fig. 2. Definition of hue of (a) trichromats, (b) protanopia, and (c) deuteranopia.

The hue β is defined as the angle around these white points, where it ranges from $140°$ direction to $200°$ direction for protanopia and ranges from $140°$ direction to $170°$ direction for deuteranopia. The hue angle β of protanopia is calculated as follows.

$$\beta = \frac{\pi}{180}\left(140 + \frac{\alpha}{2\pi}(200 - 140)\right),\qquad(4)$$

and the hue angle β of deuteranopia is calculated as follows.

$$\beta = \frac{\pi}{180}\left(140 + \frac{\alpha}{2\pi}(170 - 140)\right).\qquad(5)$$

Here, the hue angle α ranges from 0 to $360°$. The direction of $0°$ in hue angle α is casually defined (*i.e.*, $45°$); however, it does not matter for our purpose as explained mathematically in Sect. 3. Section 3 explains that our method uses the relative value for representing the hue instead of the absolute value. This is because that the hue of trichromats ranges from 0 to $360°$, but the $360°$ is cyclically connected to 0, and because that the hue of dichromats ranges in a limited range.

3 Color Enhancement for Dichromat

The purpose of the method is to enhance the visibility of the image for dichromats. As shown in Sect. 2, we represent the color as the hue angle shown in Fig. 2.

sRGB value of the input image is converted to CIE-XYZ. After that, CIE-XYZ value is converted to xy-chromaticity as follows.

$$\tilde{x} = \frac{\tilde{X}}{\tilde{X} + \tilde{Y} + \tilde{Z}}, \tag{6}$$

$$\tilde{y} = \frac{\tilde{Y}}{\tilde{X} + \tilde{Y} + \tilde{Z}}, \tag{7}$$

$$\tilde{z} = \frac{\tilde{Z}}{\tilde{X} + \tilde{Y} + \tilde{Z}}. \tag{8}$$

The vector from the white point $(1/3, 1/3)$ of xy chromaticity to the chromaticity of image pixel is represented as Eq. (9).

$$\mathbf{a}(u, v) = \begin{pmatrix} \tilde{x}(u, v) - 0.33 \\ \tilde{y}(u, v) - 0.33 \\ 0 \end{pmatrix}. \tag{9}$$

Here, we use (u, v) for representing the x and y components of pixel position represented in Euclidean coordinates with x and y axes.

We denote the 4-neighbor pixel position as $(u + \Delta v, u + \Delta v)$, where the integer values Δu and Δv obey $|\Delta u| + |\Delta v| = 1$. The color vectors of neighboring pixels are also calculated as Eq. (10).

$$\tilde{\mathbf{a}}(u + \Delta u, v + \Delta v) = \begin{pmatrix} \tilde{x}(u + \Delta u, v + \Delta v) - 0.33 \\ \tilde{y}(u + \Delta u, v + \Delta v) - 0.33 \\ 0 \end{pmatrix}. \tag{10}$$

We normalize these vectors and denote them as $\hat{\mathbf{a}}(u, v)$ and $\hat{\mathbf{a}}(u + \Delta u, v + \Delta v)$ (Fig. 3). We denote the cross product of these two vectors as $\mathbf{a}$.

$$\mathbf{a}(u + \Delta u, v + \Delta v) = \hat{\mathbf{a}}(u + \Delta u, v + \Delta v) \times \hat{\mathbf{a}}(u, v). \tag{11}$$

Calculating the arcsine of $\mathbf{a}$ results in the signed angle between $\hat{\mathbf{a}}(u + \Delta u, v + \Delta v)$ and $\hat{\mathbf{a}}(u, v)$. We denote this angle as $\Delta\alpha(u + \Delta u, v + \Delta v)$ (Fig. 4).

$$\Delta\alpha(u + \Delta u, v + \Delta v) = \sin^{-1}(\mathbf{a}(u + \Delta u, v + \Delta v)). \tag{12}$$

The discretized representation of the Laplacian of the hue angle $\tilde{\beta}$ for dichromats is as follows.

$$\Delta\tilde{\beta}(u, v) = -\Big\{ \tilde{\beta}(u, v)$$
$$-\frac{1}{4}\tilde{\beta}(u - 1, v) - \frac{1}{4}\tilde{\beta}(u + 1, v) - \frac{1}{4}\tilde{\beta}(u, v - 1) - \frac{1}{4}\tilde{\beta}(u, v + 1) \Big\}. \tag{13}$$

Same goes to α.

$$\Delta\alpha(u, v) = -\Big\{ \alpha(u, v)$$
$$-\frac{1}{4}\alpha(u - 1, v) - \frac{1}{4}\alpha(u + 1, v) - \frac{1}{4}\alpha(u, v - 1) - \frac{1}{4}\alpha(u, v + 1) \Big\}. \tag{14}$$

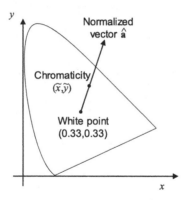

Fig. 3. Chromaticity vector.

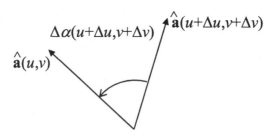

Fig. 4. Relative hue angle between two neighboring pixels.

Equation (14) is also represented as follows.

$$\triangle\alpha(u,v) = -\left\{\frac{1}{4}\left(\alpha(u,v) - \alpha(u-1,v)\right) + \frac{1}{4}\left(\alpha(u,v) - \alpha(u+1,v)\right)\right.$$
$$\left. +\frac{1}{4}\left(\alpha(u,v) - \alpha(u,v-1)\right) + \frac{1}{4}\left(\alpha(u,v) - \alpha(u,v+1)\right)\right\}. \tag{15}$$

If we simply subtract two angles, the calculation will fail since the angle has a cycle of 360°. For example, 5° minus 355° should be 10°, not −350°. If we convert an angle to a vector and calculate the angle between two vectors, this problem will not occur. Unlike dot product of two vectors, cross product of two vectors can calculate the angle with signed value. Using Eq. (11), Eq. (15) can be rewritten as follows.

$$\triangle\alpha(u,v)$$
$$= -\left\{\frac{1}{4}\Delta\tilde{\alpha}(u-1,v) + \frac{1}{4}\Delta\tilde{\alpha}(u+1,v) + \frac{1}{4}\Delta\tilde{\alpha}(u,v-1) + \frac{1}{4}\Delta\tilde{\alpha}(u,v+1)\right\}. \tag{16}$$

The difference of hue angle $\tilde{\beta}$ between neighboring pixels should be proportional to the difference of hue angle α between neighboring pixels. Namely, the Laplacian of $\tilde{\beta}$ should be the same as the Laplacian of α (Fig. 5), scaled with a certain constant value.

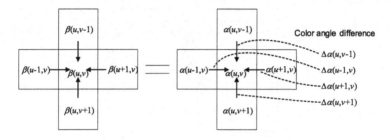

Fig. 5. Color difference between neighboring pixels.

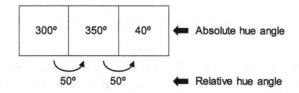

Fig. 6. Specific example of absolute and relative hue angles.

$$\triangle \tilde{\beta}(u,v) = \triangle\alpha(u,v). \tag{17}$$

This type of formula is called Poisson equation. From Eq. (13) and Eq. (16), Eq. (17) is represented as follows.

$$\tilde{\beta}(u,v) - \frac{1}{4}\tilde{\beta}(u-1,v) - \frac{1}{4}\tilde{\beta}(u+1,v)$$
$$- \frac{1}{4}\tilde{\beta}(u,v-1) - \frac{1}{4}\tilde{\beta}(u,v+1)$$
$$= \frac{1}{4}\triangle\tilde{\alpha}(u-1,v) + \frac{1}{4}\triangle\tilde{\alpha}(u+1,v) + \frac{1}{4}\triangle\tilde{\alpha}(u,v-1) + \frac{1}{4}\triangle\tilde{\alpha}(u,v+1). \tag{18}$$

The angle $\tilde{\beta}$ between neighboring pixels will become the same as the angle α between neighboring pixels if we solve Eq. (18). Although $\tilde{\beta}$ becomes similar to α, the calculated $\tilde{\beta}$ becomes free from the cycle of 360°. Unlike an identity equation $\tilde{\beta} = \alpha$ which copies the absolute angle, Eq. (17) preserves the relative angle among neighboring pixels.

Suppose that the image is consisted of three pixels, and has hue angles α which are 300°, 350°, and 40° (Fig. 6). The colors for trichromats will be blue, purple, and red. If we simply map these angles to the angle $\tilde{\beta}$, the color for dichromats becomes faint blue, deep blue, and yellow. However, if we solve the above mentioned Poisson equation, the calculated angle will be 300°, 350°, and 400°. If we map these angles to the angle $\tilde{\beta}$, for example, to 150°, 160°, and 170°, the color for dichromats becomes faintly yellow color, faintly cyan color, and faintly blue color. The color difference between neighboring pixels will be preserved if we solve the Poisson equation.

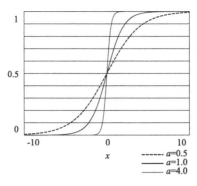

Fig. 7. Sigmoid function.

Unlike existing method [18], our method weights the color difference $\Delta\tilde{\alpha}$ of 4-neighbor using the sigmoid function (Fig. 7) subtracted by 0.5 (Eq. (19)).

$$f(x) = \frac{1}{1 + \exp\left(-ax\right)} - \frac{1}{2}. \tag{19}$$

The real number a is called gain. Sigmoid function $(0 < y < 1)$ (Fig. 7) is a monotonically increasing function which is symmetric at the point $(0, 0.5)$. The sigmoid function becomes sharp if the gain is large, and becomes smooth if that is small. Therefore, the gain can adjust the color exaggeration.

The sigmoid function $f(\Delta\tilde{\alpha}(u + \Delta u, v + \Delta v))$ when the gain is a and the color difference is $\Delta\tilde{\alpha}(u + \Delta u, v + \Delta v)$ is shown in Eq. (20).

$$f(\Delta\tilde{\alpha}(u + \Delta u, v + \Delta v)) = \frac{1}{1 + \exp\left(-a\Delta\tilde{\alpha}(u + \Delta u, v + \Delta v)\right)} - \frac{1}{2}. \tag{20}$$

The Poisson equation (Eq. (18)) considering the sigmoid function becomes Eq. (21).

$$\tilde{\beta}(x, y) - \tfrac{1}{4}\tilde{\beta}(u, v - 1) - \tfrac{1}{4}\tilde{\beta}(u - 1, v) - \tfrac{1}{4}\tilde{\beta}(u + 1, v) - \tfrac{1}{4}\tilde{\beta}(u, v + 1)$$
$$= \tfrac{1}{4}f(\Delta\tilde{\alpha}(u, v - 1)) + \tfrac{1}{4}f(\Delta\tilde{\alpha}(u - 1, v))$$
$$+ \tfrac{1}{4}f(\Delta\tilde{\alpha}(u + 1, v)) + \tfrac{1}{4}f(\Delta\tilde{\alpha}(u, v + 1)). \tag{21}$$

The closed-form solution to $\tilde{\beta}$ (Eq. (21)) can be obtained using the LU decomposition implemented in sparse matrix library.

The followings explain the process to reconvert the angle $\tilde{\beta}$ to an RGB image.

We create the cumulative histogram of $\tilde{\beta}$. Using this cumulative histogram, we converted the angle $\tilde{\beta}$ to the angle $\hat{\beta}$ (Fig. 8). The distance from the white point of protanopia is denoted as p and that from the white point of deuteranopia is denoted as d in Eqs. (22)–(23).

$$x_p(u, v) = p\cos\hat{\beta} + 0.747,$$
$$y_p(u, v) = p\sin\hat{\beta} + 0.278,$$
$$z_p(u, v) = 1.0 - x_p(u, v) - y_p(u, v). \tag{22}$$

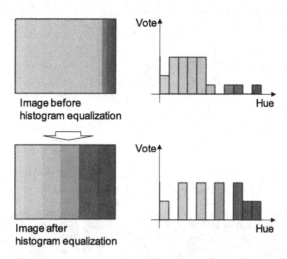

Fig. 8. Histogram equalization of dichromatic hue.

$$x_d(u, v) = d \cos \hat{\beta} + 1.000 \,,$$
$$y_d(u, v) = d \sin \hat{\beta} + 0.000 \,,$$
$$z_d(u, v) = 1.0 - x_d(u, v) - y_d(u, v) \,. \tag{23}$$

We set p and d as follows. We denote the original xy-chromaticities of the interest pixel as $\overline{x}(u, v)$ and $\overline{y}(u, v)$, and the post-processed xy-chromaticities as $x(u, v)$ and $y(u, v)$. The following t minimizes the difference between the input chromaticity and the output chromaticity.

$$\begin{pmatrix} \overline{x}(u, v) \\ \overline{y}(u, v) \end{pmatrix} = \begin{pmatrix} C_x \\ C_y \end{pmatrix} + \begin{pmatrix} \cos \hat{\beta}(u, v) \\ \sin \hat{\beta}(u, v) \end{pmatrix} t \,. \tag{24}$$

Therefore, the following is derived by solving Eq. (24).

$$t = (\overline{x} - C_x) \cos \hat{\beta} + (\overline{y} - C_y) \sin \hat{\beta} \,. \tag{25}$$

Note that, the white point of protanopia is defined as $(C_x, C_y) = (0.747, 0.278)$, and the white point of deuteranopia is defined as $(C_x, C_y) = (1.000, 0.000)$. From estimated t, Eq. (22), and Eq. (23), the final values of x, y, z are determined. This process is schematically depicted in Fig. 9.

At the beginning of our method, we convert the RGB of input image to XYZ, and calculate $W(u, v) = X(u, v) + Y(u, v) + Z(u, v)$. Equation (26) converts the chromaticities $x(u, v)$, $y(u, v)$, and $z(u, v)$ calculated from the hue β to the XYZ values $\overline{X}$, $\overline{Y}$, and $\overline{Z}$.

$$\overline{X}(u, v) = x(u, v) W(u, v) \,,$$
$$\overline{Y}(u, v) = y(u, v) W(u, v) \,,$$
$$\overline{Z}(u, v) = z(u, v) W(u, v) \,. \tag{26}$$

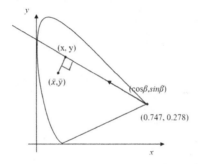

Fig. 9. Post-processing for protanopia.

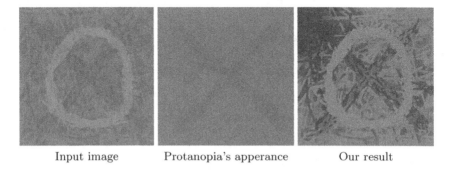

Input image   Protanopia's apperance   Our result

Fig. 10. Our result (protanopia) [symbolic illustration].

XYZ values are obtained now, and we convert it to the dichromats' view and convert its XYZ to RGB.

4 Experiment

Figure 10 shows one example of the result. The result of our method can represent the symbolic structure rather than the appearance of protanopia.

The dichromat's appearance of Fig. 11 (a) is shown in Fig. 11 (b)–(c). Note that some of the patches are indistinguishable. The output image of the gain $a = 0.1$ is shown in Fig. 11 (d)–(e), that of the gain $a = 5$ is shown in Fig. 11 (f)–(g), and that of the gain $a = 100$ is shown in Fig. 11 (h)–(i). Figure 11 (d)–(i) show that the gain can adjust the amount of exaggeration of the color difference thanks to the characteristics of the sigmoid function.

The dichromat's appearance of Fig. 12 (a) is shown in Fig. 12 (b)–(c). The output image without gain is shown in Fig. 12 (d)–(e), that of the gain $a = 0.1$ is shown in Fig. 12 (f)–(g), that of the gain $a = 5$ is shown in Fig. 12 (h)–(i), and that of the gain $a = 100$ is shown in Fig. 12 (j)–(k). Our method can distinguish red and green leaves.

The dichromat's appearance of Fig. 13 (a) is shown in Fig. 13 (b)–(c). The output image without gain is shown in Fig. 13 (d)–(e), that of the gain $a = 0.1$

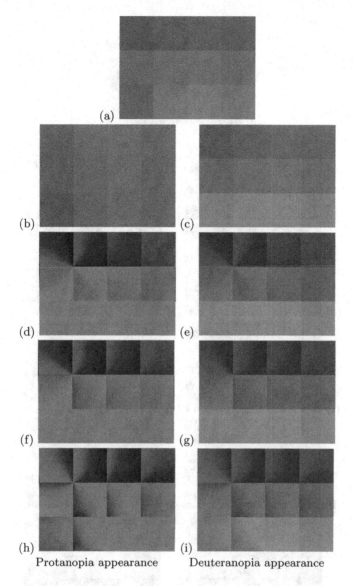

Protanopia appearance   Deuteranopia appearance

Fig. 11. Result [color patch]: (a) input, (b) perceived color of protanopia, (c) perceived color of deuteranopia, (d) our result of gain 0.1 (protanopia), (e) our result of gain 0.1 (deuteranopia), (f) our result of gain 5 (protanopia), (g) our result of gain 5 (deuteranopia), (h) our result of gain 100 (protanopia), and (i) our result of gain 100 (deuteranopia).

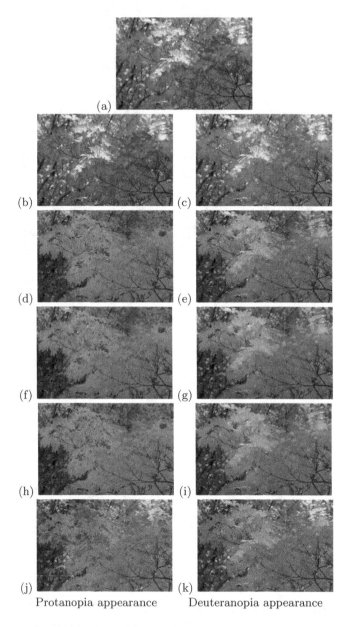

(a)

(b) (c)

(d) (e)

(f) (g)

(h) (i)

(j) (k)

Protanopia appearance   Deuteranopia appearance

Fig. 12. Result [leaf]: (a) input, (b) perceived color of protanopia, (c) perceived color of deuteranopia, (d) previous result without gain (protanopia), (e) previous result without gain (deuteranopia), (f) our result of gain 0.1 (protanopia), (g) our result of gain 0.1 (deuteranopia), (h) our result of gain 5 (protanopia), (i) our result of gain 5 (deuteranopia), (j) our result of gain 100 (protanopia), and (k) our result of gain 100 (deuteranopia).

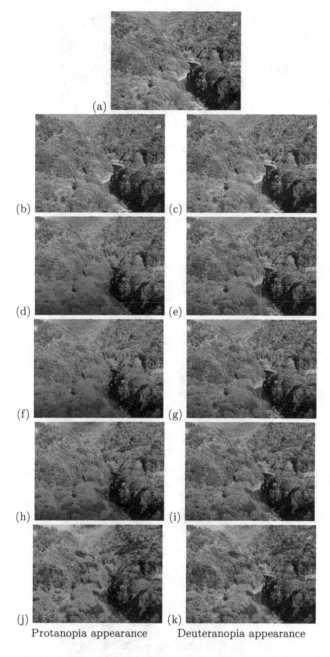

Fig. 13. Result [mountain]: (a) input, (b) perceived color of protanopia, (c) perceived color of deuteranopia, (d) previous result without gain (protanopia), (e) previous result without gain (deuteranopia), (f) our result of gain 0.1 (protanopia), (g) our result of gain 0.1 (deuteranopia), (h) our result of gain 5 (protanopia), (i) our result of gain 5 (deuteranopia), (j) our result of gain 100 (protanopia), and (k) our result of gain 100 (deuteranopia).

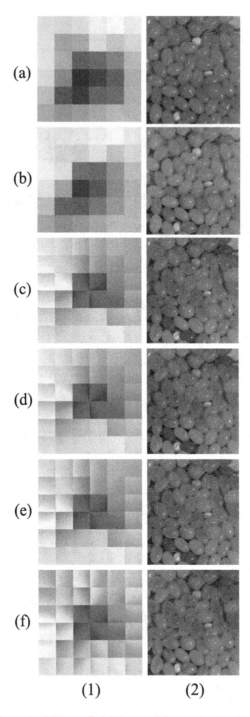

Fig. 14. Result [(1) patch, (2) beans]: (a) input, (b) perceived color of deuteranopia, (c) previous result without gain (deuteranopia), (d) our result of gain 0.1 (deuteranopia), (e) our result of gain 5 (deuteranopia), (f) our result of gain 100 (deuteranopia).

is shown in Fig. 13 (f)–(g), that of the gain $a = 5$ is shown in Fig. 13 (h)–(i), and that of the gain $a = 100$ is shown in Fig. 13 (j)–(k). If we set the gain small, the original appearance is preserved, while if we set the gain large, the color differences become large. This result empirically proves the benefit of our method compared to the methods without gain (such as Miyazaki's method [18]). Miyazaki's method does not weigh by sigmoid function, while we can exaggerate the color difference by sigmoid function.

Other results are shown in Fig. 14.

The adequate amount of color exaggeration depends on the user, the situation, and the purpose. Strong exaggeration is favored in some cases, while slight exaggeration (with naturalness preserved) is favored in other cases. As a result, the proposed method is beneficial for actual purposes, which can tune the amount of color exaggeration.

As shown in our experiments, our method successfully works for both artificial images and natural images. Our method is not sensitive to the image types, whether it is an artificial image or a natural image. However, our method is sensitive to achromatic pixels. Our method exaggerates the color difference between neighboring pixels. Therefore, if the neighboring pixel is black, gray, or white, we cannot represent the color difference between neighboring pixels, and thus, the result images might not have satisfactory color representation.

5 Conclusion

In this paper, we have proposed a method that enhances the visibility of dichromats. Our method converts the color of an image so that the image will be clear for dichromats. We have formulated the color difference of trichromat as a Poisson equation and solved it to preserve the color difference which can also be perceived by dichromats. The Poisson equation formulated in chromaticity space exaggerates the color difference of neighboring pixels, and at the same time, it preserves the chromaticity difference of trichromats. Experimental results show that our method is robust and beneficial. Also, our result has shown that the exaggeration of the color difference for dichromats can be tuned by the weighting parameter. The disadvantage of our method is that it cannot be applied to the achromatic images (black, gray, and white). Some kind of preprocessing or postprocessing may avoid such a problem, however, such processes do not fundamentally solve the problem. We are planning to theoretically solve this problem in the future.

References

1. Bao, S., Tanaka, G., Tamukoh, H., Suetake, N.: Improvement of lightness modification method based on Craik-O'Brien effect for dichromats. In: International Symposium on Intelligent Signal Processing and Communication Systems, pp. 75–78 (2015)

2. Bao, J., Wang, Y., Ma, Y., Gu, X.: Re-coloring images for dichromats based on an improved adaptive mapping algorithm. In: International Conference on Audio, Language and Image Processing , pp. 152–156 (2008)
3. Brettel, H., Viénot, F., Mollon, J.D.: Computerized simulation of color appearance for dichromats. J. Opt. Soc. Am. A **14**(10), 2647–2655 (1997)
4. Chen, W., Chen, W., Bao, H.: An efficient direct volume rendering approach for dichromats. IEEE Trans. Vis. Comput. Graph. **17**(12), 2144–2152 (2011)
5. Farup, I.: Individualised halo-free gradient-domain color image daltonisation. J. Imaging **6**(116), 10 p (2020)
6. Flinkman, M., Nakauchi, S.: Illuminations that improve color discrimination ability of people with red-green color vision deficiency. J. Opt. Soc. Am. **34**(10), 1914–1923 (2017)
7. Huang, C., Chiu, K., Chen, C.: Temporal color consistency-based video reproduction for dichromats. IEEE Trans. Multimedia **13**(5), 950–960 (2011)
8. Huang, J., Chen, C., Jen, T., Wang, S.: Image recolorization for the colorblind. In: IEEE International Conference on Acoustics, Speech and Signal Processing, pp. 1161–1164 (2009)
9. Huang, J., Tseng, Y., Wu, S., Wang, S.: Information preserving color transformation for protanopia and deuteranopia. IEEE Signal Process. Lett. **14**(10), 711–714 (2007)
10. Huang, J.-B., Wu, S.-Y., Chen, C.-S.: Enhancing color representation for the color vision impaired. In: Workshop on Computer Vision Applications for the Visually Impaired (2008)
11. Ichikawa, M., et al.: Preliminary study on color modification for still images to realize barrier-free color vision. In: International Conference on Systems, Man and Cybernetics, pp. 36–41 (2004)
12. Jeong, J., Kim, H., Kim, Y., Wang, T., Ko, S.: Enhanced re-coloring method with an information preserving property for color-blind person. In: International Conference on Consumer Electronics, pp. 600–601 (2012)
13. Judd, D.B.: Standard response functions for protanopic and deuteranopic vision. J. Opt. Soc. Am. **35**, 199–221 (1945)
14. Kuhn, G.R., Oliveira, M.M., Fernandes, L.A.F.: An efficient naturalness-preserving image-recoloring method for dichromats. IEEE Trans. Vis. Comput. Graph. **14**(6), 1747–1754 (2008)
15. Ma, Y., Wang, E., Wang, Y.: An embedded image processing device for color vision deficiency. In: International Conference on Biomedical Engineering and Informatics, pp. 1041–1045 (2011)
16. Meng, M., Tanaka, G.: Proposal of minimization problem based lightness modification for protanopia and deuteranopia. In: International Symposium on Intelligent Signal Processing and Communication Systems, pp. 1–6 (2016)
17. Meyer, G.W., Greenberg, D.P.: Color-defective vision and computer graphics displays. IEEE Comput. Graphics Appl. **8**(5), 28–40 (1988)
18. Miyazaki, D., Fujimura, S.: Hue enhancement for dichromats using Poisson equation. J. Imaging Sci. Technol. **66**(1), 1–8 (2021). Article No 010502. https://doi.org/10.2352/J.ImagingSci.Technol.2022.66.1.010502
19. Miyazaki, D., Taomoto, S., Hiura, S.: Extending the visibility of dichromats using histogram equalization of hue value defined for dichromats. Int. J. Image Graph. **19**(3), 13 p (2019). Article No. 1950016
20. Nakauchi, S., Onouchi, T.: Detection and modification of confusing color combinations for red-green dichromats to achieve a color universal design. Color. Res. Appl. **33**(3), 203–211 (2008)

21. Oliveira, M.M.: Towards more accessible visualizations for color-vision-deficient indificuals. Comput. Sci. Eng. **15**(5), 80–87 (2013)
22. Rasche, K., Geist, R., Westall, J.: Detail preserving reproduction of color images for monochromats and dichromats. IEEE Comput. Graphics Appl. **25**(3), 22–30 (2005)
23. Ribeiro, M.G., Gomes, A.J.P.: A skillet-based recoloring algorithm for dichromats. In: International Conference on e-Health Networking, Applications & Services, pp. 702–706 (2013)
24. Ribeiro, M., Gomes, A.J.P.: Recoloring algorithms for colorblind people: a survey. ACM Comput. Surv. **52**(4), 37 p (2019)
25. Ruminski, J., et al.: Color transformation methods for dichromats. In: 3rd Conference on Human System Interactions, pp. 634–641 (2010)
26. Sajadi, B., Majumder, A., Oliveira, M.M., Schneider, R.G., Raskar, R.: Using patterns to encode color information for dichromats. IEEE Trans. Visual Comput. Graphics **19**(1), 118–129 (2013)
27. Simon-Liedtke, J.T., Farup, I.: Multiscale daltonization in the gradient domain. J. Percept. Imaging **1**(1), 010503-1–010503-12 (2018)
28. Srividhya, J.P., Sivakumar, P., Rajaram, M.: The color blindness removal technique in image by using gradient map method. In: International Conference on Signal Processing, Communication, Computing and Networking Technologies, pp. 24–29 (2011)
29. Tanaka, G., Suetake, N., Uchino, E.: Lightness modification of color image for protanopia and deuteranopia. Opt. Rev. **17**(1), 14–23 (2010)
30. Tennenholtz, G., Zachevsky, I.: Natural contrast enhancement for dichromats using similarity maps. In: International Conference on Science of Electrical Engineering, pp. 1–5 (2016)
31. Yan, F., Liu, G., Zheng, Y.: An HTML5 based discoloration algorithm for people with low vision. In: International Conference on Biomedical Engineering and Informatics, pp. 837–842 (2015)

Uncalibrated Photometric Stereo Using Superquadrics with Texture Estimation

Tsuyoshi Migita$^{(\boxtimes)}$, Ayane Okada, and Norikazu Takahashi

Okayama University, Okayama, Japan
`migita@cs.okayama-u.ac.jp`

Abstract. When a 3D scene is captured in several 2D images, a compact description (or parameters) of the 3D scene can be estimated from the images. Such an inference is formulated as the inverse of rendering computer graphics and is important for various applications, such as object recognition, inspection, and/or VR. In the present paper, we extend a photometric stereo method in such a way as to estimate the texture of the object in addition to previous estimation of parameters describing the objects and light sources. To do so, we need a realistic minimization method, combined with a method to obtain the Jacobian of the cost function with respect to the texture. We implemented this method and verified the validity of the framework using synthetic and real-world data.

Keywords: Inverse rendering · Uncalibrated photometric stereo · Superquadrics · Levenberg-Marquardt method · Computer graphics · Two-stage rendering · Jacobian

1 Introduction

Given several 2D images of a 3D scene, some properties of the scene, such as object shapes and/or positions of light sources, can be estimated. Various such methods have been proposed and are collectively known as inverse rendering, because such a method is basically the inverse of rendering computer graphics. The present paper focuses on uncalibrated photometric stereo methods [1–7], where the given images differ only with respect to lighting conditions. Such methods can separate intrinsic characteristics of the objects from lighting effects, and have various applications, such as object recognition/inspection, photogrammetry, human behavior understanding, autonomous vehicles, and realization of VR space.

Based on the method described in [1], the scene is modeled by superquadrics [8,9] and a single light source for each image, i.e., the input images can be approximated by computer graphics processes when shape and lighting parameters are given appropriately. This method estimates the parameters by minimizing a cost function that describes the difference between the given images

Supported by JSPS KAKENHI Grant Number 20K11866.

K. Sumi et al. (Eds.): IW-FCV 2022, CCIS 1578, pp. 34–48, 2022.
https://doi.org/10.1007/978-3-031-06381-7_3

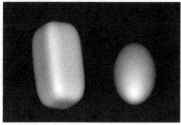

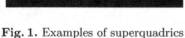

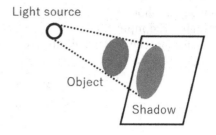

Fig. 1. Examples of superquadrics   **Fig. 2.** Example of a cast shadow

and rendered images. The minimization uses the Levenberg-Marquardt method [14,15], which is an iterative numerical optimization algorithm, and requires the Jacobian of the rendered images. In the present paper, the texture on the object surfaces is also estimated in addition to the scene parameters dealt with in the previous study. This requires an efficient method for calculation of the Jacobian and minimization methods using the Jacobian. Since the cost function involves computer graphics processes, the Jacobian should also be calculated using modern graphics APIs, such as Direct3D 12 [10], which are usually accelerated by a GPU. The method is verified on sets of synthetic and real images and is shown to be able to attain lower cost function values than previously possible.

2 Formulation and Algorithms

2.1 Minimization on Two Sets of Parameters

In the present paper, we focus on estimating two sets of parameters from images by minimizing a cost function defined as:

$$E(\boldsymbol{p}, \boldsymbol{t}) = (1/2)||\boldsymbol{r}||^2, \quad \text{where} \quad \boldsymbol{r} = (\boldsymbol{t} \circ F(\boldsymbol{p})) - \boldsymbol{e}'. \tag{1}$$

Here, $\boldsymbol{r}$, or the residual, is the difference between synthesized and given input images $\boldsymbol{e}'$. The synthesis is performed through a computer graphics algorithm modeled as the pixel-wise product, denoted by the $\circ$ symbol, of a texture $\boldsymbol{t}$ and a shading/lighting effect $F(\boldsymbol{p})$. Figure 1 shows an example of $F(\boldsymbol{p})$, where superquadrics are shown with shading effects, but without any texture. The object could cast a shadow if objects and the light source are aligned as shown in Fig. 2, and, in this case, the value of F becomes small. Usually, the texture should be warped according to the object geometry, but we do not assume any warping because of the basic assumption of photometric stereo, where the objects and camera are fixed throughout input images, and generally this assumption enables photometric stereo to provide a very accurate 3D reconstruction. We also use the term 'reflectance map' to refer to $\boldsymbol{t}$. The set of parameters $\boldsymbol{p}$ consists of object shapes and lighting conditions, as before [1]. The texture $\boldsymbol{t}$ usually consists of more than 10^5 parameters and is not iteratively estimated in the previous method, but is rather fixed after being roughly estimated by simply averaging the input images.

Consider the following update rule based on the Levenberg-Marquardt method [14, 15]:

$$x \leftarrow x - (H + \mu I)^{-1} g, \tag{2}$$

$$H = J^T J, \tag{3}$$

$$g = J^T r, \tag{4}$$

$$\text{because} \quad E(x) = (1/2)\|r(x)\|^2, \tag{5}$$

$$r(x + \Delta x) = r(x) + J \Delta x + O(\|\Delta x\|^2), \tag{6}$$

where E is a cost function, x is a vector of parameters to be estimated, J is the Jacobian of the residual r, g is the gradient $\partial E/\partial x$ of the cost function, and H is an approximated Hessian $\partial^2 E/\partial x \partial x$ of the cost function.

Since we assumed in (1) that the parameters are divided into two distinct sets, the update rule becomes

$$\begin{pmatrix} p \\ t \end{pmatrix} \leftarrow \begin{pmatrix} p \\ t \end{pmatrix} - \begin{pmatrix} \Delta p \\ \Delta t \end{pmatrix}, \quad \text{where} \tag{7}$$

$$\begin{pmatrix} \Delta p \\ \Delta t \end{pmatrix} = \left(\begin{pmatrix} H_{pp} & H_{pt} \\ H_{tp} & H_{tt} \end{pmatrix} + \begin{pmatrix} \mu_p I & \\ & \mu_t I \end{pmatrix} \right)^{-1} \begin{pmatrix} g_p \\ g_t \end{pmatrix}, \tag{8}$$

where g and H are divided into two or four parts, and subscripts indicate the set of parameters by which the cost function E is differentiated, e.g., $g_p = \partial g/\partial p$.

We do not directly calculate g and H, but rather calculate g and H from r and J. In addition, J is also divided and thus

$$g = \begin{pmatrix} J_p^T r \\ J_t^T r \end{pmatrix}, \tag{9}$$

$$H = \begin{pmatrix} J_p^T J_p & J_p^T J_t \\ J_t^T J_p & J_t^T J_t \end{pmatrix}, \tag{10}$$

$$\text{since} \quad J = (J_p | J_t). \tag{11}$$

Although the sizes of g and/or H with subscript(s) t are very large, e.g., H_{tt} is a square matrix of size $10^5 \times 10^5$ or larger, only diagonal entries are nonzero in the matrix, because J_t is very sparse due to the model (1). This makes the update rule quite feasible. Applying block-wise LU decomposition to (8), we obtain

$$\begin{pmatrix} \Delta p \\ \Delta t \end{pmatrix} = \begin{pmatrix} \hat{H}_{pp} - H_{pt} \hat{H}_{tt}^{-1} H_{tp} & 0 \\ \hat{H}_{tt}^{-1} H_{tp} & I \end{pmatrix}^{-1} \begin{pmatrix} g_p - H_{pt} \hat{H}_{tt}^{-1} g_t \\ \hat{H}_{tt}^{-1} g_t \end{pmatrix} \tag{12}$$

where $\hat{H}_{pp} = H_{pp} + \mu_p I$ and $\hat{H}_{tt} = H_{tt} + \mu_t I$. Based on the first row, Δp is easily calculated, because the upper half of the equation does not involve Δt. The result is then used to calculate Δt. Note that the upper-left part of the coefficient matrix is the Schur complement [16] and is small, 32×32 for our experiments, although intermediate J has more than $10^5 \times (32 + 1)$ possibly nonzero elements.

2.2   Three-Step Algorithm

It is well known that a non-linear optimization process can be trapped in a physically implausible local minima, or diverge, or is even undefined because the coefficient matrix becomes singular. Such risks are often mitigated by the μ_* parameters in (12) in that larger values of the parameters slow down the process and guide the process to a nearby local solution. However, since large values of μ_* actually slow down the process, the values should be as small as possible.

Instead of using large μ_* values, there is a well-known alternative method, which alternately optimizes each of the parameters at a time. With this method, p and t are updated by

$$
\begin{aligned}
p &\leftarrow p - \hat{H}_{pp}^{-1} g_p, \\
t &\leftarrow t - \hat{H}_{tt}^{-1} g_t.
\end{aligned}
\tag{13}
$$

There are two differences from the Schur-complement-based method.

(i) The alternating optimization method only uses diagonal blocks of the Hessian, H_{pp} and H_{tt}. The process may be slowed down by ignoring 'interaction' terms H_{pt}, but the required amount of computation per iteration is far smaller than that for the Schur-complement. (ii) The partial Hessian and corresponding gradient are calculated after the other parameters are updated, whereas all entities on the right-hand side of (12) are calculated simultaneously. This means that residuals should be calculated twice for (13), whereas the calculation time of the Jacobian does not increase, because only each part of the Jacobian is required for each equation.

Therefore, the performance of (12) and (13) is generally difficult to compare. After some preliminary experiments, we decided to use the following three-step algorithm, keeping both efficiency and stability in mind.

1. Using only the first equation of (13), i.e., as in the previous method, for several iterations.
2. Using both equations of (13) with relatively large μ_* for several iterations.
3. Using (12) with the smallest possible μ_*, which is typically 100.

2.3   Jacobian

The matrix J is the Jacobian of the residual r:

$$
J = (J_p | J_t) = \left(\frac{\partial r}{\partial p_0}, \frac{\partial r}{\partial p_1}, \cdots \frac{\partial r}{\partial t_0}, \frac{\partial r}{\partial t_1}, \cdots \right),
\tag{14}
$$

with $p = (p_0, p_1, \cdots)^T$ and $t = (t_0, t_1, \cdots)^T$.

We can replace the residual r in the equation with rendered images $t \circ F$, because input images do not depend on any parameters, as defined in (1).

Each column of J_p is approximated by a finite difference as

$$
\frac{\partial r}{\partial p_k} = \frac{r(p + \varepsilon_k b_k) - r(p - \varepsilon_k b_k)}{2\varepsilon_k},
\tag{15}
$$

where $\boldsymbol{b}_k$ is a vector with the same dimension as $\boldsymbol{p}$, where the value of the kth row is 1, and the other values are 0. The value of ε_k is chosen such that a certain minimum difference is produced between images, but the difference should not be too large or too small. This value is usually 2^{-7} for a parameter having a typical range of $[-1 : 1]$, e.g., an element of a 3D unit vector, and is otherwise roughly proportional to the typical range of a parameter. The choice is the result of an observation that the finite difference (15) typically cancels out seven bits of image intensity and has $O(\varepsilon^3)$ errors after 21st bit. Thus, entries of the Jacobian are expected to have 14-bit accuracy, which is optimal when using the IEEE754 32-bit floating-point format with a 23-bit mantissa. Therefore, we need to configure a graphics API to calculate and store pixel values in float32 precision, not as 8-bit integers, as is usually the case.

For $\boldsymbol{J}_t$, it is not realistic to apply finite differences, but a straightforward calculation is possible because

$$\boldsymbol{J}_t = \frac{\partial (t \circ F)}{\partial t}, \tag{16}$$

suggests that the result is almost a diagonal matrix $\text{diag}(F)$ having entries of F as its diagonal entries.

More precisely, since we have several input images, the cost function is the sum over several images. Thus, $\boldsymbol{r}$ is actually formed by stacking residual vectors $\boldsymbol{r}_f$ for each image, where f is the index of the image. So is $\boldsymbol{J}$. In this case, it is convenient to reinterpret (3) and (4) as

$$\boldsymbol{H} = \sum_f \boldsymbol{J}_f^T \boldsymbol{J}_f, \tag{17}$$

$$\boldsymbol{g} = \sum_f \boldsymbol{J}_f^T \boldsymbol{r}_f, \tag{18}$$

because this requires less memory for intermediate $\boldsymbol{J}_f$, which is a part of $\boldsymbol{J}$ instead of an entire $\boldsymbol{J}$.

In this form,

$$\begin{aligned} \boldsymbol{H}_t &= \text{diag}\left(\sum_f F_f \circ F_f\right), \\ \boldsymbol{g}_t &= \sum_f F_f \circ \boldsymbol{r}_f. \end{aligned} \tag{19}$$

Note that, F has subscript f because F depends on image index f or the lighting condition corresponding to the fth image, The other part $\boldsymbol{H}_{pt}$ can be similarly calculated. The above gradient and Hessian were calculated in 64-bit floating-point format, in order to avoid possible numerical instability in, for example, (12). This calculation is possible on a GPU using a compute shader.

A problem to consider is that F_f is an intermediate entity calculated in a pixel shader in the graphics pipeline, and, usually, we can obtain the final result $t \circ F_f$ only. It is preferable to obtain both images at once, instead of running two graphics paths separately. There are two ways to do this: post-processing and enabling multiple rendering targets, and the former is described later in Sect. 3.4.

3   Image Formation Model

In this section, details and/or extensions of our image formation model are given.

3.1   Superquadric Surfaces and Coordinate Systems

The scene is assumed to consist of superquadrics and a light source.
We use the following superquadric surface equation:

$$\Phi = \left|\frac{x}{a}\right|^r + \left|\frac{y}{b}\right|^s + \left|\frac{z}{c}\right|^t - 1 = 0. \tag{20}$$

where $(x, y, z)^T$ represents the coordinates of the point of interest in the object coordinate system (object coordinates), (a, b, c) is a set of shape parameters taking $a > 0$, $b > 0$, and $c > 0$, and (r, s, t) is also a set of shape parameters taking either $r = s = t = 2$ or 4 in the present paper. Figure 1 demonstrates shapes when $r = s = t = 4$ on the left, along with an ellipsoid on the right, where $r = s = t = 2$.

Using an orthographic camera at the coordinate origin, assuming the image coordinates are denoted by (u, v) and the possibly unknown depth of the pixel is denoted by w, the object coordinates $(x, y, z)^T$ are expressed as follows using a rotation matrix $\boldsymbol{R}$ and a position $\boldsymbol{c} = (c_x, c_y, c_z)^T$:

$$\begin{pmatrix} x \\ y \\ z \end{pmatrix} = \boldsymbol{R}^T \begin{pmatrix} u - c_x \\ v - c_y \\ w - c_z \end{pmatrix}. \tag{21}$$

3.2   Rendering Superquadric Surfaces

In standard graphics libraries, an object is usually approximated by a set of triangles. When estimating the shape of the object, obviously the parameters are not fixed but rather change constantly. Therefore, some modification to the usual computer graphics code is required. Instead of using pre-calculated superquadrics, a unit sphere is given as the graphics pipeline input, and a GPU-based code (vertex shader [10]) transforms the sphere into the designated superquadrics and projects onto the image plane. In the shader, each vertex is scaled so that it satisfies (20) or

$$(\sigma\xi)^r + (\sigma\eta)^s + (\sigma\zeta)^t = 1 \tag{22}$$

where (ξ, η, ζ) is a vertex on a unit sphere and σ is the vertex-wise scale, which is easy to obtain when $r = s = t = 2$ or 4. At the same time, the surface normal is calculated by normalizing the following vector:

$$\boldsymbol{N} = \begin{pmatrix} \frac{\partial}{\partial u} \\ \frac{\partial}{\partial v} \\ \frac{\partial}{\partial w} \end{pmatrix} \Phi \left(\boldsymbol{R}^T \begin{pmatrix} u - c_u \\ v - c_v \\ w - c_w \end{pmatrix} \right). \tag{23}$$

3.3   Shading Model

Based on the Lambertian diffuse reflection model [11] and the Blinn-Phong specular reflection model [12], the intensity of each pixel is expressed as

$$e = dc_d + sc_s \tag{24}$$
$$\text{where}\quad d = \max(0, n^T l) \tag{25}$$
$$s = \max(0, n^T ((l + v)/||l + v||))^{64}, \tag{26}$$

where n, l, and v are unit 3-vectors representing the outgoing surface normal, the vector pointing to the light source, and the vector pointing to the view point, respectively. The e is the intensity of the generated image, consisting of three elements (r, g, b) ranging from 0 to 1, and c_d and c_s are rgb vectors representing colors of diffuse and specular reflections, respectively. In our image formation model, c_d is sampled from the texture image t and thus depends on the image coordinates (no warping), whereas the other vector c_s represents the color of the light source, which is usually assumed to be white, and is fixed across images. The model is slightly extended from the previously described model $t \circ F$ by adding a specular term. However, this extension does not require extension of the methods for calculating the Jacobian.

In addition, we further extend the model to deal with cast shadows, and light attenuation that is inversely proportional to the squared distance between the light source and the object as

$$e = d_2 c_d + s_2 c_s, \quad \text{where} \quad (d_2, s_2) = \alpha ||l||^{-2} ((1 - 0.5S)d, (1 - S)s), \tag{27}$$

and S is 1 if there is an object between the point and the light source, and is otherwise 0. A specific method is described later in Sect. 3.6 to determine whether a superquadric exists between a point and a light source. The α compensates the attenuation factor $||l||^{-2}$ so that the product of these is 1 for a typical light position. The value 0.5, as in $(1 - 0.5S)$, for the diffuse component is for ambient lighting, i.e., an object in shadow is not completely black. Attenuation or a weight per image is required because each of the input images often exhibits a different overall brightness, as shown in Fig. 11, which is mainly caused by differences in light positions.

3.4   Two-Stage Shading and Jacobian

In order to efficiently calculate the Jacobian for an image with respect to the intensity values for each pixel in the texture, we use a two-stage rendering method, similar to methods that are often used to add blur or shadow or produce other lighting effects on an image. The proposed method consists of the following stages:

1. A pixel shader calculates intermediate coefficients d and s, defined in (25) and (26), respectively, or d_2 and s_2 in (27), for each pixel and stores these values in the frame buffer without calculating a final rgb color e. The frame buffer should be in float32 format.

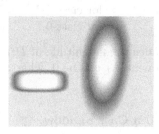

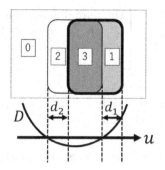

Fig. 3. Signed distance from the pixel to the nearest contour

Fig. 4. Pixel distinction based on the contours of the input images and estimated superquadric surfaces

2. The final rendering result e is calculated in a post-process compute shader. Based on (24), the d-component of the intermediate image is the Jacobian of interest, or F_f in (19), because the Jacobian of the residual essentially depends on the differentiation of (24) with respect to c_d and is obviously d, or d_2 when using (27).

3.5 Dealing with Contour Mismatch

The basic formulation sometimes suffers from a lack of information, i.e., when the contours of the object do not match between the input and estimated images, the cost function is not differentiable [13]. Therefore, it is not sufficient to use pure differences between rendered and input images. Instead, the solution in [1] is to introduce an alternative function for pixels near the object contours. Figure 3 shows an example of the function, which is basically the signed distance from the contour of the nearest superquadric surface. The formal definition of the function $D(u, v)$ is given in Sect. 3.6. The yellow region is inside the estimated object with $D(u, v) < 0$, whereas the cyan region is outside with $D(u, v) > 0$. The gradation between these regions indicates $D(u, v) = 0$ at the contour of the object and smoothly changes near the contour. The yellow region is expected to perfectly match the foreground objects in input images. However, in the early stages of the minimization process, the contour $D(u, v) = 0$ could be far from the actual contour in input images, and the process requires a cost function to guide the estimated contour to the actual position.

To do so, each pixel is classified into one of four classes, as shown in the Venn diagram in Fig. 4, where classes 1 and 3 represent the target object in the input image, and classes 2 and 3 represent the estimated superquadric surface, thus corresponding to the yellow region. The lower part of Fig. 4 illustrates a typical behavior of $D(u, v)$ with respect to coordinate u. Then, the residual r_{fi} is defined differently for each class.

$$r_{fi} = \begin{cases} \text{the pure difference in intensity values} & \text{for class-3} \\ h_1 \cdot D(u,v) \cdot (1,1,1)^T & \text{for class-1} \\ h_2 \cdot D(u,v) \cdot (1,1,1)^T & \text{for class-2} \\ 0 & \text{for class-0} \end{cases} , \quad (28)$$

where h_1 and h_2 are multiplicative factors to balance the magnitude of $D(u,v)$ and the pure differences. According to our experiment, h_1 can be 0, whereas it is preferable that $h_2 = 1$ or larger.

3.6   Contour of a Superquadric Surface and a Cast Shadow

The signed distance $D(u,v)$ is the minimum value of Φ along a semi-straight line emanating from the viewpoint and passing through pixel (u,v). When there are two or more objects, the minimum value of $D_j(u,v)$ should be taken, where D_j is the D function corresponding to the jth object.

Consider a general form

$$D(u,v) = \min_{w} \Phi(w), \quad (29)$$

$$\text{where} \quad \Phi(w) = \left| \frac{x_1 + x_0 w}{a} \right|^r + \left| \frac{y_1 + y_0 w}{b} \right|^s + \left| \frac{z_1 + z_0 w}{c} \right|^t - 1 = 0, \quad (30)$$

where $x_1 = (x_1, y_1, z_1)^T$ is the starting point and $x_0 = (x_0, y_0, z_0)^T$ is the direction of the semi-straight line, both of which are described in the object coordinate system of the superquadrics of interest. The function $\Phi(w)$ is quartic in w, and thus the minimum value is found where $\Phi'(w) = 0$, which involves solving a cubic equation. The cubic is monotonically increasing and has only one real solution. Therefore, it is relatively easy [1] to obtain the solution and the minimum value $D(u,v)$. If $D(u,v) < 0$, the semi-straight line corresponding to the pixel (u,v) intersects with the superquadric.

This is also used to determine whether the light is blocked by any other superquadric at a specified point. In this case, x_1 is the point of interest, and x_0 is the light source direction. Then, $D(u,v) < 0$ indicates that the light is blocked.

4   Experimental Results

4.1   Datasets and Implementation

We evaluated the proposed method using the set of simulated images in Fig. 5 and the set of real-world images in Fig. 11, which are hereinafter referred to as Simulation and Grapes, respectively. Each set consists of four images taken from a fixed viewpoint under different lighting conditions.

Our current implementation can handle two objects in up to four images. The shape of the object is modeled as an ellipsoid or a superquadric with $a = b = c = 4$. The images are assumed to be of size 384×288. Real images were resized and padded to become this size when the resolution and aspect ratio of the camera did not match these specifications.

4.2   Entries of p

The vector p contains parameters of multiple objects and positions of a moving light source.

In this experiment, there are 32 parameters to be estimated.

- Four light position vectors, each corresponding to the fth image.
- Two sets of shape and configuration parameters. Namely, (a_m, b_m, c_m) in (20), four parameters of the rotation matrix R_m, and translation vector $(c_{mx}, c_{my}, c_{mz})^T$ for the mth object.

The rotation matrix R_m is parameterized by a quaternion [17] as

$$R = \frac{1}{|q|^2} \begin{pmatrix} q_0^2 + q_1^2 - q_2^2 - q_3^2 & 2(q_1 q_2 - q_0 q_3) & 2(q_1 q_3 + q_0 q_2) \\ 2(q_1 q_2 + q_0 q_3) & q_0^2 - q_1^2 + q_2^2 - q_3^2 & 2(q_2 q_3 - q_0 q_1) \\ 2(q_1 q_3 - q_0 q_2) & 2(q_2 q_3 + q_0 q_1) & q_0^2 - q_1^2 - q_2^2 + q_3^2 \end{pmatrix}, \quad (31)$$

where $|q|^2 = q_0^2 + q_1^2 + q_2^2 + q_3^2$.

4.3   Initial Reflectance Map

The texture t is only estimated in later stages of the algorithm. At the beginning of the process, it is approximated by the average of the input images. However, unlike the previous method, the average is multiplied by 2, because, according to the image formation model $F_f \circ t$, the average is much smaller than t, since F_f is smaller than 1.

4.4   Simulation

The target objects in Fig. 5 are superquadric surfaces with a stripe texture. The light source vector of the 4th image was chosen so that one object casts a shadow on the other object.

The initial values for objects and lights were chosen by slightly altering the ground truth parameters used to create the input images. Figure 8(a) shows the initial reflectance map, or the texture, calculated as the weighted average of input images shown in Fig. 5. Apparently, the image is affected by shading, specular reflections, and cast shadows, so that it is not exactly the same as the original texture, which has only two colors: white and magenta. Using these parameters, initial reconstructions are created, which are shown in Fig. 6. Note that the left object is horizontally longer and the right object is slightly tilted. In addition, colors presented on the objects differ from the input images. In particular, the lower part is darker than the original because of the non-uniformity of the initial texture. The cost function value corresponding to the initial reconstruction is above 5,000, as shown in Figs. 9 and 10. The cost function is the squared sum of residuals over a varying number of effective pixels, which depends on the area of the estimated objects and is roughly between 20,000 and 24,000, out of $384 \times 288 = 110,592$ pixels.

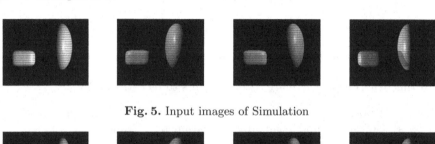

Fig. 5. Input images of Simulation

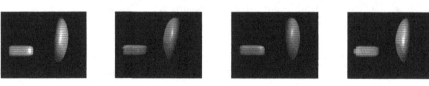

Fig. 6. Synthesized images of Simulation under initial values

Fig. 7. Synthesized images of Simulation after 322 iterations

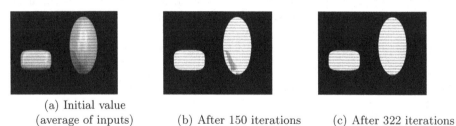

(a) Initial value
(average of inputs)   (b) After 150 iterations   (c) After 322 iterations

Fig. 8. Estimated texture (reflectance map)

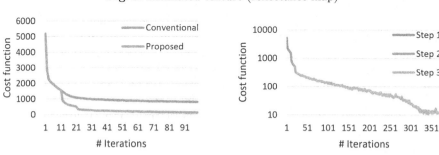

Fig. 9. Cost function comparison between proposed and conventional methods

Fig. 10. Cost function evolution over steps of proposed method

Figure 9 compares the evolution of the cost function value during iterative application of the proposed and conventional methods. Both methods start by updating parameters p only, and in the proposed method after the 10th iteration, both parameters p and t are alternately and/or simultaneously updated. Therefore, the proposed method produced much lower cost function values after the 10th iteration. Figure 10 gives a much closer look, where the behavior of the proposed method is plotted in three colors, each of which corresponds to one of three steps: (1) estimating p only, (2) estimating p and t alternately, and (3) estimating both p and t simultaneously. A total of 322 iterations were required to reconstruct an almost uniform texture, as shown in Fig. 8(c). Until then, the estimated texture t had non-uniformity caused by the cast shadow present in the initial values. For example, the estimated texture at 150th iteration is shown in Fig. 8(b), where the shading and specular reflection effects almost disappear but the false cast shadow is still visible on the bottom left of the right object. The final images are shown in Fig. 7. The images are almost indistinguishable from the input images in Fig. 5, and the cost function is no longer improving just above 10.

4.5   Grapes

Figure 11 shows a bunch of grapes photographed by a fixed camera. Since our implementation can only handle two objects, the input images are masked to pick up only two berries by using a manually created binary mask. The mask is shown as the colored area over the weighted average image (Fig. 14) of the input images. The image (fully masked version, not translucent one) is used as the initial texture.

The initial values for objects and lights were manually provided so that the 2D images of the objects are fairly close to the target objects in the input images. Using these parameters, an initial reconstruction is created, as shown in Fig. 12. Note that the objects look like circles because the initial shapes were chosen to be spheres and that lighting directions are coarsely aligned to produce similar shades on the berries. In addition, the 4th image is dark because the initial light position is slightly farther from the objects, as compared to the other images. The cost function value corresponding to the initial reconstruction is nearly 5,000, as shown in Fig. 15. The cost function is the squared sum of residuals over roughly 10,000 effective points.

For the real dataset, we focus on comparison of the cost function between the proposed and conventional methods, as shown in Fig. 15. The proposed method estimated parameters p only until the 20th iteration. It then alternately estimated p and texture t until the 50th iteration, and finally simultaneously estimated both p and t. The orange plot shows noticeable changes in the shape of the curve after the 20th and 50th iterations, and it is clear that the proposed method produces much lower cost function values than the conventional method shown by the blue plot. On the other hand, it is difficult to evaluate the resulting parameters because we do not have ground truths for any parameters of the dataset. In addition, the image formation models employed here, the Lambertian

Fig. 11. Input images of Grapes

Fig. 12. Synthesized images of Grapes under initial values

Fig. 13. Synthesized images of Grapes after 100 iterations

Fig. 14. Average image of Grapes   **Fig. 15.** Cost function for Grapes

and Blinn-Phong models with the point light source model and a single camera, do not provide sufficient clues for very reliable estimation of parameters and textures. Therefore, it is required, in the future, to use more sophisticated models and ground-truth-ready images to evaluate the other aspects of the methods.

5   Conclusions

In the present paper, we proposed an uncalibrated photometric stereo method that estimated the surface texture in addition to parameters of the superquadrics and lighting conditions. The method consists of up to three steps to gradually upgrade the estimation accuracy. We first verified the proposed method on a set of simulated images and obtained an almost perfect texture separated from lighting effects, such as shading and cast shadows, depending on the geometry or configuration of the objects and light sources. Then, the method was also tested on a set of real images, and the proposed method was shown to attain lower cost function values than the conventional method. Future directions in research may include using multiple cameras to capture the objects in order to provide more clues, and using more realistic models for shape, reflection, projection, and lighting in order to deal with real-world objects with improved accuracy.

References

1. Nasu, T., Migita, T., Takahashi, N.: Uncalibrated photometric stereo using superquadrics with cast shadow. In: Jeong, H., Sumi, K. (eds.) IW-FCV 2021. CCIS, vol. 1405, pp. 267–280 (2021)
2. Nasu, T., Migita, T., Shakunaga, T., Takahashi, N.: Uncalibrated photometric stereo using quadric surfaces with two cameras. In: Ohyama, W., Jung, S.K. (eds.) IW-FCV 2020. CCIS, vol. 1212, pp. 318–332 (2020)
3. Ramamoorthi, R., Hanrahan, P.: A signal-processing framework for inverse rendering. In: SIGGRAPH 2001, pp. 117–128 (2001)
4. Shi, B., Mo, Z., Wu, Z., Duan, D., Yeung, S.-K., Tan, P.: A benchmark dataset and evaluation for non-lambertian and uncalibrated photometric stereo. IEEE Trans. Pattern Anal. Mach. Intell. (TPAMI) 41(2), 271–284 (2019)
5. Migita, T., Ogino, S., Shakunaga, T.: Direct bundle estimation for recovery of shape, reflectance property and light position. In: Forsyth, D., Torr, P., Zisserman, A. (eds.) ECCV 2008. LNCS, vol. 5304, pp. 412–425. Springer, Heidelberg (2008). https://doi.org/10.1007/978-3-540-88690-7_31
6. Belhumeur, P.N., Kriegman, D.J., Yuille, A.L.: The bas-relief ambiguity. Int. J. Comput. Vision 35(1), 33–44 (1999)
7. Matusik, W., Pfister, H., Brand, M., McMillan, L.: A data-driven reflectance model. ACM Trans. Graph. 22(3), 759–769 (2003)
8. Paschalidou, D, Van Gool, L., Geiger, A.: Learning unsupervised hierarchical part decomposition of 3D objects from a single RGB image. In: Proceedings of 2020 IEEE/CVF Conference on Computer Vision and Pattern Recognition (CVPR) (2020)
9. Barr, A.H.: Superquadrics and angle-preserving transformations. IEEE Comput. Graphics Appl. 1(1), 11–23 (1981)
10. https://docs.microsoft.com/en-us/windows/win32/direct3d12/direct3d-12-graphics
11. Koppal, S.J.: Lambertian reflectance. In: Ikeuchi, K. (ed.) Computer Vision. Springer, Boston (2014). https://doi.org/10.1007/978-0-387-31439-6_534
12. Blinn, J.F.: Models of light reflection for computer synthesized pictures. In: Proceedings of 4th Annual Conference on Computer Graphics and Interactive Techniques, pp. 192–198 (1977)
13. Liu, S., Li, T., Chen, W., Li, H.: Soft rasterizer: a differentiable renderer for image-based 3D reasoning. In: Proceedings of International Conference on Computer Vision (2019)
14. Levenberg, K.: A method for the solution of certain non-linear problems in least squares. Q. Appl. Math. 2(2), 164–168 (1944)

15. Marquardt, D.: An algorithm for least-squares estimation of nonlinear parameters. SIAM J. Appl. Math. **11**(2), 431–441 (1963)
16. Boyd, S., Vandenberghe, L.: Convex Optimization. Cambridge University Press, Cambridge (2004)
17. Diebel, J.: Representing attitude: euler angles, unit quaternions, and rotation vectors. Technical report, Stanford University (2006)

3D Shape Reconstruction of Japanese Traditional Puppet Head from CT Images

Hiroyuki Ukida[1]([✉]), Kouki Yamazoe[1], Masahide Tominaga[2], Tomoyo Sasao[3], and Kenji Terada[1]

[1] Graduate School of Technology, Industrial and Social Sciences, Tokushima University, Tokushima, Japan
ukida@tokushima-u.ac.jp
[2] Graduate School of Biomedical Sciences, Tokushima University, Tokushima, Japan
[3] Graduate School of Frontier Sciences, The University of Tokyo, Tokyo, Japan

Abstract. In this paper, we discuss a 3D shape reconstruction method of Japanese traditional puppet heads for a digital archiving. Especially, to reconstruct an inner shape of head, we use CT images. First, we divide four regions (wood, hair, paint, and air) by thresholds based on manual directed regions. After that, we divide these regions by a graph cut method. And we also present a method to estimate 3D shape of parts in puppet head. This method is also based on a graph cut method. Moreover, we also discuss a method to distinguish material of puppet head by machine learning. Here we use "U-Net" to extract wood parts of puppet head from its CT images. And we show experimental results by these methods.

Keywords: X-ray CT images · Puppets · Shape reconstruction · Graph cut method · Machine learning

1 Introduction

"Awa Ningyo Joruri" is traditional Japanese puppet theater, especially, it has been played in Tokushima prefecture. In recent years, however, there has been a shortage of successors to the Ningyo Joruri. To preserve this culture and pass it on to future generations, this research challenges a digital archive of puppets.

"Digital archiving" [1] is a technique to preserve an object's data such as, 3D shapes, color, gloss, and so on semi permanently. This technique has been studied and applied to the national treasures, the important cultural properties, old documents, etc. We have also discussed methods to measure 3D outer shape of puppet heads precisely using a 3D scanner, a turn table, and an arm robot [2, 3].

Figure 1 shows examples of puppet heads. As a characteristic of "Awa Ningyo Joruri" puppets, many of them have some mechanisms in their heads such as moving eyes or opening/closing mouth and so on. Therefore, to archive puppet information more precisely, we must reconstruct inner parts of puppet head. Figure 2 shows an inside of puppet head in production. We can see parts of eyes and neck in it. But it is difficult to see the inside of completed head because we cannot disassemble it. To observe the

K. Sumi et al. (Eds.): IW-FCV 2022, CCIS 1578, pp. 49–63, 2022.
https://doi.org/10.1007/978-3-031-06381-7_4

inner construction of puppet head, we use X-ray Computer Tomography (CT) imaging system. And we discuss a method to reconstruct a shape of puppet head from CT images.

Main material of puppet head is the dry wood. However, it is not displayed clearly in CT images because of a low moisture. Moreover, some other materials are used in a puppet head which are hair wig, whitewash paint on the surface and metal nail to fix wig on a puppet head. The ranges of intensities of these materials in CT images are partly overlapped that of dry wood. Therefore, to reconstruct the shape of puppet head, we must discuss a method to distinguish materials in CT images. In this paper, we propose a method to distinguish and extract materials in CT images using thresholding and graph cut method. And we also present a method to estimate 3D shape of parts in puppet head. This method is also based on a graph cut method.

Moreover, we also discuss a method to distinguish material of puppet head by machine learning. Here we use "U-Net" to extract wood parts of puppet head from its CT images. And we show experimental results by these methods.

Fig. 1. Examples of puppet head.

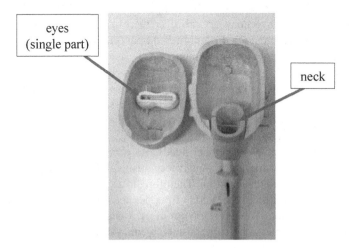

Fig. 2. Inside of puppet head.

2 3D Shape Reconstruction from CT Images

2.1 Extracted Regions in CT Images

Figure 3 shows an example of a CT image of a puppet head. In this study, we assume four regions in CT images of a puppet head.

1. Air region inside and outside of the head.
2. Hair wig region put on the head.
3. Dry wood region of the head.
4. Paint region on the surface of head.

In an actual puppet head, other materials (ex. metal nails) are also included. But the sizes of these materials are not large. Therefore, we distinguish above four regions from CT images.

Material extraction methods we propose consist of two methods as following:

1. Rough region segmentation using thresholds obtained from histogram of intensities in manual directed area in a CT image.
2. Precise region extraction using a graph cut method from the result of 1.

We explain these methods in next subsections.

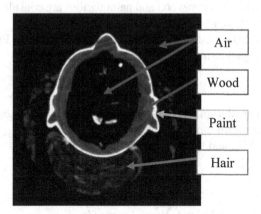

Fig. 3. A CT image of a puppet head.

2.2 Extracting Materials Based on Histogram

This subsection shows a material extracting method based on histogram.

- Step 1-1. About four regions (air, hair, wood, and paint), we obtain histograms from areas directed by manual in some CT images.
- Step 1-2. Each histogram is approximated to the normal distribution by Eq. (1):

$$f_k(x) = \frac{1}{\sqrt{2\pi\sigma_k^2}}\exp\left(-\frac{(x-\mu_k)^2}{2\sigma_k^2}\right) \tag{1}$$

where k is a kind of region, x is intensity, μ_k and σ_k are mean and standard deviation of region k.
- Step 1-3. Estimate thresholds as cross points of normal distributions which are neighboring two regions.

By using estimated thresholds, we can divide four regions in CT images roughly.

2.3 Precise Extraction by Graph Cut Method

The graph cut method estimates the combination of pixel's label (object or background) in images in a criterion of a cost minimization efficiently under the condition in which some parts in image are assigned labels beforehand [4].

In this study, we reconstruct 3D shape of dry wood and paint parts only. Because the shape of hair wig deforms depend to the attitude of puppet head, it is difficult to model the 3D hair shape. Hence, the dry wood and paint regions are considered as object label and hair and air regions are background.

The cost function $E(L)$ used in the graph cut method is shown in Eq. (2) as the linear combination of the region term $R(L)$ and the boundary term $B(L)$:

$$E(L) = R(L) + \lambda \cdot B(L) \tag{2}$$

where L is label assigned to pixels ($L \in \{obj, bkg\}$), λ is a weight between the region term and the boundary term (non-negative value).

The region term $R(L)$ and the boundary term $B(L)$ are described as:

$$R(L) = \sum_{u\in U} f_u(L_u) \tag{3}$$

$$B(L) = \sum_{\{u,v\}\in N} g_{u,v}(L_u, L_v) \tag{4}$$

where f_u is a likelihood of a region, $g_{u,v}$ is a likelihood of a boundary between neighboring pixels. U is a set of pixels and u shows a pixel. N is a set of neighboring two pixels and $\{u, v\}$ is a tuple of pixels. f_u and $g_{u,v}$ are described as follows:

$$f_u(L_u) = -\ln\Pr(I_u|L_u) \tag{5}$$

$$g_{u,v}(L_u, L_v) = \begin{cases} \frac{\exp\{-\beta(I_u-I_v)^2\}}{\text{dist}(u,v)} & (L_u \neq L_v) \\ 0 & (L_u = L_v) \end{cases} \tag{6}$$

$\Pr(I_u|L_u)$ is a likelihood of pixel I_u in each region. This is approximated to a normal distribution. β is constant and $\text{dist}(u, v)$ is a distance between neighboring pixels.

Figure 4 shows a process of graph cut method. In this figure, the node u is corresponding to a pixel, and it connected to a neighbor pixel (node) v. We call this linkage "n-link" and we assume that this link has a cost estimated by Eq. (6). The node u is also connected to the node s labeled object ("obj") and the node t labeled background ("bkg"). These linkages are called "t-link" and they have costs estimated by Eq. (5). Cutting off a link from u to t or s can be regarded as labeling "obj" or "bkg" to u. Therefore, when the sum of costs of these linkages is minimum, the label assigned u minimize Eq. (2). In this study, we apply the minimum cut/maximum flow algorithm by Boykov [5] to the cost minimization method.

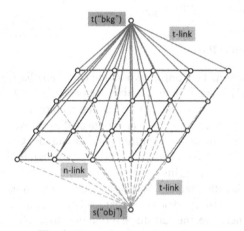

Fig. 4. Example of graph structure.

In the method of region extraction by graph cut, we must assign the object or background labels to some parts of regions as "seed" certainly. In general, this "seed" is usually assigned by user manually in graph cut method. But, in this study, we try to assign "seed" without user input by using following steps.

- Step 2-1. By applying a method in Subsect. 2.2 to a CT image, dry wood and paint regions are extracted in this image.
- Step 2-2. By using morphologic methods (dilation and erosion), we fill holes and eliminate small regions (about 10 by 10 pixels) in the image of Step 2-1.
- Step 2-3. We estimate a distance transformation image from the result of Step 2-2, and extract two regions which are:
  - One region consists of some pixels which distance is from maximum distance (D_{max}) to $D_{max} - \Delta_1$,
  - Other region consists of some pixels which distance is from minimum distance (D_{min}) to $D_{min} + \Delta_2$,

where Δ_1 and Δ_2 are distance thresholds and they are assigned some values previously. As a result, we can get two seeds for graph cut method.

Moreover, CT images of a puppet has many images, and they are aligned perpendicular to the image plane, so to assign seeds to all CT images, we use following steps:

- Step 3-1. In a neighbor (upper of lower) CT image of a labeled CT image, firstly, the region extraction based on histogram is applied. After that, we obtain an overlapped region as "seed" in which the dry wood region in this image and the object region in a labeled CT image. By using this seed region, we apply the graph cut method.
- Step 3-2. By propagating results of Step 3-1 to the upper and lower CT images, we extract object regions in all CT images.

2.4 Extraction of Inner Parts

In Subsect. 2.3, we explained the object (wood and paint) and background (hair and air) extraction method in CT images. In this section, we present a parts extraction method in puppet head. Herein, we show an eye part extraction method as an example. In puppet head, its eye is one part because two eyes are connected as shown in Fig. 2.

In a preliminary experiment, we confirmed that the sagittal CT images (from left to right) could obtain the 3D shape of the eye part more accurately than the normal axial CT image (from bottom to top). This is because that the 2D shape of eye part is simple in sagittal plane. On the other hand, CT images can be used in three directions: axial, sagittal, and coronal (from front to back). For parts other than the eyes, other orientations may be appropriate. Therefore, the part shape is obtained for each of the three directions, and the final part shape is reconstructed by integrating them.

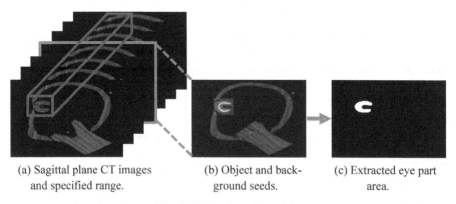

(a) Sagittal plane CT images   (b) Object and back-   (c) Extracted eye part
and specified range.   ground seeds.   area.

Fig. 5. Extraction of eye part.

In the following, the method using the case of extracting an eye from a sagittal CT image as an example is illustrated. The range of an eye part is specified manually in advance as shown as red lines in Fig. 5(a).

- Step 4-1. Select a CT image including an eye part and specify seed regions of object (eye part) and background (otherwise) manually. In Fig. 5(b), white line is object seed and black line is background seed.
- Step 4-2. By using these seed regions and the graph cut method, we extract eye part area in selected CT image (Fig. 5(c)).

By using results of Step 4-2 and following method, we estimate object and background seeds automatically in CT images adjacent to the left and right sides of the selected CT image and extract the eye part.

- Step 5-1. Estimate binarized images of object and background from eye part extracted image in Step 4-2.
- Step 5-2. Estimate a distance transform image from an object image in Step 5-1, and extract pixels whose values are from D_{min} to D_{max}.
- Step 5-3. In an adjacent CT image, we estimate object seeds in which the object region extracted in Subsect. 2.3 and extracted pixels in Step 5-2 overlap.
- Step 5-4. Similarly, we estimate a distance transform image from a background image, and extract pixels whose values are from D_{min} to D_{max}.
- Step 5-5. In the adjacent CT image, we estimate background seeds in which the background region extracted in Subsect. 2.3 and extracted pixels in Step 5-4 overlap.
- Step 5-6. By using the object and background seeds, we estimate eye part area in the adjacent CT image.

By applying the method from Step 5-1 to Step 5-6 in specified CT images, we can extract the 3D shape of eye part. In addition, the above method is applied to CT images of the axial and coronal direction to obtain the shape of the eye in each case. For the three eye shapes obtained, the common part is used as the final eye shape. The same process is applied to other parts to obtain their shapes.

2.5 Extraction by Machine Learning

In this section, we explain the method to distinguish materials from CT images by machine learning. Here, we extract only wood parts by dividing CT images into wood and other regions. As a method of two-class segmentation, we use "U-Net" [6] in this study.

U-Net is a network based on convolutional neural networks (CNNs). Figure 6 shows the configuration of the U-Net used in this study. U-Net consists of an encoder part and a decoder part. It has eight layers in both the encoder and decoder parts. The layers are joined in U-shape. In the encoder part, features are extracted from the input image by convolutional and pooling layers. In the decoder part, the extracted features are used to restore the image by the inverse convolution layer.

However, in general, the feature extraction in the encoder part discards the positional information in the image, so even if the decoder part restores the image, it will not be able to recover the same image as the original. Therefore, U-Net introduces shortcut joints. This is a method that concatenates the output from one reverse convolution layer of the decoder part with the features from the encoder part at the same level to perform the next reverse convolution process. By using this method, we can restore the image including the positional information.

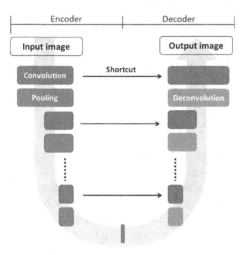

Fig. 6. Configuration of U-Net.

3 Experiments

3.1 Puppet Head and CT Images

Figure 7 shows a puppet head we use in this experiment. There is a mechanism to rotate eye up and down in this head. Figure 7 shows two of CT images of this head. These are intersection of puppet head at red lines A and B in Fig. 8. ((b) is as same as Fig. 3.) The black parts are air, the gray parts are dry wood and hair wig, and the white parts are paint on the wood surface.

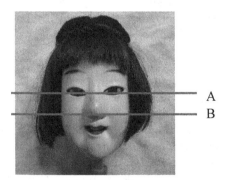

Fig. 7. Puppet head for experiments.

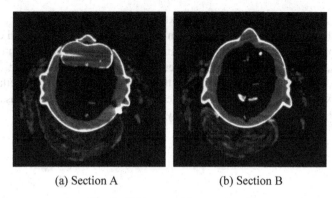

(a) Section A   (b) Section B

Fig. 8. CT images of puppet head.

3.2 Experimental Results of Puppet Shape Extraction

Figure 9 shows histograms and normal distributions of four regions (air, hair wig, dry wood, and paint) denoted in Sect. 2.2. Table 1 shows means and variances of normal distributions and thresholds to divide these regions. Figure 10 shows results of region segmentation of Fig. 8. As shown in Fig. 9, some parts of dry wood (red) are estimated as hair wig (green), and some parts of hair wig are also estimated as dry wood.

Figure 11 shows separated wood and paint region from Fig. 10(a) denoted in Subsect. 2.3. Figure 12 shows result of dilation and erosion method. Figure 13 shows result of distance transformation. In Fig. 14(a), white pixels are a region which assigns label "obj". In Fig. 14(b), white pixels are regions which assigns label "bkg".

Figure 15 shows the segmentation results by the graph cut method. The object part (dry wood and paint) is white, and the background part (air and hair wig) is black. In these images, most of hair wig regions can be extracted as the background, but some parts of hair wig regions are extracted as the object.

Figure 16 shows reconstructed 3D shape of puppet head. (a) shows extracted dry wood, paint, and hair wig from histogram thresholds. (b) shows extracted objects (dry wood and paint) by the graph cut method. In the result of (b), at the top of puppet head, the region of hair wig is remained. This is because that the hair wig is dense at this part to fix hair wig to wood parts, the intensity of hair wig is almost as same as the dry wood. Hence, we must discuss another method to segment these parts.

3.3 Experimental Results of Inner Parts Extraction

Figure 17 shows a result of eye part extraction by a method in Subsect. 2.4. (a) shows the shape obtained from CT images in the axial direction. Similarly, (b) is the shape obtained from the CT images in the sagittal direction and (c) is the shape obtained from the CT images in the coronal direction. (d) is the shape extracted only from the common part of (a), (b), and (c). In Fig. 17(a), (b) and (c), some wood parts of face are added. Because of the existence of wood parts around these parts, the proposed graph cut method cannot distinguish pixels which are parts or not. However, as shown in (d), by obtaining only the common part, the unnecessary part is removed, and the eye shape is obtained correctly.

Figure 18 shows a result of neck part extraction by same method. (a), (b), and (c) show the results obtained from CT images in the axial, sagittal, and coronal directions. (d) is the shape extracted only from the common part of (a), (b), and (c). In the case of the neck parts, contrary to the case of the eyes, a part of the neck shape is missing in all the results (a), (b), and (c). This case is also that the proposed graph cut method cannot distinguish pixels which are parts or not. Therefore, it is necessary to discuss a method how to extract the wood part more accurately.

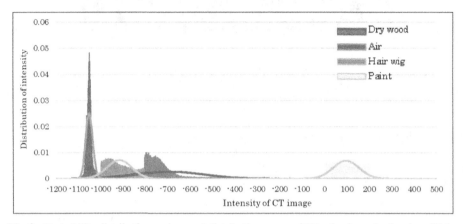

Fig. 9. Probability distribution and normal distribution curve of CT value in each of region. (Color figure online)

Table 1. Estimated means, variances, and thresholds.

	Air	Hair wig		Dry wood		Paint
Mean	−1051.9	−916.1		−689.4		96.3
Variance	253.0	3166.9		22796.7		3347.3
Threshold	−1014		−822		−131	

3.4 Experimental Results of Puppet Shape Extraction by U-Net

In this section, we show the extraction results of wood parts using machine learning (U-Net). First, 18 CT images are selected as training data from the 341 CT images used in Sect. 3.2. These images are selected from the entire CT image at equal intervals. For these CT images, only the wood part is extracted using the histogram thresholds shown in Sect. 2.2, and then the region of the wood part is manually modified to make the image data representing the ground truth in the training data. In practice, the ground truth is manually estimated for all CT images (341 images) to obtain the extraction accuracy.

Next, we train the U-Net model shown in Sect. 2.5 using the training data. Then, we identify the wood parts in 341 CT images including the training data.

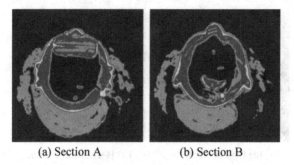

(a) Section A   (b) Section B

Fig. 10. Results of region segmentation by histogram.

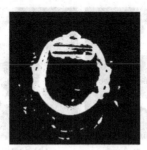

Fig. 11. Extracted wood and paint regions from Fig. 10(a).

Fig. 12. Result of dilation and erosion method.

Fig. 13. Result of distance transformation image.

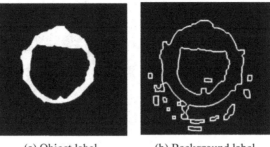

(a) Object label.   (b) Background label.

Fig. 14. Seeds of labels for graph cut.

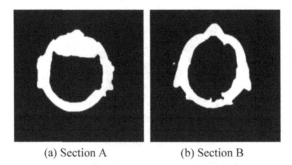

(a) Section A   (b) Section B

Fig. 15. Results of extracted regions by graph cut method.

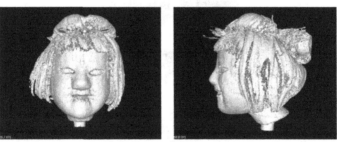

(a) Before applying graph cut.

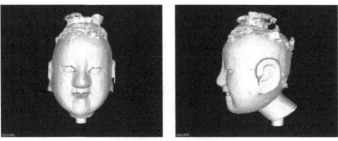

(b) After applying graph cut.

Fig. 16. Reconstructed 3D shape of puppet head.

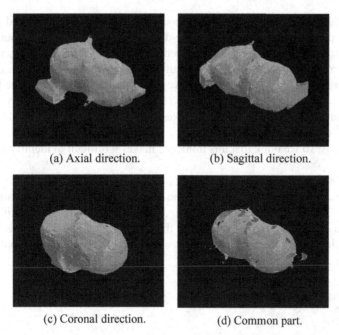

(a) Axial direction.   (b) Sagittal direction.

(c) Coronal direction.   (d) Common part.

Fig. 17. Reconstructed 3D shape of eye part.

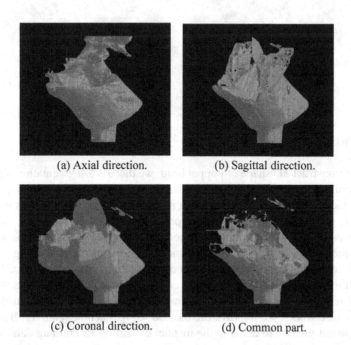

(a) Axial direction.   (b) Sagittal direction.

(c) Coronal direction.   (d) Common part.

Fig. 18. Reconstructed 3D shape of neck part.

Figure 19(a) shows the 3D shape of wood parts extracted by U-Net and Fig. 19(b) shows wood parts of the ground truth. The discrimination rate for the ground truth is 99.33%. On the other hand, for the experimental results in Sect. 3.2, the discrimination rate for the ground truth is 96.07%. This result shows that the machine learning method is more accurate to extract wood parts. However, as shown in Fig. 19(a), the hair at the top of the head is still present. The bundled hair is dense and the intensity in the CT image is similar to that of wood, which makes it difficult to identify. In addition, metal nails are used on the top of the head to hold the hair in place. It changes the pixel intensity around the nails, so we think that this influence makes it difficult to identify wood parts correctly.

In Fig. 19(a), the handle under the neck is not extracted. This part can be extracted by the graph cut method. The surface of the wood is often coated with paint, but the handle is not. Therefore, in machine learning, the part adjacent to the paint is identified as wood. But areas that are not adjacent to the paint are not identified as wood. From these points, it is also necessary to consider what kind of CT images are appropriate as training data.

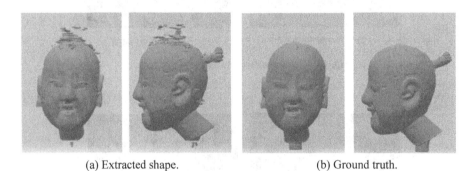

(a) Extracted shape.   (b) Ground truth.

Fig. 19. Reconstructed 3D shape by U-Net.

4   Conclusion

In order to reconstruct 3D shape of puppet head, we discuss a segmentation method for some materials of the puppet head in CT images. We propose two extraction methods to estimate the puppet head shape: one is a rough extraction based on histogram, and the other the graph cut method to extract precisely. We also propose the inner parts extraction method based on the graph cut method. Moreover, we discuss the wood part distinguish method by U-Net which is a framework of the machine learning.

From the results of experimental results using real puppet head and its CT images, 3D shape of the dry wood and paint region can be extracted but some parts of the hair wig are still remained in cases of both the graph cut and machine learning methods.

As the future works, we improve the method using machine learning. But we also use the graph cut method to assist in the manual extraction for training data. We study how to extract materials other than wood, and how to extract various puppets with high accuracy.

Acknowledgment. We would like to offer our special thanks to Mr. Kenji Sato (Tokushima Prefectural Awa Jurobe Yashiki (Puppet Theater and Museum)) and Mr. Yoichiro Amari (Joruri puppet producer) to lend us puppet heads. We would like to thank to Mr. Yoshitaka Hatakenaka and Hinata Ikeda to cooperate with experiments. This work was supported by JSPS KAKENHI Grant Number JP18K18483.

References

1. Ikeuchi, K., Oishi, T., et al.: 3D Digital Archiving. University of Tokyo Press (2010). (in Japanese)
2. Ukida, H.: 3D shape measurement system by integration of partial shapes and automatic defects detection. J. JSNDI **67**(7), 324–328 (2018). (in Japanese)
3. Ukida, H., Sasao, T., Terada, K., Yoshida, A.: Calibration method of 3D shape measurement system using 3D scanner, turn-table and arm-robot. In: Proceedings of the SICE Annual Conference 2019, pp. 136–141 (2019)
4. Ishikawa, H.: Graph cut. IPSJ SIG Technical report, 2007-CVIM-158, no. 26, pp. 193–204 (2007). (in Japanese)
5. Boykov, Y., Kolmogorov, V.: An experimental comparison of min-cut/max-flow algorithms for energy minimization in vision. IEEE Trans. Pattern Anal. Mach. Intell. **26**(9), 1124–1137 (2004)
6. Fujita, H., et al.: Introduction to Medical Image Processing in Python, Ohmsha, Tokyo (2020). (in Japanese)

Multi-band Photometric Stereo Using Random Sampling of Channels and Pixels

Daisuke Miyazaki[1(✉)] and Koumei Hamaen[1,2P]

[1] Hiroshima City University, Hiroshima 731-3194, Japan
miyazaki@hiroshima-cu.ac.jp
[2] Fujitsu Frontech Ltd., Tokyo, Japan
http://www.info.hiroshima-cu.ac.jp/~miyazaki/

Abstract. One of the main problems faced by the photometric stereo method is that several measurements are required, as this method needs illumination from light sources from different directions. A solution to this problem is the color photometric stereo method, which conducts one-shot measurements by simultaneously illuminating lights of different wavelengths. However, the classic color photometric stereo method only allows measurements of white objects, while a surface-normal estimation of a multicolored object using this method is theoretically impossible. This paper estimates the surface normal of a multi-colored object under multi-spectral lighting. This is a difficult problem since the albedo is different for each pixel and each channel. We solve this problem by sampling some pixels randomly. If we randomly sample neighboring pixels, the probability of picking the same albedo pixels may be high. Therefore, if the sampled pixels all have the same albedo, we can determine the surface normal uniquely. To demonstrate the effectiveness of this study, a measurement device with seven colors is used.

Keywords: Photometric stereo · Color photometric stereo · Multispectral camera · Multiple albedo · Random sampling

1 Introduction

The color photometric stereo method involves placing light sources of red, green, and blue colors in three different directions, which simultaneously illuminate the target object. This paper proposes a technique that employs a random sampling approach so that it can be applied to colored objects, which is impossible for conventional color photometric stereo.

The photometric stereo method [23, 26] requires capturing three pictures with different light source directions. Therefore, it is impossible to measure a dynamic object. This problem can be resolved using the color photometric stereo method [1–8, 11–16, 19, 21, 22, 24, 25, 27]. In this method, lights are simultaneously illuminated from red, green, and blue light sources, and one picture photographed with an RGB color camera is captured. The principle problem of the color photometric stereo method is the fact that it can only be used with white objects.

K. Sumi et al. (Eds.): IW-FCV 2022, CCIS 1578, pp. 64–79, 2022.
https://doi.org/10.1007/978-3-031-06381-7_5

Recently, some amount of techniques have been proposed to apply the color photometric stereo method to multicolored objects [1,3,8–10,13,14,17,22].

In this paper, we solve the problem by sampling some pixels randomly. If we randomly sample neighboring pixels, the probability of picking the same albedo pixels may be high. Therefore, if the sampled pixels all have the same albedo, we can determine the surface normal uniquely. We try the sampling process multiple times with different combinations, and we choose the representative surface normal among the multiple trials.

Unlike existing methods, we neither apply optical flow algorithm [9,14,22], nor apply region segmentation algorithm [8]. Unlike existing methods, our method is not limited to achromatic objects [10], and is not oversmoothed by median filtering [17]. Unlike existing methods, we neither need reflectance database [8], nor need shape from other sensors [1].

2 Multispectral Color Photometric Stereo Method

2.1 Image Formulation

Suppose that we lit a single parallel light source (infinite-far point light source) whose spectral distribution is represented as delta function, the pixel brightness I_c of channel c can be represented as follows using the Lambertian reflection model.

$$I_c = A_c \max(\mathbf{n} \cdot \mathbf{l}_c, 0). \tag{1}$$

Here, $\mathbf{n}$ is a normal vector and $\mathbf{l}_c$ is the light source direction vector of channel c. Hereinafter, we call A_c albedo. Note that the camera sensitivity and light source brightness are included in A_c.

As shown in Fig. 1, this study conducts a photoshoot of a multicolored object using seven channels. Following Eq. (1), the brightness is obtained from this photoshoot as follows.

$$I_0 = A_0 \max(\mathbf{n} \cdot \mathbf{l}_0, 0),$$
$$I_1 = A_1 \max(\mathbf{n} \cdot \mathbf{l}_1, 0),$$
$$\vdots$$
$$I_6 = A_6 \max(\mathbf{n} \cdot \mathbf{l}_6, 0). \tag{2}$$

The surface normal $\mathbf{n}$ is a 3D vector; however, the degree-of-freedom is two because it is constrained to be a unit vector (such constraint reduces one degree-of-freedom). Albedo A_c is represented by seven parameters. There are seven equations, as shown in Eq. (2), and nine unknown parameters (A_0, A_1, ..., A_6, n_x, n_y, n_z, s.t., $n_x^2 + n_y^2 + n_z^2 = 1$, namely seven for albedo and two for surface normal). Therefore, color photometric stereo, without any assumption or constraint, is an ill-posed problem.

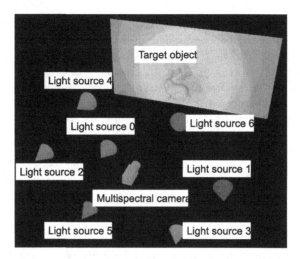

Fig. 1. Conceptual explanation of multispectral color photometric stereo. Target object is illuminated by multiple light sources whose wavelengths are different. One image is taken using multispectral camera.

The most commonly used assumption is to limit the color of the target objects to white ($A_0 = A_1 = \cdots = A_6$). The color photometric stereo for white objects, or in other words, the conventional photometric stereo can directly solve the surface normal.

However, this paper analyzes the methods with multi-colored objects. Therefore, we randomly sample some pixels that can be assumed to be the same albedo. The unknown normal parameters (n_x, n_y, n_z) increase if we use multiple pixels. The unknown albedo parameters $(A_0, A_1, \ldots, A_6)$ also increase if the chosen pixels have a different albedo, while they do not increase if the chosen pixels have the same albedo because $A_0, A_1, \ldots, A_6$ are the same for all chosen pixels. In the latter case, the number of equations is more than the number of unknowns, thus, the problem becomes solvable. If the chosen pixels have the same albedo, the correct surface normal can be estimated. However, the surface normal cannot be estimated correctly if the chosen pixels have different albedo. To overcome this problem (Fig. 1), Sect. 2.2 shows our method which can be applied to the object surface of non-uniform albedo.

2.2 Multiple Albedo with 4 Channels and 8 Pixels

Our method chooses some channels and some pixels randomly, and estimates the surface normal from chosen data. The problem is that the albedo of chosen pixels might be different from that of the pixel of interest (Fig. 2). Figure 3 is the example of randomly chosen pixels.

Another problem is that the estimation will fail if we choose the channels that contain shadow or specular reflection (Fig. 4).

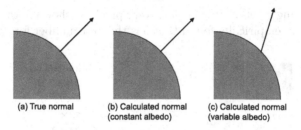

(a) True normal   (b) Calculated normal   (c) Calculated normal
                   (constant albedo)   (variable albedo)

Fig. 2. Example of estimated surface normal.

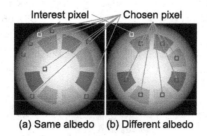

Interest pixel   Chosen pixel

(a) Same albedo   (b) Different albedo

Fig. 3. Chosen pixels: (a) Pixels chosen from same albedo and (b) pixels chosen from different albedo.

Chosen pixels should be the same albedo, thus, we choose the pixels which are spatially close to the pixel of interest. Suppose that we choose 8 pixels (Fig. 5). First, we denote the pixel of interest as P_0. Next, we choose 1 pixel P_1 from 3×3 pixels surrounding the pixel of interest. Similarly, we choose P_2 from 7×7 area. And, we choose P_3, P_4, P_5, P_6, and P_7 from 13×13, 21×21, 29×29, 41×41, and 55×55, respectively. As shown in Fig. 6, even if the interest pixel is at the boundary of multiple albedos, it is likely to choose the pixels with the same albedo. Usually, the object is painted with the same paint for a certain amount of region. Thus, it is statistically apparent that neighboring pixels have a high probability to be the same albedo.

This paper uses 8 for the number of pixels to be chosen. The optimal number to be chosen depends on the surrounding pixels whether they have uniform albedo or they have various albedos. Therefore, we cannot determine a constant

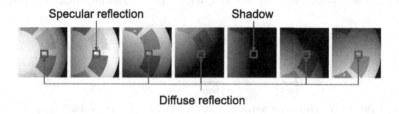

Specular reflection   Shadow

Diffuse reflection

Fig. 4. Example of pixel brightness for each channel.

number for chosing pixels that works for every pixel. As shown in the experiments (Sect. 3), we have empirically found that 8 is the best number for chosing pixels.

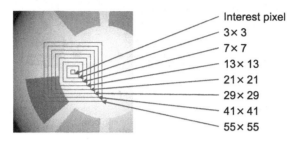

Fig. 5. Selecting area of pixels.

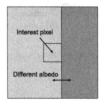

Fig. 6. Interest pixel at the boundary of multiple albedo.

To avoid shadow, we choose the channels that have large brightness. We choose the channels randomly to avoid specular reflection. Suppose that we choose 4 channels from 7 channels. First, we sum up the brightness of the pixel of interest for each channel.

$$I_{sum} = I_{0,0} + I_{0,1} + \cdots + I_{0,6}. \tag{3}$$

We represent the probability P_c as Eq. (4), which is the brightness of each channel divided by the sum.

$$P_c = \frac{I_{0,c}}{I_{sum}}. \tag{4}$$

We choose the channel a using Eq. (5), where R is a random number from 0 to 1.

$$0 \leq R < P_1 \ (a = 0),$$

$$\sum_{i=0}^{a-1} P_i \leq R < \sum_{i=0}^{a} P_i \ \text{(otherwise)}. \tag{5}$$

Let us denote the chosen channel a as C_0. We set the value I_{0,C_0} to be 0, recalculate Eq. (3) and Eq. (4), and we determine C_1 from Eq. (5). Similarly, we determine C_2 and C_3.

2.3 Computing Albedo and Surface Normal

The cost function for 4 channels and 8 pixels is shown in Eq. (6).

$$\arg\min \sum_{a=0}^{7} \sum_{b=0}^{3}$$
$$(I_{P_a,C_b} - A_{C_b}(n_{P_a,x}l_{C_b,x} + n_{P_a,y}l_{C_b,y} + n_{P_a,z}l_{C_b,z}))^2. \tag{6}$$
$$\text{s.t.} \quad n_{P_a,x}^2 + n_{P_a,y}^2 + n_{P_a,z}^2 = 1 \quad (a = 0, 1, \cdots, 7).$$

Equation (6) has 20 unknown parameters, which are the albedo $(A_{C_0}, A_{C_1}, A_{C_2}, A_{C_3})$ (4 parameters) and the normal $\mathbf{n}_p$ (2×8 parameters). Pixel brightness $I_{P,C}$ is the input, and the light source direction l_C is known. Therefore, Eq. (6) is solvable since the number of equations is 32 and the number of unknowns is 20. We minimize Eq. (6) using alternative minimization. We fix albedo and compute surface normal, next we fix surface normal and compute albedo, and we repeat this alternating minimization until convergence. This alternating minimization approach is proved to converge.

If we assume that the albedo A_C is known, we have a closed-form solution of Eq. (6), and we obtain the surface normal $\mathbf{n}$ as $\mathbf{n} = \mathbf{L}^{-1}\mathbf{s}$.

$$\mathbf{Ln} = \mathbf{s}, \tag{7}$$

$$\mathbf{L} = \begin{pmatrix} l_{C_0,x} & l_{C_0,y} & l_{C_0,z} \\ l_{C_1,x} & l_{C_1,y} & l_{C_1,z} \\ l_{C_2,x} & l_{C_2,y} & l_{C_2,z} \\ l_{C_3,x} & l_{C_3,y} & l_{C_3,z} \\ & l_{C_0,x} \cdots & \\ \vdots & & \ddots \end{pmatrix}, \mathbf{n} = \begin{pmatrix} n_{P_0,x} \\ n_{P_0,y} \\ n_{P_0,z} \\ n_{P_1,x} \\ \vdots \\ n_{P_7,z} \end{pmatrix}, \mathbf{s} = \begin{pmatrix} \frac{I_{P_0,C_0}}{A_{C_0}} \\ \frac{I_{P_0,C_1}}{A_{C_1}} \\ \frac{I_{P_0,C_2}}{A_{C_2}} \\ \frac{I_{P_0,C_3}}{A_{C_3}} \\ \frac{I_{P_1,C_0}}{A_{C_0}} \\ \vdots \\ \frac{I_{P_7,C_3}}{A_{C_3}} \end{pmatrix}.$$

If we assume that the surface normal $n_{P_a,x}, n_{P_a,y}, n_{P_a,z}$ is known, we have a closed-form solution of Eq. (6), and we obtain the albedo as Eq. (8).

$$A_{C_b} = \text{median}(\frac{I_{P_0,C_b}}{n_{P_0,x}l_{C_b,x} + n_{P_0,y}l_{C_b,y} + n_{P_0,z}l_{C_b,z}},$$
$$\frac{I_{P_1,C_b}}{n_{P_1,x}l_{C_b,x} + n_{P_1,y}l_{C_b,y} + n_{P_1,z}l_{C_b,z}},$$
$$\cdots, \frac{I_{P_7,C_b}}{n_{P_7,x}l_{C_b,x} + n_{P_7,y}l_{C_b,y} + n_{P_7,z}l_{C_b,z}}). \tag{8}$$

If the surface normal $\tilde{n}_{P_a,x}, \tilde{n}_{P_a,y}, \tilde{n}_{P_a,z}$ is given, the closed-from solution $n_{P_a,x}, n_{P_a,y}, n_{P_a,z}$ of Eq. (9) will be Eq. (10).

$$\min\{(n_{P_a,x} - \tilde{n}_{P_a,x})^2 + (n_{P_a,y} - \tilde{n}_{P_a,y})^2 + (n_{P_a,z} - \tilde{n}_{P_a,z})^2\}, \tag{9}$$
$$\text{s.t.} \quad n_{P_a,x}^2 + n_{P_a,y}^2 + n_{P_a,z}^2 = 1.$$

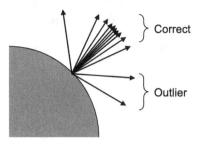

Fig. 7. Candidate surface normals.

$$(n_{P_a,x}, n_{P_a,y}, n_{P_a,z}) = \frac{\tilde{n}_{P_a,x}, \tilde{n}_{P_a,y}, \tilde{n}_{P_a,z}}{\sqrt{\tilde{n}_{P_a,x}^2 + \tilde{n}_{P_a,y}^2 + \tilde{n}_{P_a,y}^2}}. \tag{10}$$

As a result, if the initial values of $A_{C_0}, A_{C_1}, A_{C_2}, A_{C_3}$ are given, the albedo $A_{C_0}, A_{C_1}, A_{C_2}, A_{C_3}$ and the surface normal $n_{P_0,x}, n_{P_0,y}, \cdots, n_{P_7,z}$ are obtained by iteratively calculating Eq. (7), Eq. (8), and Eq. (10).

The chosen pixels and channels do not always contain the diffuse reflection with constant albedo. Therefore, we choose the set of channels and pixels 64 times. For each set of 64 sets, the candidates of surface normal can be obtained (Fig. 7). The surface normal $\mathbf{n}_m$ ($m = 1, \ldots, a$) is calculated for each set when we make a numbers of sets with randomly chosen channels and pixels. Surface normal is calculated by Eq. (11).

$$\mathbf{n} = \mathrm{median}(\mathbf{n}_m | m = 1, \ldots, a). \tag{11}$$

The pseudo-code of the algorithm is shown in Algorithm 1.

3 Experiment

Figure 8 shows a diagram of the experiment.

The camera used for this experiment is an FD-1665 (FluxData, Inc., USA) multi-spectral camera. Figure 9 shows the spectral sensitivity of the camera. As shown in Fig. 9, channel crosstalk occurred among all camera channels. Therefore, the method shown in Miyazaki et al. [17] is used to remove the channel crosstalk in the photographed input image.

Table 1 shows the full width at half maximum (FWHM) for each light source used in this experiment. Although our algorithm can be applied to natural illumination, most natural scene does not contain the variety of lights with different wavelengths. Our method cannot be applied to natural illumination due to the hardware problem, and thus, we used the system shown in Fig. 8.

Figure 10(a) shows the albedo of synthetic object, and Fig. 10(b) shows its input image. Figure 11(a)–(d) show the result of the surface normal when 3 channels 4 pixels, 4 channels 8 pixels, 4 channels 16 pixels, and 7 channels 16

Algorithm 1. Proposed algorithm

1: **for** object region **do**
2:      List $\Leftarrow$ empty
3:      **for** 64 sets **do**
4:          Choose 4 channels
5:          Choose 8 pixels
6:          $A_{C_0}, A_{C_1}, A_{C_2}, A_{C_3} \Leftarrow$ initial value
7:          $\mathbf{L} \Leftarrow$ light source direction
8:          **for** Until convergence **do**
9:              **for** $a = 0, 1, \cdots, 7$ **do**
10:                 **for** $b = 0, 1, 2, 3$ **do**
11:                     $\mathbf{s} \Leftarrow \frac{I_{P_a, C_b}}{A_{C_b}}$
12:                 **end for**
13:             **end for**
14:             $\mathbf{n} \Leftarrow \mathbf{L}^+ \mathbf{s}$
15:             **for** $p = 0, 1, \cdots, 7$ **do**
16:                 $\mathbf{n}_{P_a} \Leftarrow \frac{\mathbf{n}_{P_a}}{\|\mathbf{n}_{P_a}\|}$
17:             **end for**
18:             **for** $c = 0, 1, 2, 3$ **do**
19:                 $A_{C_b} \Leftarrow \text{median}(\frac{I_{P_0, C_b}}{\mathbf{n}_{P_0} l_{C_b}}, \frac{I_{P_1, C_b}}{\mathbf{n}_{P_1} l_{C_b}}, \cdots, \frac{I_{P_7, C_b}}{\mathbf{n}_{P_7} l_{C_b}})$
20:             **end for**
21:             $List \Leftarrow List + \mathbf{n}_{P_0}$
22:         **end for**
23:     **end for**
24:     Normal $\Leftarrow$ median($List$)
25: **end for**

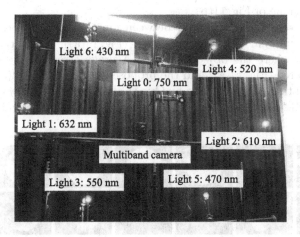

Fig. 8. Experimental setup with 7 light sources with different wavelengths and a single 7-band multispectral camera.

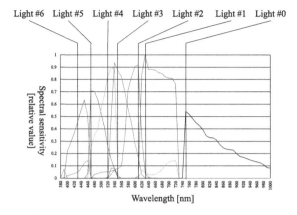

Fig. 9. Spectral sensitivity of multispectral camera and peak wavelength of each light sources.

Table 1. Peak wavelength and FWHM for each light source.

Light	0	1	2	3	4	5	6
Peak	750 nm	632 nm	610 nm	550 nm	520 nm	470 nm	430 nm
FWHM	10 nm	10 nm	10 nm	10 nm	10 nm	10 nm	10 nm

pixels are chosen, respectively. Figure 11(e) is the ground truth where R, G, and B colors represent x, y, and z axes, respectively. The average error depending on the number of channels and pixels is shown in Fig. 12. Figure 13 shows the reconstructed shape of Fig. 11(b).

Figure 14 shows the comparison between our method and other methods. Here, the conventional photometric stereo (Fig. 14(a)) means the color photometric stereo where the object is white. Average errors of the conventional photometric stereo (Fig. 14(a)) and the proposed method (Fig. 14(c)) were both 0.064 [rad], and that of the method by Guo et al. [10](Fig. 14(b)) was 0.213 [rad]. Compared to the color photometric stereo for white objects (Fig. 14(a)), where

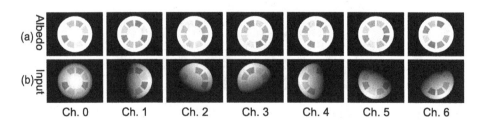

Fig. 10. Virtual sphere for each channel: (a) The albedo and (b) input image.

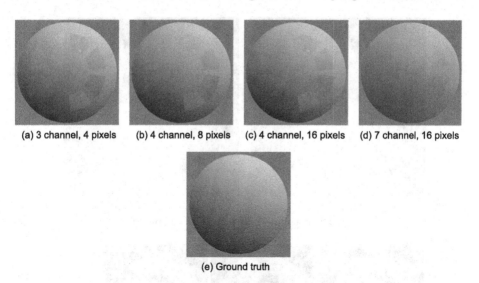

(a) 3 channel, 4 pixels   (b) 4 channel, 8 pixels   (c) 4 channel, 16 pixels   (d) 7 channel, 16 pixels

(e) Ground truth

Fig. 11. Estimated normal of virtual sphere: (a) 3 channels 4 pixels, (b) 4 channels 8 pixels, (c) 4 channels 16 pixels, (d) 7 channels 16 pixels, and (e) ground truth.

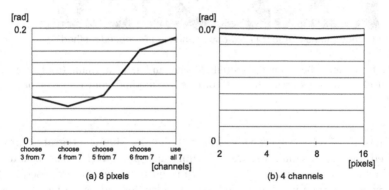

Fig. 12. The average error for different number of channels and pixels: (a) Error of 8 pixels and (b) error of 4 channels.

the shadow boundary is apparent, the proposed method (Fig. 14(c)) produces the result which is not affected by outliers such as shadows.

Figure 11(a) has more noise than Fig. 11(b) since the number of selected pixels is not enough. The color of Fig. 11(d) is vague compared to Fig. 11(c), which means that the estimated shape of Fig. 11(d) is flat. The reason that Fig. 11(c) is better than Fig. 11(d) is that the channels including shadow are chosen. Therefore, also considering Fig. 12, it is adequate to choose 4 channels and 8 pixels.

The input image of a glove is shown in Fig. 15. Figure 16(a)–(d) show the result of 3 channels 4 pixels, 4 channels 8 pixels, 4 channels 16 pixels, and

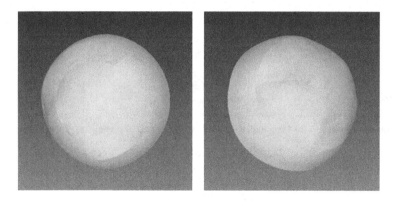

Fig. 13. Estimated shape of virtual sphere.

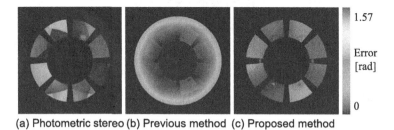

(a) Photometric stereo (b) Previous method (c) Proposed method

Fig. 14. Error map between estimated normal and true normal: (a) Error of conventional photometric stereo, (b) error of existing method, and (c) error of proposed method.

7 channels 16 pixels, respectively. Figure 17 is the shape integrated from the estimated surface normal. Figure 17 empirically proved that the dynamically deforming object such as hand can be estimated by using the proposed method. The glove can change its shape such as wrinckles depending on the motion of a human hand. If we take multiple photos of the target glove, the glove cannot be stably fixed. On the other hand, our system can take one photo, thus, we can estimate the moving objects.

Ch. 0   Ch. 1   Ch. 2   Ch. 3   Ch. 4   Ch. 5   Ch. 6

Fig. 15. Hand of each channel.

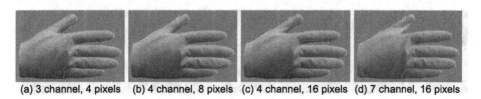

(a) 3 channel, 4 pixels   (b) 4 channel, 8 pixels   (c) 4 channel, 16 pixels   (d) 7 channel, 16 pixels

Fig. 16. Estimated normal of hand: (a) 3 channels 4 pixels, (b) 4 channels 8 pixels, (c) 4 channels 16 pixels, (d) 7 channels 16 pixels.

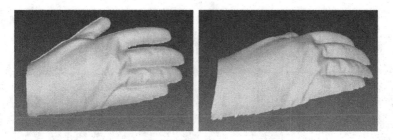

Fig. 17. Estimated shape of hand.

An object of a doll is shown in Fig. 18. The input image of a doll is shown in Fig. 19. Figure 20(a)–(d) show the result of 3 channels 4 pixels, 4 channels 8 pixels, 4 channels 16 pixels, and 7 channels 16 pixels, respectively. Figure 21 is the shape integrated from the surface normal shown in Fig. 20(b). Figure 20(b) empirically proved that the proposed method successfully estimated the surface normal even if the object has multiple albedos.

One failure part of our method can be the red basket placed in the lower part of the doll. In addition, the noise contained in the result is also the problem of our method. Median filtering can solve the problem, but the result will be oversmoothed. To overcome the problem fundamentally, our future work will be to increase the number of light sources (channels).

Fig. 18. Target object.

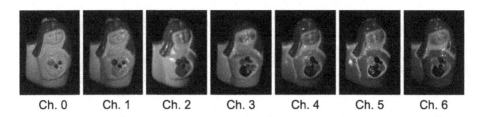

Ch. 0   Ch. 1   Ch. 2   Ch. 3   Ch. 4   Ch. 5   Ch. 6

Fig. 19. Doll of each channel.

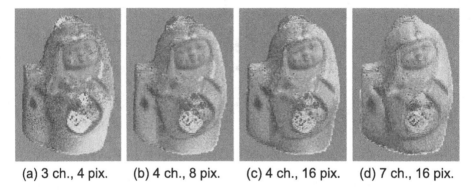

(a) 3 ch., 4 pix.   (b) 4 ch., 8 pix.   (c) 4 ch., 16 pix.   (d) 7 ch., 16 pix.

Fig. 20. Estimated normal of doll: (a) 3 channels 4 pixels, (b) 4 channels 8 pixels, (c) 4 channels 16 pixels, (d) 7 channels 16 pixels.

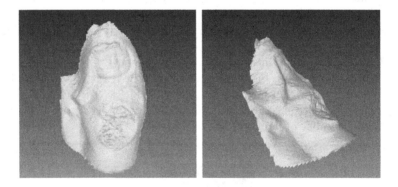

Fig. 21. Estimated shape of doll.

4   Conclusion

In this study, surface normal estimation of multicolored objects was conducted by the multi-spectral color photometric stereo method. We estimated the surface normal using randomly chosen channels and pixels.

Our approach which randomly selects the pixels and the channels is statistically convincing, however, it is not assured to choose the best combination.

An alternative approach to random selection is to apply region segmentation a priori. However, we cannot use the color information for region segmentation because each light source has different colors, and thus, we cannot distinguish between the object color and the light color. This is why we did not apply region segmentation. However, if the neighboring pixels have the same albedo and similar normal, we can apply the region-growing method to segment the image since the neighboring pixels have similar data. One of our plans is to apply a region-growing method to improve the performance of our method.

Ideally, the specular reflection only appears in one channel, and thus our approach is reliable. However, actual specular reflection does not have a spiky shape but is broadened widely. Therefore, multiple channels may contain specular reflection which violates our assumption. To overcome this problem, we are planning to increase the number of channels (*i.e.*, the number of light sources) so that the number of diffuse channels becomes larger than the number of specular channels.

Considering that the color photometric stereo is an ill-posed problem (Sect. 2.1), our method is enough good to solve this difficult problem. However, we still think that our method is not outputting a satisfactory result. Due to the difficult problem tackling, drastic update is needed, and the fundamental improvement of this work will be our future goal.

References

1. Anderson, R., Stenger, B., Cipolla, R.: Color photometric stereo for multicolored surfaces. In: International Conference on Computer Vision, pp. 2182–2189 (2011)
2. Brostow, G.J., Stenger, B., Vogiatzis, G., Hernández, C., Cipolla, R.: Video normals from colored lights. IEEE Trans. Pattern Anal. Mach. Intell. **33**(10), 2104–2114 (2011)
3. Chakrabarti, A., Sunkavalli, K.: Single-image RGB photometric stereo with spatially-varying albedo. In: International Conference on 3D Vision, pp. 258–266 (2016)
4. Drew, M.S.: Reduction of rank-reduced orientation-from-color problem with many unknown lights to two-image known-illuminant photometric stereo. In: Proceedings of International Symposium on Computer Vision, pp. 419–424 (1995)
5. Drew, M.S.: Direct solution of orientation-from-color problem using a modification of Pentland's light source direction estimator. Comput. Vis. Image Underst. **64**(2), 286–299 (1996)
6. Drew, M.S., Brill, M.H.: Color from shape from color: a simple formalism with known light sources. J. Opt. Soc. Am. A **17**(8), 1371–1381 (2000)
7. Drew, M., Kontsevich, L.: Closed-form attitude determination under spectrally varying illumination. In: IEEE Conference on Computer Vision and Pattern Recognition, pp. 985–990 (1994)
8. Fyffe, G., Yu, X., Debevec, P.: Single-shot photometric stereo by spectral multiplexing. In: IEEE International Conference on Computational Photography, pp. 1–6 (2011)
9. Gotardo, P.F.U., Simon, T., Sheikh, Y., Mathews, I.: Photogeometric scene flow for high-detail dynamic 3D reconstruction. In: IEEE International Conference on Computer Vision, pp. 846–854 (2015)

10. Guo, H., Okura, F., Shi, B., Funatomi, T., Mukaigawa, Y., Matsushita, Y.: Multi-spectral photometric stereo for spatially-varying spectral reflectances: a well posed problem? In: IEEE/CVF Conference on Computer Vision and Pattern Recognition, pp. 963–971 (2021)
11. Hernandez, C., Vogiatzis, G., Brostow, G.J., Stenger, B., Cipolla, R.: Non-rigid photometric stereo with colored lights. In: IEEE International Conference on Computer Vision, p. 8 (2007)
12. Hernández, C., Vogiatzis, G., Cipolla, R.: Shadows in three-source photometric stereo. In: Forsyth, D., Torr, P., Zisserman, A. (eds.) ECCV 2008. LNCS, vol. 5302, pp. 290–303. Springer, Heidelberg (2008). https://doi.org/10.1007/978-3-540-88682-2_23
13. Jiao, H., Luo, Y., Wang, N., Qi, L., Dong, J., Lei, H.: Underwater multi-spectral photometric stereo reconstruction from a single RGBD image. In: Asia-Pacific Signal and Information Processing Association Annual Summit and Conference, pp. 1–4 (2016)
14. Kim, H., Wilburn, B., Ben-Ezra, M.: Photometric stereo for dynamic surface orientations. In: Daniilidis, K., Maragos, P., Paragios, N. (eds.) ECCV 2010. LNCS, vol. 6311, pp. 59–72. Springer, Heidelberg (2010). https://doi.org/10.1007/978-3-642-15549-9_5
15. Kontsevich, L., Petrov, A., Vergelskaya, I.: Reconstruction of shape from shading in color images. J. Opt. Soc. Am. A 11, 1047–1052 (1994)
16. Landstrom, A., Thurley, M.J., Jonsson, H.: Sub-millimeter crack detection in casted steel using color photometric stereo. In: International Conference on Digital Image Computing: Techniques and Applications, pp. 1–7 (2013)
17. Miyazaki, D., Onishi, Y., Hiura, S.: Color photometric stereo using multi-band camera constrained by median filter and occluding boundary. J. Imaging 5(7), 29 (2019). Article no. 64
18. Nicodemus, F.E., Richmond, J.C., Hsia, J.J., Ginsberg, I.W., Limperis, T.: Geometrical considerations and nomenclature of reflectance. In: Wolff, L.B., Shafer, S.A., Healey, G. (eds.) Radiometry, pp. 940–145. Jones and Bartlett Publishers Inc. (1992)
19. Petrov, A.P., Kontsevich, L.L.: Properties of color images of surfaces under multiple illuminants. J. Opt. Soc. Am. A 11(10), 2745–2749 (1994)
20. Quéau, Y., Mecca, R., Durou, J.-D.: Unbiased photometric stereo for colored surfaces: a variational approach. In: IEEE Conference on Computer Vision and Pattern Recognition, pp. 4359–4368 (2016)
21. Rahman, S., Lam, A., Sato, I., Robles-Kelly, A.: Color photometric stereo using a rainbow light for non-Lambertian multicolored surfaces. In: Cremers, D., Reid, I., Saito, H., Yang, M.-H. (eds.) ACCV 2014. LNCS, vol. 9003, pp. 335–350. Springer, Cham (2015). https://doi.org/10.1007/978-3-319-16865-4_22
22. Roubtsova, N., Guillemaut, J.Y.: Colour Helmholtz stereopsis for reconstruction of complex dynamic scenes. In: International Conference on 3D Vision, pp. 251–258 (2014)
23. Silver, W.M.: Determining shape and reflectance using multiple images. Master's thesis, Massachusetts Institute of Technology (1980)
24. Vogiatzis, G., Hernández, C.: Practical 3D reconstruction based on photometric stereo. In: Cipolla, R., Battiato, S., Farinella, G.M. (eds.) Computer Vision: Detection, Recognition and Reconstruction. SCI, vol. 285, pp. 313–345. Springer, Heidelberg (2010). https://doi.org/10.1007/978-3-642-12848-6_12

25. Vogiatzis, G., Hernandez, C.: Self-calibrated, multi-spectral photometric stereo for 3D face capture. Int. J. Comput. Vis. **97**, 91–103 (2012). https://doi.org/10.1007/s11263-011-0482-7
26. Woodham, R.J.: Photometric method for determining surface orientation from multiple images. Opt. Eng. **19**(1), 139–144 (1980)
27. Woodham, R.J.: Gradient and curvature from photometric stereo including local confidence estimation. J. Opt. Soc. Am. **11**, 3050–3068 (1994)

Online Illumination Planning for Shadow-Robust Photometric Stereo

Hirochika Tanikawa, Ryo Kawahara⬡, and Takahiro Okabe(✉)⬡

Department of Artificial Intelligence, Kyushu Institute of Technology,
680-4 Kawazu, Iizuka, Fukuoka 820-8502, Japan
okabe@ai.kyutech.ac.jp

Abstract. Photometric stereo is a technique for estimating normals of an object surface from its images taken under different light source directions. In general, photometric stereo suffers from shadows, because almost no information on surface normals is available from shadowed pixels. In this paper, we propose an illumination planning for shadow-robust Lambertian photometric stereo; it optimizes the light source directions adaptively for an object of interest, because cast shadows depend on the entire shape of the object. More specifically, our proposed method iteratively adds the optimal light source for surface normal estimation by taking the visibility and linear independence of light source directions into consideration on the basis of the previously captured images of the object. We implemented our illumination planning with a programmable light source in an online manner, and achieve shadow-robust surface normal estimation from a small number of images.

Keywords: Photometric stereo · Illumination planning · Attached shadow · Cast shadow · Visibility

1 Introduction

Photometric stereo is a technique for estimating surface normals of an object of interest from its images taken from a fixed viewpoint but under different light source directions. The classical photometric stereo [15,18] assumes the Lambert model and known light sources, and then estimates surface normals from at least three images. The extension of the classical photometric stereo to non-Lambertian surfaces, unknown light sources, and so on is still one of the most actively studied topics in computer vision [1,14].

In this paper, we focus on shadows, *i.e.* another aspect of the extension of the classical photometric stereo, and propose photometric stereo robust to shadows. In general, shadows are classified into *attached shadows* and *cast shadows*; attached shadow is local effect and occurs when the angle between a surface normal and a light source direction is obtuse, but cast shadow is global effect and occurs when a light source is blocked by another part of an object surface. Because almost no information on surface normals is available from shadowed pixels[1], we need to illuminate an object surface by using appropriate light sources so that each pixel on the surface is sufficiently illuminated.

Optimizing light sources, so-called *illumination planning* [11] is studied also in the context of photometric stereo. Drbohlav and Chantler [6] address the optimal light source configurations for the Lambertian photometric stereo on the basis of the noise propagation analysis. For example, they show that, when the number of light sources is three, the three light sources should be placed so that those directions are orthogonal to each other. Unfortunately, however, their analysis does not take shadows into consideration, although attached shadows occur even on convex objects in practice. More importantly, they find the optimal light source directions *a priori* independent of the shape of an object. Actually, cast shadows occur on non-convex objects depending on the entire shapes of the objects.

Accordingly, we propose an *online* illumination planning for shadow-robust Lambertian photometric stereo. Our proposed method estimates surface normals of an object of interest by iteratively adding a novel image of the object taken under the optimal light source direction. More specifically, we take the visibility and linear independence of light source directions into consideration, and propose a method for optimizing the light source direction adaptively for an object of interest on the basis of the previously captured images of the object. We implemented our illumination planning by using a Liquid Crystal Display (LCD) as a programmable light source, and confirmed the effectiveness of our method through a number of experiments using synthetic and real images.

The main contributions of this study are twofold. First, we propose a novel illumination planning for shadow-robust Lambertian photometric stereo. Our proposed method iteratively adds the optimal light source according to an object of interest on the basis of the previous observations of the object. Second, we implemented our illumination planning with a programmable light source in an online manner, and achieve shadow-robust surface normal estimation from a small number of images.

2   Related Work

Conventional Approach: Outlier Removal

Both attached shadows and cast shadows are considered as outliers, because the pixel values in those shadows deviate from the Lambert model. Therefore, a number of methods are proposed for detecting shadows in the images for photometric stereo and removing them as outliers from surface normal estimation. For example, the shadows in photometric stereo images are detected by selecting the optimal three light sources out of four [2], by using RANdom SAmple Consensus (RANSAC) [10,13,16], graph cut [3], and low-rank and sparse decomposition [8,19].

---

[1] It is known that surface normals can be recovered from attached shadows if a large number of images taken under varying light source directions are given [12].

Our objective is to achieve shadow-robust photometric stereo too. In contrast to the above methods, however, our focus is not on detecting shadows but on illuminating an object surface in the context of active illumination. Specifically, we illuminate an object surface so that each pixel is sufficiently illuminated for surface normal estimation.

Learning-Based Approach

The learning-based approach is getting more common also in photometric stereo. There are a number of learning-based methods for non-Lambertian photometric stereo and uncalibrated photometric stereo [4,5,17,20]. It is certain that the learning-based approach is suitable for dealing with non-Lambertian BRDFs because the reflectance is local effect. Unfortunately, however, cast shadows depend on the entire shape of an object, and then they are global effects. Therefore, efficiently handling cast shadows is difficult for the learning-based approach; a huge amount of training data is required in general.

Recently, Ikehata [7] and Li *et al.* [9] propose methods for efficiently handling cast shadows in the learning-based approach by incorporating cast shadows into so-called observation map. Similar to the conventional approach, their objective is to remove the impact of cast shadows from surface normal estimation implicitly. On the other hand, our focus is on illuminating an object surface so that sufficient information is available for surface normal estimation.

Illumination Planning

Drbohlav and Chantler [6] address the optimal light source configurations for the Lambertian photometric stereo. Specifically, they reveal the relationship between the noises in pixel values and the expected errors of estimated surface normals on the basis of noise propagation analysis, and derive the optimal light source configurations for given numbers of light sources. Unfortunately, however, their analysis does not take shadows into consideration and finds the optimal light source directions *a priori* independent of the shape of an object.

In contrast to their method, we take account of shadows for optimizing light source directions in the Lambertian photometric stereo. In particular, our method optimizes the light source directions adaptively for an object of interest on the basis of the previously captured images of the object in an online manner, because cast shadows are global effects depending on the entire shapes of the objects.

3 Proposed Method

3.1 Overview

Our proposed method aims to illuminate an object surface from the optimal light source directions so that each pixel on the surface is *sufficiently* illuminated. To this end, our method iteratively finds the optimal light source direction on the basis of the previously captured images of the object, and then capture a novel image of the object under the optimal light source direction. The pipeline of our method is as follows; our proposed illumination planning

1. randomly selects three initial light source directions, and then captures three images of the object under each of those light source directions,
2. finds out **the pixel with the worst accuracy** in surface normal estimation,
3. finds out **the optimal light source direction** for improving the accuracy of surface normal estimation at the worst pixel, and then captures a novel image under the optimal light source direction,
4. repeats 2 and 3 a number of times,

and finally estimates surface normals from all of the captured images.

In Sect. 3.2, we describe how to estimate surface normals from images with shadows. Then, we explain the way of finding the worst pixel and the optimal light source direction in Sects. 3.3 and 3.4 respectively.

3.2 Estimating Surface Normals from Images with Shadows

Here, we explicitly formulate the Lambertian photometric stereo from images with shadows. Let us denote the pixel value at the p-th pixel $(p = 1, 2, 3, ..., P)$ on an object surface under the l-th light source direction $(l = 1, 2, 3, ..., L)$ by i_{pl}. According to the Lambert model, the pixel value i_{pl} is represented by

$$i_{pl} = v_{pl} {s'_l}^\top n'_p. \tag{1}$$

Here, s'_l is the product of the direction s_l and intensity of the l-th light source, and n'_p is the product of the surface normal n_p and albedo at the p-th pixel. Both s_l and n_p are unit vectors. We denote the visibility of the p-th pixel from the l-th light source direction by v_{pl}; $v_{pl} = 0$ if the p-th pixel is in attached shadow or cast shadow and $v_{pl} = 1$ otherwise[2].

We can rewrite Eq. (1) at the p-th surface point under the L different light source directions by using matrices as

$$\begin{pmatrix} i_{p1} \\ i_{p2} \\ \vdots \\ i_{pL} \end{pmatrix} = \begin{pmatrix} v_{p1} {s'_1}^\top \\ v_{p2} {s'_2}^\top \\ \vdots \\ v_{pL} {s'_L}^\top \end{pmatrix} n'_p = \begin{pmatrix} v_{p1} & 0 & \cdots & 0 \\ 0 & v_{p2} & \cdots & 0 \\ & & \ddots & \\ 0 & 0 & \cdots & v_{pL} \end{pmatrix} \begin{pmatrix} {s'_1}^\top \\ {s'_2}^\top \\ \vdots \\ {s'_L}^\top \end{pmatrix} n'_p, \tag{2}$$

$$i_{pL} = V_{pL} S_L n'_p. \tag{3}$$

Therefore, we can compute the scaled surface normal n'_p by using the pseudo-inverse matrix $(V_{pL} S_L)^\dagger$ as

$$n'_p = (V_{pL} S_L)^\dagger i_{pL} = \{(V_{pL} S_L)^\top (V_{pL} S_L)\}^{-1} (V_{pL} S_L)^\top i_{pL}, \tag{4}$$

if $\{(V_{pL} S_L)^\top (V_{pL} S_L)\}$ is a regular matrix. Note that the surface normal n_p with unit length is given by $n_p = n'_p / |n'_p|$. When V_{pL} is the $L \times L$ identity matrix, the estimation of the surface normal in Eq. (4) results in the estimation from images without shadows.

---

[2] The visibility is often used for representing cast shadows, but we use it for representing both attached shadows and cast shadows in this paper.

3.3 Finding Pixel with Worst Accuracy

In a similar manner to Drbohlav and Chantler [6], we can estimate the accuracy of the estimated surface normal via noise propagation analysis. Let us denote the estimated and ground truth scaled surface normals by n'_p and $\bar{n}'_p$ respectively. Then, we study the variance-covariance matrix Σ of the surface normal defined by

$$\Sigma = E\left[(n'_p - \bar{n}'_p)(n'_p - \bar{n}'_p)^\top\right], \tag{5}$$

where $E[\ ]$ stands for the expectation value.

Suppose that the observed pixel value $\tilde{i}_{pl}$ is contaminated by additive noise δ_{pl} and deviates from the ideal pixel value $i_{pl}{}^3$ as

$$\tilde{i}_{pl} = i_{pl} + \delta_{pl}, \tag{6}$$

we can derive

$$\begin{aligned}
\Sigma &= E\left[\{(V_{pL}S_L)^\dagger \delta_{pL}\}\{(V_{pL}S_L)^\dagger \delta_{pL})\}^\top\right] \\
&= \sigma^2 (V_{pL}S_L)^\dagger \{(V_{pL}S_L)^\dagger\}^\top \\
&= \sigma^2 \{(V_{pL}S_L)^\top (V_{pL}S_L)\}^{-\top}.
\end{aligned} \tag{7}$$

Here, $\delta_{pL} = (\delta_{p1}, \delta_{p2}, \delta_{p3}, \cdots, \delta_{pL})^\top$, and we assume independent and identically distributed noises whose mean and variance are 0 and σ^2 respectively. Since the Mean Square Error (MSE) is proportional to the trace of the variance-covariance matrix, we obtain the MSE of the estimated surface normal as

$$\mathrm{MSE} \propto \mathrm{Tr}\left[\{(V_{pL}S_L)^\top (V_{pL}S_L)\}^{-1}\right]. \tag{8}$$

Therefore, our proposed method finds out the pixel $\hat{p}$ with the worst accuracy in surface normal estimation as

$$\hat{p} = \arg\max_p \mathrm{Tr}\left[\{(V_{pL}S_L)^\top (V_{pL}S_L)\}^{-1}\right]. \tag{9}$$

Note that the MSE depends on the surface points via the visibility matrix $V_{pL}{}^4$. Intuitively, the MSE is larger for the pixel that is illuminated by a smaller number of light sources with smaller linear independence. When V_{pL} is the $L \times L$ identity matrix, $i.e.$ when we do not take account of shadows, the MSE results in that of Drbohlav and Chantler [6].

3.4 Finding Optimal Light Source Direction

Suppose that the L images of an object are captured and the $\hat{p}$-th pixel is selected as the pixel with the worst accuracy according to Eq. (9). Our proposed

---

[3] Note that not the noise δ_{pl} but the visibility v_{pl} is used for representing shadows as shown in Eq. (1).

[4] When multiple pixels have the same visibility matrix and therefore have the same MSE, we randomly select one of the pixels as the worst pixel.

method finds the optimal light source direction, *i.e.* the $(L+1)$-th light source direction under which a novel image of the object is captured for improving the accuracy of the estimated surface normal at the $\hat{p}$-th pixel. Our clue to the optimal light source direction is the visibility and linear independence; the optimal light source direction should be visible from the $\hat{p}$-th pixel and have the largest linear independence from the previous light source directions with $v_{\hat{p}l} = 1$.

As mentioned in Sect. 1, our implementation makes use of an LCD as a programmable light source. Then, we represent the direction of a light source by the 2-D coordinate system of the display. We assume that our setup is geometrically calibrated in advance, and represent a light source by using the 2-D coordinate (x, y) of the display and the 3-D vector $s(x, y)$ interchangeably. Our proposed method maximizes the cost function $C(x, y)$ defined as

$$C(x, y) = C_{\text{vis}}(x, y) \times C_{\text{lin}}(x, y) \tag{10}$$

with respect to (x, y). Here, $C_{\text{vis}}(x, y)$ and $C_{\text{lin}}(x, y)$ are the cost functions for the visibility and linear independence of the light source $s(x, y)$ respectively.

The cost function for the visibility has larger value if the light source direction (x, y) is likely visible from the $\hat{p}$-th pixel and vice versa. More specifically, if the direction (x_l, y_l) of the l-th light source is visible from the $\hat{p}$-th pixel, its neighboring directions are also considered to be visible. On the other hand, if the direction of the l-th light source is invisible, its neighboring directions are also considered to be invisible. Therefore, we define the cost function for the visibility by the linear combination of the Gaussian distributions as

$$C_{\text{vis}}(x, y) = \frac{1}{2\pi w^2} \left[e^{-\frac{(x-x_c)^2 + (y-y_c)^2}{2w^2}} + \sum_{l=1}^{L} (2v_{\hat{p}l} - 1) e^{-\frac{(x-x_l)^2 + (y-y_l)^2}{2w^2}} \right]. \tag{11}$$

Here, the first term corresponds to the direction of a camera (x_c, y_c), and the second term corresponds to the previous L light sources. The coefficient $(2v_{\hat{p}l} - 1) = 1$ for visible light sources from the $\hat{p}$-th pixel, and $(2v_{\hat{p}l} - 1) = -1$ for invisible light sources. Because we consider an object surface visible from the camera, the coefficient of the first term is 1. Since the cost function for the visibility is considered as a likelihood, we adopt the upper and lower limits; we set $C_{\text{vis}}(x, y) = 1$ if $C_{\text{vis}}(x, y) > 1$, and $C_{\text{vis}}(x, y) = -1$ if $C_{\text{vis}}(x, y) < -1$[5].

The cost function for the linear independence has larger value if the light source direction (x, y) has larger linear independence from the previous light source directions with $v_{\hat{p}l} = 1$. Therefore, we compute the principal directions of those previous light sources, and define the cost function for the linear independence as

$$C_{\text{lin}}(x, y) = \max[s_{\min}^{\top} s(x, y), -s_{\min}^{\top} s(x, y)]. \tag{12}$$

Here, we denote the 3-D eigenvector corresponding to the smallest eigenvalue of $(V_{\hat{p}L} S_L)$ by $s_{\min}$, and $\max[\ ]$ returns the maximum argument.

---

[5] We set the lower limit not to 0 but to 1 so that the gradient of the cost function $C(x, y)$ does not vanish for gradient-based optimization.

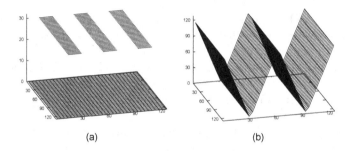

Fig. 1. Two objects used in the experiments with synthetic images: (a) a slit and (b) a wave. The camera and display are located above the objects.

Since the cost function in Eq. (10) is nonlinear with respect to (x, y), the optimization depends on the initial conditions. In our current implementation, we used the interior point algorithm (fmincon in MATLAB), and tested multiple random initial conditions and then selected the best solution that maximizes the cost function.

4   Experiments

To confirm the effectiveness of our proposed method, we conducted a number of experiments using both synthetic and real images. In the experiments using synthetic images, we assumed a similar setup to our prototype system for the experiments using real images shown in Fig. 8. We assumed that the visibility v_{pl} is 0 if the pixel value i_{pl} is smaller than a threshold depending on the noise level of images, and v_{pl} is 1 otherwise.

We changed the standard deviation w of the Gaussian distributions in Eq. (11) as $w = w_0/\sqrt{L}$ so that the cost function for the visibility can represent finer details as the number of light sources L increases. As shown in Fig. 8, we used an ultra wide display and normalized the scale of the coordinate system as the height of the display is 1, *i.e.* the range of x is $[0, 1]$, and we empirically set $w_0 = 0.7$.

4.1   Synthetic Images

Visibility
First, we show how the cost function for the visibility behaves actually. We used a slit shown in Fig. 1(a) as an object of interest. For the sake of simplicity, we investigated the visibility at a fixed point on the lower plane of the object, and the light source directions are randomly selected instead of using our illumination planning.

Figure 2 visualizes the cost function for the visibility in the display domain (x, y): (a) the ground truth and the visibilities when the numbers of light sources

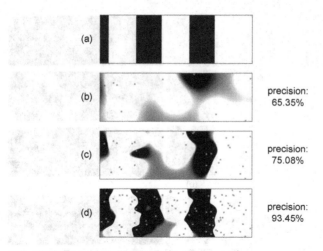

Fig. 2. The cost function for the visibility in the display domain (x, y): (a) the ground truth and the visibilities when the numbers of light sources L are (b) 10, (c) 30, and (d) 100 respectively. (Color figure online)

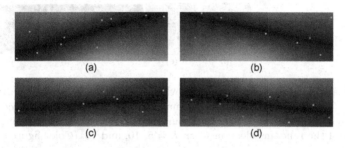

Fig. 3. The cost function for the linear independence for different sets of 10 light source directions. (Color figure online)

L are (b) 10, (c) 30, and (d) 100 respectively. Here, the visibility v_{pl} is $1/0$ at white/black pixels in (a) the ground truth, and C_{vis} is $1/-1$ at white/black pixels from (b) to (d). The selected light source directions are superimposed in those images: orange/light blue points correspond to $v_{pl} = 1/0$ respectively. We can see that the cost function for the visibility gets closer to the ground truth as the number of light sources increases. In addition, we binarize the cost function for the visibility to $1/0$ when $C_{\text{vis}} \geq 0/ < 0$, and computed the precision of the visibility, *i.e.* the fraction of the light source directions with $v_{pl} = 1$ among those with $C_{\text{vis}} \geq 0$, when $L = 10$, 30, and 100. We can see quantitatively that our cost function for the visibility works well; the precision gets closer to 100% as the number of light sources increases.

Linear Independence
Second, we show how the cost function for the linear independence behaves actually. For the sake of simplicity, we investigated the linear independence by using

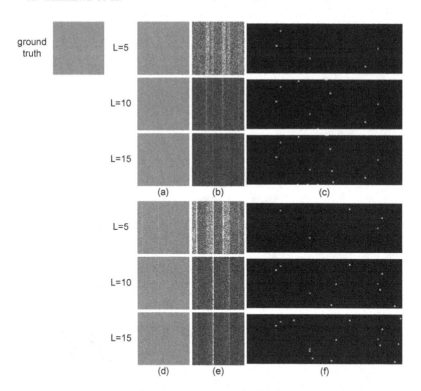

Fig. 4. The qualitative results of the slit when $\sigma = 0.02$: the ground truth surface normals and (a) the estimated surface normals, (b) the errors of the surface normals, and (c) the selected light sources by using our proposed illumination planning, and (d) (e) (f) those of the random selection when $L = 5$, 10, and 15. (Color figure online)

dummy data. More specifically, we randomly selected 10 light source directions and assumed that a surface point of attention is shadowed under some of them.

Figure 3 visualizes the cost function for the linear independence for different sets of 10 light source directions. Here, the linear independence C_{lin} is 1/0 at white/black pixels in the images. The selected light source directions are superimposed in those images: orange/light blue points correspond to $v_{pl} = 1/0$ respectively. We can see that the cost function for the linear independence takes larger values at the orthogonal directions to the visible light source directions illuminating the surface point of attention as expected.

Surface Normal Estimation

Third, we compare the performance of our proposed illumination planning with the random selection of light source directions for surface normal estimation. We tested two objects: a slit and a wave in Fig. 1. The camera and display are

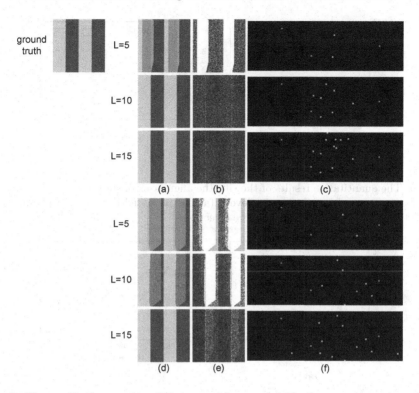

Fig. 5. The qualitative results of the wave when $\sigma = 0.02$: the ground truth surface normals and (a) the estimated surface normals, (b) the errors of the surface normals, and (c) the selected light sources by using our proposed illumination planning, and (d) (e) (f) those of the random selection when $L = 5$, 10, and 15.

located above the objects. In order to investigate the robustness to noises in pixel values, we added zero-mean Gaussian noises, whose standard deviations σ are 0.01, 0.02, and 0.04 for pixel values normalized to $[0, 1]$, to the synthetic images.

Figure 4 shows the qualitative results of the slit when $\sigma = 0.02$: the ground truth surface normals and (a) the estimated surface normals, (b) the errors of the surface normals, and (c) the selected light sources by using our proposed illumination planning, and (d) (e) (f) those of the random selection when $L = 5$, 10, and 15. The whiter the pixels in (b) and (e) are, the larger the errors in surface normal estimation are. We can see that our illumination planning works better than the random selection; our illumination planning achieves better accuracy by using smaller number of light sources than the random selection. We can also see that the light source directions selected by our illumination planning are different from those of the random selection. Here, the light blue points stand for the initial three light source directions, and the orange points stand for the iteratively added light source directions.

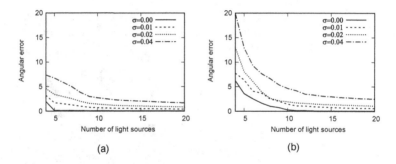

Fig. 6. The quantitative results of the slit; the angular error in degree vs. the number of light sources under various noise levels: (a) our proposed illumination planing and (b) the random selection of light source directions.

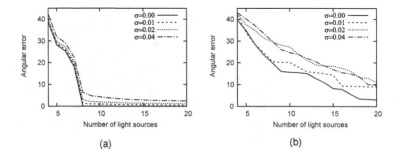

Fig. 7. The quantitative results of the wave; the angular error in degree vs. the number of light sources under various noise levels: (a) our proposed illumination planing and (b) the random selection of light source directions.

Figure 6 shows the quantitative results of the slit; the angular error in degree vs. the number of light sources under various noise levels: (a) our proposed illumination planing and (b) the random selection of light source directions. We can see that the angular errors of our illumination planning converges to smaller values for smaller number of light sources than the random selection. Those results quantitatively show that our illumination planning works better than the random selection.

The qualitative and quantitative results of the wave are shown in Fig. 5 and Fig. 7 respectively. We can see that we obtain the similar results to those of the slit. Those results for the wave also support that our proposed illumination planning works better than the random selection. It is interesting that the light source directions selected by our illumination planning for the slit and the wave are different from each other. This is because our method finds out the optimal light source directions depending on the shape of an object of interest. Actually, the optimal light source directions for the wave mainly distribute around the center column of the display in order to illuminate the deep valleys of the wave.

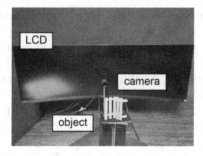

Fig. 8. Our prototype system for the experiments using real images.

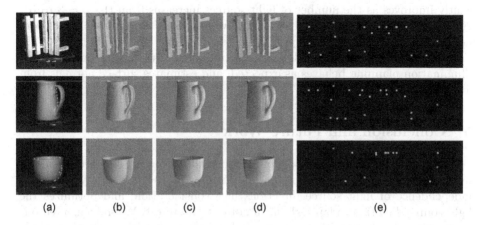

(a)   (b)   (c)   (d)   (e)

Fig. 9. The qualitative results using real images: (a) the images of target objects under ambient light, the estimated surface normals when (b) $L = 3$, (c) 10, and (d) 20, and (e) the selected optimal light source directions: light blue points ($L = 1$ to 3) and orange points ($L = 4$ to 20). (Color figure online)

4.2   Real Images

Figure 8 shows our prototype system for the experiments using real images. It consists of an ultra wide LCD 439P9H1/11 from PHILIPS and a polarimetric camera BFS-U3-51S5P-C from FLIR. We assume sufficiently smaller objects than the distance between the display and the objects, and consider the small white spots displayed on the LCD as distant light sources. The directions and intensities of those light sources are calibrated in advance by using the images of a mirror sphere and a diffuse reflector.

Our proposed online illumination planning, consisting of controlling the LCD and camera, separating reflection components, finding the worst pixel, and finding the optimal light source, is implemented by using MATLAB. We separated the diffuse and specular reflection components in the captured images on the basis of polarization, and used the former for the Lambertian photometric stereo. The optimization of the cost function in Eq. (10) takes about 0.05 sec for a single initial condition. Therefore, we can test 80 initial conditions during typical exposure time of 4 s.

We qualitatively show how our proposed illumination planning behaves for real images, since the ground truth surface normals are unknown for real objects. We tested three objects; a toy bench made of plastics, a milk pitcher and a cup made of ceramic. Figure 9 shows (a) the images of those objects under ambient light, the estimated surface normals when (b) $L = 3$, (c) 10, and (d) 20, and (e) the selected optimal light source directions: light blue points ($L = 1$ to 3) and orange points ($L = 4$ to 20). Here, the orange points in (a) the images of the objects stand for the selected worst pixels from $L = 4$ to 20.

The estimated surface normals qualitatively show that the accuracy significantly improves as the number of light sources increases from (b) $L = 3$ to (d) 20. Interestingly, we can see that (a) the worst pixels are often selected from non-convex areas, and (e) the optimal light source directions are selected so that they can illuminate those pixels. Those results demonstrate that our proposed illumination planning behaves as expected, and estimates surface normals from a small number of images.

5   Conclusion and Future Work

We proposed an illumination planning for shadow-robust Lambertian photometric stereo. Our proposed illumination planning takes the visibility and linear independence of light source directions into consideration, and optimizes the light source directions adaptively for an object of interest. We implemented our illumination planning with a programmable light source in an online manner, and achieve shadow-robust surface normal estimation from a small number of images.

One direction of our future study is to incorporate interreflections into our proposed illumination planning, because they are often observed on non-convex surfaces but our illumination planning does not take account of them. The other direction is the integration with view planning; it optimizes both the light source directions and the viewing directions for modeling an object of interest.

Acknowledgement. This work was supported by JSPS KAKENHI Grant Number JP20H00612.

References

1. Ackermann, J., Michael, G.: A survey of photometric stereo techniques. Found. Trends Comput. Graph. Vis. **9**(3–4), 149–254 (2015)
2. Barsky, S., Petrou, M.: The 4-source photometric stereo technique for three-dimensional surfaces in the presence of highlights and shadows. IEEE Trans. PAMI **25**(10), 1239–1252 (2003)
3. Chandraker, M., Agarwal, S., Kriegman, D.: ShadowCuts: photometric stereo with shadows. In: Proceedings of the IEEE CVPR 2007, pp. 1–8 (2007)

4. Chen, G., Han, K., Shi, B., Matsushita, Y., Wong, K.Y.K.: Self-calibrating deep photometric stereo networks. In: Proceedings of the IEEE CVPR 2019, pp. 8739–8747 (2019)
5. Chen, G., Han, K., Wong, K.-Y.K.: PS-FCN: a flexible learning framework for photometric stereo. In: Ferrari, V., Hebert, M., Sminchisescu, C., Weiss, Y. (eds.) ECCV 2018. LNCS, vol. 11213, pp. 3–19. Springer, Cham (2018). https://doi.org/10.1007/978-3-030-01240-3_1
6. Drbohlav, O., Chantler, M.: On optimal light configurations in photometric stereo. In: Proceedings of the IEEE ICCV 2005, vol. 2, pp. 1707–1712 (2005)
7. Ikehata, S.: CNN-PS: CNN-based photometric stereo for general non-convex surfaces. In: Ferrari, V., Hebert, M., Sminchisescu, C., Weiss, Y. (eds.) ECCV 2018. LNCS, vol. 11219, pp. 3–19. Springer, Cham (2018). https://doi.org/10.1007/978-3-030-01267-0_1
8. Ikehata, S., Wipf, D., Matsushita, Y., Aizawa, K.: Robust photometric stereo using sparse regression. In: Proceedings of the IEEE CVPR 2012, pp. 318–325 (2012)
9. Li, J., Robles-Kelly, A., You, S., Matsushita, Y.: Learning to minify photometric stereo. In: Proceedings of the IEEE CVPR 2019, pp. 7568–7576 (2019)
10. Mukaigawa, Y., Ishii, Y., Shakunaga, T.: Analysis of photometric factors based on photometric linearization. JOSA A 24(10), 3326–3334 (2007)
11. Murase, H., Nayar, S.K.: Illumination planning for object recognition using parametric eigenspaces. IEEE Trans. PAMI 16(12), 1219–1227 (1994)
12. Okabe, T., Sato, I., Sato, Y.: Attached shadow coding: estimating surface normals from shadows under unknown reflectance and lighting conditions. In: Proceedings of the IEEE ICCV 2009, pp. 1693–1700 (2009)
13. Okabe, T., Sato, Y.: Object recognition based on photometric alignment using RANSAC. In: Proceedings of the IEEE CVPR 2003, pp. 221–228 (2003)
14. Shi, B., Mo, Z., Wu, Z., Duan, D., Yeung, S.K., Tan, P.: A benchmark dataset and evaluation for non-Lambertian and uncalibrated photometric stereo. In: Proceedings of the IEEE CVPR 2016, pp. 3707–3716 (2016)
15. Silver, W.M.: Determining shape and reflectance using multiple images. Master's thesis, MIT (1980)
16. Sunkavalli, K., Zickler, T., Pfister, H.: Visibility subspaces: uncalibrated photometric stereo with shadows. In: Daniilidis, K., Maragos, P., Paragios, N. (eds.) ECCV 2010. LNCS, vol. 6312, pp. 251–264. Springer, Heidelberg (2010). https://doi.org/10.1007/978-3-642-15552-9_19
17. Taniai, T., Maehara, T.: Neural inverse rendering for general reflectance photometric stereo. In: Proceedings of the ICML 2018, pp. 4857–4866 (2018)
18. Woodham, R.J.: Photometric method for determining surface orientation from multiple images. Opt. Eng. 19(1), 139–144 (1980)
19. Wu, L., Ganesh, A., Shi, B., Matsushita, Y., Wang, Y., Ma, Y.: Robust photometric stereo via low-rank matrix completion and recovery. In: Kimmel, R., Klette, R., Sugimoto, A. (eds.) ACCV 2010. LNCS, vol. 6494, pp. 703–717. Springer, Heidelberg (2011). https://doi.org/10.1007/978-3-642-19318-7_55
20. Zheng, Q., Jia, Y., Shi, B., Jiang, X., Duan, L.Y., Kot, A.C.: SPLINE-Net: sparse photometric stereo through lighting interpolation and normal estimation networks. In: Proceedings of the IEEE ICCV 2019, pp. 8549–8558 (2019)

Learning Algorithm

Decomposition of Invariant and Variant Features by Using Convolutional Autoencoder

Hidenori Ide[✉], Hiromu Fujishige, Junichi Miyao, and Takio Kurita

Hiroshima University, Higashi-Hiroshima, Japan
wate2263@gmail.com, {miyao,tkurita}@hiroshima-u.ac.jp

Abstract. In our brain, the visual information captured by the retina is processed by the two different visual pathways known as ventral stream and the dorsal stream. The ventral stream known as the "what pathway" is involved with object and visual identification and recognition and the dorsal stream known as "where pathway" is involved with processing the object's spatial location relative to the viewer. This means that the human brain decomposes the visual information captured by the retina into the invariant information and the variant information. In this paper, we propose two network architectures based on the convolutional autoencoder in order to decompose the input information into invariant information and variant information. The decomposition of variant and invariant information is realized by decomposing the feature vectors obtained in the hidden layer of the convolutional autoencoder. To extract invariant information, the classifier or the estimator of the invariant image are combined with the convolutional autoencoder. Effectiveness of the proposed architectures are experimentally confirmed by visualizing the extracted feature vectors.

Keywords: Invariant feature · Variant feature · Autoencoder · Visual pathway · Decomposition · Character recognition · White balance correction

1 Introduction

In the human brain, it is known that visual information is processed by the different visual pathways. The visual information entered from the retina is recognized in the primary visual cortex (V1) of the occipital lobe firstly. Thereafter, the information is processed on two different pathways [1]. One is a path called ventral stream and the other is called dorsal stream. The ventral stream (known as the "what pathway") is involved with object and visual identification and recognition. On the other hand, the dorsal stream (known as "where pathway") is involved with processing the object's spatial location relative to the viewer. This means that the human brain decomposes the visual information captured by the retina into the invariant information and the variant information.

Invariant feature extraction is necessary for recognition. If the recognition target in an input image is spatially shifted, the feature vector calculated by the

© The Author(s), under exclusive license to Springer Nature Switzerland AG 2022
K. Sumi et al. (Eds.): IW-FCV 2022, CCIS 1578, pp. 97–111, 2022.
https://doi.org/10.1007/978-3-031-06381-7_7

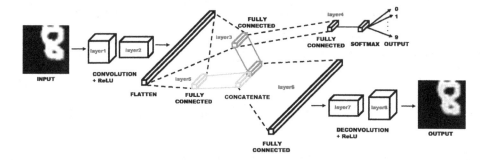

Fig. 1. Overview of the network by autoencoder and classifier.

classifier is usually different from the feature vector of the original image. If we can extract shift invariant feature vectors, the design of the classifier become very easy.

The variant information is also important to understand the arrangement of the multiple objects in the input image. For example, the meaning of the photograph may change depending on where an object is located in a photograph. In other words, the combination of invariant and variant information gives the whole contextual meaning of the input image. So it is important to simultaneously extract invariant and variant features from the input image.

In order to realize this mechanism with a neural network, in this paper, we proposed two neural network architectures based on the convolutional autoencoder. These architectures have two pathways (what pathway and where pathway) like the mechanism of the human brain as shown in Fig. 1 and Fig. 2. The decomposition of invariant and variant information is realized by decomposing the feature vectors obtained in the hidden layer of the convolutional autoencoder. To extract invariant information, the classifier or the estimator of the invariant image are combined with the convolutional autoencoder.

The paper is structured as follows. In Sect. 2, the related works are briefly reviewed. The proposed approaches are explained in Sect. 3 and experimental results are shown in Sect. 4. Section 5 is for conclusion and future works.

2   Related Works

2.1   Autoencoder

The autoencoder is a method to efficiently extract dimension reduced representation (encoding) for the training samples in an unsupervised manner [2]. It is closely related with the principal component analysis (PCA). The autoencoder can be considered as a nonlinear extension of PCA by using the neural network.

There are two main uses of the autoencoder. The first way to use is to build a network which has the ability to represent dimension reduced features that can be restored to the original input vectors. By this network, an input vector can

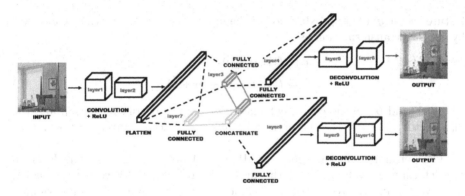

Fig. 2. Overview of the network by two autoencoders. (Color figure online)

be transformed into a dimension reduced feature vector and an approximation of the input vectors can be recalled. If the autoencoder is trained using the training samples with noises, the network can remove the noises. This network is called the denoising autoencoder [3,4]. Takahashi et al. used this functionality of autoencoder to improve the recognition accuracy of partly occluded image [5]. Also, it is possible to generate virtual samples by simply adding the noises to the dimension reduced features of the autoencoder. By sharing the feature vector of the classifier with the autoencoder and adding the noises to the feature vector in the learning process, we can realize the automatic data augmentation [6]. Effectiveness of the combination of the noise injection with the autoencoder in deep learning is shown in [7]. If we introduce the competition in the elements of the reduced feature vector, the autoencoder can achieve clustering of the training samples. Kurita et al. used this functionality of the autoencoder for the gating in the mixture of classifiers [8].

Another way is to determine the initial parameters for deep neural networks. Hinton et al. proposed to use the stacked autoencoders for pre-training of the deep belief nets [9]. In this method, at first the stacked autoencoders are trained by using the training samples and then the weights of the forward connections are used as the initial weights of the deep belief nets. To train the classification problem, the weights of the deep belief nets are further tuned by the usual supervised learning.

As a basic form of autoencoder, consider a network with three layers. Let an M-dimensional input vector be $\boldsymbol{x}$. The encoded feature vector $\boldsymbol{y} \in R^H$ $(H < M)$ in the hidden layer of the three layer Perceptron is computed by a transformation of $\boldsymbol{x}$ as

$$\boldsymbol{y} = f(W\boldsymbol{x} + \boldsymbol{b}) \tag{1}$$

where W and $\boldsymbol{b}$ are the coefficient matrix of the linear transformation and the bias vector respectively. The function $f(x)$ is the activation function of the neurons in the hidden layer. To reconstruct the input vector $\boldsymbol{x}$ from the extracted feature vector $\boldsymbol{y}$, the approximation of the input vector $\tilde{\boldsymbol{x}} \in R^M$ is also computed by another transformation as

$$\tilde{\boldsymbol{x}} = \tilde{f}(\tilde{W}\boldsymbol{y} + \tilde{\boldsymbol{b}})$$
$$= \tilde{f}(\tilde{W}f(W\boldsymbol{x} + \boldsymbol{b}) + \tilde{\boldsymbol{b}}) \qquad (2)$$

where $\tilde{W}$ and $\tilde{\boldsymbol{b}}$ are the coefficient matrix of the linear transformation and the bias vector respectively. The activation function of the neurons in the output layer is denoted as $\tilde{f}$.

The optimal coefficients matrices W and $\tilde{W}$ and the bias vectors $\boldsymbol{b}$ and $\tilde{\boldsymbol{b}}$ are determined by minimizing the mean squared errors between the original input vector and the reconstructed vector. The mean squared errors for training samples $\{\boldsymbol{x}_n | n = 1, \ldots, N\}$ is given as

$$J = \frac{1}{N} \sum_{n=1}^{N} \{||\boldsymbol{x}_n - \tilde{\boldsymbol{x}}_n||^2\} \qquad (3)$$

where $\tilde{\boldsymbol{x}}_n$ is the output of the network for the n-th image in the training samples. Usually the Stochastic Gradient Descent (SGD) is used to determine these parameters of the network.

If both activation functions f and $\tilde{f}$ are linear, then the autoencoder becomes equivalent to the principal component analysis (PCA) except for the rotation of the principal axes.

2.2   Invariant Features

Invariant feature extraction is one of the very important topics in pattern recognition. If the recognition target in an image is spatially shifted, the feature vector calculated by the classifier is usually different from the feature vector of the original image. If we can extract a shift invariant feature vectors, the design of the classifier become easy.

For the case of an ordinary autoencoder, an image and the one shifted spatially are encoded into different feature vectors. This will be a problem when classifying the target in the image. To solve this problem, Matsuo et al. proposed Transform Invariant Autoencoder [10]. This autoencoder separates an input into a shift invariant feature vector and transform parameters. By this method, they can extract a shift invariant feature vector from an input image.

Kobayashi proposed methods to improve performance of action classification by taking into account the invariance against the horizontal flipping [11].

3   Proposed Network Architecture

In this paper, we experimentally investigate how to extract invariant and variant features by using autoencorder and propose two network architectures which can extract both invariant and variant features from the training samples. The first architecture consists of the combination of classifier and autoencoder. The second architecture consists of the combination of two autoencoders.

3.1   Combination of Classifier and Autoencoder

In this paper, we use the convolutional autoencoder with 8 layers (two convolution layers, three fully-connected layers, a classification layer and two deconvolution layers). Figure 1 shows the network architecture which combines the classifier and the autoencoder. The images shifted vertically and horizontally are used as the training samples of this network.

In this network architecture, first two convolution layers are denoted as layer1 and layer2. Layer1 and layer2 extract the features from input images by convolution at each layer. Rectified Linear Unit (ReLU) function is used as the activation function of the neuron in the convolution layers layer1 and layer2. Then, it is divided into two different streams. One is the classification stream which corresponds to "what pathway". The other stream is used to reconstruct an input image which corresponds to "where pathway".

The classification stream is realized by using the standard multi-layered Perceptron with two fully-connected layers. They are denoted as layer3 (green layer) and layer4 in Fig. 1. The soft max function is used at the output layer of the classification stream. The cross entropy is used as the loss function for classification. In this stream, it is expected that the features on what is the object, namely shift invariant feature, can be extracted in layer3. This is because only information on what is the target object is necessary to classify the object and the information on the target shift is not necessary.

The reconstruction stream is realized as the decoder of the standard convolutional autoencoder. The dimension reduced feature vector is decomposed into two feature vectors which are shown as layer3 (green layer) and layer5 (yellow layer). For reconstruction, the outputs of layer3 and layer5 are concatenated and the concatenated features are used as the feature vector for reconstruction. The fully-connected layer6 is the reconstructed feature vector of the autoencoder. Then the approximation of the original input image are reconstructed by using two deconvolution layers denoted as layer7 and layer8. ReLU function is also used as the activation function of the neuron in the deconvolution layers layer7 and layer8. The mean squared errors between the reconstructed image by this reconstruction stream and the input image is used as the loss function. In this stream, all the information of the input image is necessary to reconstruct the original image but the information on what is the target object is extracted in the feature vector at the layer3. Thus it is expected that the feature vector at the layer5 includes only the information which is not related to what is the target object such as shift of the target.

The sum of cross entropy in the classification stream and mean squared error in the reconstruction stream is used as the loss function for training. The loss function of the proposed network architecture is given as

$$J_C = \frac{1}{N} \sum_{n=1}^{N} \{ - \sum_{k=1}^{K} t_{nk} \log y_{nk} + \lambda ||\boldsymbol{p}_n - \tilde{\boldsymbol{p}}_n||^2 \} \tag{4}$$

where t_{nk} and y_{nk} are the correct label and the output in the classification stream and $\boldsymbol{p}_n$ and $\tilde{\boldsymbol{p}}_n$ are the input image and the reconstructed image in the reconstruction stream. λ is a tuning parameter which controls the balance between the classifier and the autoencoder.

3.2 Combination of Two Autoencoders

The second network architecture uses two autoencoders with sharing the encoder network. We use the convolutional auto-encoder with 10 layers (two convolution layers, three fully-connected layers and a pair of deconvolution layers). Figure 2 shows the network architecture.

Similar with the previous network architecture, first two convolution layers are used to extract the features from input images by convolution at each layer. They are denoted as layer1 and layer2. ReLU function is used as the activation function of the neuron in these layers. Then, it is divided into two different streams for the estimation of the invariant image and the reconstruction of the input image.

The estimation stream is used to estimate the invariant images as shown as upper pathway in Fig. 2. This estimation network is realized by using the decoder of the standard convolutional autoencoder. The two fully-connected layers denoted as layer3 and layer4 are used to extract invariant features. The two deconvolution layers are used to estimate the invariant images which are denoted as layer5 and layer6. Rectified Linear Unit (ReLU) function is used as the activation function of the neuron in convolution layers and deconvolution layers. The mean squared error between the output of this stream and the invariant image is used as the loss function. In this stream, it is expected that the invariant features can be extracted in layer3.

The reconstruction stream is also realized as the decoder of the standard convolutional autoencoder. The dimension reduced feature vector is decomposed into two feature vectors which are shown as layer3 (green layer) and layer7 (yellow layer) in Fig. 2. The outputs of layer3 and layer7 are concatenated and the concatenated feature vector is used for the feature vector for the reconstruction of the input image. The fully-connected layer8 is the reconstructed feature vector of the autoencoder. Then the approximation of the original input image are reconstructed by using two deconvolution layers denoted as layer9 and layer10. ReLU function is also used as the activation function of the neuron in these deconvolution layers. The mean squared error between the output of this stream and the input image is used as the loss function. In this stream, it is expected that the variant features can be extracted in layer7.

The sum of two mean squared errors is used as the loss function to train the parameters of this network architecture. The loss function of this network is given by

$$J_E = \frac{1}{N} \sum_{n=1}^{N} \{||\boldsymbol{q}_n - \tilde{\boldsymbol{q}}_n||^2 + \lambda||\boldsymbol{p}_n - \tilde{\boldsymbol{p}}_n||^2\} \tag{5}$$

where $\boldsymbol{q}_n$ and $\tilde{\boldsymbol{q}}_n$ are the invariant image and the estimated image by the estimation stream respectively.

Table 1. Architecture of first proposed method using MNIST.

	Type	Filter	Stride	Outputs
layer1	conv	5×5	1	32
layer2	conv	5×5	1	64
layer3	FC	–	–	100
layer4	FC	–	–	10
layer5	FC	–	–	100
	link	–	–	200
layer6	FC	–	–	50176
layer7	deconv	5×5	1	32
layer8	deconv	5×5	1	1

Table 2. Architecture of second proposed method using SUN database or MNIST. Some hyperparameters in SUN database and MNIST are denoted as · or · (e.g., 2 or 1), respectively.

	Type	Filter	Stride	Outputs
layer1	conv	5×5	2 or 1	32
layer2	conv	5×5	2 or 1	64
layer3	FC	–	–	100 or 9
layer4	FC	–	–	53824 or 50176
layer5	deconv	5×5	2 or 1	32
layer6	deconv	5×5	2 or 1	3 or 1
layer7	FC	–	–	100 or 9
	link	–	–	200 or 18
layer8	FC	–	–	53824 or 50176
layer9	deconv	5×5	2 or 1	32
layer10	deconv	5×5	2 or 1	3 or 1

4   Experiments

To investigate the effectiveness of proposed method for extraction of invariant and variant features, we have performed the experiments using two datasets, MNIST and SUN Database. MNIST was used for two proposed methods, and SUN Database was used for second proposed method.

4.1   Combination of Classifier and Autoencoder

At first, we have performed an experiment using MNIST dataset to confirm the ability of the proposed network architecture to extract the shift invariant information and the shift variant information simultaneously. The first architecture which combines the classifier with the convolutional autoencoder is used in this experiment. The details of the network architecture is shown in Table 1.

MNIST is the well known dataset of handwritten character images for character recognition. The training dataset consists of 60000 images and the number of classes is 10. All the images in this dataset are the same size (28×28 pixels). In this experiment, all images are converted to gray scale and normalized in the range from 0 to 1.

The images are shifted randomly up to 5 pixels in the vertical and horizontal directions and shifted images are used as training samples. Adam optimizer is used for training.

We have also implemented simple convolutional autoencoder for comparison. Its network architecture is same as the autoencoder part of our proposed architecture. It consists of two convolutional neural network layers, two full-connected layers and two deconvolution layers. We used a ReLU as an activation function after each convolution and deconvolution layers.

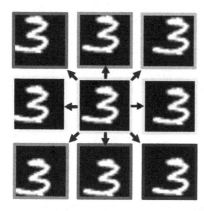

Fig. 3. The examples of input shifted data. The images are shifted randomly up to 5 pixels in the vertical and horizontal directions.

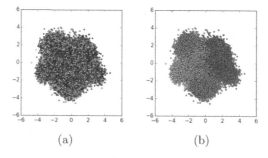

Fig. 4. The distribution by taking first two principal components of the features acquired from layer3 (green layer) in proposed autoencoder. (a) is colored by shifted position (Fig. 3). (b) is colored by class of the dataset. (Color figure online)

Figure 4 shows the distribution by taking first two principal components of the features acquired from layer3 (green layer) in proposed autoencoder. Figure 4(a) is colored by shifted position as shown in Fig. 3. For example, when input image is shifted more than 3 pixels vertically upwards and horizontally to the right, the point on the graph is colored as orange. It is noticed that any regularity is not seen in this plot. This means that the information on shift is not included in this feature vector, namely shift invariant feature vector is extracted at the layer3. Figure 4(b) is colored by class of the dataset. We can find that it is distributed collectively for each class. This means that only class information (shift invariant features) is extracted in layer3.

Figure 5 shows the distribution by taking first two principal components of the features acquired from layer5 (yellow layer) in proposed autoencoder. Figure 5(a) is colored by shifted position (Fig. 3). We can find that it is distributed collectively for each shifted position. Figure 5(b) is colored by the class. It is noticed that any regularity is not seen in plotting colored by the class.

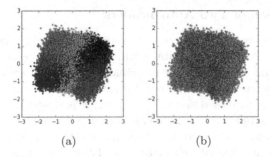

Fig. 5. The distribution by taking first two principal components of the features acquired from layer5 (yellow layer) in proposed autoencoder. (a) is colored by shifted position (Fig. 3). (b) is colored by class of the dataset. (Color figure online)

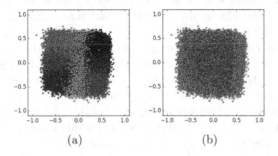

Fig. 6. The distribution of features by autoencoder used principal components analysis. (a) is colored by shifted position (Fig. 3). (b) is colored by class of the dataset. (Color figure online)

This means that only information representing the shift (shift variant features) is extracted in layer5.

Figure 6 shows the distribution by taking first two principal components of the features in the simple convolutional autoencoder. Figure 6(a) is colored by shifted position (Fig. 3). We can find that it is distributed collectively for each shifted position. Figure 6(b) is colored by class of the dataset. It seems that regularity is not seen in plotting colored by the class. This means that the simple convolutional autoencoder can extract only variant information.

From Fig. 4, Fig. 5 and Fig. 6, only the shift invariant features can be extracted at layer3 of the proposed architecture. Also, the shift variant information is extracted at layer5. This means that the decomposition of the shift invariant and shift variant information is achieved by the proposed network architecture.

4.2 Combination of Two Autoencoders

We have also performed an experiment to confirm the effectiveness of the second network architecture using SUN Database for white balance correction. The task is to estimate the image in which the illuminant information are removed. In this experiments, the white balance corrected image is used as the invariant image.

The detail of the proposed network architecture is shown in Table 2. We have also implemented simple convolutional autoencoder for comparison. Its network architecture is same as the autoencoder part of our proposed architecture. It consists of two convolutional neural network layers, two full-connected layers and two deconvolution layers. ReLU is used as an activation function after each convolution and deconvolution layers.

SUN Database [12] contains more than 900 variety of scene categories such as indoor, urban, nature etc. It is mainly used for scene recognition. To generate variations of the illuminant, the illuminant information is added to each of the images in the database. Here we assume that the images are uniformly influenced by only one light source and produce illuminated images from the original image based on this assumption. The color of the light source used for the preparation of the training samples is randomly generated on each image, whereas its illuminant value is not perfectly random. The value is selected based on the range of values that corresponding to natural scenes and their frequencies. To generate random values of distributions for suitable illuminant colors, we use NUS 8-Camera Dataset [13]. This dataset contains 1736 images and color information corresponding to each illuminant. We assume the distribution of that illuminant information as shown in the top of Fig. 7 which is equivalent to the distribution of illuminant information that influences the natural image. The illuminated image is generated using illuminant information of this dataset. The color values for preparing the synthetic dataset to get illumination is given by

$$\boldsymbol{p}_{filt} = \boldsymbol{p}_{orig} \circ \boldsymbol{p}_{coef} \tag{6}$$

where $\boldsymbol{p}_{filt} = \begin{bmatrix} r_{filt} & g_{filt} & b_{filt} \end{bmatrix}^T$ is a pixel value of the illuminated image obtained by Hadamard's product of a simple original image pixel value $\boldsymbol{p}_{orig} = \begin{bmatrix} r_{orig} & g_{orig} & b_{orig} \end{bmatrix}^T$ with the coefficient of illuminant information as $\boldsymbol{p}_{coef} = \begin{bmatrix} r_{coef} & g_{coef} & b_{coef} \end{bmatrix}^T$. The coefficient value is generated for each image using a random number of distribution of illuminant information as shown in the bottom of Fig. 7. The distribution is calculated by dividing the RGB values of each image as shown in the top of Fig. 7 by using the median value of each channel. Figure 8 shows the examples of the original image and the image with illuminant variation.

We used 10000 images for training. All the images are the same size (128×128 pixels) and normalized in the range from 0 to 1. The images with illuminant variations are used as the input of the network and the original images are used as the invariant images.

Figure 9 shows the distribution by taking first two principal components of the features acquired from layer3 (green layer) in the proposed architecture show

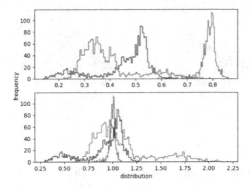

Fig. 7. Histogram for distributions of illuminant information based on NUS 8-Camera Dataset. The top is original distributions, and the bottom is a random number of distributions of illuminant information.

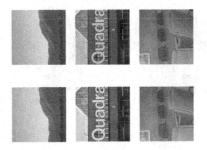

Fig. 8. The examples of SUN database. The top row are the original image in SUN database. The bottom row are the images with illuminant variation.

in Fig. 2. Figure 9(a) shows the scatter plot of the original images which don't have illuminant variation. Figure 9(b) is the scatter plot of the images with illuminant variations. From Fig. 9(a), we can find that the bright images on the bottom are distributed in the upper part and the bright ones on the top are distributed in the lower part. We can also find overall dark images are placed in the left part and bright ones are in the right part. From Fig. 9(b), it is noticed that illuminant variations do not affect this distribution. This means that the illuminant invariant features are extracted in this layer.

Figure 10 shows the distribution by taking first two principal components of the features acquired from layer7 (yellow layer) in the proposed architecture. Figure 10(a) shows the scatter plot of the original images which don't have illuminant variations. Figure 10(b) is the scatter plot of the illuminant variant images. From Fig. 10(a), we can find that the orange images are appeared in the upper part and the dark ones are in the left part. But we cannot find the regularity on the contents of the images. We can also find that it is distributed collectively for each illuminant filters in Fig. 10(b). This means that the illuminant variant features are extracted in this layer.

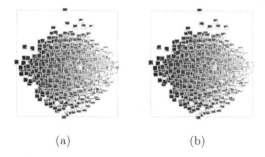

(a)   (b)

Fig. 9. The distribution by taking first two principal components of the features acquired from layer3 (green layer) in the proposed architecture (Fig. 2). (a) is the scatter plot of the original images. (b) is the scatter plot of the images with illuminat variations. (Color figure online)

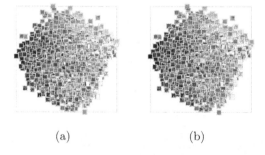

(a)   (b)

Fig. 10. The distribution by taking first two principal components of the features acquired from layer7 (yellow layer) in the proposed architecture (Fig. 2). (a) is the scatter plot of the original images. (b) is the scatter plot of the images with illuminant variations. (Color figure online)

Figure 11 shows the distribution by taking first two principal components of the features in autoencoder. Figure 11(a) is the scatter plots of the original images and Fig. 11(b) is the scatter plot of the images with illuminant variations. From Fig. 11(a), we can find that the orange images are appeared in the upper part and the dark ones are in the right part. From Fig. 11(b), it is also noticed that it is distributed collectively for each illuminant filters. These results shows that the standard autoencoder can extract only the illuminant variant features.

From Fig. 9, Fig. 10 and Fig. 11, only the illuminant invariant features can be extracted in the layer3 of the proposed architecture. Also the illuminant variant information is extracted at layer7. This means that the proposed architecture can separately extract the illuminant invariant and variant features.

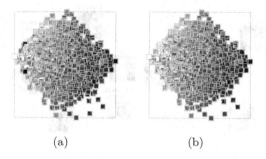

(a)   (b)

Fig. 11. The distribution by taking first two principal components of the features in the standard autoencoder. (a) is the scatter plot of the original images. (b) is the scatter plot of the images with illuminant variations.

4.3   Image Reconstruction

Finally, we have performed an experiment to generate shifted images by manipulating the shift variant feature vector extracted by the second proposed architecture (Fig. 2). The details of the architecture is shown in Table 2. The parameters of the network are trained by using the shifted MNIST images. The shifted images are used as the input of the network and the original images are used as the invariant images for training.

Then the shifted images are fed to the trained network and shift invariant features and shift variant features are calculated. To generate shifted images, only the shift variant feature vector (yellow layer in Fig. 2) is changed by using the first 2 dimensional principal components while the shift invariant feature vector is kept the same.

Figure 12(a) shows the examples of the generated images by this method. For example, INPUT1 in Fig. 12(a) is the input image shifted vertically upwards and horizontally to the left. The shift variant features of this image is located in the brown region in the scatter plot of the 2 dimensional principal components. When the shift variant features are changed so that it is located in the green region, OUTPUT1 in Fig. 12(a) is generated. It is noticed that the character "0" in OUTPUT1 is located in the center and the shape of the character is not changed.

Similarly, we can generate the images with different shapes by changing the shift invariant features (green layer in Fig. 2). Figure 12(b) shows the examples of the generated images. For example, INPUT1 in Fig. 12(b) is the input image which shows the character "1". The shift invariant features of this image is located in the blue region in the scatter plot of the 2 dimensional principal components. By changing the shift invariant features to the green region which is corresponding to the charager "8", the generated output becomes OUTPUT1 in Fig. 12(b). The shape of the character in this images becomes close to the "8". Also, the location of the character in the generated images is kept to the same as the input image.

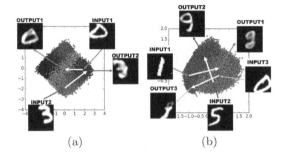

(a)   (b)

Fig. 12. The examples of reconstructed images by second proposed method and the distribution (scatter points) by taking first two principal components of their features. (a) shows examples of the shift variant features acquired from yellow layer in Fig. 2. (b) shows examples of the shift invariant features acquired from green layer in Fig. 2.

5   Conclusion and Future Works

In this paper, we experimentally investigated how to extract invariant and variant features by using autoencorder which can extract both invariant and variant features from the training samples. Two approaches (combination of classifier and autoencoder and combination of two autoencoders) were proposed for extracting both invariant and variant features. Through some experiments, we found that only the variant features can be extracted in autoencoder, whereas the invariant and variant features are separately extracted in the proposed methods.

As the future work, we would like to construct tangent space [14] in the space where the geometric invariance like shift is removed by using the proposed methods. Also we would like to reconstruct images using the obtained features by proposed methods and apply it to data augmentation.

Acknowledgement. This work was partly supported by JSPS KAKENHI Grant Number 16K00239.

References

1. Goodale, M.A., Milner, A.D.: Separate visual pathways for perception and action. Trends Neurosci. **15**, 20–25 (1992)
2. Hinton, G.E., Salakhutdinov, R.R.: Reducing the dimensionality of data with neural networks. Science **313**(5786), 504–507 (2006)
3. Takahashi, T., Kurita, T.: Robust de-noising by kernel PCA. In: Dorronsoro, J.R. (ed.) ICANN 2002. LNCS, vol. 2415, pp. 739–744. Springer, Heidelberg (2002). https://doi.org/10.1007/3-540-46084-5_120
4. Vincent, P., Larochelle, H., Bengio, Y., Manzagol, P.A.: Extracting and composing robust features with denoising autoencoder. In: Proceedings of the 25th International Conference on Machine Learning, pp. 1096–1103 (2008)
5. Takahashi, T., Kurita, T.: A robust classifier combined with an auto-associative network for completing partly occluded images. Neural Netw. **18**, 958–966 (2005)

6. Inayoshi, H., Kurita, T.: Improved generalization by adding both auto-association and hidden-layer-noise to neural-network-based-classifiers. In: Proceedings of 2005 IEEE International Workshop on Machine Learning for Signal Processing (MLSP 2005), pp. 141–146 (2005)

7. Sabri, M., Kurita T.: Effect of additive noise for multi-layered perceptron with autoencoders. IEICE Trans. Inform. Syst. **E100-D**(7), 1494–1504 (2017)

8. Kurita, T., Takahashi, T.: Viewpoint independent face recognition by competition of the viewpoint dependent classifiers. Neurocomputing **51**, 181–195 (2003)

9. Hinton, G.E., Simon, O., Yee-Whye, T.: A fast learning algorithm for deep belief nets. Neural Comput. **18**(7), 1527–1554 (2006)

10. Matsuo, T., Shimada, N.: Auto-encoder for generating a transform invariant descriptor and transform parameters. In: Meeting on Image Recognition and Understanding, vol. 1, p. 4 (2018)

11. Kobayashi, T.: Flip-invariant motion representation. In: Proceedings of 2017 IEEE International Conference on Computer Vision (ICCV), pp. 5628–5637 (2017)

12. Xiao, J., Hays, J., Ehinger, K.A., Oliva, A., Torralba, A.: SUN database: large-scale scene recognition from abbey to zoo. In: Computer Vision and Pattern Recognition (CVPR), pp. 3485–3492 (2010)

13. Cheng, D., Prasad, D.K., Brown, M.S.: Illuminant estimation for color constancy: why spatial-domain methods work and the role of the color distribution. J. Opt. Soc. Am. A **31**(5), 1049–1058 (2014)

14. Simard, P.Y., LeCun, Y.A., Denker, J.S., Victorri, B.: Transformation invariance in pattern recognition—tangent distance and tangent propagation. In: Orr, G.B., Müller, K.-R. (eds.) Neural Networks: Tricks of the Trade. LNCS, vol. 1524, pp. 239–274. Springer, Heidelberg (1998). https://doi.org/10.1007/3-540-49430-8_13

Deep Automatic Control of Learning Rates for GANs

Toshiki Kamiya, Fumihiko Sakaue, and Jun Sato$^{(\boxtimes)}$

Nagoya Institute of Technology, Nagoya 466-8555, Japan
kamiya@cv.nitech.ac.jp, {sakaue,junsato}@nitech.ac.jp

Abstract. In this paper, we propose a method for automatically controlling the learning rate of Generative Adversarial Networks (GANs) so as to stabilize the training of GANs. In recent years, GAN has been successful in various types of image generation tasks. Since GAN trains Generators and Discriminators adversarially, it is very important to keep the balance of their learning progress. However, it is known that the adjustment of learning rate of GAN is extremely difficult compared to conventional networks. Thus, we in this paper propose a method for predicting the future training progress of GANs from the current state of Generators and Discriminators, and for automatically controlling the learning rate of GANs appropriately. The proposed method has been tested using several different GANs, and the results show the proposed method can control the learning rate of GANs appropriately for a variety of tasks.

Keywords: GAN · Learning rate · Hyperparameter · Automatic control · Adversarial training

1 Introduction

GAN [4,12] is a network in which the generator and the Discriminator learn from each other adversarially so that the generator acquires a high generation ability. In recent years, GAN has attracted particular attention in the field of image generation, since it has the advantage of obtaining high performance from a small amount of training data [7,16].

While having these advantages, GAN is known to be more difficult to train stably than other networks. This is because GAN has to control the balance of Generator training and Discriminator training. Therefore, the learning rate that determines the training balance is an important hyperparameter that determines whether GAN can be trained successfully.

For example, Fig. 1 shows the result of training GAN to generate an image of Fashion-MNIST [15]. If the learning rate of Generator and Discriminator is set appropriately, the training will proceed properly and the image will be generated successfully as shown in Fig. 1(a). However, if the learning rate is inappropriate, the training balance will be lost, and proper image generation will not be performed as shown in Fig. 1(b). Although the learning rate is an important parameter in GAN training, no method for adjusting it has been established, and many people adjust

© The Author(s), under exclusive license to Springer Nature Switzerland AG 2022
K. Sumi et al. (Eds.): IW-FCV 2022, CCIS 1578, pp. 112–126, 2022.
https://doi.org/10.1007/978-3-031-06381-7_8

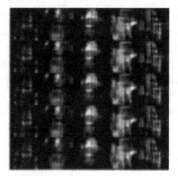

(a) Appropriate learning rate   (b) Inappropriate learning rate

Fig. 1. Difference in generated images due to difference in learning rate in GAN that generates Fashion-MNIST images [15]. If the learning rate of Generator and Discriminator is set appropriately, the training will proceed properly and the image will be generated successfully as shown in (a). However, if the learning rate is inappropriate, the training balance will be lost, and image generation fails as shown in (b).

the learning rate empirically or experimentally. As a result, a lot of costs are spent for adjusting the learning rate in many GAN studies.

Thus, in this paper, we propose a method to automatically control the learning rate appropriately for training GANs successfully. For this objective, we predict the future training success from current and past behavior of GAN training, and control the learning rate so that it maximizes the future training success degree. For predicting the future training success, we introduce a network called training success predictor, and train this network using various GANs and datasets. Thus, our method can be used for various GANs and datasets.

GAN is divided into two types, that is unconditional GANs trained on unlabeled image datasets and conditional GANs [9] trained on labeled datasets. In this paper, we propose a method for stabilizing GAN training for both unconditional GANs and conditional GANs.

2   Related Work

Many methods for adjusting hyperparameters have been studied as optimization problems in various studies. Grid search and random search are examples of naive methods for adjusting hyperparameters, and Nelder-Mead [10] and CMA-ES [5] were introduced for more sophisticated hyperparameter adjusting. Also, in recent years, Bayesian optimization [13] that considers the variance and narrows down where the appropriate parameters are, and TPE c̃itetpe that manages the state with a tree structure and efficiently prunes candidates have been proposed. Optimizations such as hyperopt [2] and optuna [11], which apply TPE and others, are beginning to be used.

However, although they work well in networks like CNN [3], they are difficult to apply to GANs with complex structures. In addition, these methods search for better hyperparameters by repeating trial and error while changing hyper-parameters. Therefore, a large amount of computational time is required to find an appropriate hyperparameter.

Thus, we in this paper propose a method for stabilizing GAN training by appropriately controlling hyperparameters, i.e. learning rates, in a single GAN training. Our method can control the learning rate without repeating trial and error since we introduce a predictor for future training success. The predictor enables us to find the best learning rate for future success of GANs at each epoch of training. As a result, our method can control the learning rate appropriately at each epoch of GAN training.

3   Prediction of Training Success Degree

In order to control the learning rate and improve the GAN training, we need a measure of how much the training is progressing in the network. We call it the training success degree of the network.

It seems that the network loss can be used as such a measure. However, the network loss varies depending on the task in general, and thus it cannot be used for comparing the network training progress across different tasks.

In recent years, the output of a pre-trained classifier trained with a large amount of data has been used as a quality measure of generated images. Thus, in this research, we define the training success degree by using the output value of the pre-trained classifier obtained by inputting the images generated by GAN during training.

3.1   Training Success Degree of Conditional GAN

In conditional GAN, it can be said that the more the image matches the label, the more advanced the training. Therefore, a pre-trained classifier is used for the evaluation network, and the classification accuracy of the images generated by the Generator can be considered as the learning success degree of the conditional GAN. Let u be the generated image, and let $C_k(u)$ be the probability that the image u will be classified into class k by the pre-trained classifier. Then, if the ground truth label of the image u is $l(u)$, the training success degree y_c of conditional GAN can be defined as follows:

$$y_c = \frac{1}{N_u} \sum_{i=1}^{N_u} C_{l(u_i)}(u_i) \tag{1}$$

where, N_u is the number of generated images, and u_i represents the ith image. The range of y_c is $y_c \in [0, 1]$, and the larger the value, the more advanced the training.

3.2   Training Success Degree of Unconditional GAN

In unconditional GAN, it can be said that the more similar the characteristics of the data set and the generated image are, the more advanced the training

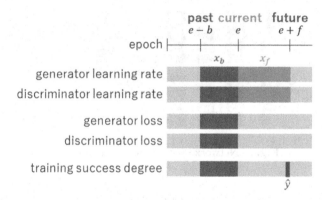

Fig. 2. Behavior dataset $\{x_b, x_f, y\}$ in our method. x_b is a 5-channel time series data consisting of the learning rate of Generator and Discriminator, the training error of Generator and Discriminator, and the training success degree in the past b epoch. x_f is a 2-channel time series data consisting of the learning rate of Generator and Discriminator to be used in the next f epoch, and y is the ground truth of training success degree after f epoch.

is. Therefore, the Inception Network [14] is used as the evaluation network, and the FID [6] between the image of the dataset and the image generated by the Generator is defined as the learning success degree. When the image dataset is D and a set of generated images is U, the training success degree y_u of unconditional GAN can be described as follows:

$$y_u = FID(U, D) \tag{2}$$

where, FID represents the Fréchet Inception Distance. The range of y_u is $y_u \in \mathbb{R}$, and the smaller the value, the more advanced the training.

3.3   Prediction of Training Success Degree

We next consider the prediction of training success degree at some point in the future. To predict the training success degree, we use the training loss and the training success degree under the learning rate used in the past training. Based on these past training behaviors, we predict the training success degree for the learning rate used in future training.

We define the behavior dataset $\{x_b, x_f, y\}$ as shown in Fig. 2. x_b is a 5-channel time series data consisting of the learning rate of the Generator and Discriminator, the training error of the Generator and Discriminator, and the training success degree in the past b epoch. x_f is a 2-channel time series data consisting of the learning rate of the Generator and Discriminator to be used in the next f epoch, and y is the ground truth of training success degree after f epoch.

For predicting the training success degree y, we use a training success predictor P. This is a network that predicts the training success degree after f epoch from x_b and x_f as follows:

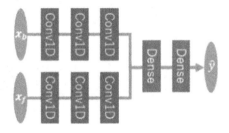

Fig. 3. Network structure of predictor P

$$\hat{y} = P(\boldsymbol{x}_b, \boldsymbol{x}_f) \tag{3}$$

The network structure of the predictor P is as shown in Fig. 3. The inputs of $\boldsymbol{x}_b$ and $\boldsymbol{x}_f$ are convolved three times with kernel size 3, and the number of filters increases in order of 10, 20, and 30. Each convoluted tensor is flattened and concatenated into one vector. Then, the output $\hat{y}$ is obtained after full connection with 128 units and full connection with 1 unit. ReLU was used as the activation function in the intermediate layers, and the sigmoid function was used as the activation function of the output layer.

3.4   Training of the Training Success Predictor

The training of the predictor P is conducted by minimizing the squared error between the output of the predictor $P(\boldsymbol{x}_b, \boldsymbol{x}_f)$ and the ground truth training success degree y as follows:

$$P^* = \arg \min_P \sum_i \|y_i - P(\boldsymbol{x}_{bi}, \boldsymbol{x}_{fi})\|^2 \tag{4}$$

where, y_i is the ground truth training success degree in the ith training data, and $\boldsymbol{x}_{bi}$ and $\boldsymbol{x}_{fi}$ represent $\boldsymbol{x}_b$ and $\boldsymbol{x}_f$ in the ith training data respectively.

For this training, we need a training dataset consisting of $\mathbf{x}_b$, $\mathbf{x}_f$ and y. The training dataset can be obtained by training a variety of GANs and datasets at many different learning rates. First, the learning rate is randomly determined, and GAN training is performed with b epoch. The generated images in this training step are used for computing the training success degree by using Eq. (1) or Eq. (2). This provides us $\boldsymbol{x}_b$, which represents the behavior of the training so far. We next set the learning rate $\boldsymbol{x}_f$ for the next f epoch, and train the GAN f epoch. Then, the real, i.e. ground truth, training success degree y is obtained after the training by using Eq. (1) or Eq. (2). By performing this training procedure on a variety of GANs and datasets changing the learning rate, we can obtain the training dataset consisting of $\mathbf{x}_b$, $\mathbf{x}_f$ and y.

By training the predictor P using the dataset, the predictor P can be trained to predict the training success degree after f epoch.

4   Learning Rate Control

4.1   Estimating the Optimal Learning Rate

We next explain a method for estimating the pair of learning rates for Generator and Discriminator x_f^* that will maximize the learning success of GAN in the future by using the predictor P.

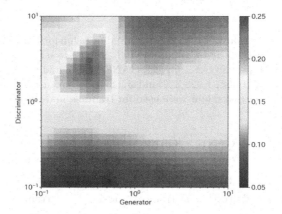

Fig. 4. Example of estimating the optimum learning rate. The figure shows how the training success degree after f epoch changes when the learning rate is changed in the range of $\frac{1}{10}$ to 10 times at the current training stage. We find that the Generator should reduce the learning rate and the Discriminator should increase the learning rate in this case.

Let us consider a 2D space S consisting of the generator learning rate g and the Discriminator learning rate d. Then, a set of the learning rates of Generator and Discriminator (g, d) used in the training can be considered as a point in this 2D space S. The future training success of GAN can be predicted from x_b and x_f obtained by arranging (g, d) along the time axis by using the predictor P as shown in Eq. (3). Thus, the learning rate x_f^* that maximizes the training success after f epoch can be obtained by solving the following maximization problem.

$$x_f^* = \arg \max_{x_f} P(x_b, x_f) \qquad (5)$$

In this research, we solve this maximization problem as a point selection problem in a discretized space.

First, the 2D space S consisting of the learning rate (g, d) is discretized. Next, the training success degree $\hat{y}$ is computed from Eq. (3) at each point in this discretized space. Then, a set of discrete points (g, d) where $\hat{y}$ becomes the maximum is the optimum learning rate x_f^*.

For example, Fig. 4 shows the result of estimating how the training success degree after f epoch changes when the learning rate is changed in the range of

$\frac{1}{10}$ to 10 times at the current training stage. In this case, we can see that the Generator should reduce the learning rate and the Discriminator should increase the learning rate.

4.2 Learning Rate Control in GAN Training

We next explain how to automatically control the learning rate by using the predictor P. Here, we assume that the learning rate is controlled for each s epoch.

Table 1. Image generation tasks used for obtaining behavior datasets. Two types of image datasets, MNIST [8] and Fashion-MNIST [15], were used as target images for generation, and four types of GANs, GAN1, GAN2, GAN3 and GAN4, with parameter numbers of 254,754, 661,058, 1,928,322 and 3,240,578 were used as GANs for image generation. Of the eight tasks, four were used for training, and the remaining four were used for testing.

	GAN1 (254,754)	GAN2 (661,058)	GAN3 (1,928,322)	GAN4 (3,240,578)
MNIST	Training	Test	Training	Test
F-MNIST	Test	Training	Test	Training

First, we determine an appropriate initial learning rate and perform GAN training for b epoch. Next, we compute the optimal learning rate $\boldsymbol{x}_f^*$ from $\boldsymbol{x}_b$ by using Eq. (5). Then, by using the obtained optimal learning rate $\boldsymbol{x}_f^*$, GAN training is performed by s epoch. After that, GAN training is continued in the same manner, and the learning rate is updated to the optimum learning rate for each s epoch.

By sequentially computing the optimum learning rate with the predictor P and controlling the learning rate of GAN in this way, it is possible to train GAN stably.

5 Experiments

We next show the experimental results of training success degree prediction and automatic control of learning rate. All code was implemented by tensorflow [1].

5.1 Prediction of Training Success Degree in Conditional GAN

We first conducted an experiment to predict the training success degree for conditional GAN.

Two types of image datasets, MNIST [8] and Fashion-MNIST [15], were used as target images for image generation, and four types of conditional GANs, GAN1, GAN2, GAN3 and GAN4, with parameter numbers of 254754, 661058, 1928322, and 3240578 were used for this image generation. These GANs and

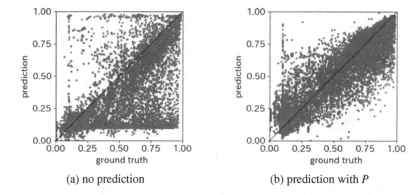

(a) no prediction   (b) prediction with P

Fig. 5. Relationship between the predicted training success degree and its ground truth in conditional GAN. (a) shows the result when the prediction was not performed, and (b) shows the result when the training success degree is predicted by the predictor P in the proposed method. We find that the correlation between the predicted value and the ground truth value increases by using the proposed method.

image datasets were combined as shown in Table 1, and eight different tasks were defined. Of the eight tasks, four were used for training the predictor, and the remaining four were used for testing the predictor as shown in Table 1. Training of GAN in these tasks was repeated with different learning rates, and 16000 training data and 16000 test data were obtained for training and testing the predictor P.

The predictor P is set to predict the training success degree after $f = 20$ epoch from the past $b = 10$ epoch training. The batch size was 128, the learning rate was 0.001, and the predictor P was trained by 25 epochs. Then, the training success degree after $f = 20$ epoch training was predicted by using the predictor P. The case of no prediction was also conducted for comparison. In this case, the training success degree at the current epoch is used as the predicted training success degree after $f = 20$ epoch.

Figure 5 shows the relationship between the ground truth value and the predicted value of the training success degree, in which a single point corresponds to one training of GAN. Figure 5(a) shows the result when the prediction was not performed. As shown in this figure, the correlation between the predicted value and the ground truth value was low, and the RMSE between the ground truth value and the predicted value was 0.24. On the other hand, Fig. 5(b) shows the result when the training success degree is predicted by the predictor P. From this figure, we find that the correlation between the predicted value and the ground truth value is high. The RMSE was 0.13, and the error was reduced by 46% compared to the case without prediction.

5.2 Prediction of Training Success Degree in Unconditional GAN

We next conducted an experiment to predict the training success degree for unconditional GAN.

120   T. Kamiya et al.

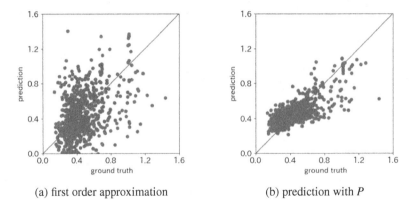

(a) first order approximation   (b) prediction with P

Fig. 6. Relationship between the predicted training success degree and its ground truth in unconditional GAN. (a) shows the result of prediction by first-order approximation, and (b) shows the result when the training success degree is predicted by the predictor P. We find that the correlation between the predicted value and the true value increases in the proposed method.

Fashion-MNIST was used as the target images to be generated, and three types of unconditional GAN with the number of parameters of 580,000, 1,300,000, and 2,100,000 were used as the network for image generation. Training was repeated for these tasks with different learning rates, and 720 training data and 75 test data were obtained.

The predictor P is set to predict the training success degree after $f = 5$ epoch from the past $b = 10$ epoch training. The batch size was 32, the learning rate was 0.001, and the predictor P was trained in 100 epochs. Then, the training success degree after $f = 5$ epoch training was predicted using the trained predictor P. For comparison, the first-order approximation was also used for predicting the training success degree. For each prediction of the predictor P and the first-order approximation, the RMSE of the predicted training success degree is computed.

Figure 6 shows the relationship between the ground truth value and the predicted value of the training success degree. Figure 6(a) shows the result of prediction by first-order approximation, and the RMSE between the ground truth value and the predicted value is 7.23. Figure 6(b) shows the result when the training success degree is predicted by the predictor P in the proposed method. From this figure, we find that the correlation between the predicted value and the true value increases in the proposed method. The RMSE was 3.66, which was a 49.4% reduction in error compared to the first-order approximation. From these results, we find that the training success degree can be predicted accurately by using the predictor P in the proposed method.

5.3   Learning Rate Control

We next show the results of learning rate control in conditional GAN.

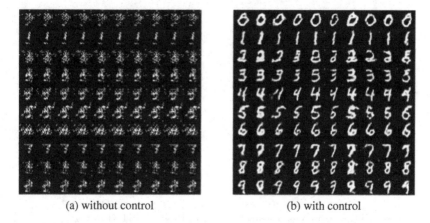

<table>
<tr><td>(a) without control</td><td>(b) with control</td></tr>
</table>

Fig. 7. Images obtained by training MNIST. Each row shows images generated in the same class, and each column shows images generated by using the same noise. As shown in (a), the numbers were not generated properly when the learning rate was not controlled. As shown in (b), the numbers were generated accurately when the learning rate was controlled by using the proposed method, and the GAN training for image generation was successful.

In this experiment, GAN is trained by 50 epochs for each of MNIST and Fashion-MNIST, and 10 images corresponding to 10 types of labels are generated for a total of 100 images. Then, we compare the generated images with and without learning rate control.

The interval of learning rate control was set to $s = 1$, so the learning rate was controlled every epoch. For comparison, we also evaluated a conventional method in which the learning rate is not changed from the initial learning rate. In the MNIST training, the initial learning rate of the Generator was set to 10^{-3} and the initial learning rate of the Discriminator was set to 10^{-6}, so the learning rate of the Discriminator was set to be smaller than the learning rate of the Generator. In the Fashion-MNIST training, the initial learning rate of the Generator was 10^{-5} and the initial learning rate of the Discriminator was 10^{-3}, and the learning rate of the Discriminator was larger than the learning rate of the Generator.

After training with the MNIST dataset, GAN output the images shown in Fig. 7. In this figure, each row shows images generated in the same class, and each column shows images generated by using the same noise. As shown in Fig. 7(a), the numbers are not generated properly when the learning rate is not controlled, and we find that the GAN training was not performed properly. On the other hand, when the learning rate was controlled by using the proposed method, the numbers were generated accurately as shown in Fig. 7(b), and the GAN training for image generation was successful.

The changes in the learning rate, network loss, and the training success degree in the learning rate control are as shown in Fig. 8, Fig. 9, and Fig. 10 respectively. In the first 10 epochs without learning rate control, the Discriminator loss

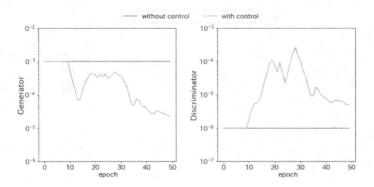

Fig. 8. Changes in learning rate during MNIST training

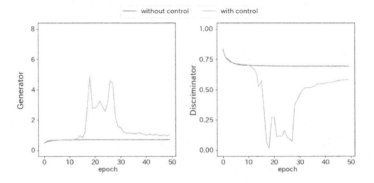

Fig. 9. Changes in generator loss and discriminator loss during MNIST training

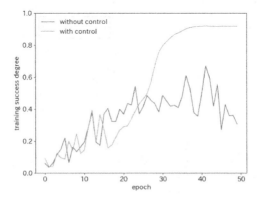

Fig. 10. Changes in training success degree during MNIST training

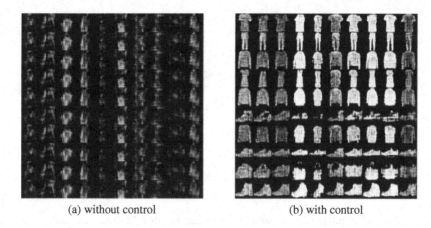

(a) without control   (b) with control

Fig. 11. Images obtained by training Fashion-MNIST

Table 2. Success rate of GAN training in 4 test tasks shown in Table 1. In each test task, we performed GAN training 100 times changing the initial learning rate of Generator and Discriminator, and computed the average training success degree for the trained Generator. The training success rate of the proposed method is much higher than that of the uncontrolled method.

	GAN1	GAN2	GAN3	GAN4
	F-MNIST	MNIST	F-MNIST	MNIST
Proposed	**0.71**	**0.91**	**0.78**	**0.86**
Uncontrolled	0.37	0.58	0.57	0.46

remains high. On the other hand, after the 10 epoch, the learning rate of the Generator is controlled to be small, and the learning rate of the Discriminator is controlled to be large. Furthermore, after 15 epochs, the learning rate of the Generator is controlled to increase as the loss of the Generator increases, and we find that the learning rate is controlled appropriately according to the changes in loss. By controlling the learning rate in this way, the training success degree finally increased to 0.92 as shown in Fig. 10.

On the other hand, after training with the Fashion-MNIST dataset, GAN output the images shown in Fig. 11. The labels correspond to T-shirts, trousers, pullovers, dresses, coats, sandals, shirts, sneakers, bags and ankle boots, from top to bottom. When training without learning rate control, the output images strongly depend on noise as shown in each column in Fig. 11(a), and we can see that the GAN training has failed. On the other hand, when the learning rate was controlled, the object of each class appeared appropriately as shown in Fig. 11(b), and we can see that the GAN training was successful. The changes in learning rate and loss during the training are as shown in Fig. 12 and Fig. 13 respectively. Since the first 10 epochs do not control the learning rate, the error of the Generator remains high. From the 10th epoch to the 20th epoch, the learning

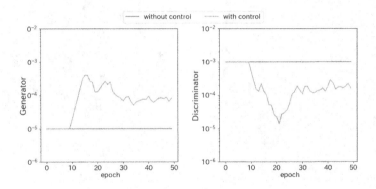

Fig. 12. Changes in learning rate during Fashion-MNIST training

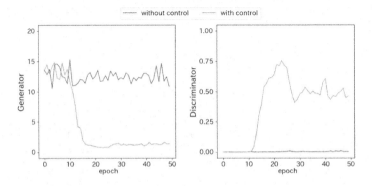

Fig. 13. Changes in generator loss and discriminator loss during Fashion-MNIST training

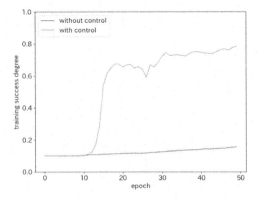

Fig. 14. Changes in training success degree during Fashion-MNIST training

rate of the Generator becomes large and the learning rate of the Discriminator becomes small. As a result, the generator loss is reduced and the discriminator loss is increased. Along with this, the learning rate of the Discriminator is controlled to increase from the 20th epoch to the 30th epoch. By this operation, the discriminator loss is reduced. As a result of controlling the learning rate as described above, the training success degree finally increased to 0.79 as shown in Fig. 14.

We next evaluated the success rate of GAN training by conducting the GAN training with various initial learning rates in various tasks. We chose 100 random initial learning rates of Generator and Discriminator in each test task in Table 1 and conducted GAN trainings. Then, the training success rate, i.e. the average training success degree for the trained Generator, was computed. For comparison we also conducted the GAN trainings without learning rate control. Table 2 shows the training success rate of the proposed method and the uncontrolled method respectively. As shown in this table, the training success rate of the proposed method is much higher than that of the uncontrolled method. From these results, we find that the proposed method can control the learning rate properly in various GAN tasks.

6   Conclusion

In this paper, we proposed a method for stabilizing GAN training by automatically controlling the GAN learning rate based on the prediction of training success degree.

We showed that it is possible to predict future training success degree in both conditional GANs and unconditional GANs by using the predictor P introduced in this research. We trained the predictor P using training behavior data of various GANs and image datasets, so that it can predict future training success degree for various GANs and datasets. By using the predictor, we controlled the learning rate of GANs to maximize the future success of GAN training.

In our experiments, we showed that even if the training is started from an inappropriate initial learning rate that would otherwise fail, the learning rate can be appropriately controlled by using the proposed method and stable training of GAN is possible. We also compared the proposed method with an uncontrolled method quantitatively, and showed that the proposed method outperformed the uncontrolled method in the success rate of GAN training.

By training the predictor P with a wider variety of GANs and datasets, it will be possible to use our method in wider class of GANs and datasets.

References

1. Abadi, M., et al.: Large-scale machine learning on heterogeneous systems (2015). https://www.tensorflow.org/

2. Bergstra, J., Yamins, D., Cox, D.D.: Making a science of model search: hyperparameter optimization in hundreds of dimensions for vision architectures. In:Proceedings of the 30th International Conference on Machine Learning (ICML 2013), pp. I-115–I-123 (2013)
3. Fukushima, K., Miyake, S.: Neocognitron: a new algorithm for pattern recognition tolerant of deformations and shifts in position. Pattern Recogn. **15**(6), 455–469 (1982)
4. Goodfellow, I., et al.: Generative adversarial nets. In: Advances in Neural Information Processing Systems, pp. 2672–2680 (2014)
5. Hansen, N., Ostermeier, A.: Adapting arbitrary normal mutation distributions in evolution strategies: the covariance matrix adaptation. In: Proceedings of IEEE International Conference on Evolutionary Computation, pp. 312–317 (1996)
6. Heusel, M., Ramsauer, H., Unterthiner, T., Nessler, B., Hochreiter, S.: GANs trained by a two time-scale update rule converge to a local Nash equilibrium. In: Conference on Neural Information Processing Systems (NIPS) (2017)
7. Isola, P., Zhu, J.Y., Zhou, T., Efros, A.A.: Image-to-image translation with conditional adversarial networks. In: IEEE Conference on Computer Vision and Pattern Recognition (CVPR), pp. 1125–1134 (2017)
8. LeCun, Y., Cortes, C., Burges, C.J.: MNIST handwritten digit database, yann lecun, corinna cortes and chris burges. http://yann.lecun.com/exdb/mnist/
9. Mirza, M., Osindero, S.: Conditional generative adversarial nets. arXiv preprint arXiv:1411.1784, pp. 1–7 (2014)
10. Nelder, J.A., Mead, R.: A simplex method for function minimization. Comput. J. **7**, 308–313 (1965)
11. Preferred Networks, I.: Automatic hyperparameter optimization framework for machine learning. https://www.preferred.jp/en/projects/optuna/
12. Salimans, T., Goodfellow, I., Zaremba, W., Cheung, V., Radford, A., Chen, X.: Improved techniques for training GANs. In: NIPS 2016 (2016)
13. Snoek, J., Larochelle, H., Adams, R.P.: Practical Bayesian optimization of machine learning algorithms. In: NIPS 2012: Proceedings of the 25th International Conference on Neural Information Processing Systems, vol. 2, pp. 2951–2959 (2012)
14. Szegedy, C., et al.: Going deeper with convolutions. In: IEEE Conference on Computer Vision and Pattern Recognition (CVPR) (2015)
15. Xiao, H., Rasul, K., Vollgraf, R.: Fashion-MNIST: a novel image dataset for benchmarking machine learning algorithms (2017)
16. Zhu, J., Park, T., Isola, P., Efros, A.: Unpaired image-to-image translation using cycle-consistent adversarial networks. In: Proceedings of the International Conference on Computer Vision, pp. 2223–2232 (2017)

Multimodal Pseudo-Labeling Under Various Shooting Conditions: Case Study on RGB and IR Images

Hiroki Kojima$^{(\boxtimes)}$, Naoshi Kaneko, Seiya Ito, and Kazuhiko Sumi

Aoyama Gakuin University, 5-10-1 Fuchinobe, Chuo-ku,
Sagamihara, Kanagawa, Japan
kojima.hiroki@vss.it.aoyama.ac.jp

Abstract. In recent years, large-scale datasets with accurate labels have been an extremely important factor in the progress of computer vision. One typical example is object detection in outdoor scenes, where data captured under various conditions such as lighting, weather, and temperature are essential to increase the robustness of object detectors. However, such is time-consuming. In addition, under conditions such as extremely low luminance, it is difficult to assign accurate labels, even manually. When even a small amount of labeled data is available, pseudo-labeling can be used to effectively assign labels to unlabeled data, but if the labeled data is captured under only a single condition (e.g., day-time), it is difficult to perform pseudo-labeling to images under different conditions (e.g., nighttime). In this paper, we propose a pseudo-labeling method under various conditions by using multimodal images. If one of which has a small change in texture depending on the conditions and the other has a large change, we can perform pseudo-labeling and self-training by projecting the outputs mutually. Using videos taken by RGB and IR cameras on a road as a case study, we show the effectiveness of the proposed method in object detection.

Keywords: Pseudo-labeling · Self-training · Multimodal · RGB and IR · Object detection

1 Introduction

With the recent development of deep learning, large-scale datasets with accurate labels are becoming more and more important. For example, in object detection, which is one of the major topics in computer vision, data captured under various conditions including lighting, temperatures, and weather are essential for detection in various scenes. However, the process of capturing data under various conditions and assigning labels to the data is a time-consuming. In addition, some cases are difficult to label even manually. For example, under conditions such as extremely low luminance, data captured under various conditions including lighting, temperatures, and weather are essential for detection in various scenes.

© The Author(s), under exclusive license to Springer Nature Switzerland AG 2022
K. Sumi et al. (Eds.): IW-FCV 2022, CCIS 1578, pp. 127–140, 2022.
https://doi.org/10.1007/978-3-031-06381-7_9

In order to perform labeling efficiently, pseudo-labeling, which automatically assigns labels to unlabeled data utilizing a small number of data with ground truth labels, has been studied [1–4]. While it may be a practical solution, if the labeled data is captured under only a single condition, it is difficult to perform pseudo-labeling to images under different conditions. Therefore, pseudo-labeling that can handle a variety of conditions is required.

In this paper, we propose a pseudo-labeling method under various shooting conditions by using multimodal images. For the case where one modality correctly recognizes an object but fails to recognize it under other conditions, the proposed method performs pseudo-labeling through different modalities to cope with those conditions. We first train a model with a small amount of labeled data collected in one modality, and then transform the object detection results of the trained model to another modality. As a case study, we apply our method to RGB and IR images to address the object detection task of detecting the back of vehicles for vehicle tracking in road images under different lighting conditions. We first train a model with a small amount of labeled data collected in one modality, and then transform the object detection results of the trained model to another modality.

The contributions of this paper are as follows:

- We propose a pseudo-labeling method under various shooting conditions such as lighting, temperature, and weather by using multimodal images.
- As a case study, we apply our method to RGB images with IR images under different lighting conditions and show quantitative improvements.

2   Related Work

In this chapter, we first introduce related techniques for object detection, which are the main topics of this paper. Next, we introduce typical datasets for object detection to access multimodal information. Finally, we describe related techniques for pseudo-labeling.

2.1   Object Detection

Many methods exist for object detection, which predicts the classes and rectangular regions of objects in an image. There are two types of methods for object detection: two-stage methods [5,6] that perform candidate region prediction and class estimation in stages, and one-stage methods that perform both simultaneously.

Faster R-CNN [7] is a representative method of the former, estimates the candidate regions from the feature map after convolution of the whole input image, and then classifying each candidate region. However, while the two-stage method has high accuracy, it has a problem of slow processing speed, and therefore, the one-stage method has been attracting more attention in recent years.

YOLO [8] is a representative method of the one-stage method. YOLO first divides the whole input image into $S \times S$ grid cells. Then, for all grids, it predicts the bounding box centered on the grid and its confidence level, as well as the conditional probabilities for all grid classes, and outputs the result by multiplying the confidence level and conditional probability. SSD [9] improved the detection accuracy of small objects, which was difficult to achieve with YOLO, by fitting bounding boxes to features of various scales obtained in the convolution layers.

More recently, the transformer technique has been gaining attention in object detection. DETR [10] is one of the major methods of it, in which a feature map of the entire image is segmented and input to an encoder-decoder using a transformer to output object regions and class probabilities. It is particularly effective for detecting large objects because it can take the attention between features that are far apart in the image. Whereas the method described above used the Non-Maximum-Suppression to suppress thousands of duplicate predictions, this method outputs only a small number of predictions, making it completely end-to-end.

2.2   Multimodal Dataset

KAIST Dataset [11] is a major multispectral dataset consisting of pairs of RGB and IR images for pedestrian detection. This dataset contains both daytime and nighttime images. Since pedestrians are harder to see at night due to the reduced brightness, such data is displayed alongside infrared images for labeling. In other words, it is difficult to accurately label nighttime images using only visible images.

The AAU RainSnow Traffic Surveillance Dataset[1] is also one of the major datasets consisting of RGB and IR images where vehicles are labeled. This dataset includes multiple climatic conditions, such as rain and snow; in contrast to the KAIST Dataset, rainy weather makes labeling on the infrared side of the image more difficult, as the contours are obscured due to the proximity of the road and body heat on the infrared image.

2.3   Pseudo-Labeling and Self-training

Pseudo-labeling and Self-training are one of the popular methods to deal with a small amount of labeled data and a large amount of unlabeled data. First, train a model with a small number of labeled data. Then input unlabeled data into the model and use the outputs as pseudo-labels, which are treated like GT labels and used for training data. The most important advantage of pseudo-labeling is that it can use most of the existing Supervised Learning methods as the base model without any modification.

Self-training [1] is the most simple and popular method, which uses a single model for the base model. Co-training [2] allows multiple models to be used, where the labeled data is divided into multiple model training data, and the pseudo-label output from each model is used as training data for another model. Passing information from multiple models to each other is expected to avoid

---

[1] https://bitbucket.org/aauvap/aau-rainsnow-eval.

biased learning, but this method is only suitable when the features of the divided labeled training data are independent.

ASSEMBLE [3] is one of the Boosting methods that uses multiple weak models, and uses pseudo-labels as the GT labels of the next weak model.

In recent years, there have been some methods that aim to improve the accuracy of pseudo-label by using multimodal information in a complementary manner, such as [4] which uses RGB, Optical Flow, and Temporal Gradient.

2.4   Problem of Existing Methods

In order to detect objects under various conditions, such as lighting and weather, we need a model trained with data taken under various conditions. Even if it is possible to manually label the images for each condition like KAIST Dataset and RainSnow Dataset, explained in Sect. 2.2, it is a time-consuming task, and it is difficult to label accurately when the scene is very dark or the weather is bad. Although pseudo-labeling is considered to be an effective method to avoid manual labeling, if the labeled data contains only a single condition and the conditions of the unlabeled data are different, pseudo-labeling is difficult to perform, and there are still cases where labeling is difficult.

3   Method

In this paper, we propose a pseudo-labeling method under various conditions using multimodal images. As shown in Fig. 1, the core idea is to acquire data from the same scene with multimodal sensors and use the limited labeled data to perform pseudo-labeling while taking advantage of each modality to accommodate various shooting conditions. In multimodal images under certain conditions, if one modality has a small difference in texture or appearance and the other modality has a large difference, it is possible to obtain pseudo labels for the other modality by going through the modality with the small difference, since the small difference does not affect the detection accuracy. Using the transformation matrix obtained by the calibration between the multimodal cameras, the coordinates of the bounding box obtained by object detection in one modality can be transformed to the coordinates of another modality. Here, although the multimodal cameras are asynchronous, the timestamp information is used to eliminate the time gap by adopting the frame with the smallest time difference. By using the pseudo-labels obtained in this way and training models independently for each modality, models that accommodate a variety of conditions can be learned from a small amount of labeled data and a large amount of unlabeled data.

As a case study, we address object detection using two modalities: RGB images (mod-A) and IR images (mod-B) under different lighting conditions due to sunlight. Whereas the texture and appearance of RGB images change dramatically with daylight, IR images change only slightly.

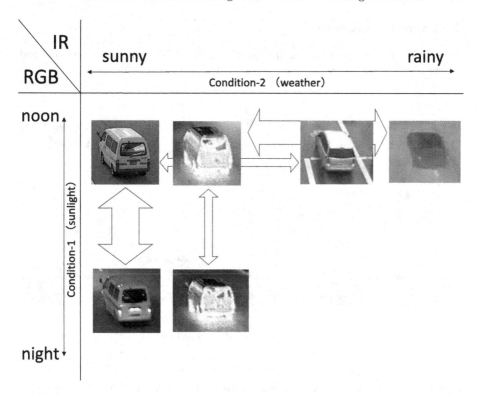

Fig. 1. Intuition of our idea. The thickness of the arrows mean the magnitudes of the change in texture. Rainy images are cropped from AAU RainSnow Trafic Surveillance Dataset.

In the following subsections, we first explain the prerequisite for applying the proposed method (Sect. 3.1). Then, we provide an overall procedure of the proposed method (Sect. 3.2). Finally, we describe the transformation between the two modalities (Sect. 3.3).

3.1 Prerequisite

We assume that the same scene is captured by multiple multimodal sensors. In our case study, we use an RGB camera and an IR camera as sensors to detect vehicles. These cameras are fixed, and calibration can be used to obtain the transformation matrix between them.

We employ homography transformation, which is a transformation associated with two planes, because it can be used even when the axes of the two cameras are different. Homography transformation requires at least four correspondences between two images. The correspondence points between the modalities used to compute the transformation matrix H are assigned manually.

3.2 Overall Procedure

Figure 2 shows an overview of the proposed method. The proposed method consists of three steps.

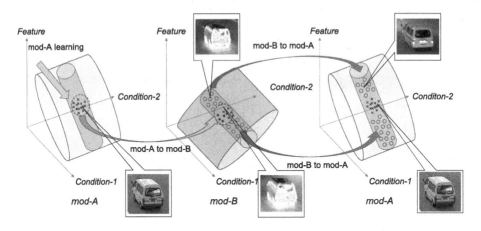

Fig. 2. Overview of our method

Training mod-A Using Manually Labeled mod-A Images. The first process is to manually label mod-A in order to train a model of mod-A under a certain condition (condition-1 in Fig. 2). Since this process is manual, only a small amount of data may be available. If a model is trained from such data, the trained model will be able to detect objects with high accuracy only under the same condition as training. In contrast, the detection accuracy for images under different conditions will be greatly reduced.

Pseudo-Labeling of mod-B Images Using mod-A Detection Model. Even under conditions where mod-A can detect objects with high accuracy, mod-B cannot easily label them. Therefore, the second process uses the detection results of mod-A to perform pseudo-labeling of mod-B. As mentioned in Sect. 3.1, we assume that the transformation matrix of mod-A and mod-B are available. Using this transformation matrix, we obtain the pseudo-label of mod-B by transforming the detection result of mod-A to mod-B. The pseudo-labels obtained in this process are used to train the model of mod-B. By training with the pseudo-labels obtained in this process, we can obtain a model of mod-B that can handle condition-1.

Pseudo-Labeling of mod-A Images Using mod-B Detection Model. Here, we note that mod-A and mod-B are different modalities. Since condition-1 in mod-A does not exactly encompass condition-1 in mod-B, condition-1 in mod-B may encompass both condition-1 and condition-2 in mod-A. There-fore, the third process transforms the detection results of mod-B into mod-A again for pseudo-labeling. By training the model of mod-A with pseudo-labeling, the model of mod-A can accommodate the two conditions of condition-1 and condition-2. In the next subsection, we explain details of transformation between two modalities.

3.3   Transformation Between Two Modalities

The proposed method automatically generates data for various conditions by pseudo-labeling while taking advantage of each modality. In our case study, we train a model for each modality by performing pseudo-labeling between two cameras with different characteristics. In the following, we explain how to transform between the two modalities.

mod-A to mod-B. The proposed method first trains the object detection model of mod-A D_A using a small amount of labeled data $\mathcal{D}_A^l$. Each image x_A^i in unlabeled data of mod-A D_A^u is then fed into the model to obtain bounding boxes $b_A \in \mathcal{B}_A^i$ and class labels $l_A \in L_A^i$. To transform the detection result of mod-A to mod-B, the homography matrix H is used:

$$\hat{b}_B = H\hat{b}_A \tag{1}$$

where $\hat{b}_A$ and $\hat{b}_B$ are the homogeneous coordinates of the points comprising the bounding box b_A in mod-A and mod-B. The coordinates obtained by the homography transformation b_B^i and the labels L_A^i obtained from the detection are used as pseudo labels. Here, the mod-B image x_B^i to which the pseudo-label l_A is assigned is the one whose shooting time is closest to the mod-A image x_A^i.

mod-B to mod-A. Next, we train the object detection model of mod-B D_B using pseudo-labeled data $\mathcal{D}_B^p$. As described in Sect. 3.2, The model D_B trained by mod-B has the potential to detect not only the conditions under which the model D_A can detect objects, but also the conditions under which the model D_A cannot detect objects. Hence, we use the model D_B to perform pseudo-labeling on mod-A. Similar to the mod-A to mod-B transformation, each image of mod-B x_B^i id fed into the model D_B. The resulting bounding boxes $b_B' \in \mathcal{B}_B^i$ and class labels $l_B \in L_B^i$ are used for pseudo-labeling of mod-A. The transformation from mod-B to mod-A can be written using the inverse homography matrix H^{-1} as:

$$\hat{b}_A' = H^{-1}\hat{b}_B' \tag{2}$$

where $\hat{b}_A'$ and $\hat{b}_B'$ are the homogeneous coordinates of the points comprising the bounding box b_B' in mod-A and mod-B. By combining this data with manu-ally labeled data as training data, self-training can be performed on data with multiple conditions.

4 Experiments

4.1 Dataset

We used RGB and IR cameras to capture videos of two roads, and cut out frames from the videos at regular intervals. We assigned a single label, "behind the car." One consists of daytime data only, and the other consists of both daytime and nighttime data, which we call them data R1 and R2 respectively. Therefore, the data R1 were used in the processes of Sect. 3.1 and Sect. 3.2, and the data R2 were used in Sect. 3.3. Details of produced data are as shown in Table 1.

Table 1. Details of assigned instances

Step	Modality	Time	Label	Instances	Images	Procedure	Data
1. mod-A	RGB	Noon	1	1,877	1,000	Manually	R1
2. mod-A to mod-B	IR	Noon	1	4,888	2,943	Automatically	R1
3. mod-B to mod-A	RGB	Night	1	4,124	1,380	Automatically	R2

To show the effectiveness of our method, we first train the model with only labeled daytime data in the first row of Table 1. Then, we combine manually labeled RGB daytime data in the first row and the pseudo-labeled RGB nighttime data in the third row as training data in order to perform self-training. For quantitative comparison between these models, test labels are assigned to data R2 with daytime and nighttime data in the same way as in step 3. 1,704 labels are assigned to the 595 images in the daytime data, and 636 labels are assigned to the 254 images in the nighttime data.

4.2 Implementation Details

For the detection model, we used YOLOv5[2], which is a faster and more accurate version of YOLO described in Sect. 2.1. We train the model with the SGD optimizer, setting the learning rate to 1e–2, weight decay to 5e–4, and epochs to 100. The model's parameters are initialized with the COCO-pretrained model.

4.3 Quantitative Results

We used Average Precision (AP) with 0.5 IoU threshold for the evaluation metrics.

---

[2] https://github.com/ultralytics/yolov5. Last accessed 1 December 2021

Table 2. Results of trained model

Training data	AP	
	Daytime	Nighttime
Labeled data	0.358	0.109
Labeled & pseudo-labeled data	0.545	0.679

The first row of Table 2 shows that detection at nighttime is difficult when only manually labeled daytime data is used for training.

From the second line of Table 2, we can see that the nighttime detection accuracy is greatly improved by adding the pseudo-labeled data generated by our method to the training data. Furthermore, we can see that the detection accuracy during the daytime has also improved due to the increase in the number of training data.

However, there is a difference of more than 10% mAP between the daytime and nighttime test data. One possible reason for this is because the number of labels in the nighttime pseudo-labeled data is more than twice as large as that in the daytime labeled data, resulting in learning biased toward the nighttime data. Therefore, we reduced the number of labels in the nighttime data to 1,893, almost the same as the daytime data, and trained the model again.

Table 3. Results of trained model on balanced data

Training data	AP	
	Daytime	Nighttime
Labeled & pseudo-labeled data	0.612	0.667

From Table 3, we can see that the difference in accuracy between daytime and nighttime becomes smaller than the second line of Table 2 because the imbalance in the number of data has been eliminated. The daytime performance is still lower than the nighttime because the daytime evaluation uses different roads for training and testing. On the other hand, nighttime is only included in data R2, so the same roads are used for training and testing. As a result, we think that the difference is since the models have already seen the road or not.

4.4 Qualitative Results

Figure 3 shows examples of the labels assigned in step 3. These labels are assigned by projecting labels of IR images. Still, labeling IR images is a difficult problem even by hand because it is difficult to grasp the exact boundary when the temperature of the area in contact with the road is close. In our method, however, we project the detection results of the daytime RGB image, which has a clear boundary, so we can accurately label IR images. Since the results of the accurate IR detection model are projected, nighttime RGB images are also accurately labeled.

Fig. 3. Examples of labels assigned in step 3.

Fig. 4. Example of failed labeling

Figure 4 shows an example of a pseudo-label that failed to be assigned in step 3. The rightmost box is assigned to the front of the vehicle, not the behind. This is the result of projecting what was detected in the IR image, so the cause of the failure is the IR model. False positives are more likely to occur in IR images, which are represented in grayscale and have less texture information. This problem can be expected to be solved by generating labels for the front and side of the vehicle as negative samples in step 2 in advance. The second box from the right, which should be placed slightly in front of the vehicle, is placed at a different location. This is due to the thermal calibration of the IR image. The thermal calibration occurs about once every three minutes, and the IR camera returns the same frame for about one second during that time. On the other hand, the RGB camera does not undergo thermal calibration, so the frames do not correspond to each other for about one second. As a result, these failures occur. Although failures due to thermal calibration are negligible, they can be handled by comparing the previous and next frames during processing to determine if they occur.

Fig. 5. Detection results of the model trained only with daytime labeled data. The top two images show the detection results at nighttime, and the bottom two images show the detection results at daytime.

Figure 5 shows the detection results of the model trained only with daytime labeled data. In the nighttime testing data, the model fails to detect the behind areas of the vehicles because the light conditions are very different from the

Fig. 6. Detection results of the model trained with balanced daytime labeled data and nighttime pseudo-labeled data

training data. In the daytime testing data, the behind areas are relatively well detected, but distant vehicles are not detected, and the front part is inaccurately detected. For the problem of false front detection, the addition of a negative sample, as described above, may be effective.

Figure 6 shows the detection results of the model trained with daytime labeled data and nighttime pseudo-labeled data. In the nighttime testing data, the model can detect most of the behind areas of the vehicles. In the daytime test image, while there is still a problem with false detection of the front, the model can detect more distant vehicles. This is probably due to the fact that the pseudo-labeled data contains a wider variety of sizes.

5   Conclusion

We proposed a pseudo-labeling method under various conditions by mutually utilizing multimodal images. In our experiments, we confirmed that pseudo-labeling data can be automatically generated under different conditions by mutually transforming the detection coordinates of each modality. In addition, self-learning with both manually labeled and pseudo-labeled data shows that the method can achieve high detection accuracy under multiple conditions.

In future work, we will apply our method to a variety of labeling problems for various conditions by combining RGB and IR images or other modalities. For example, IR images could be labeled using RGB images for weather and seasonal changes. In addition, if the object and the background are similar in color, the depth image could be used to label the RGB image.

Acknowledgements. We thank Takuya Matsumoto and Tatsuya Oshiro of the Sohatsu Systems Laboratory for their cooperation in taking the data. Part of this research was operated as the project of Center for Advanced Information technology Research, Aoyama Gakuin University.

References

1. Yarowsky, D.: Unsupervised word sense disambiguation rivaling supervised methods. In: Proceedings of the 33rd Annual Meeting of the Association for Computational Linguistics (ACL), pp. 189–196 (1995)
2. Blum, A., Mitchell, T.M.: Combining labeled and unlabeled data with co-training. In: Proceedings of the Eleventh Annual Conference on Computational Learning Theory (COLT), pp. 92–100 (1998)
3. Bennett, K. P., Demiriz, A., and Maclin, R.: Exploiting unlabeled data in ensemble methods. In: Proceedings of the eighth ACM SIGKDD International Conference on Knowledge Discovery and Data Mining (KDD), pp. 289–296 (2002)
4. Xiong, B., Fan, H., Grauman, K., Feichtenhofer, C.: Multiview pseudo-labeling for semi-supervised learning from video. In: Proceedings of the IEEE/CVF International Conference on Computer Vision (ICCV), pp. 7189–7199 (2021)
5. Girshick, R., Donahue, J., Darrell, T., Malik, J.: Rich feature hierarchies for accurate object detection and semantic segmentation, In: Proceedings of the IEEE Conference on Computer Vision and Pattern Recognition (CVPR), pp. 580–587 (2014)
6. Girshick, R.B.: Fast R-CNN, In: Proceedings of the IEEE International Conference on Computer Vision (ICCV), pp. 1440–1448 (2015)
7. Ren, S., He, K., Girshick, R.B., Sun, J.: Faster R-CNN: towards real-time object detection with region proposal networks. In: Proceedings of the Advances in Neural Information Processing Systems (NeurIPS), pp. 91–99 (2015)
8. Redmon, J., Divvala, S., Girshick, R., Farhadi, A.: You only look once: unified, real-time object detection, In: Proceedings of the IEEE Conference on Computer Vision and Pattern Recognition (CVPR), pp. 779–788 (2016)
9. Liu, W., et al.: SSD: single shot multibox detector. In: Leibe, B., Matas, J., Sebe, N., Welling, M. (eds.) ECCV 2016, Part I. LNCS, vol. 9905, pp. 21–37. Springer, Cham (2016). https://doi.org/10.1007/978-3-319-46448-0_2

10. Carion, N., Massa, F., Synnaeve, G., Usunier, N., Kirillov, A., Zagoruyko, S.: End-to-end object detection with transformers. In: Vedaldi, A., Bischof, H., Brox, T., Frahm, J.-M. (eds.) ECCV 2020. LNCS, vol. 12346, pp. 213–229. Springer, Cham (2020). https://doi.org/10.1007/978-3-030-58452-8_13
11. Hwang, S., Park, J., Kim, N., Choi, Y., Kweon, I.S.: Multispectral pedestrian detection: benchmark dataset and baseline. In: Proceedings of the IEEE Conference on Computer Vision and Pattern Recognition (CVPR), pp. 1037–1045 (2015)

Object Detection/Segmentation

Convolutional Neural Network Design for Eye Detection Under Low-Illumination

Duy-Linh Nguyen⑩, Muhamad Dwisnanto Putro⑩, Xuan-Thuy Vo⑩, and Kang-Hyun Jo$^{(\boxtimes)}$⑩

Department of Electrical, Electronic and Computer Engineering, University of Ulsan, Ulsan 44610, South Korea
{ndlinh301,dputro}@mail.ulsan.ac.kr, xthuy@islab.ulsan.ac.kr, acejo@ulsan.ac.kr

Abstract. The eye is an important organ in the human body for sensing and communicating with the outside world. The development of human eye detectors is essential for applications in the computer vision field, especially under low illumination. This paper proposes a convolutional neural network to detect the position of the eye in the acquired image. This network architecture exploits the advantages of convolutional neural networks combined with the concatenated rectified linear unit (C.ReLU), inception module, and Bottleneck Attention Module (BAM) to extract feature maps. Then it uses two detectors to localize the eye area using bounding boxes. The experiment was trained, evaluated on the BioID Face and Yale Face Dataset B (YALEB) dataset. As a result, the network achieves 99.71% and 99.37% of Average Precision (AP) on YALEB and BioID Face datasets, respectively.

Keywords: Attention module · Convolutional neural network (CNN) · Concatenated rectified linear unit (C.ReLU) · Eye detection · Inception module

1 Introduction

The computer vision field has been focusing on exploiting the structural features of the human body to develop application and support tools. In which, eye detection is a topic of extensive research interest. The location of the human eye and related components provides useful information for many fields such as psychological analysis, biomedical device development, medical diagnostics [12], assistance devices [14], and tracking technology [5]. However, the eye is a quite small organ with a complex structure, so detecting eye position faces many challenges. In particular, lighting conditions, distance, and camera placement can distort the acquired image area and make it difficult to detect. In addition, real-time applications require network architectures that work smoothly with mobile and embedded devices. Based on the above observations and inspired by the drowsiness warning system, this study proposes an eye detector based

K. Sumi et al. (Eds.): IW-FCV 2022, CCIS 1578, pp. 143–154, 2022.
https://doi.org/10.1007/978-3-031-06381-7_10

on a convolutional neural network under low-illumination. Experiments were performed on BioID Face, YALEB proposed image datasets and tested on a real-time system. The main contributions of this paper are shown as follows:

1 - Propose a convolutional neural network design for eye detection based on a combination of convolution layer, max pooling layer, C.ReLU module, inception module, and Bottleneck Attention Module.
2 - Built datasets for eye detection under low-illumination conditions from BioID Face and YALEB datasets.

The rest of the paper is organized as follows: Sect. 2 presents methods related to eye position detection. Section 3 describes the proposed method in detail. Section 4 discusses and analyzes the test results. Section 5 concludes the issue and direction development for future research.

2   Related Work

This section introduces the methods used in eye detection and eye-related components. These methods can be considered in two aspects: the traditional-based and machine learning-based methods. The traditional-based method mainly exploits the geometrical features of the eye to detect the eye area and its related components. The methods focus on extracting features of eyes and neighborhoods using classical geometric algorithms. A set of stochastic regressions was used by the authors in [17], the image gradients, and squared dot products in [4] to locate the pupil. The isophote curve is used in [24] to detect the position of the eye and the pupil. Later, several methods used pattern matching algorithms to replace classical algorithms. Specifically, [23] used the elliptical equation, [13] used the inner product detector to locate the eye. These traditional methods can achieve quite accurate results and are easy to deploy. However, their application may be limited by several conditions such as illumination, image resolution, and hardware devices. The machine learning-based methods can be divided into two groups, traditional machine learning-based, and CNN-based methods. The traditional machine learning-based mainly uses classical image processing algorithms to extract eye and face features. With the advent and development of the OpenCV open-source library, the application of these algorithms has become even more convenient and easy. Some of these algorithms include self-similarity information and shape analysis [3], Haar Wavelet and Support Vector Machine (SVM) [20], Histogram of Oriented Gradients (HOG) features combine with Support Vector Machine [22]. The explosion of convolutional neural networks in the computer vision field has spurred the development of applications for eye detection, eye segmentation, and eye classification. The CNN-based methods focus on studying the central position of the eye or pupil. In [10], the authors used a simple convolutional neural network to detect the central part of the eye. A set of convolutional neural networks is combined to locate the pupil [2]. In addition, several methods are also applied to detect the eye areas using twelve feature points [16] and then use transform operations [19] to localize the eyes. The CNN-based methods have proved superior ability in feature extraction and flexibility compared to other methods. However, in order to increase performance precision, networks need to be designed with more depth and incorporate many other additional algorithms. This increases the computational memory which hinders the application to real-time systems. Especially, when the system is deployed in low light conditions such as operating at night.

3   Methodology

As depicted in Fig. 1, the eye detection network consists of two main modules: feature extraction and detection.

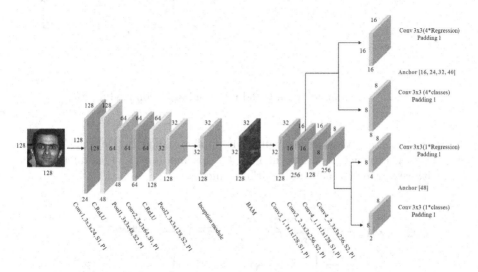

Fig. 1. The proposed eye detection network.

3.1   Feature Extraction Module

This module is designed based on the advantages of convolution layer, max pooling layer, C.ReLU module [6], inception module [18], and Bottleneck Attention Module [15] to extract feature maps. In the first stage, the network extracts low-level feature maps using two convolutions with kernel size of 3×3 followed by each convolution layer a C.ReLU module and a max pooling layer. As shown in Fig. 1, Conv1, Pool1, Conv2 and Pool2 use strides 1, 2, 1 and 2 so it reduces the input image space size from 128×128 to 32×32. In this phase, the C.ReLU module plays the role of ensuring useful information for the feature maps. The architecture of the C.ReLU module is shown in Fig. 2(a).

In the next stage, the inception module is used as a multi-scale block according to the width to enrich the receptive field of the network. This block is designed with four convolution branches, each of which uses convolutions with kernel size 1×1 or 3×3 and a number of kernels 24 or 32. The detailed description of the inception module is in Fig.2(b). The feature map after going through this module continues to be enriched and maintains the size $32 \times 32 \times 128$.

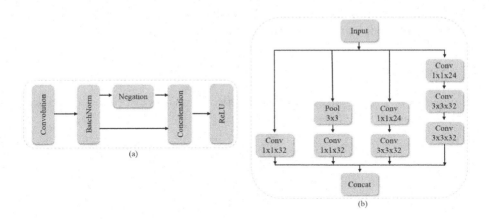

Fig. 2. The architecture of C.ReLu (a) and inception module (b).

After that, an attention mechanism is applied called Bottleneck Attention Module (BAM) which is shown in Fig. 3. This module provides an attention map with separate channels and spatial branches.

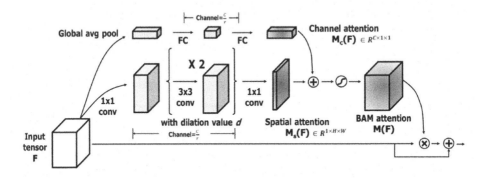

Fig. 3. The architecture of Bottleneck Attention Module [15].

The processing of BAM can be expressed as follows:

$$M(F) = \sigma(M_c(F) + M_c(F)), \tag{1}$$

where $M_c(F)$ is the channel attention, $M_s(F)$ is the spatial attention, σ is a sigmoid function.

The channel attention branch uses global average pooling on input feature map F and generates a channel vector F_c of size $C \times 1 \times 1$. Then, estimate attention across channels using a multi-layer perceptron (MLP) with one hidden layer. The hidden activation size is set to $\frac{c}{r} \times 1 \times 1$ with r is the reduction ratio. The end is a batch normalization (BN) layer.

$$M_c(F) = BN(MLP(AvgPool(F))), \tag{2}$$

The spatial attention branch uses 1×1 convolution (f_3) to compress the feature map F ($C \times H \times W$) across the channel dimension. Thus, the feature map F is reduced to $\frac{C}{r}$ (r is reduction ratio, it's the same as the channel attention branch). As a next step, this branch applies two 3×3 dilated convolutions (f_2, f_1) to take advantage of contextual information. Then the feature map was further reduced to $1 \times H \times W$ using 1×1 convolution (f_0) and a batch normalization layer was also used at the end of the branch.

$$M_s(F) = BN(f_3^{1\times1}(f_2^{3\times3}(f_1^{3\times3}(f_0^{1\times1}(F))))) \tag{3}$$

Finally, the two branches are extended to CxHxW and combined using element-wise summation operation. Furthermore, a sigmoid function is applied to produce the attention map. BAM only increases the learning capacity of the network and maintains the dimension of the feature map.

In the final stage of the extraction module, four conventional convolutions with 1×1 and 3×3 kernel sizes are used to further reduce the dimension and increase the number of channels of the feature map. Specifically, the first and third convolutions use 1×1 kernel size with 128 channels, the second and fourth convolutions use 3×3 kernel size with 256 channels. As a result, the final feature map is generated with size $8 \times 8 \times 256$ this shows that the feature map is reduced by four times, and the number of channels is increased by two times from 128 to 256.

3.2   Detection Module

This module consists of two detectors to detect eyes at different scales. Each detector uses two 3×3 sibling convolutions for classification and bounding box regression. These two detectors are applied on the last two feature maps in the feature extraction module (at 16×16 and 8×8 feature maps). A set of square anchors of different sizes are used to localize the eyes in the input image. The proposed network uses five square anchors of which four (16, 24, 32, 40) are for small and medium eyes on 16×16 and one (48) for large eyes on 8×8 feature maps. The output of this module is a four-dimensional vector (x, y, w, h) as the position offset and a two-dimensional vector (eye or non eye) as the label classification. Where (x, y) is the coordinate of the center point, w is the width and h is the height of the bounding box.

3.3 Loss Function

The loss function in this paper comprises the loss from two tasks, classification and bounding box regression. In this case, the softmax loss function is used for classification and smooth $L1$ loss is used for regression. The loss function is defined as follows:

$$L(p_i, t_i) = \frac{1}{N_{cls}} \sum_i L_{cls}(p_i, p_i^*) + \lambda \frac{1}{N_{reg}} \sum_i p_i^* L_{reg}(t_i, t_i^*), \tag{4}$$

where $L_{cls}(p_i, p_i^*)$ is the classification loss using the softmax loss defined as in Eq. (5), $L_{reg}(t_i, t_i^*)$ is regression loss, $L_{reg}(t_i, t_i^*) = H(t_i - t_i^*)$ and H is the smooth $L1$ loss defined as in Eq. (6), i is the index of an anchor bounding box, p_i is the predicted score of anchor i being an object, p_i^* is ground truth label and $p_i^* = 1$ (the anchor is positive) or $p_i^* = 0$ (the anchor is negative). t_i is the coordinates predicted bounding box and t_i^* is the coordinates of ground truth bounding box. N_{cls} is normalized by the mini-batch size, N_{reg} is normalized by the number of anchor locations, λ is balancing parameter and it is assigned by 10.

The softmax loss function:

$$L_{cls}(p_i, p_i^*) = - \sum_{i \in Pos} x_i^p log(p_i) - \sum_{i \in Neg} log(p_i^0), \tag{5}$$

where $x_i^p = \{0, 1\}$ is indicator for matching the $i - th$ anchor bounding box to ground truth bounding box of category p, p_i^0 is the probability for non eye classification.

The smooth $L1$ loss:

$$H(x) = \begin{cases} 0.5x^2 & if \; |x| < 1 \\ |x| - 0.5 & otherwise \end{cases} \tag{6}$$

4 Experiments

4.1 Dataset Preparation

Besides designing a CNN network architecture for eye detection, this work also proposes datasets for training and evaluating eye detection under low-illumination based on BioID Face [1] and Yale Face Dataset B [7] (YALEB) datasets. Specifically, 1,521 gray-scale images with 384×286 pixels resolution were selected from the BioID Face dataset. The images show the front view of 23 different people. From the eye's center coordinates, a square bounding box of size 36×36 is generated using Python code. The total number of labeled bounding boxes is 3,042. For the YALEB dataset, a set of 2,679 images with different lighting conditions and head poses were randomly selected and annotated manually using the LabelImg tool. The total number of labels assigned is 5,358 labels. The datasets are divided into 80% for training and 20% for evaluation. Table 1 shows detailed proposed datasets for eye location detection under low-illumination.

Table 1. The proposed datasets for eye location detection under low-illumination.

Dataset	Image size	Format	Images	Annotations
BioID Face	384×286	PGM	1,521	3,042
YALEB	256×256	JPG	2,679	5,358

4.2   Experimental Setup

The proposed network is implemented by the Pytorch framework. The network was trained with 300 epochs and evaluated on a GeForce GTX 1080Ti GPU, 32 GB of RAM. It applies some training configuration like a batch size = 16, weight decay = 5.10^{-4}, momentum = 0.9. The learning rate is initially set to 10^{-3}. The stochastic Gradient Descent technique is used to optimize the weight during the back-propagation stage. The Non Maximum Suppression algorithm was applied with a threshold of 0.5.

4.3   Experimental Result

The eye detection network is trained and evaluated on two datasets, BioID Face and YALEB. In order to make a fair comparison with other CNN network archi-tectures, this work also implemented similar experiments with FaceBoxes [25], SSD [9] and several variants of the proposed eye detection network. As a result, this network achieved Average Precision (AP) up to 99.71% and 99.37% on YALEB and BioID Face datasets, respectively. This result shows that the pro-posed network outperforms other mobile networks under the same experimental conditions with only 780,383 network parameters. This study also replaces dif-ferent attention modules to evaluate the eye detection ability of the network. The proposed method with Bottleneck Attention Module (BAM) also achieved the highest performance compared with network variants using Squeeze-and-Excitation (SE) [8], Convolutional Block Attention Module (CBAM) [21], and Triple Attention Module (TAM) [11] with a network parameter that is insignif-icantly larger. Table 2 shows the comparison result of eye detection network on two datasets with different CNN architectures. The several qualitative results of the eye detection network on BioID Face and YALEB datasets are shown in Fig. 4. However, under low light or uneven illumination conditions, the network may incorrectly detect several surrounding objects (pictures, shirt button) or the part on the face (mouth, lips) because they are similar in shape and color to the eyes, as shown in Fig. 5.

BioID Face dataset

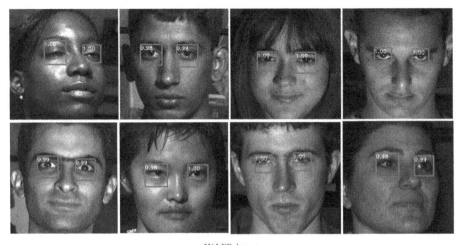

YALEB dataset

Fig. 4. The qualitative results of the eye detection network on the BioID Face and YALEB datasets. The first two rows are the BioID Face dataset and the second two rows are the YALEB dataset.

4.4 Ablation Study

This study evaluates the effectiveness of the modules in the eye detection network by several ablation studies on the YALEB dataset shown in Table 3. This experiment removes the Inception Module and the Bottleneck Attention Module, respectively, and then compares the results with the proposed network. The results show that, when removing the Inception Module and using only the Bottleneck Attention Module, the network parameters decreased by 37,792 parameters and the AP decreased by 1.14%. When using only the Inception Module

BioID Face dataset

YALEB dataset

Fig. 5. The mistake results of the eye detection network on the BioID Face and YALEB datasets. The first two rows are the BioID Face dataset and the second two rows are the YALEB dataset.

and removing Bottleneck Attention Module, the network parameters and AP only decreased by 4,457 parameters and 0.28%, respectively. Thus, the Bottleneck Attention Module plays an important role in improving the efficiency of eye position detection.

Table 2. Comparison result of eye detection network on two datasets. SE presents the Squeeze-and-Excitation, CBAM presents the Convolutional Block Attention Module, and TAM presents the Triple Attention Module. The red color is the best competitor.

Model	Number of parameters	Average precision (%)	
		BioID Face	YALEB
Mobile architectures			
FaceBoxes	844,610	98.23	99.70
SSD300	23,745,908	90.90	90.90
SSD512	23,745,908	90.80	90.00
Our architectures			
Proposed	**780,383**	**99.37**	**99.71**
Our (SE)	778,110	96.31	99.56
Our (CBAM)	780,394	96.55	99.07
Our (TAM)	776,226	98.18	95.63

Table 3. Ablation studies on the YALEB dataset.

Module	Network		
Inception Module		✓	✓
Bottleneck Attention Module	✓		✓
Parameter	742,591	775,926	780,383
Average Precision (%)	98.57	99.43	99.71

5 Conclusion

This paper presents a convolutional neural network design for eye detection. The proposed network consists of two main modules: feature extraction and detection. Feature extraction module exploited the advantage of convolution, C.ReLu, max pooling layers, inception, and Bottleneck Attention Modules to extract multi-scale feature maps. Based on the extracted feature maps, the detection module learns and locates the eyes using square anchor boxes. The network is trained and evaluated on two datasets YALEB and BioID Face with low or uneven illumination image sets. It scored 99.71% and 99.37% of AP on YALEB and BioID Face, respectively. In the future, this network will be developed and integrated into the drowsiness alert system for night operating conditions.

Acknowledgement. This results was supported by "Regional Innovation Strategy (RIS)" through the National Research Foundation of Korea (NRF) funded by the Ministry of Education (MOE) (2021RIS-003).

References

1. The BioID Face Database. https://www.bioid.com/facedb. Accessed 23 Oct 2010
2. Araujo, G., Ribeiro, F., da Silva, E., Goldenstein, S.: Fast eye localization without a face model using inner product detectors. In: 2014 IEEE International Conference on Image Processing, ICIP 2014, pp. 1366–1370, January 2015. https://doi.org/10.1109/ICIP.2014.7025273
3. Chen, S., Liu, C.: Eye detection using discriminatory Haar features and a new efficient SVM. Image Vision Comput. **33**(C), 68–77 (2015). https://doi.org/10.1016/j.imavis.2014.10.007, https://doi.org/10.1016/j.imavis.2014.10.007
4. Deng, J., et al.: The Menpo benchmark for multi-pose 2D and 3D facial landmark localisation and tracking. Int. J. Comput. Vis. **127**(6–7), 599–624 (2019)
5. Fu, H., Wei, Y., Camastra, F., Arico, P., Sheng, H.: Advances in eye tracking technology: theory, algorithms, and applications. Comput. Intell. Neurosci. **2016** (2016)
6. Fuhl, W., Santini, T., Kasneci, G., Kasneci, E.: Pupilnet: convolutional neural networks for robust pupil detection. CoRR abs/1601.04902 (2016). http://arxiv.org/abs/1601.04902
7. Georghiades, A., Belhumeur, P., Kriegman, D.: From few to many: Illumination cone models for face recognition under variable lighting and pose. IEEE Trans. Pattern Anal. Mach. Intell. **23**(6), 643–660 (2001)
8. Hu, J., Shen, L., Sun, G.: Squeeze-and-excitation networks. CoRR abs/1709.01507 (2017). http://arxiv.org/abs/1709.01507
9. Liu, W., et al.: SSD: single shot multibox detector. CoRR abs/1512.02325 (2015). http://arxiv.org/abs/1512.02325
10. Markuš, N., Frljak, M., Pandžić, I., Ahlberg, J., Forchheimer, R.: Eye pupil localization with an ensemble randomized trees. Pattern Recogn. **47**, 578–587 (2014). https://doi.org/10.1016/j.patcog.2013.08.008
11. Misra, D., Nalamada, T., Arasanipalai, A.U., Hou, Q.: Rotate to attend: convolutional triplet attention module. CoRR abs/2010.03045 (2020). https://arxiv.org/abs/2010.03045
12. Mosa, A.H., Ali, M., Kyamakya, K.: A computerized method to diagnose strabismus based on a novel method for pupil segmentation. In: Proceedings of the International Symposium on Theoretical Electrical Engineering (ISTET 2013) (2013)
13. Mosa, A.H., Ali, M., Kyamakya, K.: A computerized method to diagnose strabismus based on a novel method for pupil segmentation. In: Proceedings of the International Symposium on Theoretical Electrical Engineering (ISTET 2013) (2013)
14. Nguyen, D.-L., Putro, M.D., Jo, K.-H.: Eye state recognizer using light-weight architecture for drowsiness warning. In: Nguyen, N.T., Chittayasothorn, S., Niyato, D., Trawiński, B. (eds.) ACIIDS 2021. LNCS (LNAI), vol. 12672, pp. 518–530. Springer, Cham (2021). https://doi.org/10.1007/978-3-030-73280-6_41
15. Park, J., Woo, S., Lee, J.Y., Kweon, I.S.: Bam: Bottleneck attention module (2018)
16. Shang, W., Sohn, K., Almeida, D., Lee, H.: Understanding and improving convolutional neural networks via concatenated rectified linear units. CoRR abs/1603.05201 (2016), http://arxiv.org/abs/1603.05201
17. Sharma, R., Savakis, A.: Lean histogram of oriented gradients features for effective eye detection. J. Electr. Imaging **24**, 063007 (2015). https://doi.org/10.1117/1.JEI.24.6.063007
18. Szegedy, C., et al.: Going deeper with convolutions. CoRR abs/1409.4842 (2014). http://arxiv.org/abs/1409.4842

19. Timm, F., Barth, E.: Accurate eye centre localisation by means of gradients. In: VISAPP (2011)
20. Valenti, R., Gevers, T.: Accurate eye center location through invariant isocentric patterns. IEEE Trans. Pattern Anal. Mach. Intell. **34**, 1785–1798 (2012). https://doi.org/10.1109/TPAMI.2011.251
21. Woo, S., Park, J., Lee, J., Kweon, I.S.: CBAM: convolutional block attention module. CoRR abs/1807.06521 (2018). http://arxiv.org/abs/1807.06521
22. Wu, Y., Ji, Q.: Facial landmark detection: a literature survey. CoRR abs/1805.05563 (2018). http://arxiv.org/abs/1805.05563
23. Xiao, S., Feng, J., Xing, J., Lai, H., Yan, S., Kassim, A.: Robust facial landmark detection via recurrent attentive-refinement networks. In: Leibe, B., Matas, J., Sebe, N., Welling, M. (eds.) ECCV 2016. LNCS, vol. 9905, pp. 57–72. Springer, Cham (2016). https://doi.org/10.1007/978-3-319-46448-0_4
24. Zadeh, A., Chong Lim, Y., Baltrusaitis, T., Morency, L.P.: Convolutional experts constrained local model for 3d facial landmark detection. In: Proceedings of the IEEE International Conference on Computer Vision Workshops, pp. 2519–2528 (2017)
25. Zhang, S., Zhu, X., Lei, Z., Shi, H., Wang, X., Li, S.Z.: Faceboxes: a CPU real-time face detector with high accuracy. CoRR abs/1708.05234 (2017), http://arxiv.org/abs/1708.05234

Pedestrian Head Detection and Tracking via Global Vision Transformer

Xuan-Thuy Vo[1], Van-Dung Hoang[2], Duy-Linh Nguyen[1],
and Kang-Hyun Jo[1]([✉])

[1] Department of Electrical, Electronic and Computer Engineering,
University of Ulsan, Ulsan 44610, South Korea
`xthuy@islab.ulsan.ac.kr, ndlinh301@mail.ulsan.ac.kr, acejo@ulsan.ac.kr`
[2] Ho Chi Minh City University of Technology and Education,
Ho Chi Minh City, Vietnam
`dunghv@hcmute.edu.vn`

Abstract. In recent years, pedestrian detection and tracking have significant progress in both performance and latency. However, detecting and tracking pedestrian human-body in highly crowded environments is a complicated task in the computer vision field because pedestrians are partly or fully occluded by each other. That needs much human effort for annotation works and complex trackers to identify invisible pedestrians in spatial and temporal domains. To alleviate the aforementioned problems, previous methods tried to detect and track visible parts of pedestrians (e.g., heads, pedestrian visible-region), which achieved remarkable performances and can enlarge the scalability of tracking models and data sizes. Inspired by this purpose, this paper proposes simple but effective methods to detect and track pedestrian heads in crowded scenes, called PHDTT (Pedestrian Head Detection and Tracking with Transformer). Firstly, powerful encoder-decoder Transformer networks are integrated into the tracker, which learns relations between object queries and image global features to reason about detection results in each frame, and also matches object queries and track objects between adjacent frames to perform data association instead of further motion predictions, IoU-based methods, and Re-ID based methods. Both components are formed into single end-to-end networks that simplify the tracker to be more efficient and effective. Secondly, the proposed Transformer-based tracker is conducted and evaluated on the challenging benchmark dataset CroHD. Without bells and whistles, PHDTT achieves 60.6 MOTA, which outperforms the recent methods by a large margin. Testing videos are available at https://bit.ly/3eOPQ2d.

Keywords: Pedestrian head detection · Pedestrian head tracking · Vision transformer · Crowded scenes · Surveillance systems

1 Introduction

Pedestrian detection and tracking are fundamental tasks in visual image and video understanding, which have attracted much attention in recent years.

K. Sumi et al. (Eds.): IW-FCV 2022, CCIS 1578, pp. 155–167, 2022.
https://doi.org/10.1007/978-3-031-06381-7_11

These two tasks have widely applied to many real-world applications such as surveillance systems, action recognition, abnormal detection, robot navigation, human-machine interaction, and autonomous vehicles.

In crowded scenes, pedestrian detection and tracking are challenging missions in computer vision research due to the high density of pedestrians on the road. The tracking performances rely on the level of crowd occlusion. When increasing the high density of pedestrians, trackers produce mislocalized results because a pedestrian is largely occluded with other pedestrians, and the models are ambiguously learned to determine the boundaries of each pedestrian since the appearance features are very identical. As a result, ambiguous learning makes the networks generate more false positives and identity changes during tracking. This reason causes performance degradation. Moreover, annotating pedestrian full-body bounding boxes takes a high cost, and it is difficult to enlarge the scalability of the model and data size. Existing methods [21,23] provide efficient annotations only localizing visible regions of pedestrians and give us a promising opportunity to investigate pedestrian heads detection and tracking in crowded scenes.

Current trends in computer vision utilizing vision Transformer for visual understanding tasks such as object classification [7,14,28], object localization [5,42], multiple object tracking [16,22,33,34], object segmentation [8,29,35] bring promising advantages of self-attention and cross-attention mechanisms, and general modeling capacities. Transformer is originally designed for machine translation in natural language processing task, which achieves significant improvements in modeling long-range dependencies in input data. ViT [7] was the first method applying Transformer encoder architecture to vision tasks, which shows its simpleness and effectiveness. To fully leverage both Transformer encoder and decoder into the detector, DETR [5] uses self-attention blocks in Transformer encoder to model the global image features extracted from Convolutional Neural Networks (CNNs) backbone. And then, DETR considers a set of object queries as a set of predictions and learns the relation between image global features and the set of object prediction through cross-attention blocks in Transformer decoder and Hungarian matching to reason about object categories and locations. According to DETR, this work investigate the benefits of Transformer into pedestrian heads detection and tracking tasks, called PHDTT. Firstly, PHDTT performs detection in the adjacent frames based on correlation learning of object queries and image global features. Secondly, PHDTT associates detection results between previous frame and current frame based on track queries. Each object query indicates one object in the current and each track query represents one object in the previous frame. It means PHDTT considers both detection predictions and association between frames as queries into single end-to-end network to reason about tracking results via global Transformer. Thus, the proposed method is simple and consistent compared to ReID-based methods [12,30,37], and motion-based methods [18,32,39].

We conduct and evaluate the proposed PHDTT on benchmark CroHD [23] for pedestrian detection and tracking tasks in crowded scenes. Without bells and whistles, PHDTT achieves the 60.6 MOTA on the CroHD test set, which surpasses the state-of-the-art head trackers by a clear margin. It is noteworthy that PHDTT is the first method leveraging the Transformer encoder and decoder into pedestrian heads detection and tracking. We hope the researcher can use our PHDTT as the baseline for improvement and comparison.

2   Related Works

The pedestrian heads detection and tracking are strongly correlated to multiple object tracking (MOT) tasks. Hence, we briefly summarize the method-based taxonomy of the MOT task based on milestones. Both pedestrian heads tracking and MOT include two essential steps: detection and data association. Therefore, we also provide a review of these two steps.

Multiple Object Tracking. In tracking literature, MOT is grouped into two methods that are tracking by detection and detection by tracking. Firstly, tracking-by-detection methods employ advanced object detectors [5,9,13,19,20, 40] to improve tracking performance since data association procedure heavily relies on detection results. Most state-of-the-art trackers [27,30,37–39] use CenterNet [40] as the detector. Recent methods [18,26] utilize the single-stage object detector RetinaNet [13] for the detection step. Due to high efficiency, some existing methods [12,30] use YOLO [19] as the detector, and ByteTrack [36] employs the simple and effective YOLOX [9] for producing detection results. Secondly, detection-by-tracking methods [6,41] adopt the tracking model such as single object tracking and Kalman filter to improve detection performance.

Data Association. Data association is the crucial step in MOT, matching detection results based on similarity scores and ReID-based methods. SORT [3], DeepSORT [31] predicts future object location via Kalman filter and computes the IoU scores between predicted objects and detected objects. And then, these methods apply the Hungarian algorithm to assign each identity to each object based on IoU cost. In the most popular methods [12,17,30,37] add a new ReID branch to the detection network for predicting appearance features and also use the Hungarian algorithm to perform a one-to-one assignment.

Pedestrian Heads Tracking. In recent years, many researchers [10,24] have paid much attention to pedestrian full-body detection by introducing multi-scale features, loss-based anchor assignments. However, head detection is paid less attention by researchers and needs more investigations. Head detection has been widely used in crowd counting and intelligent surveillance systems. HeadHunter [23] was the first method to solve pedestrian heads detection and tracking in crowded environments, applying Faster R-CNN [20] for performing detection. Since the head regions are very small, HeadHunter uses high input resolution to detect small heads. To do that, extracted features from the backbone are upsampled to higher resolutions via the Context Sensitive module and transposed convolutions. For data association, HeadHunter utilizes IoU and center distance similarity and Hungarian matching to perform assignments between the same targets.

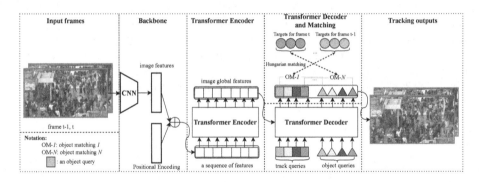

Fig. 1. The general pipeline of the proposed PHDTT. This network includes six essential procedures: input frames, backbone, transformer encoder, transformer decoder, object matching, and tracking outputs.

Vision Transformer. ViT [7] was the first method that brings the original Transformer encoder from NLP (natural language processing) to visual understanding research, which shows the promising improvements in both modeling capacity and performance on par with advanced CNNs. DETR [5] applies Transformer encoder and decoder and Hungarian matching to reason about detection prediction through the relation between object queries and image global features, which achieves high efficiency and simple architecture.

3   Methodology

The general network of the proposed PHDTT is described in Fig. 1. The input of this system takes adjacent frames e.g., frame $t-1$: $I^{t-1} \in \mathbb{R}^{3 \times H \times W}$ and frame t: $I^t \in \mathbb{R}^{3 \times H \times W}$. The input features are extracted by CNNs network, denoted by $F \in \mathbb{R}^{2048 \times \frac{H}{32} \times \frac{W}{32}}$. We take this feature F from stage 5 of the backbone network, and this feature has a low resolution suitable for generating a sequence of features. Because the model complexity of Transformer encoder and decoder networks [5] quadratically grows with the increase of the input feature sizes.

Transformer Encoder. Firstly, the extracted feature F is mapped from channel 2048 to 256 by using 1×1 convolution and flatten to dimension $S \in \mathbb{R}^{N \times d_{model}}$, where $N = \frac{H}{32} * \frac{W}{32}$ is a sequence dimension and $d_{model} = 256$ is embedding dimension. Secondly, because of the flattened features, the order of sequences is lost. Accordingly, positional encoding is supplemented with input features to learn the relationship between sequences, followed by [25]. The core element of the Transformer encoder is the self-attention module that models long-range dependencies in the input sequences. The detailed architecture of the self-attention operation and Transformer encoder are illustrated in Fig. 2(a) and Fig. 2(b), respectively.

Similar to [5,7,25], the proposed PHDTT creates the query matrix Q, key matrix K, and value matrix V from the feature F. And then, we linearly project

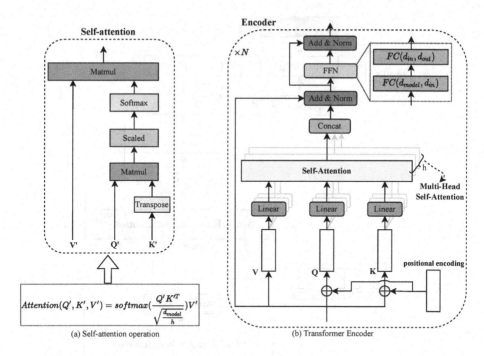

Fig. 2. The detailed architecture of the self-attention operation (a) and Transformer encoder (b). V, Q, K are value matrix, query matrix, and key matrix. Matmul indicates matrix multiplication. h denotes the number of self-attention blocks inside the multi-head self-attention module. concat is concatenation oepration. FFN is feed-forward network, contains two stacked fully-connected layers to transform the low dimension d_{model} to high dimension d_{in} and map back to original dimension d_{model}. N is the number of multi-head self-attention modules in one Transformer encoder network.

each matrix embedding to lower dimension $\frac{d_{model}}{h}$ and the model can perform all self-attention blocks in a parallel way. Multi-Head self-attention module includes h self-attention blocks. In each self-attention block, we compute attention weights defined as follows,

$$Attention(Q^{'}, K^{'}, V^{'}) = softmax(\frac{Q^{'}K^{'}}{\sqrt{\frac{d_{model}}{h}}})V^{'}, \qquad (1)$$

where the notation $Q^{'}, K^{'}, V^{'}$ are the projected query, key, and value matrices, respectively. The core idea of self-attention block is to learn correlation between query-key elements through dot-product operation. Generally speaking, one query position globally gathers all information of key positions and output which positions are important to be emphasized in value features. After using FFN, we can model image global features.

Transformer Decoder. The detailed architecture of the Transformer decoder is illustrated in Fig. 3. The main purpose of the Transformer decoder is to

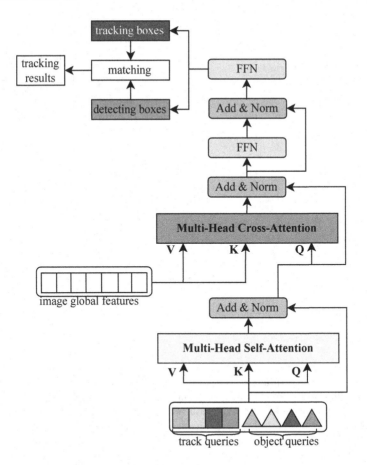

Fig. 3. The detailed architecture of the transformer decoder. Multi-head self-attention block is computed similar to the computation in the Transformer encoder. The main component of the Transformer decoder is the multi-head cross-attention block that learns the relation between image global features and combined queries.

learn the relation between object queries *vs.* image global features to reason about detecting boxes for frame t, track queries *vs.* image global features to reason about tracking boxes, and object queries *vs.* track queries to facilitate data association step and also improve detection task. Firstly, we generate a set of learned object queries with dimension N responsible for predicting N objects at frame t. Detected objects at the previous frame $t - 1$ (i.e., track queries) are combined with object queries and passed to Transformer decoder architecture to model the object similarities of two adjacent frames through multi-head self-attention. These similar features are set as query matrix in the multi-head cross-attention module, and the image global features are set as key and value matrices. Secondly, FFN is used to generate the final prediction with $2N$ bounding boxes: N detecting boxes and N tracking boxes. To match objects with the same targets, we compute IoU scores between each paired prediction (i.e., tracking box *vs.* detecting box). If the IoU score is greater than a certain threshold, this paired box is assigned as the positive sample otherwise. Finally, we apply the Hungarian matching algorithm for assigning positive samples to box targets that follow the procedure in DETR [5].

Matching Algorithm. N detecting boxes, and N tracking boxes are assigned to ground truth boxes via Hungarian matching. The cost for the assignment is linear combination of classification and localization losses, defined as,

$$\mathcal{L}_{match} = \lambda_{cls}\mathcal{L}_{cls} + \lambda_{loc}\mathcal{L}_{loc}, \tag{2}$$

where $\mathcal{L}_{cls} = -\log\hat{p}(c_i)$ is a negative log-likelihood for computing classification cost in which $\hat{p}(c_i)$ denotes the probability of class c_i. $\mathcal{L}_{loc} = \lambda_{L1}\left\|b_{i,t} - \hat{b}_{i,t}\right\| + \lambda_{giou}\mathcal{L}_{giou}(b_{i,t}, \hat{b}_{i,t})$ is the localization cost that is linear combination of $\mathcal{L}1$ and $\mathcal{L}_{giou}$ costs. $\lambda_{cls}, \lambda_{L1}, \lambda_{giou}$ are the balancing terms.

4   Experiments

4.1   Dataset and Evaluation Metrics

We conduct and evaluate the proposed PHDTT on the challenging benchmark dataset CroHD [23]. This dataset recorded in crowded scenarios consists of four training videos corresponding to 5740 training frames and five testing videos corresponding to 5723 testing frames. The average of pedestrian head density over all videos is approximately 178 pedestrians per frame. The performances on the test set are submitted to the evaluation system[1], and our evaluated results under the name PHDTT are available at this link[2].

For performance evaluation, the tracking performance is measured by standard metrics: Multiple Object Tracking Accuracy (MOTA) proposed by [2], the ratio of correctly identified detections IDF1 [2], Higher Order Tracking Accuracy (HOTA) defined by [15], and IDEucl [23]. Extra metrics used to evaluate all aspects of the proposed PHDTT are MT - Mostly tracked targets, ML - Mostly lost targets, FP - false positives, FN - false negatives (FN), and ID Sw. - identity switches (ID Sw.).

4.2   Implementation Details

The deep learning Pytorch framework is used to conduct the experiments. The used backbone network for feature extraction is ResNet-50 [11] pre-trained on ImageNet dataset for weight initialization in tracking model. The model is trained on the additional dataset Crowdhuman [21] for 150 epochs and the trained model is fine-tuned on the training set of CroHD for 20 epochs. We use

---

[1] https://motchallenge.net/.
[2] https://motchallenge.net/results/Head_Tracking_21/.

Table 1. Comparison with state-of-the-art tracking methods on CroHD test set

Method	MOTA	IDF1	IDEucl	HOTA	MT	ML	FP	FN	ID Sw.
SORT [3]	46.4	48.4	58.0	-	2.1	9.2	-	-	**649**
V_IOU [4]	53.4	35.4	34.3	-	3.4	7.8	-	-	1,890
Tracktor [1]	58.9	38.5	31.8	-	5.3	**5.0**	-	-	3,474
HeadHunter [23]	57.8	**53.9**	**54.2**	**36.8**	31.9	19.9	**51,840**	**299,459**	4,394
Our PHDTT	**60.6**	47.9	52.6	36.1	**47.1**	8.0	132,714	184,215	15,004

Table 2. The detailed performance on each video of the CroHD test set

Video	MOTA	IDF1	IDEucl	HOTA	MT	ML	FP	FN	ID Sw.
HT21-11	79.0	63.7	65.5	47.8	84	4	1,485	4,620	232
HT21-12	72.0	57.6	63.1	40.7	514	11	36,824	48,584	2,352
HT21-13	37.3	24.9	27.0	20.2	192	63	66,256	60,498	19,005
HT21-14	68.4	59.7	55.1	43.4	223	59	11,514	46,604	2,551
HT21-15	55.1	44.3	52.4	33.1	91	51	16,635	23,909	4,863

the GPU Tesla V100 device with Cuda 10.2, and CuDNN 7.6.5 to train the tracking model with batch size of 16 and learning rate schedule followed by [5]. The number of object queries $N = 500$ is set for all experiments. The optimizer is AdamW to minimize the training objectives,

$$\mathcal{L}_{training} = \lambda_{cls}\mathcal{L}_{focal} + \lambda_{giou}\mathcal{L}_{giou}, \tag{3}$$

where $\mathcal{L}_{focal}$ is the Focal loss [13] for classification loss and $\mathcal{L}_{giou}$ is the GIoU localization loss.

5 Results

As shown in Table 1, our proposed PHDTT surpasses all state-of-the-art trackers by a clear margin. More specifically, the proposed method achieves 60.6 MOTA that outperforms SORT [3] by 14.2 MOTA, V_IOU [4] by 7.2 MOTA, Tracktor [1] by 1.7 MOTA, and HeadHunter [23] by 2.8 MOTA. It verifies the effectiveness and generalization capacity of the tracker PHDTT. The proposed method joins both detection and association tasks into the single end-to-end model that each task can help to learn another task efficiently. While all methods treat two tasks independently, the total inference time is a sum of two tasks. Based on predicted bounding boxes, SORT [3] exploits the Kalman filter to generate future motion and the Hungarian matching algorithm to associate future predicted boxes and detected boxes. V_IOU [4] reduces the tracking fragmentation and ID switches by combining a single object tracker into Hungarian matching, improving the data association task. Instead of using available detection results, HeadHunter [23] utilizes the two-stage network Faster R-CNN as the object detector. To meet

Frame 1   Frame 20

Fig. 4. The qualitative visualization of our PHDTT on the CroHD testing set with various crowded scenes. Each number indicates each identity of each person.

the requirement of small head sizes, Headhunter introduces a Context-Sensitive Prediction Module and uses transposed convolutions to balance the multi-level features of the backbone and to upsample these multi-level features to higher spatial resolutions.

Table 2 shows the detailed performances on five sequences of the CroHD test set. Specifically, PHDTT achieves 79.0 MOTA, 72.0 MOTA, 37.3 MOTA, 68.4 MOTA, and 55.1 MOTA on video HT21-11, HT21-12, HT21-13, HT21-14, and HT21-15, respectively. The proposed method poorly performs on the sequence HT21-15 and HT21-13 because both videos contain the highest pedestrian density, motion blur, and crowd occlusion problem. We will consider this challenging problem for future researches.

The qualitative visualization of our proposed PHDTT are illustrated in Fig. 4. The visualization performances are evaluated under crowded conditions with different scenes such as indoor, outdoor night, and day. As a result, the PHDTT model can detect small pedestrian heads and track assigned pedestrian heads accordingly. It is noteworthy that our PHDTT only uses the single-level feature and does not increase the spatial resolution for detecting small objects. Thus, our approach is efficient while HeadHunter [23] uses transposed convolution to upsample the multi-level features to higher spatial dimensions.

6   Conclusion

This paper leverages the powerful Transformer encoder and decoder architectures into pedestrian head detection and tracking tasks. The track queries and object queries are responsible for detection predictions in adjacent frames. The Transformer network not only extracts the long-range dependencies in image features but also learns the object relations between frames to reason about tracking boxes and detecting boxes. The query-key mechanism facilitates the data association procedure since the object similarity across frames is learned through the Transformer decoder. Integrating the matching step into the detection network can improve the overall performance and enhance the model's capacity learning at the current frame. Without bells and whistles, the proposed PHDTT surpasses the existing trackers by a clear margin, becomes the state-of-the-art tracker. To the best of our knowledge, no prior methods are presented, that apply the benefits of the Transformer encoder and decoder to solve pedestrian head detection and tracking researches. We believe that our proposed PHDTT can serve as the simple baseline for pedestrian head detection and tracking tasks.

Acknowledgement. This results was supported by "Region Innovation Strategy (RIS)" through the National Research Foundation of Korea (NRF) funded by the Ministry of Education (MOE) (2021RIS-003).

References

1. Bergmann, P., Meinhardt, T., Leal-Taixe, L.: Tracking without bells and whistles. In: Proceedings of the IEEE/CVF International Conference on Computer Vision, pp. 941–951 (2019)
2. Bernardin, K., Stiefelhagen, R.: Evaluating multiple object tracking performance: the clear mot metrics. EURASIP J. Image Video Process. **2008**, 1–10 (2008)
3. Bewley, A., Ge, Z., Ott, L., Ramos, F., Upcroft, B.: Simple online and realtime tracking. In: 2016 IEEE International Conference on Image Processing (ICIP), pp. 3464–3468. IEEE (2016)
4. Bochinski, E., Senst, T., Sikora, T.: Extending IOU based multi-object tracking by visual information. In: 2018 15th IEEE International Conference on Advanced Video and Signal Based Surveillance (AVSS), pp. 1–6. IEEE (2018)

5. Carion, N., Massa, F., Synnaeve, G., Usunier, N., Kirillov, A., Zagoruyko, S.: End-to-end object detection with transformers. In: Vedaldi, A., Bischof, H., Brox, T., Frahm, J.-M. (eds.) ECCV 2020. LNCS, vol. 12346, pp. 213–229. Springer, Cham (2020). https://doi.org/10.1007/978-3-030-58452-8_13

6. Chu, P., Wang, J., You, Q., Ling, H., Liu, Z.: TransMOT: spatial-temporal graph transformer for multiple object tracking. arXiv preprint arXiv:2104.00194 (2021)

7. Dosovitskiy, A., et al.: An image is worth 16 × 16 words: transformers for image recognition at scale. In: International Conference on Learning Representations (2021)

8. Fang, Y., et al.: Instances as queries. In: Proceedings of the IEEE/CVF International Conference on Computer Vision, pp. 6910–6919 (2021)

9. Ge, Z., Liu, S., Wang, F., Li, Z., Sun, J.: YOLOX: exceeding yolo series in 2021. arXiv preprint arXiv:2107.08430 (2021)

10. Ge, Z., Wang, J., Huang, X., Liu, S., Yoshie, O.: Lla: Loss-aware label assignment for dense pedestrian detection. arXiv preprint arXiv:2101.04307 (2021)

11. He, K., Zhang, X., Ren, S., Sun, J.: Deep residual learning for image recognition. In: Proceedings of the IEEE Conference on Computer Vision and Pattern Recognition, pp. 770–778 (2016)

12. Liang, C., et al.: Rethinking the competition between detection and ReID in multi-object tracking. arXiv preprint arXiv:2010.12138 (2020)

13. Lin, T.Y., Goyal, P., Girshick, R., He, K., Dollár, P.: Focal loss for dense object detection. In: Proceedings of the IEEE International Conference on Computer Vision, pp. 2980–2988 (2017)

14. Liu, Z., et al.: Swin transformer: hierarchical vision transformer using shifted windows. In: Proceedings of the IEEE/CVF International Conference on Computer Vision (ICCV), pp. 10012–10022, October 2021

15. Luiten, I., et al.: HOTA: a higher order metric for evaluating multi-object tracking. Int. J. Comput. Vision 129(2), 548–578 (2021)

16. Meinhardt, T., Kirillov, A., Leal-Taixe, L., Feichtenhofer, C.: Trackformer: multi-object tracking with transformers. arXiv preprint arXiv:2101.02702 (2021)

17. Pang, J., et al.: Quasi-dense similarity learning for multiple object tracking. In: Proceedings of the IEEE/CVF Conference on Computer Vision and Pattern Recognition, pp. 164–173 (2021)

18. Peng, J., et al.: Chained-tracker: chaining paired attentive regression results for end-to-end joint multiple-object detection and tracking. In: Vedaldi, A., Bischof, H., Brox, T., Frahm, J.-M. (eds.) ECCV 2020. LNCS, vol. 12349, pp. 145–161. Springer, Cham (2020). https://doi.org/10.1007/978-3-030-58548-8_9

19. Redmon, J., Farhadi, A.: Yolov3: an incremental improvement. arXiv preprint arXiv:1804.02767 (2018)

20. Ren, S., He, K., Girshick, R., Sun, J.: Faster R-CNN: towards real-time object detection with region proposal networks. Adv. Neural Inf. Process. Syst. 28, 91–99 (2015)

21. Shao, S., et al.: CrowdHuman: a benchmark for detecting human in a crowd. arXiv preprint arXiv:1805.00123 (2018)

22. Sun, P., et al.: TransTrack: multiple-object tracking with transformer. arXiv preprint arXiv:2012.15460 (2020)

23. Sundararaman, R., De Almeida Braga, C., Marchand, E., Pettre, J.: Tracking pedestrian heads in dense crowd. In: Proceedings of the IEEE/CVF Conference on Computer Vision and Pattern Recognition, pp. 3865–3875 (2021)

24. Tian, Z., Shen, C., Chen, H., He, T.: FCOS: a simple and strong anchor-free object detector. In: IEEE Transactions on Pattern Analysis and Machine Intelligence (2020)
25. Vaswani, A., Shazeer, N., Parmar, N., Uszkoreit, J., Jones, L., Gomez, A.N., Kaiser, L., Polosukhin, I.: Attention is all you need. In: Advances in Neural Information Processing Systems, pp. 5998–6008 (2017)
26. Vo, X.-T., Tran, T.-D., Nguyen, D.-L., Jo, K.-H.: Regression-aware classification feature for pedestrian detection and tracking in video surveillance systems. In: Huang, D.-S., Jo, K.-H., Li, J., Gribova, V., Bevilacqua, V. (eds.) ICIC 2021. LNCS, vol. 12836, pp. 816–828. Springer, Cham (2021). https://doi.org/10.1007/978-3-030-84522-3_66
27. Wang, Q., Zheng, Y., Pan, P., Xu, Y.: Multiple object tracking with correlation learning. In: Proceedings of the IEEE/CVF Conference on Computer Vision and Pattern Recognition, pp. 3876–3886 (2021)
28. Wang, W., et al.: Pyramid vision transformer: a versatile backbone for dense prediction without convolutions. In: Proceedings of the IEEE/CVF International Conference on Computer Vision (ICCV), pp. 568–578, October 2021
29. Wang, Y., Xu, Z., Wang, X., Shen, C., Cheng, B., Shen, H., Xia, H.: End-to-end video instance segmentation with transformers. In: Proceedings of the IEEE/CVF Conference on Computer Vision and Pattern Recognition, pp. 8741–8750 (2021)
30. Wang, Z., Zheng, L., Liu, Y., Li, Y., Wang, S.: Towards real-time multi-object tracking. In: Vedaldi, A., Bischof, H., Brox, T., Frahm, J.-M. (eds.) ECCV 2020. LNCS, vol. 12356, pp. 107–122. Springer, Cham (2020). https://doi.org/10.1007/978-3-030-58621-8_7
31. Wojke, N., Bewley, A., Paulus, D.: Simple online and realtime tracking with a deep association metric. In: 2017 IEEE International Conference on Image Processing (ICIP), pp. 3645–3649. IEEE (2017)
32. Wu, J., Cao, J., Song, L., Wang, Y., Yang, M., Yuan, J.: Track to detect and segment: an online multi-object tracker. In: Proceedings of the IEEE/CVF Conference on Computer Vision and Pattern Recognition, pp. 12352–12361 (2021)
33. Xu, Y., Ban, Y., Delorme, G., Gan, C., Rus, D., Alameda-Pineda, X.: TransCenter: transformers with dense queries for multiple-object tracking. arXiv preprint arXiv:2103.15145 (2021)
34. Zeng, F., Dong, B., Wang, T., Chen, C., Zhang, X., Wei, Y.: MOTR: end-to-end multiple-object tracking with transformer. arXiv preprint arXiv:2105.03247 (2021)
35. Zhang, W., Pang, J., Chen, K., Loy, C.C.: K-Net: towards unified image segmentation. In: Beygelzimer, A., Dauphin, Y., Liang, P., Vaughan, J.W. (eds.) Advances in Neural Information Processing Systems, MIT Press, London (2021)
36. Zhang, Y., et al.: ByteTrack: multi-object tracking by associating every detection box. arXiv preprint arXiv:2110.06864 (2021)
37. Zhang, Y., Wang, C., Wang, X., Zeng, W., Liu, W.: FairMOT: on the fairness of detection and re-identification in multiple object tracking. Int. J. Comput. Vision **129**(11), 3069–3087 (2021)
38. Zheng, L., Tang, M., Chen, Y., Zhu, G., Wang, J., Lu, H.: Improving multiple object tracking with single object tracking. In: Proceedings of the IEEE/CVF Conference on Computer Vision and Pattern Recognition, pp. 2453–2462 (2021)
39. Zhou, X., Koltun, V., Krähenbühl, P.: tracking objects as points. In: Vedaldi, A., Bischof, H., Brox, T., Frahm, J.-M. (eds.) ECCV 2020. LNCS, vol. 12349, pp. 474–490. Springer, Cham (2020). https://doi.org/10.1007/978-3-030-58548-8_28
40. Zhou, X., Wang, D., Krähenbühl, P.: Objects as points. arXiv preprint arXiv:1904.07850 (2019)

41. Zhu, J., Yang, H., Liu, N., Kim, M., Zhang, W., Yang, M.H.: Online multi-object tracking with dual matching attention networks. In: Proceedings of the European Conference on Computer Vision (ECCV), pp. 366–382 (2018)
42. Zhu, X., Su, W., Lu, L., Li, B., Wang, X., Dai, J.: Deformable DETR: deformable transformers for end-to-end object detection. In: International Conference on Learning Representations (2021)

Proposal of a Method to Identify Vascular Endothelial Cells from Images of Mouse Myocardial Tissue

Shotaro Kaneko[1]($\boxtimes$), Yuichiro Arima[2], Masahiro Migita[3], and Masashi Toda[3]

[1] Department of Computer Science and Electrical Engineering, Kumamoto University, Kumamoto 860-8555, Japan
182t3139@gmail.com
[2] Department of Cardiovascular Medicine, Kumamoto University, Kumamoto 860-0811, Japan
[3] Center for Management of Information Technologies, Kumamoto University, Kumamoto 860-8555, Japan

Abstract. Three-dimensional (3D) analysis of cardiomyocytes using computers is urgently required to elucidate the pathogenesis of cardiac diseases. As there exists several different types of cells in microscopic images, it is necessary to classify the cells prior to analysis. To classify cells, the fact that the cell nuclei of vascular endothelial cells are covered by vascular endothelial cell membrane is considered. In this study, the cell nuclei and areas of the vascular endothelial cell membrane are extracted from microscopic images of myocardial tissue in the left atrium of newborn mice and classified into vascular endothelial cell nuclei and non-endothelial cell nuclei based on the quantity of the cell nuclei that is covered by the vascular endothelium. The accuracy was calculated from the experimental results, and it was more than 85%. Future studies will include improving the accuracy of the classification and further classifying the cell nuclei that were determined to be other than endothelial cell nuclei to analyze the cells. These are expected to contribute to the research to clarify the mechanism of blood vessels and cells in myocardium.

Keywords: 3D analysis · Cell classification · Cell nuclei · Medical images · Vascular endothelial cell

1 Introduction

Heart disease accounts for 15% of all deaths in Japan, second only to malignant neoplasms (tumors), and the mortality rate is increasing every year [1]. In addition, heart failure accounts for approximately half of all deaths from heart disease [1]. Although the treatment of heart failure with medication has made steady progress, it is often ineffective in cases of severe heart failure, and there is currently no established treatment other than heart transplantation [2]. Although heart transplantation has been taking place in

Japan, the number of donors remains far fewer than the number of patients eligible for transplantation. Moreover, the likelihood of utilizing this kind of treatment in the future is low [2]. Therefore, there is an urgent requirement to understand the pathogenesis of heart failure and establish new treatment methods.

In recent years, the development of computer technology has elucidated the pathogenesis of heart failure at the cellular level. To understand the pathogenesis of heart failure, cardiomyocytes, the primary constituent of the heart, have been utilized. However, as it is difficult to use human cardiomyocytes, mouse cardiomyocytes, which are also mammals, is popular. One representative study reported the cross-sectional area of cell nuclei from mouse cardiomyocyte images under conditions similar to those of heart failure captured using a microscope [3]. Various studies till date have discussed and reported the three-dimensional (3D) cardiomyocyte bodies in two dimensions. Therefore, a 3D analysis of the cardiomyocytes could provide more insight. Additionally, as cardiomyocytes coexist with other cells in the heart, it is desirable to classify the nucleated cells and analyze their volume and positional relationships as 3D information. Single-cell analysis [4] has demonstrated the mechanism of cardiomyocyte hypertrophy and failure via machine learning. However, single-cell analysis cannot be used to obtain the information on the shape of the cells and the positional relationship between the cells in a tissue because the analysis is performed by isolating the cells and focusing on an individual cell. In addition, there are other methods for modeling, analyzing, and classifying cell nuclei and nucleoli in three dimensions [5], however, these only utilize the morphological information, i.e., volume, surface area, etc., of cell nuclei and nucleoli. In this study, a method for classifying the cell nuclei by utilizing the positional relationship with the vascular endothelial cell membrane in a group of tissue images of mouse myocardium is investigated. Figure 1(top) shows one frame of a fluorescence microscopy image of a mouse myocardial section. In Fig. 1(top), the cell nucleus is red, the cell membrane is green, the dividing cell nucleus is blue, and the vascular endothelial cell fluoresces are white. Figure 1(bottom) shows a 3D visualization of the fluorescence microscope image with ImageJ. The fluorescence microscopy image shows four objects simultaneously, each of which can be viewed separately: the cell nucleus (Fig. 2(top left)), the cell membrane (Fig. 2(top right)), the dividing cell nucleus (Fig. 2(bottom left)), the endothelial cell membrane (Fig. 2(bottom right)), and the vascular endothelium (Fig. 2(bottom right)). The four imaging targets are the cell nucleus (Fig. 2(upper left)), the cell membrane (Fig. 2(upper right)), the dividing cell nucleus (Fig. 2(lower left)), and the vascular endothelial cell membrane (Fig. 2(lower right)).

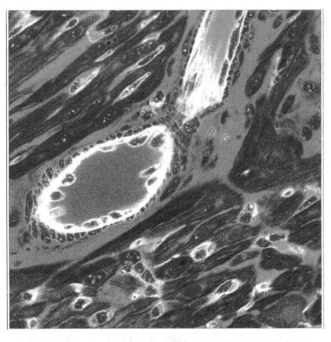

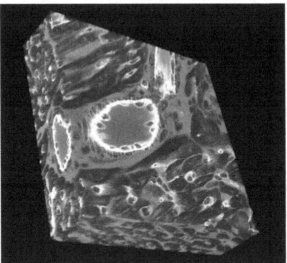

Fig. 1. Superimposed image of all the photographed objects (top) and a three-dimensional visualization of this image (bottom).

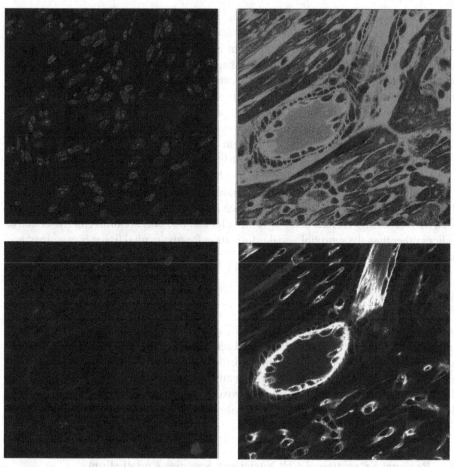

Fig. 2. Cell nucleus (top left), cell membrane (top right), dividing cell nucleus (bottom left), and vascular endothelial cell (bottom right).

2   Related Work

Several methods have been proposed to classify cells from fluorescence microscopy images. U-net [6] was developed as a region extraction method for medical images and has garnered significant attention because of its high accuracy in segmentation despite the small amount of training data, and it also supports 3D images [7]. Currently, numerous methods have been proposed to utilize and derive from these methods, and Cellpose [8] is one such method. This method is capable of segmenting a wide range of cell types and other images without the need for parameter tuning, new training datasets, or retraining of the model. In addition to analyzing the cells from microscopic images of tissue, there are other methods for analyzing cells, such as single-cell analysis, in which the cells are isolated from the tissue and analyzed individually. Single-cell analysis of cardiomyocytes has gradually elucidated their molecular mechanisms. Nomura et al. [4] used single-cell analysis of cardiomyocytes to investigate how cardiomyocyte morphology and molecular characteristics are related to cardiac function using machine learning. However, single-cell analysis is expensive and time-consuming because it involves isolating cells and focusing on an individual cell. In addition, the isolation of the cells makes it is impossible to obtain any information on their original shape and location when they existed as parts of cardiac muscle tissue. Therefore, in this study, a group of cell tissue images of the myocardium captured under a microscope is analyzed.

One of the most popular 3D analysis of nuclei is the 3D shape modeling for cell nu-clear morphological analysis and classification [5]. In this study, modeling, analysis and classification of cell nuclei and nucleoli are performed in three dimensions. The morphology of the serum-starved and proliferating fibroblasts is compared, followed by a comparison of the epithelial and mesenchymal human prostate cancer cell lines to classify the fibroblasts and epithelial and mesenchymal cells, respectively. However, in this study, the cardiac muscle is not discussed and only the morphological in-formation, such as volume and surface area, of cell nuclei and nucleoli are utilized. The effective indices other than the morphological information for myocardial tissue is examined and analyze in three dimensions.

3 Method

In this section, the methods used in this study are described. First, the respective regions are extracted from the images of fluoresced cell nuclei and fluoresced vascular endothe-lium (Sect. 3.1). Next, the voxels that are the surface portions of the extracted cell nuclei are determined (Sect. 3.2). Subsequently, the proportion of the vascular endothe-lial region that exists around the surface voxels of individual cell nuclei (Sect. 3.3) is determined. Finally, the cell nuclei is classified based on the information derived from Sect. 3.3 (Sect. 3.4).

3.1 Regional Extraction of Cell Nuclei and Vascular Endothelium

The respective regions are extracted from the images of fluoresced cell nuclei and fluo-resced vascular endothelium. For the cell nucleus regions, Cellpose was used to extract the individual cell nucleus regions [8]. However, during this extraction process several regions were found to be over-segmented. If solely the cell nucleus region is extracted from the cell nucleus image, the general binarization process is more accurate, and Cell-pose is more accurate in distinguishing the separate cells, although the region is blurred due to over-segmentation. Therefore, the cell nucleus region was extracted utilizing the method proposed by Takematsu et al. [9]. First, Otsu's binarization was used from the cell nucleus image to define the foreground area as the cell nucleus region. The bina-rization of the images was performed with a threshold of 46 for normal mice and a threshold of 19 for genetically modified mice. If the image is divided into individual cell nuclei using the watershed method after the distance transformation, the image will be mistakenly extracted as multiple cell nuclei even if originally it has one nucleus because the inside of the nucleus is insect-eaten. Therefore, in this study, the closed area of the binarized cell nucleus image is filled in for each slice in the xy, yz, and zx coordinates in the depth direction (Fig. 3). This prevents the ac-cidental extraction of a single nucleus as multiple nuclei (Fig. 4). Next, two images are prepared: one is the image after filling in the holes, which is transformed by the dis-tance and divided into individual cell nuclei by the watershed method (cell nucleus image 1), and the other is the binarized image, in which the cell nuclei extracted by Cellpose are used as markers and divided into cell nuclei by the watershed method (cell nucleus image 2). Following this, the cell nucleus image 2 is corrected with the cell nucleus image 1, because the Cellpose extraction results revealed plenty of over-segmentation. Finally, the cell nucleus image 2 is used to replace the one with ex-tremely large volume and distorted shape. Figure 5 shows the flow of the cell nucleus region extraction method.

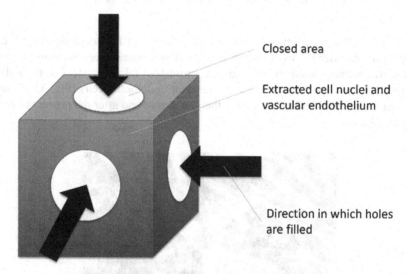

Fig. 3. How to fill in closed areas.

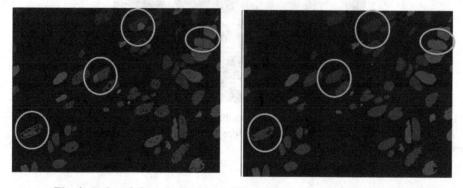

Fig. 4. Before (left) and after (right) filling the holes inside the cell nucleus.

For the vascular endothelial region, the endothelial cell image is smoothed using an anisotropic diffusion filter and then binarized using adaptive thresholding. The binarization by adaptive thresholding is used because the normal binarization could not extract

---

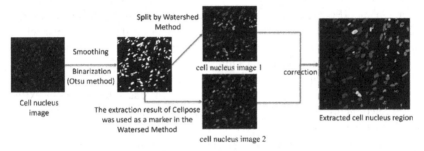

Fig. 5. Overview of the cell nucleus region extraction method.

the endothelial cells even if they are the same, due to the difference in the fluorescence intensity values. After removing the noise, the closed area of each slice in the depth direction was painted on the xy, yz, and zx coordinates of Takematsu et al. to facilitate the classification of the cell nuclei of the vascular endothelial cells (Fig. 3). Figure 6 shows a superimposed image of the endothelium before and after the process of filling the occluded area.

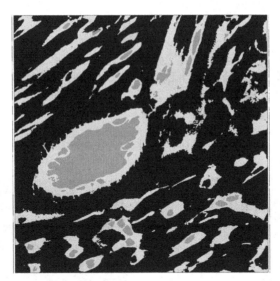

Fig. 6. Extraction image of the vascular endothelial area. The areas before and after the hole filling are shown in yellow because the areas before the hole filling were overlaid in red and after the hole filling in green. (Color figure online)

3.2 Determining the Surface of the Cell Nucleus

As shown in Fig. 7, the cell nuclei of the vascular endothelial cells are those that exist inside the blood vessel (covered by the vascular endothelium). In this experiment, it is necessary to determine the surface of the cell nuclei because the index is a measure of the portion of the vascular endothelial area the exists around the cell nuclei. From the cell nuclei extracted in Sect. 3.1, the voxels that make up the individual surfaces are obtained. For each voxel that constitutes a cell nucleus, it is determined if there exists a voxel of the same cell nucleus at ± 1 of the x, y, and z coordinates, using the six connections (Fig. 8).

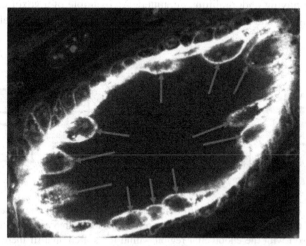

Fig. 7. Superimposed images of the cell nuclei and the vascular endothelium. The arrows indicate the cell nuclei of the vascular endothelial cells.

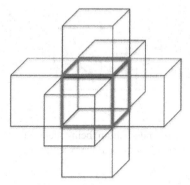

Fig. 8. An example of a group of voxels that make up a cell nucleus. The red cubes are the surface voxels. (Color figure online)

3.3 Determining Whether the Nuclei is Covered with Vascular Endothelium

The nuclei of the vascular endothelial cells are surrounded by the vascular endothelium. This is not observed in the nuclei of the cells other than the vascular endothelial cells, including cardiomyocytes. Therefore, the quantity of the vascular endothelium that exists around the surface of the cell nucleus has to be determined. First, the coordinates of the surface voxel of the cell nucleus are obtained. Next, it is determined whether there are voxels that constitute the vascular endothelial regions within the same coordinates as the surface voxel itself or within one voxel (26 connections) around it. If at least one voxel that constitutes an endothelial region exists, the sur-face voxel is classified as having an endothelium, and if none exists, it is classified as having no endothelium. This is performed for each surface voxel, and subsequently the number of voxels that are classified as having endothelium is counted. An example of a voxel judged to have endothelium (Fig. 9), and an example of a voxel judged to have no endothelium (Fig. 10) are shown.

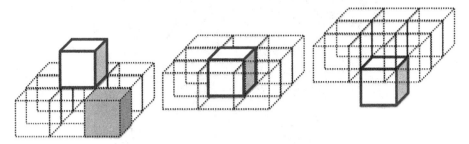

Fig. 9. Example of vascular endothelium being detected. The red cube represents one of the surface voxels of the cell nucleus, the black cube represents the search area, and the yellow cube represents the voxel with the endothelial region within the search area (if there is at least one yellow cube in the search area including the surface voxel itself). (Color figure online)

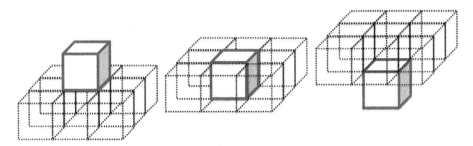

Fig. 10. Example of no vascular endothelium being detected. (When there is no vascular endothelium in the search area including the surface voxel itself.)

3.4 Classification of the Cell Nuclei Using the Percentage of Coverage

Vascular endothelial cells are characterized by the fact that their nuclei are covered by the vascular endothelium. The percentage of this coverage is determined and classified as follows. The threshold value is derived via discriminant analysis. If the percentage is greater than the threshold value, the cell is classified as an endothelial cell nucleus; whereas if it is smaller, it is not an endothelial cell nucleus.

$$\text{The percentage of coverage}(\%) = \frac{\textit{Number of voxels ''with'' vascular endothelium}}{\textit{Number of surface voxels of cell nucleus}} \times 100$$

4   Experiment

The specifications of the current experiment are presented in Table 1.

Table 1. Equipment used and development environment

OS	MS Windows10
CPU	i7-8700K (3.70 GHz)
RAM	40.0 GB
Development environment	MATLAB R2020b

4.1   Data Sets Used

Microscopic images of the mouse heart are utilized in this study. The images are captured using fluorescing cell nuclei, cell membranes, dividing cell nuclei, and vascular endothelial cell membrane, respectively. The specifications of the images are detailed in Table 2. The myocardial images of normal and genetically modified mice of the same age are considered for this experiment. Genetically engineered mice are mice that have been modified to be unable to metabolize because of which their growth is likely to be immature. Therefore, they are expected to have more cells and blood vessels and smaller cells compared to normal mice. In this experiment, fluorescence images of the cell nuclei and vascular endothelial cell membrane were used among them. One slice of the superimposed images of the cell nuclei and the vascular endothelial cells from both normal and genetically modified mice, are shown in Fig. 11.

Table 2. Supplementary information regarding the image

Format	Tiff
Number of slices	Normal mouse: 170 Genetically modified mouse: 176
Width	1,024
Height	1,024
Color type	Grayscale
Target	Neonatal murine
Shooting location	Myocardial tissue of the left atrium
Shooting object	Cell nucleus, cell membrane, dividing cell nucleus, and vascular endothelial cell membrane
Shooting equipment	Confocal laser scanning microscopy

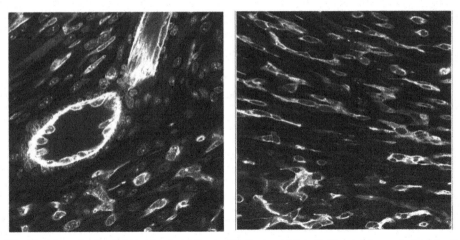

Fig. 11. Normal mice (left) and genetically modified mice (right). Cell nuclei fluoresce in red and vascular endothelial cells fluoresce in white. (Color figure online)

4.2 Experimental Details

In this experiment, the cell nucleus region and the vascular endothelial cell membrane region are extracted from the target image using the method proposed in this study. Further, binary classification is performed for the cell nuclei both belonging and not belonging to the vascular endothelial cells. A threshold value is calculated using discriminant analysis from the coverage of each cell nucleus. The cell nuclei that have a coverage greater than the threshold value are classified as vascular endothelial cell nuclei. In contrast, the cell nuclei with a coverage less than the threshold value are classified as non-vascular endothelial cell nuclei. The classification accuracy is evaluated only by the cell nuclei existing in 1~30 slices in this study. The grand truth data is prepared by the expert who cooperated in this study.

5 Results

The results of the binary classification according to the threshold value calculated from the percentage of coverage are shown in Fig. 12. One slice of the image superimposed with the image of vascular endothelial cells is depicted in Fig. 13. The cell nuclei classified as vascular endothelial cell nuclei and not vascular endothelial cell nuclei using the binary classification are presented in blue and red, respectively.

The number of cell nuclei according to the classification results are shown in Table 3. Tables 4 and 5 show the confusion matrix obtained from the prediction data and the classification results of the grand truth data for cell nuclei up to 1~30 slices for normal and genetically modified mouse, respectively, and Table 6 shows the values of the classification evaluation index calculated from Tables 4 and 5.

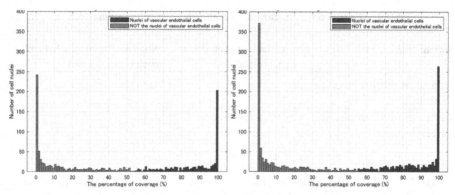

Fig. 12. Results of binary classification. Normal mice (left) and genetically modified mice (right). (Color figure online)

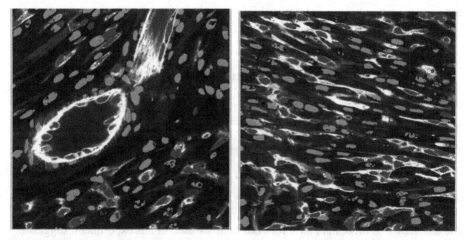

Fig. 13. Visualization of binary classification results. Normal mouse (left), genetically modified mouse (right). (Color figure online)

Table 3. The number of cell nuclei according to the classification results.

Type of mouse	Vascular endothelial cell nuclei	Not vascular endothelial cell nuclei	Total number
Normal mouse	575	721	1,296
Genetically modified mouse	804	939	1,743

Table 4. Confusion matrix showing classification results for normal mouse.

Normal mouse	Vascular endothelial cell nuclei (grand truth)	Not vascular endothelial cell nuclei (grand truth)
Vascular endothelial cell nuclei (predicted)	75	13
Not vascular endothelial cell nuclei (predicted)	16	121

Table 5. Confusion matrix showing classification results for Genetically modified mouse.

Genetically modified mouse	Vascular endothelial cell nuclei (grand truth)	Not vascular endothelial cell nuclei (grand truth)
Vascular endothelial cell nuclei (predicted)	95	8
Not vascular endothelial cell nuclei (predicted)	26	99

Table 6. Classification of experimental results value of evaluation index

	Accuracy	Precision	Recall	F-measure
Normal mouse	0.871	0.852	0.824	0.838
Genetically modified mouse	0.851	0.922	0.785	0.848

6 Conclusions and Future Work

The accuracy was more than 85% for both samples used in this experiment, suggesting that this method is effective in classifying endothelial cell nuclei. The experts who collaborated with us on this study agreed that the results were very useful. However, amongst the cell nuclei of the vascular endothelial cells in the binary classification, there were certain cell nuclei that were not vascular endothelial cells. This is believed to have occurred because the cell nuclei are located near the endothelial cell membrane even though they are not those of vascular endothelial cells. Such features were frequently observed in the cell nuclei near the threshold.

Future work will include investigating the accuracy of the classification and further attempts will be made to accurately classify the cell nuclei into those of vascular endothelial cells and non-vascular endothelial cells. In addition, as the non-endothelial cell nuclei not only originate from cardiomyocytes but also from the smooth muscle cells and fibroblasts, a plan to classify them in further detail is in progress. The ultimate objective is to compare the normal mice with the genetically modified mice and ascertain the differences to clarify the mechanisms of myocardial blood vessels and cells and to elucidate the pathogenesis of cardiac diseases.

References

1. Ministry of Health, Labour and Welfare, Summary of the 2020 Vital Statistics Monthly Report Annual Total (Approximate). https://www.mhlw.go.jp/toukei/saikin/hw/jinkou/geppo/nengai20/dl/gaikyouR2.pdf. Accessed 07 Dec 2021
2. Ministry of Education, Culture, Sports, Science and Technology (MEXT) Strategic Research on Heart Failure Elucidation of the pathogenesis of heart failure using developmental engineering and gene and cell therapy. https://www.mext.go.jp/a_menu/shinkou/hojyo/1300506.htm. Accessed 07 Dec 2021
3. Bao, N.P., et al.: The oxygen rich postnatal environment induces cardiomyocyte cell cycle arrest through DNA damage response. Cell **157**(3), 565–579 (2014)
4. Nomura, S., Satoh, M., Fujita, T., et al.: Cardiomyocyte gene programs encoding morphological and functional signatures in cardiac hypertrophy and failure. Nat. Commun. **9**, 4435 (2018)
5. Kalinin, A.A., Allyn-Feuer, A., Ade, A., et al.: 3D shape modeling for cell nuclear morphological analysis and classification. Sci. Rep. **8**, 13658 (2018)
6. Ronneberger, O., Fischer, P., Brox, T.: U-Net: convolutional networks for biomedical image segmentation. In: Navab, N., Hornegger, J., Wells, W.M., Frangi, A.F. (eds.) MICCAI 2015. LNCS, vol. 9351, pp. 234–241. Springer, Cham (2015). https://doi.org/10.1007/978-3-319-24574-4_28
7. Çiçek, Ö., Abdulkadir, A., Lienkamp, S.S., Brox, T., Ronneberger, O.: 3D U-Net: learning dense volumetric segmentation from sparse annotation. In: Ourselin, S., Joskowicz, L., Sabuncu, M.R., Unal, G., Wells, W. (eds.) MICCAI 2016. LNCS, vol. 9901, pp. 424–432. Springer, Cham (2016). https://doi.org/10.1007/978-3-319-46723-8_49
8. Stringer, C., Wang, T., Michaelos, M., et al.: Cellpose: a generalist algorithm for cellular segmentation. Nat. Methods **18**, 100–106 (2021)
9. Takematsu, A., Migita, M., Toda, M., Arima, Y.: Study on 3D extraction and analysis of blood vessels and cardiomyocytes on neonatal murine. In: Jeong, H., Sumi, K. (eds.) IW-FCV 2021. CCIS, vol. 1405, pp. 117–130. Springer, Cham (2021). https://doi.org/10.1007/978-3-030-81638-4_10

Improved Facial Keypoint Regression Using Attention Modules

Rahul Vijay Soans$^{(\boxtimes)}$ (iD) and Yohei Fukumizu (iD)

Ritsumeikan University, Kusatsu 525-8577, Shiga, Japan
`rahulvijaysoans231444@gmail.com, fukumizu@se.ritsumei.ac.jp`

Abstract. Recently, keypoint detection or pose estimation has gained a lot of applications and scope of research. However, the facial keypoint localization gives a poor prediction for low-quality and low-resolution images. Our goal is to overcome this and regress keypoint positions more accurately, the model needs to learn representations that focus more on the regions around the keypoints. In this paper, we are interested in finding the facial keypoints by regressing the gaussian heat mapped labels with distance loss and pixel-wise labels with segmentation loss functions like cross-entropy using Fully Convolution Network (FCN) and UNET segmentation models. We find the best version of the segmentation models by further refining the output features of the segmentation models by utilizing the popular channel and attention mechanisms like Convolution Block Attention Module (CBAM), Squeeze-and-Excitation Network (SENET) and Efficient Channel Attention Network (ECANET). Various experiments are performed to find the optimal position to place the attention module inside the segmentation models by monitoring the evaluation metrics. The refined features focus more on the relevant parts of the face, thereby improving the accuracy of the model. The intermediate channel activations and the final output are also visualized to observe the differences between various attention modules. Based on the quantitative and qualitative validation results, we rank the models best suited for our future applications such as facial tracking and emotion detection.

Keywords: Keypoint detection · Segmentation · Attention mechanism · Spatial Attention · Channel Attention · Facial Keypoints · Semantic landmark localization

1 Introduction

The keypoints or landmarks detection is a wide research topic and has a variety of applications in computer vision, robotics, security, augmented reality, virtual reality like human pose estimation [5, 25], facial landmark detection [4, 10], hand landmark detection [11, 19], human activity recognition, CGI, face recognition [24, 26] and 3D face reconstruction [3].

Heatmap regression is widely used in both top-down and bottom-up approaches. In heatmap regression, the ground truth heatmap is generated by a 2D Gaussian filter centered at each keypoint on each channel. Heatmap regression is widely used for face

© The Author(s), under exclusive license to Springer Nature Switzerland AG 2022
K. Sumi et al. (Eds.): IW-FCV 2022, CCIS 1578, pp. 182–196, 2022.
https://doi.org/10.1007/978-3-031-06381-7_13

alignment [9, 16] and gives much higher accuracy than coordinate regression [13]. The goal of the heatmap regression is to reconstruct the output heatmap/masks similar to the ground truth heatmap using L2 distance loss. This method has much higher accuracy than direct coordinate regression [12]. Also, the direct coordinate regression has less accuracy since humans cannot annotate the keypoints with pixel-wise accuracy [2]. So it is not a good choice to go for the direct keypoint regression. Direct regression is a difficult task since it is nonlinear in nature and requires a lot of training data to get decent performance.

Although heatmap regression gives better results, the L2 distance loss or the mean square error (MSE) loss doesn't penalize small errors and since the gaussian heatmap has the majority of pixels as background, it dominates the important foreground since all pixels have the same weights during training. This results in a blurry prediction of the heatmap. Also, the heatmap regression takes a longer time for training. So we try semantic pixel labeling schemes and find whether it outperforms the heatmap regression.

Further, we believe that for accurate keypoint regression the model should learn the representations that focus more on the joint/keypoint. We use the attention mechanisms to focus more on the pixels lying in the keypoint regions (spatial attention) and channel filters that contribute more to learning better representations of the features (channel attention). The attention mechanisms used in this paper are CBAM, SENET, and ECANET [27–29]. Without the attention modules, the model filters will learn image representations that are less meaningful for the final predictions. By using the attentions modules, we can efficiently use the model filters by focusing on the relevant spatial and channel features along with performance gains.

In summary, our main contributions include:

- Compare various mask labeling schemes and loss functions.
- Boost the model performance using spatial and channel attention modules.

Related Work. 2D keypoint detection was a popular approach before the heatmap regression came into the picture, like a multi-resolution framework that generates heat maps representing per-pixel likelihood for keypoints [6]. A repeated bottom-up, top-down Hourglass architecture that enforces intermediate supervision by applying loss on intermediate heat maps showed good keypoint detection accuracy. HRNet [5] also proved good results by maintaining high resolution throughout the network mainly used for real-time applications. Our research is intended to provide improvements for low-resolution images. Openpose network proposed to use a multi-branch approach which can relate the body parts with the body joints [23].

Coordinate regression has been widely used in semantic keypoint localization. To improve the performance of coordinate regression several methods have been proposed by using cascade refinement [14, 15], multi-task learning [17, 18], and better loss functions [20]. Many powerful models promoted the use of heatmap regression for accurate facial keypoint localization [4, 21]. There are several choices of loss function for heat maps. The most widely used is L2 distance loss/mean squared error between the predicted heat map and ground-truth heat map with a 2D Gaussian blob centered on the ground truth joint location [1, 22, 23]. We try to implement pixel-wise labeling and check its performance.

2 Proposed Method

2.1 Keypoint Regression

The semantic keypoints detection aims to find the numerical coordinates of a set of pre-defined facial landmarks (e.g., left eye, right eye, nose, left mouth corner, right mouth corner, etc.). The normal method involves direct coordinate regression using mean square error loss (MSE/L2 loss) or mean absolute error loss (MAE/L1 loss). But the direct coordinate regression gives bad results and also needs a very large number of samples for training. Heatmap Regression on the other hand tries to learn to construct the heatmaps also known as confidence maps. They are a simple and effective representation of the keypoint coordinates. The heatmap regression needs the encoded label as discussed earlier. That is the conversion of ground truth numerical coordinates to the ground truth heatmap. The model aims to construct the heatmaps given an input image. While prediction, the heatmaps are decoded back to the numerical coordinates by taking the argmax of the individual class-wise confidence maps along the channel axis. Similar to the heatmap regression, we also implement pixel-based categorical masks from the numerical coordinates which can be regressed using cross-entropy loss functions. More information regarding the ground-truth labeling methods are discussed in Sect. 3.2 below.

2.2 Proposed Model

In this section, we describe the CNN model used for keypoint detection. The architecture is based on the segmentation models of [7, 8]. The FCN-8 model consists of 5 blocks of 3×3 Conv2D with stride 1, Relu activation and Max pool layer of size 2×2 and stride 2×2 as the down-sampling layers. This is followed by Conv2D of 1×1 size to reduce the channel size same as the number of label classes. This is followed by up-sampling layers which use the Conv2D transpose filters with the skip connections from the lower pool layers. The final output layer consists of 15 channels representing confidence maps from the 15 keypoints.

The UNET model consists of 5 blocks of 2 3×3 Conv2D with stride 1, Relu activation and Max pool layer of size 2×2 and stride 2×2 as the down-sampling layers. This is followed by 4 blocks of Conv2d transpose of 2×2, concatenation or skip connection, $2 \times 3 \times 3$ Conv2D and Relu activation. Finally, a 1×1 convolution to reduce the channel size same as the number of output classes. The final output layer consists of 15 channels representing confidence maps from the 15 keypoints.

Our objective is to boost the intermediate feature representations by multiplying them with various channel/spatial attention weights for learning context information and improving the final heatmap predictions. We use two base models FCN and UNET to compare them with the attention-based models. We also experiment to find the best position to place the attention blocks to get the best results. We place the attention blocks at the down-sampling/encoder layers and at the end of the up-sampling/decoder layers of the segmentation models to observe which gives the best results. However, placing the attentions modules in the intermediate decoder layers will degrade the model performance. The FCN-8 and UNET model with optimal positions to place the attention blocks are illustrated in Figs. 1 and 2 respectively. The white arrows indicate the positions which return the best-refined feature maps that promote improved keypoint localization.

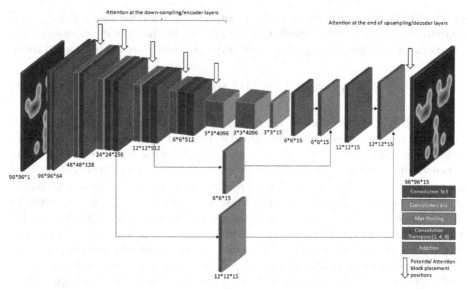

Fig. 1. The FCN-8 architecture with the best attention block placement positions

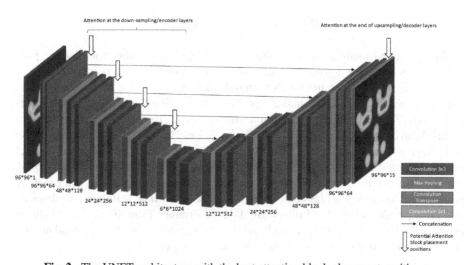

Fig. 2. The UNET architecture with the best attention block placement positions

2.3 Ground Truth Masks Encoding and Loss Functions

We use three different methods to generate ground truth labels/masks from the original keypoint annotation dataset. In the first method, we generate synthesized heatmaps for each keypoint separately by placing a 2D Gaussian filter with fixed variance at the ground truth keypoint position. We represent the keypoint coordinates of 15 keypoints as the 15-channel heatmaps. We model each keypoint as a channel heatmap with a 2D Gaussian distribution centered at the landmark. The equation of a gaussian filter is illustrated in

Eq. (1). The distribution is normalized to a range of 0 to 1 and the standard deviation σ depends on the size of the distribution. We use $\sigma = 5$, for the input image of size 96×96 so that the distribution covers the entire keypoint which is not too big nor too small.

$$G(x, y) = exp\left[-\frac{1}{2\sigma^2}\left((x - \mu_1)^2 + (y - \mu_2)^2\right)\right] \tag{1}$$

where (x, y) is the keypoint location and (μ_1, μ_2) is the center of the distribution. Each keypoint coordinate is converted to an individual heatmap, where the circular area values indicate the probability of the landmark appearing, so that the distributions can contain the uncertainty involved in the landmark locations. This way the center area of the facial keypoints has pixels close to 1 and has pixel values close to 0 as the distribution reduces around the keypoints. The face training dataset consists of 15 keypoints per image, so 15 corresponding gaussian heatmaps are generated for each image. We then use the mean squared error (MSE)/L2 distance loss over the mean absolute error/L1 distance loss because of better results. The MSE is found by calculating the squared pixel-wise difference between the predicted heatmap and the ground-truth heatmap to update the model weights as per Eq. (2) where y_i is the ground-truth and $\hat{y}_i$ is the prediction. This is viewed as the heatmap regression task.

$$MSE \text{ loss} = \frac{1}{N}\sum_{i=1}^{N}\left(y_i - \hat{y}_i\right)^2 \tag{2}$$

In the second method, we generate an individual binary mask for each keypoint separately by assigning a group of pixels around the ground truth keypoint position with pixel 1 (foreground) and other pixels with 0 (background). We use active pixels with a size similar to $\sigma = 2$ which is smaller than the Gaussian filter kernel size, which will be around 70–77 pixels around each keypoint which is enough to learn the mapping between the label and input facial parts for 96×96 input image. The face training dataset consists of 15 keypoints per image, so 15 corresponding binary masks are generated for each image. The model output layer is replaced with the sigmoid activation as per Eq. (4) and then we use the binary cross-entropy loss, by comparing each of the predicted probabilities to the actual class output which can be either 0 or 1. It then calculates the score that penalizes the probabilities based on the distance from the expected value as per Eq. (3) where y_i is the ground-truth and $\hat{y}_i$ is the prediction and N is the total number of samples. This is viewed as the binary multiclass segmentation task.

$$BCE \text{ loss} = -\frac{1}{N}\sum_{i=1}^{N}\hat{y}_i \log y_i + \left(1 - \hat{y}_i\right)\log\left(1 - \hat{y}_i\right) \tag{3}$$

$$\hat{y}_i = f(p_i) = \frac{1}{1 + e^{-p_i}} \tag{4}$$

The third method is an extension of the second method, where we generate a multi-class categorical mask for keypoints by assigning a group of pixels around the ground truth keypoint position with pixels 1 to 15 for each keypoint and other background pixels with 0 (background). The face training dataset consists of 15 keypoints per image, so 15 corresponding masks plus 1 background class are generated for each image and one-hot encoded for the multiclass segmentation task. Also, the overlapping pixels are taken care of by giving more priority to pixels with more information since each pixel can belong to only one class in the multiclass segmentation task. The model output layer is replaced with the softmax activation as per Eq. (6) and then we use the categorical cross-entropy loss, by comparing each of the predicted probabilities to actual class output which can be either 0, 1, 2…15 as per Eq. (5) where y_i is the ground-truth, $\hat{y}_i$ is the prediction, N is the total number of samples and C is the total number of classes. During the prediction, the argmax is taken along all the channel axis to get only one active class per pixel (one-hot decoding). This is viewed as the categorical multiclass segmentation task.

$$\text{CCE loss} = -\frac{1}{N} \sum_{i=1}^{N} \hat{y}_{i1} \log y_{i1} + \hat{y}_{i2} \log y_{i2} + \cdots + \hat{y}_{i16} \log y_{i16} \tag{5}$$

$$\hat{y}_i = f(p)_i = \frac{e^{p_i}}{\sum_j^{C=16} e^{p_j}} \tag{6}$$

2.4 Attention Modules

CBAM. In this section, we describe the attention modules used for keypoint detection. The first attention module is the Convolution block attention module (CBAM). Given an intermediate feature map F of dimension $C \times H \times W$ as input, CBAM sequentially infers a 1D channel attention map M_c of dimension $C \times 1 \times 1$ and a 2D spatial attention map M_s of dimension $1 \times H \times W$ as illustrated in Eq. 7. Then these attention maps/weights are element-wise multiplied with the original feature map F to get the refined feature map F′ and F″ as illustrated in Eq. (7). The spatial attention block is followed by the channel attention block serially.

$$\begin{aligned} F' &= M_c(F) \otimes F \\ F'' &= M_s(F') \otimes F' \end{aligned} \tag{7}$$

In the original paper, the authors reduce the feature dimensions from $C \times H \times W$ to $C \times 1 \times 1$ using both global average pooling and global max pooling operations across the spatial axis, generating two different spatial context descriptors which are denoted by F_{avg}^c and F_{max}^c. These 1D vectors are forwarded to a multi-layer perceptron (MLP) to learn the inter-channel relationship with one hidden layer to produce the channel attention map M_c of dimension$C \times 1 \times 1$. To reduce parameter overhead, the hidden activation size is set to $C/r \times 1 \times 1$, where r is the reduction ratio. The optimal reduction ratio is set as $r = 16$ according to the author. We use the first dense layer to reduce the channel dimension to C/r with relu activation and the second dense layer to convert the reduced channel dimension back to C. The final 1D channel attention map is the addition of two descriptors as illustrated in Eq. (8).

$$\begin{aligned} M_c(F) &= \sigma(\text{MLP}(\text{AvgPool}(F)) + \text{MLP}(\text{MaxPool}(F))) \\ &= \sigma\left(W_1\left(W_0\left(F_{avg}^c\right)\right) + W_1\left(W_0\left(F_{max}^c\right)\right)\right) \end{aligned} \tag{8}$$

where σ denotes the sigmoid function, MLP weights W_0 of dimension $C/r \times C$ and W_1 of dimension $C \times C/r$. These attention maps after sigmoid activation has values ranging from 0 to 1, which are essentially the weighted channel maps that are multiplied with the original feature map as per Eq. (7) to get the refined channel attentive feature map.

Similarly, for spatial attention, the feature dimensions are reduced from $C \times H \times W$ to $1 \times H \times W$ using both global average pooling and global max-pooling operation across the channel axis, which is denoted by F_{avg}^s and F_{max}^s. These 2D vectors are concatenated and forwarded to a convolution filter to learn the inter-spatial relationship to produce the spatial attention map M_s of dimension $1 \times H \times W$. The author used the filter of size 7×7 in their implementation, but we found that the filter size of 3×3 works better for our application. The final 2D channel attention map is shown in Eq. (9).

$$\mathbf{M_s}(\mathbf{F}) = \sigma \left(f^{3 \times 3}([\text{AvgPool(F)}; \ \text{MaxPool(F)}]) \right)$$
$$= \sigma \left(f^{3 \times 3} \left(\left[F_{avg}^s ; F_{max}^s \right] \right) \right) \tag{9}$$

where σ denotes the sigmoid function, $f^{3 \times 3}$ convolution filter size. These attention maps after sigmoid activation has values ranging from 0 to 1, which are essentially the weighted spatial maps that are multiplied with the original feature map as per Eq. (7) to get the refined spatial attentive feature map.

The channel and spatial attention blocks are placed sequentially in the model while training because of their better performance over the parallel arrangement. Hence the model can learn "what" and "where" to look in the image thereby giving the best performance.

SENET and ECANET. The second attention module is the Squeeze-and-Excitation channel attention module (**SENET**). This channel attention is similar to the CBAM channel attention module, where the feature map F of dimension $C \times H \times W$ is reduced to $C \times 1 \times 1$ but using only the global average pooling across the spatial axis, generating the weighted attention map, whereas the CBAM uses both global average pooling and global max pooling.

The third attention module is the Efficient Channel Attention Network (ECANET). According to the authors, this is an improvement over SENET attention where it solves the problem of dependent cross-channel interaction and dimensionality reduction. The SENET learns the channel weights not in a isolated way, but with respect to other channels. The ECANET solves this by using adaptive local neighborhood size and performs the cross channel interaction with respect to all other channels within this neighborhood. The first step to create the feature descriptor is similar to the SENET where the global max pooling is used to reduce the dimension of the feature map from $C \times H \times W$ is reduced to $C \times 1 \times 1$. It is then subjected to an adaptive kernel which slides over this space with the kernel size describing the neighborhood size. It is a 1D convolutional whose kernel size k is adaptive to the global channel space C and determined by the following formula:

$$k = \psi(C) = \left| \frac{\log_2(C)}{\gamma} + \frac{b}{\gamma} \right|_{odd} \tag{10}$$

where |t|odd indicates the nearest odd number of t. According to the authors, we set γ and b to 2 and 1 respectively. Thus, essentially k provides the size of the local neighborhood space which will be used to capture cross-channel interaction while mapping the per-channel attention weights. This function $\psi(C)$ essentially approximates the closest odd number as the kernel size for the 1D convolutional.

Hence with this mapping ψ, high dimensional channels have longer range interaction while low-dimensional ones undergo shorter range interaction by using a non-linear mapping. The next steps are similar to ECANET where the descriptors are passed through sigmoid activation to get the final channel attention map which is later multiplied with the original feature map to get the refined feature map.

3 Experiments

3.1 Training

Dataset. We evaluate the performance on the Kaggle face keypoints dataset which consists of 15 keypoints for each sample representing the facial parts. The train and test set consists of 7049 and 1783 samples respectively with the size of $96 \times 96 \times 1$ but, some of the target keypoint positions are missing. We only consider the samples where all the keypoint information is present. So a total of 2140 samples were used for training with a 10% validation set.

Training. The data augmentation includes random rotation ($[-10°, 10°]$), random scale ($[0.8, 1.2]$) and random shift ($[-5, 5]$) and random flipping. The augmentation is limited for a small change since the images are pre-cropped. Too much augmentation will cause the model to degrade its performance. We use the Adam optimizer [29] over SGD because of better results. The batch size is set to 16. The base learning rate of $1e^{-3}$, it is dropped at the linear decay rate of $1e^{-1}$ if the validation loss has no further improvements for 5 epochs and the training is stopped if the validation loss has no further improvements for 10 epochs (patience = 10). The PC configuration is Intel® Core™ i7–9700 CPU @ 3.00 GHz $\times$ 8 cores and NVIDIA GeForce RTX 3060 Ti GPU.

The training is performed on three different attention-based FCN and UNET architectures with three methods of labeling. We experiment on training various networks by placing the attention modules in each block of the down-sampling and up-sampling layers, end of the down-sampling and up-sampling layers. We further improve the model performance by adding spatial attention blocks in series with the SENET and ECANET channel attention module. It was found that the results differ for various attention mechanisms with different methods of labeling. Finally, we choose the best network, best attention modules and the best placement position for each labeling method.

The test set is used to compute the heatmap and visualize the pixel-wise keypoints of the original, flipped images and rotated images. The keypoints detection results were satisfactory. The quantitative results of the validation set are discussed in the next section.

3.2 Qualitative Results

Visualizing filter activations. We also provide the qualitative results of the model by visualizing the intermediate filter maps before and after using the attention modules. The filter activations illustrate how the attention mechanism improves the model performance by learning where and what to look in the image more effectively. Intermediate activations are the feature maps or output by various convolution and pooling layers in a network. Each channel encodes relatively independent features, so we plot each channel activation as a 2D image (Fig. 3).

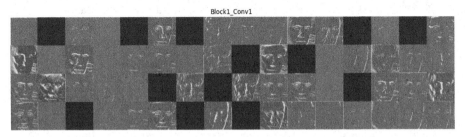

Fig. 3. Visualization of intermediate filter responses without Attention

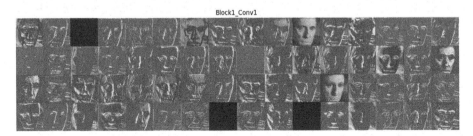

Fig. 4. Visualization of intermediate filter responses with CBAM Attention

From the illustrated Figs. 4, 5, and 6, it is evident that using the attention blocks early in the convolution block improves the kernel performance of the initial stages. From Fig. 4, CBAM can be viewed as the best response here because it contains both channel and spatial attention. It can be seen that many filters are idle when no attention is used. We then rank ECANET followed by SENET. However, during implementation, we combine the spatial attention block along with SENET and ECANET to give better performance.

Fig. 5. Visualization of intermediate filter responses with SENET Attention

Fig. 6. Visualization of intermediate filter responses with ECANET Attention

Keypoint Coordinate Decoding. We visualize the best results after using the attention modules in this section. In order to find the keypoints from the predicted heatmaps/confidence maps, we decode the individual maps by taking the argmax or maximum pixel from the given mask in case of heatmap regression. Another method is finding the center pixel from the individual binary/class mask by taking the mean of active mask data points. This may be useful in cases where there are many pixels with similar probability/intensity close to each other.

Fig. 7. Keypoint decoded from the heatmap regression

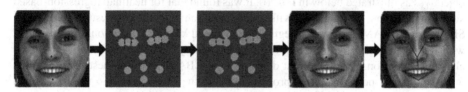

Fig. 8. Keypoints decoded from the binary segmentation

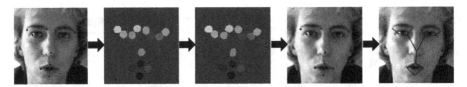

Fig. 9. Keypoints decoded from the multi-class segmentation

Figures 7, 8, and 9 illustrates the results of facial keypoint detection using heatmap regression, binary segmentation and multiclass segmentation respectively. The first image illustrates the input keypoint coordinates followed by a generated label followed by the model output prediction followed by output keypoint coordinate decoding followed by the skeleton mapping. The heatmaps/ confidence maps are summed over all the 15 channel axis for visualization. It is essentially a group of individual masks predicted.

3.3 Quantitative Results

PCK. We use the Percentage of Correct Keypoints (PCK) as the evaluation metric to compare the performance of various models. The detected joint is considered correct if the distance between the predicted and the true joint is within a certain threshold value. The Euclidian distance is calculated between the predicted and ground truth keypoint position and averaged for all the 15 keypoints and then the mean is taken over the entire validation set. The PCK scores for various labeling schemes and attention modules are presented in Table 1. In our experiments, we found that the ECANET channel attention along with spatial attention gives the best PCK accuracy for heatmap regression and keypoint regression using binary class segmentation. And CBAM attention gives the best PCK accuracy for keypoint regression using multi-class segmentation. The (enc) and (dec) denote the position of the attention block whether it is placed at the encoder/down-sampling layers or after the decoder/up-sampling layers. We do not place the attention block in between the decoder layers since it gives poor results. It can be seen from the scores that the ECANET with spatial attention works well when placed after the up-sampling layers for gaussian heatmap regression and with binary class segmentation. In the case of multiclass segmentation, the CBAM attention gives better results when placed in the encoder part.

Since the UNET model gives better results than the FCN model, we evaluate the PCK scores over a range of thresholds with various attention mechanisms for various model objectives as illustrated below in Fig. 10. It was found that for heatmap regression-based keypoint detection, the ECANET with spatial attention gives the best results followed by SENET and CBAM. For binary segmentation-based keypoint detection, the ECANET with spatial attention gives the best results followed by CBAM and SENET. For multi-class segmentation-based keypoint detection, the CBAM gives the best results. There is still room for performance improvement since the PCK scores go to 100% when the pixel distance threshold is around 3.0. The goal of the paper is to study the model performance with various labeling schemes and find the best attention mechanism for the corresponding schemes.

Table 1. PCK scores for various labeling schemes and attention modules.

Labeling method	Model	Attention module	PCK@0.8
Gaussian heatmap	FCN	None	0.4541
		CBAM (enc)	0.3137
		SENET (enc)	0.4483
		ECANET + spatial attention (dec)	**0.5887**
	UNET	None	0.4153
		CBAM (dec)	0.5240
		SENET + spatial attention (dec)	0.6522
		ECANET + spatial attention (dec)	**0.6615**
Binary class-wise masks	FCN	None	0.3317
		CBAM (dec)	0.4935
		SENET + spatial attention (dec)	0.3974
		ECANET + spatial attention (dec)	**0.5756**
	UNET	None	0.4926
		CBAM (dec)	0.5605
		SENET + spatial attention (enc)	0.5355
		ECANET + spatial attention (dec)	**0.6826**
Multi-class masks	FCN	None	0.4929
		CBAM (enc)	**0.6006**
		SENET + spatial attention (enc)	0.5189
		ECANET + spatial attention (enc)	0.5105
	UNET	None	0.5625
		CBAM (enc)	**0.6153**
		SENET + spatial attention (enc)	0.4948
		ECANET + spatial attention (enc)	0.4826

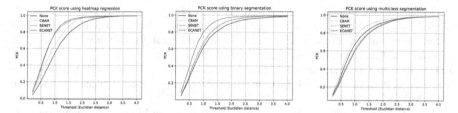

Fig. 10. Performance of Attention mechanism for various regression tasks.

IOU/Dice Score. We also use the Inter Section Over Union (IoU) and Dice scores to evaluate the segmentation scores of the binary and multiclass confidence maps predicted. Figure 11 illustrates the bar graph with segmentation scores for various attention modules. The CBAM attention seems to provide the best quality of the segmentation maps.

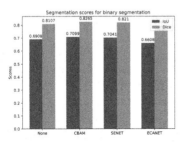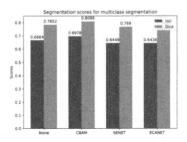

Fig. 11. Performance of Attention mechanism for segmentation task.

4 Conclusion

In this paper, we address the problem of poor keypoint localization of low-resolution images and focus on improving the segmentation models using various attention mechanisms for keypoint detection. The proposed attention-based keypoint regression improves the confidence map predictions and keypoint localization quality. Extensive experiments are conducted on the facial keypoint dataset with various labeling schemes and attention mechanisms. As a result, we found that the binary class labeling scheme with the ECANET attention module gives the best results for facial keypoint detection with the slightest difference followed by the heatmap regression. Although heatmap regression is much stronger, we can train the model quicker with segmentation tasks rather than the slower heatmap regression.

References

1. Chen, Y., Shen, C., Wei, X.-S., Liu, L., Yang, J.: Adversarial posenet: a structure-aware convolutional network for human pose estimation. In: Proceedings of the IEEE International Conference on Computer Vision, pp. 1212–1221 (2017)
2. He, Y., Zhu, C., Wang, J., Savvides, M., Zhang., X.: Bounding box regression with uncertainty for accurate object detection. In: Proceedings of the IEEE/CVF Conference on Computer Vision and Pattern Recognition, pp. 2888–2897 (2019)
3. Dou, P., Shah, S.K., Kakadiaris, I.A.: End-to-end 3D face reconstruction with deep neural networks. In: Proceedings of the IEEE Conference on Computer Vision and Pattern Recognition, pp. 5908–5917 (2017)
4. Bulat, A., Tzimiropoulos, G.: How far are we from solving the 2d and 3d face alignment problem? (and a dataset of 230,000 3d facial landmarks). In: Proceedings of the IEEE International Conference on Computer Vision, pp. 1021–1030 (2017)

5. Sun, K., Xiao, B., Liu, D., Wang, J.: Deep high-resolution representation learning for human pose estimation. In: Proceedings of the IEEE/CVF Conference on Computer Vision and Pattern Recognition, pp. 5693–5703 (2019)

6. Tompson, J.J., Jain, A., LeCun, Y., Bregler, C.: Joint training of a convolutional network and a graphical model for human pose estimation. Adv. Neural Inf. Process. Syst. **27**, 1799–1807 (2014)

7. Long, J., Shelhamer, E., Darrell, T.: Fully convolutional networks for semantic segmentation. In: Proceedings of the IEEE Conference on Computer Vision and Pattern Recognition, pp. 3431–3440 (2015)

8. Ronneberger, O., Fischer, P., Brox, T.: U-net: convolutional networks for biomedical image segmentation. In: Navab, N., Hornegger, J., Wells, W.M., Frangi, A.F. (eds.) MICCAI 2015. LNCS, vol. 9351, pp. 234–241. Springer, Cham (2015). https://doi.org/10.1007/978-3-319-24574-4_28

9. Cao, X., Wei, Y., Wen, F., Sun, J.: Face alignment by explicit shape regression. Int. J. Comput. Vision **107**(2), 177–190 (2014)

10. Kowalski, M., Naruniec, J., Trzcinski, T.: Deep alignment network: a convolutional neural network for robust face alignment. In: Proceedings of the IEEE Conference on Computer Vision and Pattern Recognition Workshops, pp. 88–97 (2017)

11. Sinha, A., Choi, C., Ramani, K.: Deephand: robust hand pose estimation by completing a matrix imputed with deep features. In: Proceedings of the IEEE Conference on Computer Vision and Pattern Recognition, pp. 4150–4158 (2016)

12. Sekii, T.: Pose proposal networks. In: Ferrari, V., Hebert, M., Sminchisescu, C., Weiss, Y. (eds.) ECCV 2018. LNCS, vol. 11217, pp. 350–366. Springer, Cham (2018). https://doi.org/10.1007/978-3-030-01261-8_21

13. Sun, X., Xiao, B., Wei, F., Liang, S., Wei, Y.: Integral human pose regression. In: Ferrari, V., Hebert, M., Sminchisescu, C., Weiss, Y. (eds.) ECCV 2018. LNCS, vol. 11210, pp. 536–553. Springer, Cham (2018). https://doi.org/10.1007/978-3-030-01231-1_33

14. Carreira, J., Agrawal, P., Fragkiadaki, K., Malik, J.: Human pose estimation with iterative error feedback. In: Proceedings of the IEEE Conference on Computer Vision and Pattern Recognition, pp. 4733–4742 (2016)

15. Belagiannis, V., Zisserman, A.: Recurrent human pose estimation. In: 2017 12th IEEE International Conference on Automatic Face and Gesture Recognition (FG 2017), pp. 468–475. IEEE (2017)

16. Bulat, A., Tzimiropulos, G.: Two-stage convolutional part heatmap regression for the 1st 3d face alignment in the wild (3dfaw) challenge. In: Hua, G., Jegou, H. (eds.) Computer Vision – ECCV 2016 Workshops. LNCS, vol. 9914, pp. 616–624. Springer, Cham (2016). https://doi.org/10.1007/978-3-319-48881-3_43

17. Zhang, K., Zhang, Z., Li, Z., Qiao, Y.: Joint face detection and alignment using multitask cascaded convolutional networks. IEEE Signal Process. Lett. **23**(10), 1499–1503 (2016)

18. Ranjan, R., Patel, V.M., Chellappa, R.: Hyperface: a deep multi-task learning framework for face detection, landmark localization, pose estimation, and gender recognition. IEEE Trans. Pattern Anal. Mach. Intell. **41**(1), 121–135 (2017)

19. Iqbal, U., Molchanov, P., Breuel, T., Gall, J., Kautz, J.: Hand pose estimation via latent 2.5 d heatmap regression. In: Proceedings of the European Conference on Computer Vision (ECCV), pp. 118–134 (2018)

20. Feng, Z.-H., Kittler, J., Awais, M., Huber, P., Wu, X.-J.: Wing loss for robust facial landmark localisation with convolutional neural networks. In: Proceedings of the IEEE Conference on Computer Vision and Pattern Recognition, pp. 2235–2245 (2018)

21. Merget, D., Rock, M., Rigoll, G.: Robust facial landmark detection via a fully-convolutional local-global context network. In: Proceedings of the IEEE Conference on Computer Vision and Pattern Recognition, pp. 781–790 (2018)

22. Wei, S.-E., Ramakrishna, V., Kanade, T., Sheikh, Y.: Convolutional pose machines. In: Proceedings of the IEEE Conference on Computer Vision and Pattern Recognition, pp. 4724–4732 (2016)

23. Cao, Z., Simon, T., Wei, S.-E., Sheikh, Y.: Realtime multi-person 2d pose estimation using part affinity fields. In: Proceedings of the IEEE Conference on Computer Vision and Pattern Recognition, pp. 7291–7299 (2017)

24. Yang, J., Ren, P., Zhang, D., Chen, D., Wen, F., Li, H., Hua, G.: Neural aggregation network for video face recognition. In: Proceedings of the IEEE Conference on Computer Vision and Pattern Recognition, pp. 4362–4371 (2017)

25. Nerwell, A., Yang, K., Jia, D.: Stacked hourglass networks for human pose estimation. In: Leibei, B., Matas, J., Nicu, S., Welling, M. (eds.) Computer Vision – ECCV 2016. LNCS, vol. 9912, pp. 483–499. Springer, Cham (2016). https://doi.org/10.1007/978-3-319-46484-8_29

26. Masi, I., Rawls, S., Medioni, G., Natarajan, P.: Pose-aware face recognition in the wild. In: Proceedings of the IEEE Conference on Computer Vision and Pattern Recognition, pp. 4838–4846 (2016)

27. Woo, S., Park, J., Lee, J.-Y., Kweon, I.S.: CBAM: convolutional block attention module. In: Ferrari, V., Hebert, M., Sminchisescu, C., Weiss, Y. (eds.) Computer Vision – ECCV 2018. LNCS, vol. 11211, pp. 3–19. Springer, Cham (2018). https://doi.org/10.1007/978-3-030-01234-2_1

28. Hu, J., Shen, L., Sun, G.: Squeeze-and-excitation networks. In: Proceedings of the IEEE Conference on Computer Vision and Pattern Recognition, pp. 7132–7141 (2018)

29. Wang, Q., Wu, B., Zhu, P., Li, P., Zuo, W., Hu, Q.: ECA-Net: efficient channel attention for deep convolutional neural networks. In: 2020 IEEE/CVF Conference on Computer Vision and Pattern Recognition (CVPR), pp. 11531–11539 (2020)

Video Object Segmentation Based on Guided Feature Transfer Learning

Mustansar Fiaz[1] , Arif Mahmood[2], Sehar Shahzad Farooq[3], Kamran Ali[4],
Muhammad Shaheryar[3], and Soon Ki Jung[3(✉)]

[1] Department of Computer Vision, Mohamed bin Zayed University of Artificial
Intelligence, Abu Dhabi, UAE
mustansar.fiaz@mbzuai.ac.ae
[2] Department of Computer Science, Information Technology University,
Lahore, Pakistan
arif.mahmood@itu.edu.pk
[3] School of Computer Science and Engineering, Kyungpook National University,
Daegu, Republic of Korea
skjung@knu.ac.kr
[4] Department of Computer Science, University of Central Florida, Orland, USA
kamran@knights.ucf.edu

Abstract. Video Object Segmentation (VOS) is a fundamental task
with many real-world computer vision applications and challenging due
to available distractors and background clutter. Many existing online
learning approaches have limited practical significance because of high
computational cost required to fine-tune network parameters. Moreover,
matching based and propagation approaches are computationally efficient but may suffer from degraded performance in cluttered backgrounds
and object drifts. In order to handle these issues, we propose an offline
end-to-end model to learn guided feature transfer for VOS. We introduce guided feature modulation based on target mask to capture the
video context information and a generative appearance model is used to
provide cues for both the target and the background. Proposed guided
feature modulation system learns the target semantic information based
on modulation activations. Generative appearance model learns the probability of a pixel to be target or background. In addition, low-resolution
features from deeper networks may not capture the global contextual
information and may reduce the performance during feature refinement.
Therefore, we also propose a guided pooled decoder to learn the global as
well as local context information for better feature refinement. Evaluation
over two VOS benchmark datasets including DAVIS2016 and DAVIS2017
have shown excellent performance of the proposed framework compared
to more than 20 existing state-of-the-art methods.

Keywords: Video Object Segmentation · Guided Feature
Modulation · Generative appearance model · Guided Pooled Decoder

K. Sumi et al. (Eds.): IW-FCV 2022, CCIS 1578, pp. 197–210, 2022.
https://doi.org/10.1007/978-3-031-06381-7_14

1   Introduction

Video Object Segmentation (VOS) aims to segment regions of interest throughout a sequence of frames. VOS plays an important role in understanding the visual contents of a video and for visual object tracking [12–14,16,34]. In this paper, we focus on semi-supervised VOS also known as one-shot learning where target mask is provided in the first frame of a sequence and model has to segment the subsequent frames [32]. VOS is a challenging problem due to various aspects such as occlusion, background clutter, and object appearance variations.

Various VOS algorithms have been proposed to tackle the aforementioned challenges using Online Learning (OL) by fine-tuning the model parameters trained on initial image-mask pair. This strategy has limited real-world applications due to high computational cost [1,2,39]. Moreover, these algorithms do not hold end-to-end segmentation property, since online model update process is separated from offline learning. On the contrary, template matching or propagation approaches are faster but exhibit sub-optimal VOS accuracy. Template matching approaches violate the temporal consistency of the target object due to appearance variations in the sequence which leads to mismatching problem [6,44]. The propagation approaches which fit the target in the current frame from previous frame, may suffer drift problem due to fast motion and occlusion [7,8,31,42,46]. Most propagation approaches either do not satisfy discriminative feature learning or these are too simple to achieve the objective. Also most of the VOS approaches follow encoder-decoder architecture where encoder part encodes the target representation using a series of convolutional layers which may dilute the contextual information. While the decoder fuses different layers to obtain high-level features from coarse-level features. During features refinement, VOS methods either utilizes convolution layers or up-sampling layers therefore these methods may loose the contextual information required for the VOS task. In short, more efficient algorithms with better trade-off between speed and accuracy for VOS task are still required.

In the current work, we present an efficient network architecture that benefits from guided feature transfer learning by following encoder-decoder architecture. We introduce a guided feature modulation approach to assist a generative appearance model to learn the target information. Our guided feature modulation approach captures the contextual information by leveraging from the conditional feature normalization and modulates using activations from the object mask. Generative appearance module predicts the foreground and background probabilities in a single forward pass. A class-conditional Gaussian Mixture Model (GMM) is employed to infer posterior class probabilities. The generative appearance model gives strong cues for target and background, therefore provides useful information for discriminative learning to avoid online learning. In contrast to the existing approaches, proposed algorithm does not require first frame fine-tuning. Furthermore, instead of utilizing conventional decoder during feature refinement, we introduce a guided pooled decoder which learns the global as well as local context information during the generation of fine-grained features from the coarse features. Proposed video segmentation framework is fully differentiable thus withholds the end-to-end learning capabilities. Experimental results on two challenging benchmark datasets including DAVIS2016 and DAVIS2017 have shown excellent performance of the proposed VOS algorithm compared the current state-of-the-art methods.

2   Related Work

Recently, video object segmentation task has surged its popularity in the community and variety of VOS methods have been proposed. Caelles et al. [2] proposed OSVOS which employs pre-trained CNN model and fine-tune it on the initial object mask of a video. This work was extended with online learning [29] and integrating instance-level semantic segmentation [39]. Ci et al. [9] extended their work by exploiting location specific embedding. Bao et al. [1] included the motion information via optical flow with model fine-tuning. Although these approaches have shown satisfactory performance but have critical drawback. These methods learn object information from the initial frame and perform extensive model update with stochastic gradient descent. Such approaches may suffer over-fitting problem due to extensive fine-tuning [23]. This phenomena results in significant delay in time before the tracking start, limiting its practical usage.

In order to avoid fine-tuning at initial frame, several VOS methods have been proposed based on propagation and matching. MaskTrack [31] handles VOS problem by utilizing image-mask pair from previous frame as input. Fiaz et al. [15,17] used guided features to exploit contextual information for video object segmentation. Optical flow is employed to guide in many VOS methods [22,36], but failed to distinguish arbitrary objects from motionless background. Li et al. [25] introduced DyeNet that uses online learning to boost the performance by adding instance re-identification and temporal propagation. Although DyeNet presents good performance but it is not casual and prediction depends on future frames. Xu et al. [45] utilizes convolutional LSTM for segmentation. Several VOS methods [6,19,23] construct lightweight generative models from initial target masks instead of fine-tuning from first frame. In this work, we efficiently utilize propagation strategy to handle mismatching and drift problem. Our guided feature modulation and generative appearance model learns appearance variations in forward pass. Furthermore, we also argue about better feature refinement from coarse-level to fine-grained features. Tian et al. [35] propose data-dependent upsampling technique during bottom-up stage for pixelwise segmentation. On the contrary, our approach learns global and local context information during feature refinement from lower-resolution feature maps.

3   Proposed Method

We propose a video object segmentation method to discriminate the target from the background in one-shot learning manner without fine-tuning. Our segmentation framework is composed of feature extractor, Guided Feature Modulation (GFM) module, Generative Appearance Module (GAM), merge module, and

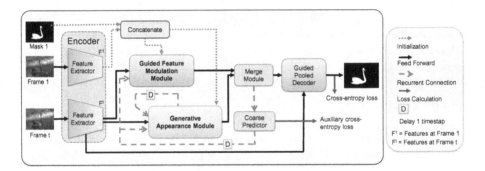

Fig. 1. The illustration of proposed video object segmentation framework. At initialization stage, features from the first frame and mask are forwarded to Guided Feature Modulation (GFM) module and Generative Appearance Module (GAM). During inference, features from the current frame are forwarded to GFM and GAM. The output from GFM and GAM is combined in merge module and passed to coarse predictor to estimate the coarse segmentation encoding. This coarse encoding is feeded back to GFM and GAM for next frame segmentation estimation. The merge module output with shallow features are forwarded to Guided Pooled Decoded (GPD) for refinement and to produce final segmentation result.

Guided Pooled Decoder (GPD) as shown in Fig. 1. Input image features are extracted using ResNet and propagated to GFM and GAM modules. The outputs from these modules are merged using a Merge module which forwards these features to a coarse predictor to construct a coarse segmentation mask which is then handed to GAM and GFM for the next frame segmentation. The merge module output is also forwarded to GPD module with shallow features in order to estimate a refined object segmentation mask. These components are explained below in more detail.

3.1   Guided Feature Modulation Module (GFM)

The objective of GFM is to learn video content in latent space. On the contrary to [17] which exploits features into key-value pair maps, the GFM learns the target and background discrimination in a modulation activation manner. The proposed module learns target context information such that it preserves semantic information. GFM is inspired from Conditional Batch Normalization (CBN) [10,20] which produces scale and bias for each layer to control the behavior of the network. Each CBN layer can be formulated as:

$$Z_c = \alpha_c \frac{X_c - \mu_{X_c}}{\sigma_{X_c}} + \beta_c, \tag{1}$$

where Z_c and X_c denotes the output and input feature maps, while α_c and β_c are the scale and bias parameters to control the network behaviour are learned from input data, and c represents the channel. The parameters μ_{X_c} and σ_{X_c} are the mean and variance of X_c.

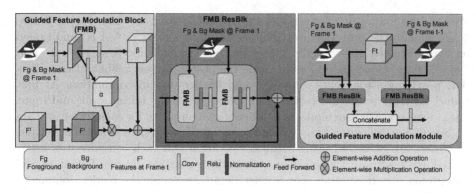

Fig. 2. The illustration of Guided Feature Modulation (GRM) module on right, guided Feature Modulation Block (FMB) on left, and FMB Residual Block (FMB ResBlk) in middle.

We employ segmentation mask $m \in \mathcal{R}^{hw}$ to compute the scale $\alpha(m)$ and bias $\beta(m)$ parameters, where $m \in [0,1]$ represents the background and the target labels, and h and w denote the height and width. Suppose $X \in \mathcal{R}^{k,h,w}$ be an input feature extracted from an encoder. The $x^{k,i,j}$ be (k,i,j)-th feature element, where $k \leq c$ denotes the channel number, and $i \leq h$ and $j \leq w$ show the spatial location in the feature map. Our guided Feature Modulation Block (FMB) yields guided semantic feature map $Z^{k,i,j}$ as:

$$Z^{k,i,j} = \alpha^{k,i,j}(m)\frac{X^{k,i,j} - \mu^k}{\sigma^k} + \beta^{k,i,j}(m), \qquad (2)$$

where μ^k and σ^k represent the mean and standard deviation

$$\mu^k = \frac{1}{hw}\sum_h\sum_w x_{k,i,j},$$

$$\sigma^k = \frac{1}{hw}\sum_h\sum_w (x_{k,i,j} - \mu^k)^2. \qquad (3)$$

The mask m contains both foreground and background labels as guidance to encode semantic feature information. We utilize two convolutional network layers to estimate α_m and β_m parameters as shown in Fig. 2 (left). In practice we compute Instance Normalization [30] and leaky Relu activation function [28] over input feature map and then feed to modulation. Two FMB are used in each residual block FMB Resblk as shown in Fig. 2 (middle). At frame t, we compute guided feature maps from previously estimated mask and the first frame mask. Finally, we merge guided features from the first frame F^1 and the current frame F^t, and feed to conv layer for propagation as shown in Fig. 2 (right).

3.2 Generative Appearance Module (GAM)

The features extracted from ResNet (Fig. 1) are sub-optimal for segmentation. Therefore, soft spatial constraints are required for accurate segmentation.

We used generative mixture model that is inhereted from [23]. The objective is to estimate the posterior probabilities for input images. GAM is conditioned on class variables to learn the target and background appearances in a deep feature space. Generative module yields the posterior class probabilities as output, providing strong cues for target and background discrimination. At first frame, generative mixture model is initialized from the initial mask and input image features. Mixture model components are computed for each frame and are updated for every coming frame based on estimated soft class labels. The output posteriors are predicted using softmax operation and each component is interpreted as a discriminative mask encoding which gives strong cues for target and background discrimination. For further details, we refer the reader Johnander et al. [23].

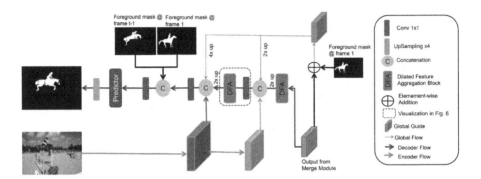

Fig. 3. The architecture of the proposed Guided Pooled Decoder (GPD). To gain refined high-resolution features, low-resolution features fused with global guide are exploited Dilated Feature Aggregation (DFA). During feature refinement, foreground maps of first frame and previous frames are also merged. Final predictions are performed by forwarding the features to a predictor.

3.3   Guided Pooled Decoder

In the encoder-decoder architecture, the encoder is responsible to generate low-resolution feature maps from a raw input image. While the decoder restores the output with the same resolution by pixel-wise estimation from encoded low-resolution features. In a light-weight decoder, a series of convolutional layers are used to generate high-resolution feature maps, and it may loose contextual information due to convolution and pooling operations. Another approach is to use bilinear up-sampling to produce the desired pixel-wise output. This approach is also not suitable because of data dependence and does not consider the accurate amount of correlation during the pixel-wise prediction. Thus, an efficient decoder is required to maintain the saliency of the target object during refinement.

In order to tackle these limitations in a decoder, similar to [15,17], we propose a Guided Pooled Decoder (GPD) which is built bottom-up pathway during refinement as shown in Fig. 3. The aim of GPD is to explicitly notice the presence of salient object features at different layers and preserve the global target information from the input feature maps during refinement. We intend to provide a global guidance information throughout the feature refinement process from coarse-level to fine-grained level. For that, we introduce global guide along with a global flow to deliver the high-level semantic information at different layers (as illustrated in Fig. 3). Moreover, similar to [4,5], we aggregate features at different scales. We introduce a Dilated Feature Aggregation (DFA) module that merges the features seamlessly as shown in Fig. 4. Given a feature map, our DFA first produces features from different receptive fields. Instead of utilizing features from lower-layers, we used different dilation rates. After that, features are down-sampled with different down-sampling rates. The down-sampled features are then merged together after up-sampling, followed by a convolution layer. Proposed DFA benefits from the following factors: (1) enlarges the receptive field, (2) views the local context information at different scales, and (3) reduces the aliasing effect due to bilinear up-sampling [17]. In order to verify the effectiveness of the proposed GPD. We visualize the features with and without proposed DFA in Fig. 5.

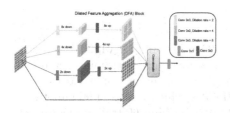

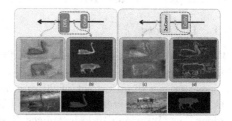

Fig. 4. Dilated Feature Aggregation (DFA) block.

Fig. 5. The illustration of effect of DFA using feature visualization.

3.4 Video Object Segmentation Architecture

We use ResNet101 [18] as backbone feature extractor which is pre-trained over ImageNet dataset. Multi-scale features are extracted from the last three blocks. The GFM module encodes the target and background information from the first frame features, given initial ground-truth mask, a feature map extracted at current frame, and an estimated mask at previous $(t-1)$ frame. The GAM returns the posterior probabilities for the target and the background. The outputs from GFM and GAM are merged with two convolutional layers in the merge module. We adopt [23] approach to estimate the coarse segmentation mask from the merge module output using coarse predictor which is further used by GFM and GAM for the next frame mask estimation. The merge module output along with shallow features are forwarded to GPD module to produce segmentation masks.

For multiple objects, we proceed with one object at a time and estimate the final segmentation mask by combining the segmentation results using soft-max aggregation [44].

3.5   Network Training Details

We implemented the proposed framework in PyTorch by utilizing ResNet101 [18] as backbone feature extractor, pre-trained on ImageNet [11] benchmark for object classification task. The model is end-to-end trainable based on a single ground-truth mask from the first frame and $n-th$ frame from a sequence. The model has to estimate the segmentation mask for the $n-th$ frame. We set input image size to 480×864 which are normalized by computing the mean and the standard deviation. We set batch size of 2 with 8 frames from a video. During training, we apply cross-entropy loss function to compute the segmentation loss and auxiliary loss for coarse segmentation. We optimize our model for 200 epochs using Adam optimizer [24] by adding these losses. The initial learning rate is 10^{-2} and it decreases exponentially till 10^{-5} with weight decay 10^{-5}.

4   Experiments and Evaluations

4.1   Datasets

We evaluate proposed algorithm over DAVIS2016 [32] and DAVIS2017 [33] validation sets. DAVIS2016 consists of 50 videos including a training set of 30 videos and a validation set of 20 unique single instance annotated videos. The DAVIS2017 is an extended version of DAVIS2016 which has total 90 annotated videos containing multiple instances. The DAVIS2017 has 60 training videos set while 30 videos for validation, each video contains 25 to 100 frames, and has one or more annotated objects. We adopted Jaccard index J (also known as mean intersection-over-union (mIoU)) and contour accuracy F to validate the proposed method [32]. We also compute the mean of J and F as $J\&F$.

4.2   Comparison Methods

We compared our algorithm with other single object VOS with 8 Online Learning (OL) methods [1,2,6,7,29,31,39]. We also compare our method with 15 other offline VOS methods including [3,8,21,23,27,38,40,41,43,44,46–49].

DAVIS-2016: We present the comparison over DAVIS2016 in Table 1 with OL and offline VOS methods. On single object segmentation, our approach beats other OL methods such as OnAVOS, OSVOS-S, and CINM in terms of J, F and $J\&F$. Due to online learning, segmentation speed is much slower than ours. Compared with offline VOS methods, our method showed excellent results. We notice

Table 1. Quantitative analysis of VOS methods over DAVIS2016. The speed is compared with the SOTA reported in their papers.

Method	OL	J&F (%)	F (%)	J (%)	Speed
OnAVOS [39]	Yes	85.5	84.9	86.1	13 s
OSVOS-S [29]	Yes	86.6	87.5	85.6	4.5 s
SFL [7]	Yes	-	-	84.7	7.9 s
CINM [1]	Yes	84.2	85.0	83.4	>30 s
MSK [31]	Yes	75.4	760	74.8	12 s
OSVOS [2]	Yes	80.2	80.6	79.8	9 s
PML [6]	Yes	77.4	79.3	75.5	0.28 s
RGMP [44]	No	79.0	79.7	78.4	0.14 s
RGMP* [44]	No	81.8	82.0	81.5	0.14 s
FAVOS [8]	No	81.8	79.5	82.4	0.6 s
FaSTGAN [3]	No	81.9	83.5	80.2	0.03
VPN [21]	No	67.9	65.5	70.2	0.63
AGAME [23]	No	82.1	82.2	82.0	0.07 s
RANet [43]	No	85.5	85.4	85.5	0.03
SiamMask [41]	No	70.0	67.8	71.7	0.06 s
BoLTVOS [40]	No	71.9	75.4	68.5	0.72 s
FEELVOS [38]	No	81.7	82.2	81.1	0.51 s
AD-Net [47]	No	81.1	80.5	81.7	-
MTN [49]	No	76.05	76.2	75.9	0.027 s
D3S [27]	No	74.0	72.6	75.4	0.04 s
Ours	No	**87.2**	**87.5**	**86.8**	0.08 s

that our approach also showed outstanding performance and ranked top compared to other offline methods for single object segmentation. Although RANet, SiamMask, D3S, FaSTGAN, FAVOS, AGAME, and MTN are faster compared to our VOS method, our method leads in objective metrics, e.g., J is 86.8%, F is 87.55% and $J\&F$ is 87.2%.

DAVIS2017: We evaluate proposed algorithm over multiple object segmentation dataset DAVIS2017 validation set which comprises of 30 videos with 61 different objects, thus it has 2 objects per video on average. This dataset is very challenging due to similar objects in a video. Thus, it makes difficult to obtain accurate segmentation results compared to single object segmentation as shown in Table 2. The methods OnAVOS [39], OSVOS-S [29], CINM [1], MSK [31], and OSVOS [2] employ fine-tuning to improve performance. FAVOS [8] uses part-based tracker to track and segment the parts. Methods RVOS [37], RANet [43], AGAME [23], OSMN [46], and RGMP [44] use mask propagation. Our algorithm has achieved excellent performance compared to the other VOS methods in terms of $J = 68.3\%$, $F = 73.5\%$, and $J\&F = 70.9\%$. AGAME relies on appearance module and achieved $J = 67.2\%$, while RANet computes the correlation ranks and obtained $J = 63.2\%$. The RGMP simply relies on concatenating image features from the first frame and secured $J\&F = 66.7\%$. While proposed method depends upon mask guided feature map and guided pooled decoder. Therefore, achieves best $J = 68.3\%$. Table 2 shows that our method has outperformed other VOS methods over multiple object segmentation task.

Table 2. Quantitative analysis of VOS methods over DAVIS2017. RGMP* trained on YouTube-VOS benchmark.

Method	OL	J&F (%)	F (%)	J (%)
OnAVOS [39]	Yes	65.4	69.1	61.6
OSVOS-S [29]	Yes	68.0	71.3	64.7
CINM [1]	Yes	67.5	70.5	64.5
MSK [31]	Yes	46.1	47.6	44.6
OSVOS [2]	Yes	60.3	63.9	56.6
RGMP [44]	No	66.7	68.6	64.8
RGMP* [44]	No	56.2	59.6	52.8
FAVOS [8]	No	58.2	61.8	54.6
RVOS [37]	No	60.6	63.6	57.5
AGSS-VOS [26]	No	66.6	69.8	63.4
AGAME [23]	No	70.0	72.7	67.2
RANet [43]	No	65.7	68.2	63.2
SiamMask [41]	No	55.8	58.5	54.3
OSMN [46]	No	54.8	57.1	52.5
FaSTGAN [3]	No	60.2	63.4	57.6
PTSNet [48]	No	68.3	70.5	66.1
MTN [49]	No	54.2	59.0	49.4
D3S [27]	No	60.8	63.8	57.8
Ours	No	**70.9**	**73.5**	**68.3**

4.3   Qualitative Analysis

We present the qualitative results on videos from DAVIS2017 to compare our approach with recent methods including [23,37,43]. For a fair comparison, we selected RVOS [37] trained for semi-supervised object segmentation. In Fig. 6, we note that our approach segmented target object better compared to the other approaches.

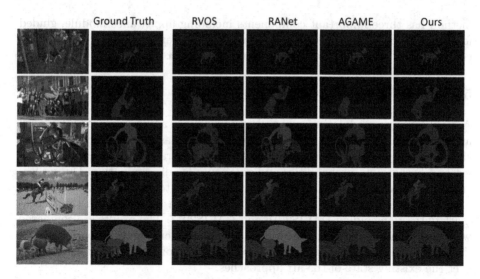

Fig. 6. Qualitative results on various videos from DAVIS2017. Compared to recent methods including RVOS [37], RANet [43], and AGAME [23], proposed approach segmented the target object quite good.

Table 3. Ablation study over DAVIS2016.

Version	F (%)	J (%)
GFM+GAM	86.4	85.9
GAM+GPD	85.7	84.3
GFM+GPD	83.1	82.6
Ours *(GFM+GAM+GPD)*	87.5	86.8

4.4 Ablation Study

We performed extensive experiments to highlight the importance of our VOS components over DAVIS2016 validation set. We retrained the whole model for each version. First we retrain our model without appearance module and it showed degradation in performance. In Table 3, *GFM+GPD* represent system without mixture model, shows that J dropped from 86.8% to 82.6% while F score decreased by 4.4%. Secondly, we investigate the effectiveness of proposed guided feature modulation module by retraining, and it is denoted as *GAM+GPD* in Table 3. We observe that J and F scores degraded to 84.3% and 85.7% respectively. This indicates that guided feature modulation module boosts the VOS performance. Finally, we also investigated our guided pooled decoder. The resulting version in Table 3 is represented with *GFM+GAM*. In this variant, we do not use the global guide and DFA during feature refinement. We notice that guided pooled decoder also improved the performance. Without this module the J and F scores reduced to 85.9% and 86.4%. Our ablation study shows that proposed method has three important components including appearance module, guided feature modulation module and guided pooled decoder. Removal of any of these component will degrade the overall system VOS performance.

5   Conclusion

A guided feature modulation approach is proposed to assist a generative appearance module for Visual Object Segmentation (VOS) task. The proposed modulation approach learns semantic information while generative model learns the target and background probabilities and gives cues for discrimination. During feature refinement, a global pooled decoder is proposed to capture both global and local context information. Extensive evaluations are performed on two benchmark datasets including DAVIS2016 and DAVIS2017. The results are compared with more than 20 existing algorithms. The experiments and comparisons have demonstrated excellent segmentation performance of the proposed algorithm over the existing state-of-the-art approaches.

Acknowledgment. This study was supported by the BK21 FOUR project (AI-driven Convergence Software Education Research Program) funded by the Ministry of Education, School of Computer Science and Engineering, Kyungpook National University, Korea (4199990214394).

References

1. Bao, L., Wu, B., Liu, W.: CNN in MRF: video object segmentation via inference in a CNN-based higher-order spatio-temporal MRF. In: CVPR, pp. 5977–5986 (2018)
2. Caelles, S., et al.: One-shot video object segmentation. In: CVPR, pp. 221–230 (2017)
3. Caelles, S., et al.: Fast video object segmentation with spatio-temporal GANs. arXiv preprint arXiv:1903.12161 (2019)
4. Chen, L.C., Papandreou, G., Kokkinos, I., Murphy, K., Yuille, A.L.: Deeplab: Semantic image segmentation with deep convolutional nets, atrous convolution, and fully connected CRFs. IEEE Trans. Pattern Anal. Mach. Intell. **40**(4), 834–848 (2017)
5. Chen, L.C., Zhu, Y., Papandreou, G., Schroff, F., Adam, H.: Encoder-decoder with atrous separable convolution for semantic image segmentation. In: ECCV, pp. 801–818 (2018)
6. Chen, Y., et al.: Blazingly fast video object segmentation with pixel-wise metric learning. In: CVPR, pp. 1189–1198 (2018)
7. Cheng, J., et al.: SegFlow: Joint learning for video object segmentation and optical flow. In: ICCV, pp. 686–695 (2017)
8. Cheng, J., et al.: Fast and accurate online video object segmentation via tracking parts. In: CVPR, pp. 7415–7424 (2018)
9. Ci, H., Wang, C., Wang, Y.: Video object segmentation by learning location-sensitive embeddings. In: ECCV, pp. 501–516 (2018)
10. De Vries, H., Strub, F., Mary, J., Larochelle, H., Pietquin, O., Courville, A.C.: Modulating early visual processing by language. In: Advances in Neural Information Processing Systems, pp. 6594–6604 (2017)

11. Deng, J., Dong, W., Socher, R., Li, L.J., Li, K., Fei-Fei, L.: ImageNet: a large-scale hierarchical image database. In: CVPR, pp. 248–255. IEEE (2009)
12. Fiaz, M., Mahmood, A., Baek, K.Y., Farooq, S.S., Jung, S.K.: Improving object tracking by added noise and channel attention. Sensors **20**(13), 3780 (2020)
13. Fiaz, M., Mahmood, A., Javed, S., Jung, S.K.: Handcrafted and deep trackers: Recent visual object tracking approaches and trends. ACM Comput. Surv. (CSUR) **52**(2), 1–44 (2019)
14. Fiaz, M., Mahmood, A., Jung, S.K.: Learning soft mask based feature fusion with channel and spatial attention for robust visual object tracking. Sensors **20**(14), 4021 (2020)
15. Fiaz, M., Mahmood, A., Jung, S.K.: Video object segmentation using guided feature and directional deep appearance learning. In: Proceedings of the 2020 DAVIS Challenge on Video Object Segmentation-CVPR, Workshops, Seattle, WA, USA, vol. 19 (2020)
16. Fiaz, M., et al.: Adaptive feature selection Siamese networks for visual tracking. In: Ohyama, W., Jung, S.K. (eds.) IW-FCV 2020. CCIS, vol. 1212, pp. 167–179. Springer, Singapore (2020). https://doi.org/10.1007/978-981-15-4818-5_13
17. Fiaz, M., Zaheer, M.Z., Mahmood, A., Lee, S.I., Jung, S.K.: 4G-VOS: video object segmentation using guided context embedding. Knowl. Based Syst. **231**, 107401 (2021)
18. He, K., Zhang, X., Ren, S., Sun, J.: Deep residual learning for image recognition. In: CVPR, pp. 770–778 (2016)
19. Hu, Y.T., Huang, J.B., Schwing, A.G.: Videomatch: Matching based video object segmentation. In: ECCV, pp. 54–70 (2018)
20. Huang, X., Belongie, S.: Arbitrary style transfer in real-time with adaptive instance normalization. In: ICCV, pp. 1501–1510 (2017)
21. Jampani, V., Gadde, R., Gehler, P.V.: Video propagation networks. In: CVPR, pp. 451–461 (2017)
22. Jang, W.D., Kim, C.S.: Online video object segmentation via convolutional trident network. In: CVPR, pp. 5849–5858 (2017)
23. Johnander, J., Danelljan, M., Brissman, E., Khan, F.S., Felsberg, M.: A generative appearance model for end-to-end video object segmentation. In: CVPR, pp. 8953–8962 (2019)
24. Kingma, D.P., Ba, J.: Adam: a method for stochastic optimization. arXiv preprint arXiv:1412.6980 (2014)
25. Li, X., C. Loy, C.: Video object segmentation with joint re-identification and attention-aware mask propagation. In: ECCV, pp. 90–105 (2018)
26. Lin, H., Qi, X., Jia, J.: AGSS-VOS: attention guided single-shot video object segmentation. In: ICCV, pp. 3949–3957 (2019)
27. Lukežič, A., Matas, J., Kristan, M.: D3s-a discriminative single shot segmentation tracker. arXiv preprint arXiv:1911.08862 (2019)
28. Maas, A.L., Hannun, A.Y., Ng, A.Y.: Rectifier nonlinearities improve neural network acoustic models. In: Proceedings of ICML, vol. 30, p. 3 (2013)
29. Maninis, K.K., et al.: Video object segmentation without temporal information. IEEE Trans. Pattern Anal. Mach. Intell. **41**(6), 1515–1530 (2018)
30. Nam, H., Kim, H.: Batch-instance normalization for adaptively style-invariant neural networks. In: Advances in Neural Information Processing System (2018)
31. Perazzi, F., Khoreva, A., Benenson, R., Schiele, B., Sorkine-Hornung, A.: Learning video object segmentation from static images. In: CVPR, pp. 2663–2672 (2017)

32. Perazzi, F., Pont-Tuset, J., McWilliams, B., Van Gool, L., Gross, M., Sorkine-Hornung, A.: A benchmark dataset and evaluation methodology for video object segmentation. In: CVPR, pp. 724–732 (2016)

33. Pont-Tuset, J., Perazzi, F., Caelles, S., Arbeláez, P., Sorkine-Hornung, A., Van Gool, L.: The 2017 davis challenge on video object segmentation. arXiv preprint arXiv:1704.00675 (2017)

34. Rahman, M.M., Fiaz, M., Jung, S.K.: Efficient visual tracking with stacked channel-spatial attention learning. IEEE Access **8**, 100857–100869 (2020)

35. Tian, Z., He, T., Shen, C., Yan, Y.: Decoders matter for semantic segmentation: Data-dependent decoding enables flexible feature aggregation. In: CVPR, pp. 3126–3135 (2019)

36. Tsai, Y.H., Yang, M.H., Black, M.J.: Video segmentation via object flow. In: CVPR, pp. 3899–3908 (2016)

37. Ventura, C., Bellver, M., Girbau, A., Salvador, A., Marques, F., Giro-i Nieto, X.: RVOS: end-to-end recurrent network for video object segmentation. In: CVPR, pp. 5277–5286 (2019)

38. Voigtlaender, P., Chai, Y., Schroff, F., Adam, H., Leibe, B., Chen, L.C.: Feelvos: fast end-to-end embedding learning for video object segmentation. In: CVPR, pp. 9481–9490 (2019)

39. Voigtlaender, P., Leibe, B.: Online adaptation of convolutional neural networks for the 2017 DAVIS challenge on video object segmentation. In: The 2017 DAVIS Challenge on VOS-CVPR Workshops, vol. 5 (2017)

40. Voigtlaender, P., Luiten, J., Leibe, B.: BoLTVOS: box-level tracking for video object segmentation. arXiv preprint arXiv:1904.04552 (2019)

41. Wang, Q., et al.: Fast online object tracking and segmentation: a unifying approach. In: CVPR, pp. 1328–1338 (2019)

42. Wang, W., Shen, J., Porikli, F., Yang, R.: Semi-supervised video object segmentation with super-trajectories. IEEE Trans. Pattern Anal. Mach. Intell. **41**(4), 985–998 (2018)

43. Wang, Z., Xu, J., Liu, L., Zhu, F., Shao, L.: RANet: ranking attention network for fast video object segmentation. In: ICCV, pp. 3978–3987 (2019)

44. Oh, S.W., et al.: Fast video object segmentation by reference-guided mask propagation. In: CVPR, pp. 7376–7385 (2018)

45. Xu, N., et al.: YouTube-VOS: a large-scale video object segmentation benchmark. arXiv preprint arXiv:1809.03327 (2018)

46. Yang, L., et al.: Efficient video object segmentation via network modulation. In: CVPR, pp. 6499–6507 (2018)

47. Yang, Z., et al.: Anchor diffusion for unsupervised video object segmentation. In: ICCV, pp. 931–940 (2019)

48. Zhou, Q., et al.: Proposal, tracking and segmentation (PTS): a cascaded network for video object segmentation. arXiv preprint arXiv:1907.01203 (2019)

49. Zhuo, T., Cheng, Z., Kankanhalli, M.: Fast video object segmentation via mask transfer network. arXiv preprint arXiv:1908.10717 (2019)

Improvement of On-Road Object Detection Using Inter-region and Intra-region Attention for Faster R-CNN

Ryunosuke Ikeda[✉] and Akinori Hidaka

Tokyo Denki University, Ishizaka, Hatoyama-machi, Hikigun, Saitama 350-0394, Japan
21RMU01@ms.dendai.ac.jp

Abstract. In this paper, we incorporate the attention module and the lambda layer into the existing object detection method, Faster R-CNN, to improve its detection accuracy. We propose three methods that incorporate mechanisms based on the attention module to capture the relationship between object candidate regions within an input frame, or a mechanism based on the lambda layer to improve the feature representation within each candidate region. We evaluated the performance of the proposed methods on BDD100K, which includes diverse scene types, weather conditions and times of the day. The results show that the detection accuracy of the proposed methods are improved compared to Faster R-CNN.

Keywords: Object detection · Faster R-CNN attention module · Lambda layer

1 Introduction

In recent years, the practical application of automated driving technology has been strongly promoted. In such technology, the automatic detection system of traffic objects on roads from onboard camera is an essential basic technology. In order to perform such detection process fast and accurate, various object detection methods based on deep learning have been proposed [1–5]. These methods have already achieved high recognition accuracy for practical use, especially in relatively good conditions such as fine daytime with low traffic volume. On the other hand, in order to prevent accidents during automated driving, it is necessary to detect objects on roads as accurately as possible even under poor conditions, e.g., when only a small part of the car body is visible due to overlapping cars in traffic jams, or when visibility is extremely unclear such as at night in dense fog. However, the recognition performance of existing object detection methods under such adverse conditions have been still insufficient.

In typical object detection methods such as Faster R-CNN [3], object classification and location estimation are performed based on feature information extracted from object candidate regions proposed by Region Proposal Network (RPN). Usually, hundreds or thousands of such candidate regions are found in a single image, and feature information extracted from each region is *individually* used to estimate object class and location. In other words, it can be said that in conventional RPN-based detection methods (such as Faster R-CNN), the estimation process never uses any information that is possibly obtained from similarity/distance between features in candidate regions which exist simultaneously in a single image.

Based on the attention approach [6], Beery et al. [7] showed that similarity between features obtained from different candidate regions proposed by RPN have rich information for object detection. They construct the memory matrix for the self attention [6] using feature information within candidate regions detected by RPN from multiple consecutive video frames. They showed that their candidate-region-based the attention module can efficiently model temporal context required for video object detection [7].

Although Beery et al. [7] used candidate regions obtained from multiple video frames to compose the memory matrix, the same approach may work well for candidate regions within a single frame. Namely, this approach may be used to learn and model *spatial context* hidden in an input frame. For example, when there is an ambiguous candidate region which is hard to classify whether it is a target object or a background, the actual appearance of surrounding target objects are expected to be an important clue to support making decision. Based on this idea, in this research, we propose attention-based Faster R-CNN to capture inter-region context within a single frame.

Also, in this paper, we propose another attention-based Faster R-CNN to capture local context within a single candidate region (i.e., intra-region context). For example, if a large part of a vehicle's body is occluded by other objects in a given candidate region, the visible part of the vehicle is *contextually* important in the region. Therefore, a mechanism to dynamically emphasize contextually important parts in a given candidate regions will be useful to increase accuracy of object classification or location estimation. For this purpose, we incorporate the lambda layer [8], which is the effective alternative to the self attention [6], into Faster R-CNN.

We valid the performance of the proposed methods, i.e., attention-based Faster R-CNN to capture inter- or intra-region context, based on several experiments using BDD100K dataset [9] which includes diverse scene types, weather conditions and times of the day. Our methods show higher average precision than usual Faster R-CNN.

2 Related Methods

In this section, we first give an overview of Faster R-CNN, which is the foundation of the object detection method proposed in this study. Next, we describe the attention module and the lambda layer introduced in the proposed methods.

2.1 Faster R-CNN

Faster R-CNN (FRCNN) [3] is one of the most fundamental object detection methods which is characterized by searching candidate regions of target objects (i.e., regions of interests: RoIs) using learnable neural network module, called "region proposal network (RPN)." Figure 1 illustrates a brief detection process of FRCNN. First, an input image is fed to a convolutional neural network (CNN) for feature extraction, which is called "backbone" network. The backbone outputs a set of feature maps as a 3-dimensional numeric array. Next, the output maps are fed into RPN to obtain a set of ROIs, which are coordinates of rectangular regions that indicate candidate regions of target objects. Then, the feature maps in each RoI are transformed into fixed-size feature vectors by applying RoI Pooling. The feature vectors are finally used for object classification and location estimation by a two-head NN architecture which has fully connected (FC) layers and classification or regression outputs.

Fig. 1. The entire architecture of Faster R-CNN.

2.2 Region Proposal Network

RPN is a simple NN module to output coordinates of object-like regions (i.e., RoIs) using the feature information extracted by the backbone CNN. In RPN, each pixel in the input feature maps is defined as an "anchor point." Each anchor point is accompanied by a certain number of "anchor boxes", which are rectangles of N_A different shapes centered at each anchor point. If the feature map size of the backbone is $H_b * W_b$ pixels, $H_b * W_b * N_A$ anchor boxes can be obtained from one input image.

RPN is typically designed as a shallow two-heads CNN which has two types of outputs, called "classification head" and "regression head." As the preprocess for both heads, 3 * 3 Conv (i.e., convolutional filtering with a kernel size of 3 * 3 pixel) is applied to the backbone feature maps C_{RPN} times to extract C_{RPN} new feature maps suitable for region proposal.

In the classification head, 1 * 1 Conv is applied to those new maps. Based on this operation, each C_{RPN}-dimensional feature vector extracted from each anchor point (i.e., each pixel location in the maps) is classified as either "a region including one of target objects" or "a background region". The output probability in this binary classification is called "objectness." The 1 * 1 Conv for this binary classification is performed independently for each anchor box. Therefore, we obtain the objectness of each anchor box at each anchor point.

Meanwhile, the regression head predicts an offset (difference) from the coordinates of each anchor box to the coordinates of an object in its neighborhood. This prediction is performed by applying a 1 * 1 Conv with $4 * N_A$ channels to the same feature maps used in the classification head. By summing the coordinates of each anchor box and corresponding predicted offset value, the estimated coordinates of the RoI for each anchor box are calculated.

Based on the above process, we obtain the objectness and RoI coordinates for each of the $H_b * W_b * N_A$ anchor boxes. To reduce the computational cost, a fixed number of RoIs with the highest objectness are selected. Finally, non-maximum suppression (NMS) [3] is applied to the selected RoIs to integrate closely overlapped RoI boxes. The output of RPN is the set of coordinates (x, y, w, h) and Objectness p_o of each integrated RoI.

2.3 Attention Module

The attention module [6] is a method that converts input feature vectors into new features by using the attention weights which are calculated by comparing the input features with a set of reference feature vectors. Figure 2 shows the calculation process of the attention module.

At first, the input feature matrix $X \in \mathbb{R}^{n \times d}$, which consists of n d-dimensional input feature vectors, is transformed into the Query matrix $Q \in \mathbb{R}^{n \times k}$ by an FC layer. Also, the memory matrix $M \in \mathbb{R}^{m \times d}$, which is a set of m d-dimensional vectors given for reference, is transformed by two different FC layers to form the Key matrix $K \in \mathbb{R}^{m \times k}$ and the Value matrix $V \in \mathbb{R}^{m \times d}$. Then, the attention weight matrix $W \in \mathbb{R}^{n \times m}$ is calculated as follows:

$$W = \text{Softmax}\left(QK^T\right) \in \mathbb{R}^{n \times m} \tag{1}$$

where $\text{Softmax}\left(QK^T\right)$ implies the soft-max operation $\exp(x_i)/\sum_k \exp(x_k)$ for each row vector $\mathbf{x} \in \mathbb{R}^{1 \times m}$ in QK^T. Finally, the output of the attention module is obtained as.

$$O_A = WV \in \mathbb{R}^{n \times d}. \tag{2}$$

The attention module is roughly divided into two types: The one in which $X = M$ is called "self attention", and the other one in which $X \neq M$ is called "source-target attention."

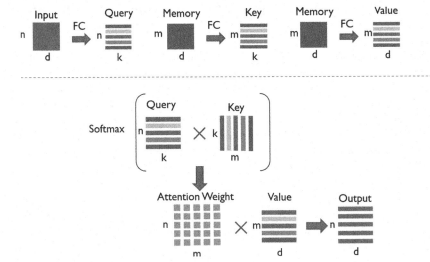

Fig. 2. Calculation process of the attention module.

2.3.1 Scaled Dot-Product Attention

In the usual attention module, when calculating the matrix product QK^T, the value of each element may become too large and adversely affect the error back propagation.

In order to reduce such the effect, the scaled dot-product attention, i.e., dividing each element of QK^T by the temperature t as shown below, is proposed.

$$W = \text{Softmax}\left(\frac{1}{t}QK^T\right), \tag{3}$$

$$O_A = WV. \tag{4}$$

In this method, the temperature t becomes a hyper-parameter which should be experimentally determined.

2.4 Lambda Layer

The lambda layer [8] is a framework to capture long-range interactions among structured contextual information, e.g., pixels surrounded by other pixels. The lambda layer is proposed as an efficient alternative to the self attention module; it can be applied to long sequences and multidimensional arrays such as images, and can model internal data structures in images (e.g., relative distances between different pixels), which is difficult to do with the self attention [8].

Figure 3 shows the calculation process of the lambda layer. At first, as in the self attention, the input feature matrix $X \in \mathbb{R}^{n \times d}$ is transformed into the Query matrix $Q \in \mathbb{R}^{n \times k}$ by an FC layer. Similarly, the feature matrix $C \in \mathbb{R}^{m \times d}$ (called Context, which is synonymous with the memory M in the self attention) is transformed into the Key matrix $K \in \mathbb{R}^{m \times k}$ and the Value matrix $V \in \mathbb{R}^{m \times v}$ by two different FC layers. Then, by applying the soft-max operation for each column of K, the normalized matrix $\overline{K} \in \mathbb{R}^{m \times k}$ is obtained. The coefficient matrix Λ^c calculated by the following equation is called "Content Lambda":

$$\Lambda^c = \overline{K}^T V \in \mathbb{R}^{k \times v}. \tag{5}$$

Content Lambda is a matrix that represents the interaction between m Context vectors in C. When we put $C = X$ as in the self attention, Λ^c can be regarded as the coefficient matrix that captures the interaction between the input feature vectors.

Also, the coefficient matrix $\Lambda^p_j \in \mathbb{R}^{k \times v}$ calculated by the following equation is called "Position Lambda":

$$\Lambda^p_j = E^T_j V \in \mathbb{R}^{k \times v} \tag{6}$$

where $E_j \in \mathbb{R}^{m \times k}$ is a learnable weight matrix for applying positional embedding to the Query vector at the j-th position.

A matrix obtained by adding the content lambda Λ^c and the position lambda Λ^p_j for the j-th Query position, i.e.,

$$\Lambda_j = \Lambda^c + \Lambda^p_j = \left(\overline{K}^T + E^T_j\right)V = \sum_{i=1}^{m}(\mathbf{k}_i + \mathbf{e}_{ji})\mathbf{v}^T_i \in \mathbb{R}^{k \times v} \tag{7}$$

is used as the coefficient matrix of linear projection for each Query vector $\mathbf{q}_j \in \mathbb{R}^{1 \times k}$, as follows:

$$\mathbf{y}_j = \mathbf{q}_j \Lambda_j = \mathbf{q}_j \left(\Lambda^c + \Lambda_j^p \right) \in \mathbb{R}^{1 \times v}. \qquad (8)$$

The output of the lambda layer is the matrix $O_\Lambda = \left[\mathbf{y}_1^T \mathbf{y}_2^T \cdots \mathbf{y}_n^T \right]^T \in \mathbb{R}^{n \times v}$.

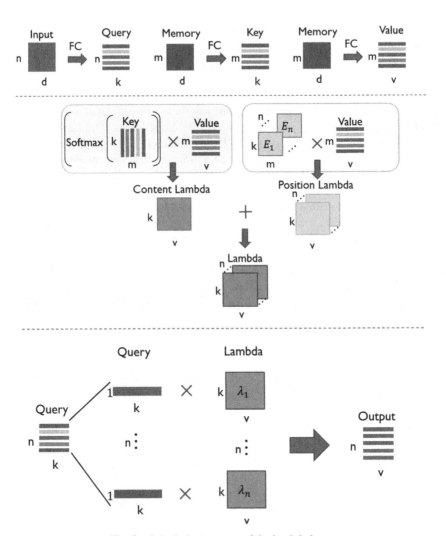

Fig. 3. Calculation process of the lambda layer.

3 Proposed Methods

In this paper, we propose three methods that incorporate the attention module [6] or the lambda layer [8] into Faster R-CNN [3]. The details of the proposed methods are described in the following sections.

3.1 Self Attention for Final Features Between High-Confidence Regions

In this section, we describe the proposed method that introduces a self attention block after RoI pooling layer in Faster R-CNN. Figure 4 shows the architecture of the proposed method. In our method, a matrix $X \in \mathbb{R}^{n \times d}$ is used as the input of the self attention; X consists of $n = N_{RPN}$ feature vectors $\mathbf{f}_1, \cdots, \mathbf{f}_n \in \mathbb{R}^{1 \times d}$ which are calculated by applying FC layer for a set of feature maps $\{M_1, \cdots, M_n\}$ obtained after RPN and RoI pooling. It implies that the attention memory is constructed from a large number of RoIs that exist simultaneously in a single image. This makes it possible to transform individual RoIs into new features capturing similarity between the query RoI and other RoIs, and to perform target classification and location estimation by incorporating the "appearance" of the neighboring objects or backgrounds.

Figure 5 shows the internal structure of the self attention block with actual parameters used in this paper. At first, a 4-dimensional feature tensor with $n \times 7 \times 7 \times 1, 280$ elements (where n RoIs, 7×7 pixel, and $1, 280$ feature channels), which is the output of RoI Pooling, is flattened and input FC layers to obtain a feature matrix X with $n \times 1, 024$ elements. The number $n = N_{RPN}$ varies roughly from 500 to 1,000 depending of the results of NMS. The matrix X is used as the input of the self attention block to obtain the matrices for the self attention: Q, K, V and O_A. By summing the output O_A and input X, the final feature matrix for object classification and location estimation are performed. We call this method self-attentional Faster R-CNN (SA-FRCNN).

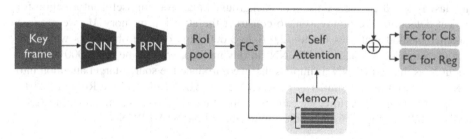

Fig. 4. The entire architecture of SA-FRCNN.

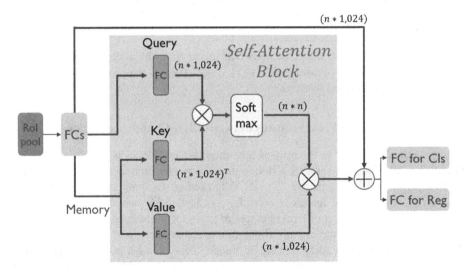

Fig. 5. Details of the self attention block.

3.2 Attention for Final Features Between Medium- and High-Confidence Regions

In this research, RoI Pooing in FRCNN is only applied to $n = 2,000$ RoIs with highest objectness among all RPN outputs. In other words, RoIs with the objectness lower than $2,000^{th}$ place are discarded and then not used for further processing. One of the proposed methods, SA-FRCNN described in Sect. 3.1, also uses only 2,000 RoIs with the highest objectness to execute the self attention module. This means that SA-FRCNN is based only on the similarity between features that have a high probability of being target objects.

On the other hand, not only RoIs with high objectness but also RoIs that are difficult to classify whether target objects or backgrounds may contain useful information for object detection. For this reason, to construct the attention memory M, we propose another method that uses the top 2,001 to 3,000 RoIs of high objectness which are not used in FRCNN and SA-FRCNN. In this method, we use the top 2,000 RoIs for input X as in SA-FRCNN. It implies that we introduce the source-target attention into FRCNN, based on the similarity between the top 2,000 RoIs and the RoIs of $2,001^{st}$ to $3,000^{th}$ places. Therefore, we call this method the source-target-attentional FRCNN (STA-FRCNN). Figure 6 shows the architecture of our STA-FRCNN.

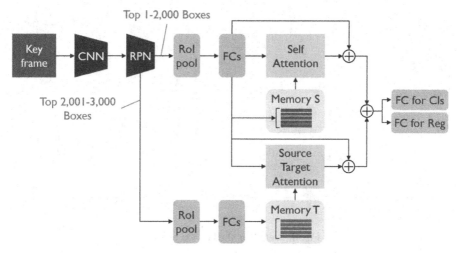

Fig. 6. The entire architecture of STA-FRCNN.

3.3 Lambda Layer for ROI Feature Maps

In order to refine feature representation obtained after RoI pooling, in this paper, we incorporate the lambda layer before final FC layers in Faster R-CNN. In this method, the pixel-to-pixel similarity between the candidate region feature maps, which are the output of RoI Pooling, is computed using the lambda layer, which is computationally less expensive than the attention module. The architecture of this method is shown in Fig. 7. By using the lambda layer, the relationships obtained from each position of the input and the memory feature maps are a set of $n \times k \times v$ dimensional vectors, where k and v are the number of dimensions of Key and Value, respectively. This makes it possible to efficiently obtain new features that contain global contextual information based on the location and similarity of feature information in the feature maps.

Figure 8 shows the internal structure of the Lambda Block actually used in this paper. First, each output of RoI Pooling, which is the $7 \times 7 \times 1,280$ pixel feature array, is reshaped to $49 \times 1,280$ feature matrix. The matrix is transformed into Query, Key, and Value by using different FC layers. In this paper, the dimensionality k of Key and v of Value are set to 128 and 512, respectively. Therefore, the shapes of Query, Key, and Value are 49×128, 49×128, and 49×512, respectively. Therefore, the output size of the lambda layer is 49×512. The object classification and the offset regression are performed with the features transformed by the subsequent FC layers. We call this method Lambda-FRCNN.

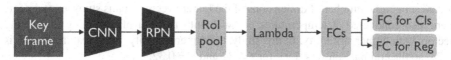

Fig. 7. The entire architecture of Lambda-FRCNN.

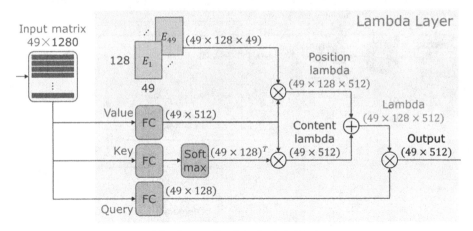

Fig. 8. Details of the lambda block.

4 Experiments

In this section, we describe our experiments and results of on-road object detection using Faster R-CNN and the proposed methods.

4.1 Experimental Setup

In this study, we used the Berkeley Deep Drive 100K (BDD100K) dataset [9], which contains many scenes with poor visibility at night and dense object data, and is more difficult to detect than Pascal VOC and MSCOCO. Although the data set composes 70,000 training images, from the viewpoint of computation amount, we made a reduced version of the data set (called BDD7K) which contains 7,000 training images and used it to train the usual and the proposed methods. To evaluate the performance of the trained models, we just used the 10,000 validation images provided by BDD100K. The numbers of objects in the BDD7K and the validation images in BDD100K are shown in Table 1.

We used MobileNetV2 [10] as the backbone of Faster R-CNN. As the optimized method, we used Stochastic Gradient Descent (SGD) with the learning rate 0.001. We set the batch size to 3, and trained all models up to 400 epochs.

In the attention calculation of SA-FRCNN and STA-FRCNN, the scaled dot-product attention with temperature t as a hyperparameter was used. When t is larger than 1, features with low similarity are emphasized more when Softmax is calculated, and the attention map becomes smoother overall. On the contrary, when t is smaller than 1, those with high similarity are emphasized. In general, the temperature t is often taken as the square root of the number of dimensions of the feature vector. In this study, experiments were also conducted at temperatures below 1 with the aim of extracting the feature vectors with higher similarity. In this study, the dimensionality of the feature vectors is 1024, so the comparison was done for $t = 32$ and $t = 0.32$.

Table 1. Numbers of objects in the training images (BDD7K, our reduced version of BDD100K) and the validation images.

Object name	Person	Traffic light	Train	Traffic sign	Rider	Car	Bike	Motor	Truck	Bus
# of Objects (Train)	24,839	259,91	136	28,690	4,517	69,903	7,210	3,002	4,014	1,792
# of Objects (Val)	13,262	26,885	15	34,908	649	102,506	1,007	452	4,245	1,597

We used COCO-style Average Precision (AP) as the evaluation metric. The performance of each method was evaluated in the following two Epochs:

(a)   The last Epoch (400Ep), or
(b)   An epoch with the best validation AP (IoU[0.05:0.95]).

Tables 2 and 3 show the results of the cases (a) and (b), respectively. Also, Tables 4 and 5 report the performance of the models in the case (b). The following sections describe the results of these comparisons.

4.2   Comparison Between Faster R-CNN and Proposed Methods

In this section, we describe the comparison results between Faster R-CNN (FRCNN) and the proposed methods (SA-FRCNN, STA-FRCNN, and Lambda-FRCNN). As shown in Table 2, FRCNN was the lowest in all metrics except AP_S in the performance at 400 epochs. Therefore, it is shown that the self attention, the source-target attention, and the lambda layer introduced into FRCNN can improve the detection performance of FRCNN. Table 3 also shows that FRCNN was the lowest in all metrics except AP_S.

Table 4 shows the average number of output boxes (which are finally classified as one of target objects) for the validation data of each model. The number of boxes was highest for FRCNN, Ground Truth, SA-FRCNN, STA-FRCNN, and Lambda-FRCNN, in that order. This implies that FRCNN is prone to false positive detection, i.e., misrecognizing the background as an object. Meanwhile, the total numbers of output boxes are reduced in the proposed methods, and their APs are higher than that of FRCNN. This means that the number of cases where the backgrounds are misclassified as target objects is reduced.

These results suggest that the attention module improves the discrimination performance between objects and backgrounds, by incorporating the similarity with surrounding similar object regions and background regions into the feature information. The results also suggest that the lambda layer captures the relationships between local regions in a single RoI and reconstructs them as feature representations suitable for object detection, which is thought to have improved the discrimination between objects and the background.

The improvements in the performance of the proposed methods are especially significant for AP_L. In the evaluation of the case (a), SA-FRCNN ($t = 0.32$) improved the performance by 4% compared to FRCNN. Also, the evaluation in the case (b) shows a 4.2% performance improvement in Lambda-FRCNN.

On the other hand, in AP_S, the performance of the proposed methods against FRCNN were within the range of $\pm 0.2\%$, and no significant difference was found. This suggests that the attention module and the lambda layer are more effective for large objects in the image.

As for the AP for small objects, the accuracy tended to decrease slightly, especially with SA-FRCNN and STA-FRCNN. The reason for this is that the small RoI area of the Query may have resulted in relatively less spatial information in the feature vectors, which may have prevented a meaningful similarity evaluation with other RoIs. In this experiment, we used a single attention module regardless of the size of RoI. However, if we introduce different the attention modules for different sizes of RoI, the detection accuracy for small objects may be improved.

4.3 Comparison Between SA-FRCNN and STA-FRCNN

In this section, we describe the comparison results between SA-FRCNN and STA-FRCNN. As shown in Table 2, the AP at 400 epochs were similar for SA-FRCNN ($t = 0.32$) and STA-FRCNN ($t = 32$). On the other hand, when compared in Table 3 (i.e., performance in the best epoch for each model), STA-FRCNN ($t = 32$) seems to show slightly better results among the SA and STA family; in particular, AP_L showed an improvement of 0.8 to 1.2% over SA-FRCNN. In STA-FRCNN, the feature information in the RoIs that RPN considered ambiguous as either object or background are also utilized to construct the attention memory. Those complex features in the memory were incorporated into difficult background RoIs in the validation images via the STA module, and then the false positive detection for such RoIs might have been prevented.

Figure 9 shows the images of the detection results of FRCNN and STA-FRCNN. It can be seen that the false positive box in the lower right corner of FRCNN image is no longer present in the STA-FRCNN image. It also shows that FRCNN tends to output multiple boxes for a single object. The number of output boxes is 36 for FRCNN, 26 for STAFRCNN, and 29 for Ground Truth. It can be seen that FRCNN outputs more boxes than Ground Truth, while STA-FRCNN outputs a number of boxes close to Ground Truth. These results suggest that STA-FRCNN is able to capture objects more accurately while reducing false positives.

4.4 Comparison Between Lambda-FRCNN and Other Methods

In this section, we discuss the comparison results between Lambda-FRCNN and other methods. As shown in Tables 2 and 3, Lambda-FRCNN showed stable and higher AP than both conventional FRCNN and our attention-based FRCNNs. In particular, Table 3 (i.e., comparison at the best epoch for each model) shows the highest APs in all evaluation metrics.

The lambda layer, like the attention module, shows remarkable effectiveness for large objects, but its performance in APs for small objects is comparable to that of conventional FRCNN. It suggests that the lambda layer may have relatively less negative impact on small objects than the attention module.

In the case of small objects, the attention module incorporates the features of other objects based on the similarity calculated with a small amount of information. Therefore, depending on the quality of the calculated similarity, there is a possibility that noisy information which has bad influence for recognition process is captured; it might have reduced the detection accuracy of our attention-based FRCNN. On the other hand, the lambda layer performs the transformation on features only referring the features in the same RoI. Therefore, the features of the other small objects were not incorporated, and the negative impact on accuracy was considered to be minimal.

4.5 Comparison in Average Recall

Table 5 shows the Average Recall (AR) for the epochs where each method showed the highest AP. In AR, Lambda-FRCNN outperformed the other methods except for small objects. In particular, AR_L showed a 3.6% performance improvement compared to FRCNN. Compared with FRCNN, Lambda-FRCNN also improved the performance of AP for large objects by 4.2%, which is a significant performance improvement in both AP and AR.

Table 2. Model comparison in 400 Epochs. The bold and italic fonts indicate the best and worst method in all methods. The underlines indicate the best method in attention-based methods. The numbers in parentheses indicate the number of times that the method ranked first among the group of SA-FRCNN and STA-FRCNN.

Model	t	AP	AP50	AP75	APS	APM	APL	# of Best	# of Worst
FRCNN		*0.152*	*0.324*	*0.126*	0.030	*0.190*	*0.345*	0	5
SA-FRCNN	32	0.156	0.328	0.133	<u>0.030</u>	*0.190*	0.372	0 (1)	1
SA-FRCNN	0.32	0.161	<u>0.334</u>	0.140	<u>0.030</u>	0.195	**0.385**	1 (3)	0
STA-FRCNN	32	<u>0.162</u>	0.333	**0.141**	0.030	0.200	0.381	1 (4)	0
STA-FRCNN	0.32	0.160	0.326	0.137	*0.029*	0.196	0.363	0 (0)	1
Lambda-FRCNN		**0.165**	**0.339**	**0.141**	**0.031**	**0.201**	0.375	5	0

Table 3. Model comparison at the best epoch for each model.

Model	t	Best epoch	AP	AP50	AP75	APS	APM	APL	# of Best	# of Worst
FRCNN		310	*0.158*	*0.330*	*0.131*	**0.032**	0.195	*0.355*	1	5
SA-FRCNN	32	260	0.162	0.331	0.142	*0.028*	0.196	0.380	0 (0)	1
SA-FRCNN	0.32	370	0.163	<u>0.336</u>	0.141	<u>0.030</u>	0.198	0.384	0 (2)	0
STA-FRCNN	32	280	<u>0.165</u>	0.333	<u>0.145</u>	0.029	<u>0.201</u>	<u>0.392</u>	0 (4)	0
STA-FRCNN	0.32	260	0.162	0.334	0.138	0.029	0.199	0.373	0 (0)	0
Lambda-FRCNN		310	**0.170**	**0.345**	**0.149**	**0.032**	**0.203**	**0.397**	6	0

Table 4. Average number of output boxes per image in evaluation data.

	Ground Truth	FRCNN	SA-FRCNN	STA-FRCNN	Lambda-FRCNN
# of boxes	17.3626	19.4387	15.6028	15.4773	14.6268

Table 5. Model comparison at maximum AP value for evaluation data (AR).

Model	t	Best epoch (for AP)	ARS	ARM	ARL	# of Best	# of Worst
FRCNN	–	310	**0.081**	0.307	*0.450*	1	1
SA-FRCNN	32	260	<u>0.075</u>	0.302	0.478	0 (1)	0
SA-FRCNN	0.32	370	*0.070*	0.300	<u>0.483</u>	0 (1)	1
STA-FRCNN	32	280	*0.070*	*0.294*	<u>0.483</u>	0 (1)	2
STA-FRCNN	0.32	260	*0.070*	<u>0.303</u>	0.478	0 (1)	1
Lambda-FRCNN	–	310	0.073	**0.311**	**0.486**	2	0

Fig. 9. (top) FRCNN detection results (36 boxes), (bottom) STA-FRCNN detection results (26 boxes).

5   Conclusions

In this paper, we proposed three methods that incorporate a mechanism to capture the relationship between the boxes proposed by RPN, and a mechanism to improve the feature representation within each box into the conventional object detection method, Faster R-CNN. We validated the performance of the proposed methods using a reduced version of BDD100K. The validation results show that the improved feature representations are effective to increase both of AP and AR especially for large objects.

In order to improve the AP and AR for small objects in the future, we need to develop an architecture that uses the attention modules for each object size, or an architecture that can capture the relationship between individual features converted by the lambda layer and the attention module.

Acknowledgement. This work was supported by Research Institute for Science and Technology of Tokyo Denki University Grant Number Q20J-02.

References

1. Girshick, R., Donahue, J., Darrell, T., Malik, J.: Rich feature hierarchies for accurate object detection and semantic segmentation. In: Proceedings of the IEEE Conference on Computer Vision and Pattern Recognition, pp. 580–587 (2014)
2. Girshick, R.: Fast R-CNN. In: Proceedings of the IEEE International Conference on Computer Vision, pp. 1440–1448 (2015)
3. Ren, S., He, K., Girshick, R., Sun, J.: Faster R-CNN: towards real-time object detection with region proposal networks. Adv. Neural. Inf. Process. Syst. **28**, 91–99 (2015)
4. Redmon, J., Divvala, S., Girshick, R., Farhadi, A.: You only look once: Unified, real-time object detection. In: Proceedings of the IEEE Conference on Computer Vision and Pattern Recognition, pp. 779–788 (2016)
5. Liu, W., et al.: SSD: single shot multibox detector. In: Leibe, B., Matas, J., Sebe, N., Welling, M. (eds.) ECCV 2016. LNCS, vol. 9905, pp. 21–37. Springer, Cham (2016). https://doi.org/10.1007/978-3-319-46448-0_2
6. Vaswani, A., et al.: Attention is all you need. In: Advances in Neural Information Processing Systems, pp. 5998–6008 (2017)
7. Beery, S., Wu, G., Rathod, V., Votel, R., Huang, J.: Context R-CNN: Long term temporal context for per-camera object detection. In: Proceedings of the IEEE/CVF Conference on Computer Vision and Pattern Recognition, pp. 13075–13085 (2020)
8. Bello, I.: Lambdanetworks: modeling long-range interactions without attention. arXiv:2102.08602 (2021)
9. Yu, F., et al.: BDD100K:: a diverse driving video database with scalable annotation tooling, vol. 2, issue 5, p. 6. arXiv:1805.04687 (2018)
10. Sandler, M., Howard, A., Zhu, M., Zhmoginov, A., Chen, L.C.: Mobilenetv2: inverted residuals and linear bottlenecks. In: Proceedings of the IEEE Conference on Computer Vision and Pattern Recognition, pp. 4510–4520 (2018)

Deep Segmentation Network Without Mask Image Supervision for 2D Image Registration

Shunsuke Yoneda[1]([✉]), Go Irie[2], Takashi Shibata[2], Masashi Nishiyama[1], and Yoshio Iwai[1]

[1] Tottori University, 101 Minami 4-chome, Koyama-cho, Tottori 680-8550, Japan
shunsukeyoneda77@gmail.com
[2] NTT Corporation, 1 Morinosato-wakamiya 3-chome, Atsugi 243-0198, Japan

Abstract. Two-dimensional (2D) image registration is a conventional technique for simultaneously performing object recognition and pose estimation tasks. Deep neural-based 2D image registration techniques recently emerged and achieved high performance in both tasks. However, these 2D image registration techniques are not designed to perform the segmentation task, which is one of the significant image processing techniques. Here, we consider introducing a deep segmentation network module into the framework of the 2D image registration. Especially, we consider training the segmentation network module with no supervision cost of mask images. To do this, we exploit the idea of the canonical plane, which is one surface observed mainly for each object in an image. We train the weakly supervised segmentation network module to perform the segmentation task of the canonical plane in the query and target images using the outputs of the 2D image registration. Experimental results show that our network can accurately perform the segmentation task without mask image supervision.

Keywords: Segmentation · Image registration · Supervision

1 Introduction

There is a strong demand for solutions in warehouses to automate the picking process of planar objects such as product boxes and books to solve the labor shortage in logistics. Recently, some object-picking systems using cameras and robot arms [5,10] have been developed as one of the automation solutions. These systems automatically infer foreground masks, class labels and pose parameters of target objects using image processing technologies to control robot arms to pick objects up. To do this, we need to perform the following tasks accurately; segmentation, object recognition and pose estimation.

We consider 2D image registration techniques, which are conventional techniques for simultaneously performing object recognition and pose estimation

K. Sumi et al. (Eds.): IW-FCV 2022, CCIS 1578, pp. 227–241, 2022.
https://doi.org/10.1007/978-3-031-06381-7_16

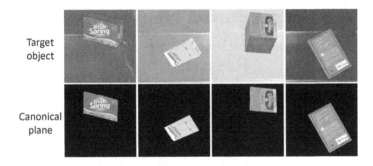

Fig. 1. Examples of the canonical plane in the target object. The canonical plane is one surface that is observed mainly for each object.

tasks. These techniques detect interest points from images containing the same object, extract local descriptors from the surroundings of the interest points, and search the correspondences between the interest points using the descriptors. The popular 2D image registration techniques are Scale-Invariant Feature Transform (SIFT) [11] + Random Sample Consensus (RANSAC) [7] and Oriented FAST and Rotated BRIEF (ORB) [13] + RANSAC. Recently, deep neural-based 2D image registration techniques, such as SuperPoint [6] + SuperGlue [14], have emerged and achieved high performance in object recognition and pose estimation tasks. However, these 2D image registration techniques [6,7,11,13,14] do not consider how to perform the segmentation task though they consider how to perform object recognition and pose estimation tasks.

Here, we propose a deep segmentation network module that is easily attached to the framework of the 2D image registration under the condition that mask image supervision is not required. Before explaining our segmentation network module, we consider a simple idea to use a fully supervised segmentation network in addition to using a 2D image registration technique. This idea requires collecting large datasets with mask image supervision, which is generally costly, to obtain high segmentation accuracy. Instead of using a fully supervised segmentation network, we introduce a weakly supervised segmentation network module into the framework of the 2D image registration. Experimental results show that our segmentation network module with no cost of mask supervision accurately performed the segmentation task with the help of pose parameters estimated by the 2D image registration technique.

2   Our Deep Segmentation Network with 2D Image Registration

2.1   Overview

Our goal is to attach the deep segmentation network module to the framework of 2D image registration without explicit mask image supervision. To train the

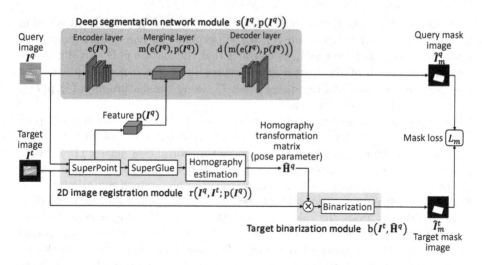

Fig. 2. Overview of our network for the training process. We introduce our deep segmentation network module s(), which does not require mask image supervision, into the framework of the 2D image registration. To predict the region of the canonical plane in the query image I^q, we train the segmentation network module s() by reducing the mask loss L_m computed between the query mask image $\hat{I}_m^q$ and the target mask image $\hat{I}_m^t$.

weakly supervised segmentation network module, we exploit the idea of the canonical plane, which has been introduced in [15]. The canonical plane is one surface that is observed mainly for each object. Figure 1 shows examples of the canonical plane when a camera acquires a rectangular or planar object image. We consider training the segmentation network module that predicts the region of the canonical plane in a query image. Our network performs the segmentation task using the output of 2D image registration between the query and target images belonging to the same canonical plane. Based on this idea, our training process can achieve no mask image supervision for the segmentation task. Figure 2 shows the overview of our network that trains the segmentation task of the canonical plane with the 2D image registration. We describe the detail of our overall network below.

In advance, we prepare the image pair as the training sample, where the pair consists of the query image I^q and target image I^t. Note that the query I^q and the target I^t belong to the same canonical plane of the same object class (but with a different pose), which are used for the deep segmentation network module and the 2D image registration module.

Our overall network consists of the deep segmentation network module s(), the 2D image registration module r(), and the target binarization module b(). First, the segmentation network module s() predicts a query mask image $\hat{I}_m^q$ from a query I^q by using the encoder layer, the merging layer, and the decoder layer. The encoder layer e() extracts the feature $e(I^q)$ from the query I^q. The merging layer m() combines the feature e($\boldsymbol{I}^q$) with the feature p($\boldsymbol{I}^q$), which is extracted in the 2D image registration module r(). We will explain this registration module r() later. In the merging layer m(), we consider that the feature p($\boldsymbol{I}^q$) highlights the informative region of the feature e($\boldsymbol{I}^q$) representing the canonical plane. The decoder layer d() predicts the query mask $\hat{\boldsymbol{I}}_m^q$ using the feature m(e($\boldsymbol{I}^q$), p($\boldsymbol{I}^q$)) combined in the merging layer.

Second, the 2D image registration module r() estimates the relative pose change from the target $\boldsymbol{I}^t$ to the query $\boldsymbol{I}^q$. According to [14,15], this pose change can be represented by a homography transformation matrix $\hat{\mathbf{H}}^q$ between the regions of the target $\boldsymbol{I}^t$ and the query $\boldsymbol{I}^q$ belonging to the same canonical plane. For this module r(), we simply use the pre-trained SuperPoint [6] + SuperGlue [14] network. SuperPoint detects interest points and extracts deep local descriptors from the query $\boldsymbol{I}^q$ and the target $\boldsymbol{I}^t$ using a convolutional network. SuperGlue searches the correspondences between the interest points of the query $\boldsymbol{I}^q$ and those of the target $\boldsymbol{I}^t$ using a graph neural network and a matching layer. Additionally, the 2D image registration module r() uses the least squares method to estimate the homography matrix $\hat{\mathbf{H}}^q$ using the correspondences searched by SuperGlue.

Third, the target binarization module b() predicts a target mask image $\hat{\boldsymbol{I}}_m^t$ from a target $\boldsymbol{I}^t$ by using the following processes. This module transforms the target $\boldsymbol{I}^t$ using the homography matrix $\hat{\mathbf{H}}^q$ estimated in the 2D image registration module r() so that the pose parameter of the canonical plane in the target $\boldsymbol{I}^t$ is the same as that of the query $\boldsymbol{I}^q$. Next, this module binarizes pixel values of the canonical plane to 1 and those of other regions to 0. To check the similarity between the query mask $\hat{\boldsymbol{I}}_m^q$ and the target mask $\hat{\boldsymbol{I}}_m^t$, we compute the mask loss L_m in our network. By reducing the mask loss L_m, we can train the segmentation network module s() without the mask image supervision.

2.2 Training Image Pairs

Our network uses the query $\boldsymbol{I}^q$ and the target $\boldsymbol{I}^t$ as the training image pair $\langle \boldsymbol{I}^q, \boldsymbol{I}^t \rangle$. The query $\boldsymbol{I}^q$ contains a rectangular or planar object with a random pose. We do not place any particular restrictions on the background of the query $\boldsymbol{I}^q$. In contrast, we assume that the pixel values of the background region outside the canonical plane in the target $\boldsymbol{I}^t$ are filled with 0, i. e., the background condition of the target $\boldsymbol{I}^t$ is black. We also assume that the target $\boldsymbol{I}^t$ contains only one canonical plane, which appears in the pair's query $\boldsymbol{I}^q$. We consider that it is reasonable to acquire the target $\boldsymbol{I}^t$ with the black background condition. Specifically, the target $\boldsymbol{I}^t$ can be acquired by placing the object parallel to the black floor and using a camera set up so that its optical axis passes through the object's center of gravity. Each of Fig. 3(a) and (b) show the examples of the target $\boldsymbol{I}^t$ representing the canonical planes for rectangular and planar objects. It is sufficient to acquire six targets per one rectangular object and two targets per one planar object for the training process.

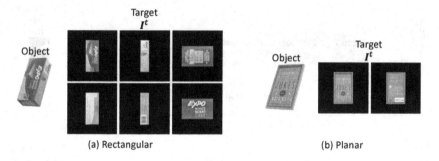

Fig. 3. Examples of the target I^t representing the canonical plane for rectangular and planar objects.

2.3 Deep Segmentation Network Module

We describe the details of the training process of the deep segmentation network module s(). As described in Sect. 2.1, this module s() performs the segmentation task with the help of the feature $p(I^q)$ extracted in the 2D image registration module r(). Hence, we first describe the pose estimation task using the module r(). This module estimates the homography matrix $\hat{\mathbf{H}}^q$ from the target I^t to the query I^q as

$$\hat{\mathbf{H}}^q = r(I^q, I^t; p(I^q)). \tag{1}$$

In the module r(), SuperPoint [6] internally extracts the feature $p(I^q)$ using a convolutional network. After performing the pose estimation task, the deep segmentation network module s() predicts the query mask $\hat{I}_m^q$ from the query I^q using $p(I^q)$ as

$$\hat{I}_m^q = s(I^q, p(I^q)) = d(m(e(I^q), p(I^q))). \tag{2}$$

As described in Sect. 2.1, the module s() uses the encoder layer e(), the merging layer m(), and the decoder layer d(). The encoder layer e() extracts the feature $e(I^q)$ that represents the region of the canonical plane in the query I^q using convolutional layers. The merging layer m() first combines the feature $e(I^q)$ with the feature $p(I^q)$ extracted by the SuperPoint network. Then, the merging layer reduces the dimensionality of the combined feature for fitting the dimensionality of the feature $e(I^q)$. The decoder layer d() predicts the query mask $\hat{I}_m^q$ from the feature $m(e(I^q), p(I^q))$ combined in the merging layer m() using deconvolutional layers. After performing the segmentation task, the target binarization module b() predicts the target mask $\hat{I}_m^t$ from the target I^t as

$$\hat{I}_m^t = t(I^t, \hat{\mathbf{H}}^q). \tag{3}$$

This module transforms the target I^t using the homography matrix $\hat{\mathbf{H}}^q$ estimated in the 2D image registration module r() and binarize the pixel value of the canonical plane to 1 and that of the other region to 0. Finally, the mask loss L_m is computed using the squared L2 norm between the query mask $\hat{I}_m^q$ and the target mask $\hat{I}_m^t$ as

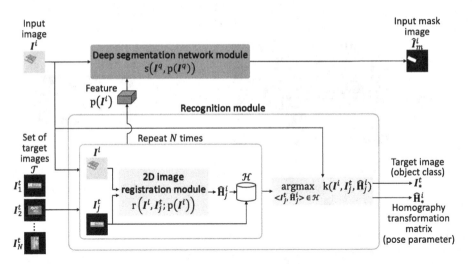

Fig. 4. Overview of our network for the inference process. The deep segmentation network module s() predicts the input mask image $\hat{I}_m^i$ of the input image I^i using the feature p(I^i) extracted in the 2D image registration module r(). The recognition module outputs the pair of the selected target image I_*^t and the homography transformation matrix $\hat{\mathbf{H}}_*^i$.

$$L_m = ||\hat{I}_m^q - \hat{I}_m^t||_2^2. \tag{4}$$

This loss L_m returns a small value when the query mask $\hat{I}_m^q$ and the target mask $\hat{I}_m^t$ are similar, i.e. when the prediction of the query mask $\hat{I}_m^q$ is close to a correct solution.

2.4 Inference

Figure 4 shows the overview of our network for the inference process. Our inference process consists of the deep segmentation network module s() and the recognition module. We initially perform the object recognition and pose estimation tasks for an input image I^i using the recognition module and then perform the segmentation task using our module s(). We store a set of target images $\mathcal{T} = \{I_j^t\}_{j=1}^N$ in advance. Note that each target I_j^t stored in the set $\mathcal{T}$ contains only one canonical plane belonging to a target object.

We describe the detail of the recognition module. The 2D image registration module r() in the recognition module estimates the homography transformation matrix $\hat{\mathbf{H}}_j^i$ for transforming the image from the target I_j^t to the input I^i. We store a pair of the target I_j^t and the homography matrix $\hat{\mathbf{H}}_j^i$ in the set of the pairs $\mathcal{H}$ for all N target images. Here, the recognition module performs the object recognition task for the input I^i as

$$\langle I_*^t, \hat{\mathbf{H}}_*^i \rangle = \underset{\langle I_j^t, \hat{\mathbf{H}}_j^i \rangle \in \mathcal{H}}{\operatorname{argmax}} \ \mathrm{k}(I^i, I_j^t, \hat{\mathbf{H}}_j^i). \tag{5}$$

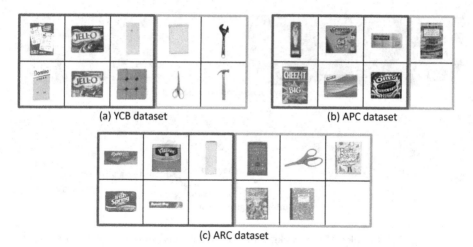

(a) YCB dataset   (b) APC dataset

(c) ARC dataset

Fig. 5. Target objects from YCB dataset, APC dataset, and ARC dataset used in our experiments. The color frame indicates the type of the object shape (Red: rectangular, Orange: planar) (Color figure online).

This equation means that a pair of a target image I_*^t and a homography transformation matrix $\hat{\mathbf{H}}_*^i$ is selected from the set $\mathcal{H}$, where the target I_*^t has the largest number of interest points corresponding to the input I^i. The function k() counts the number of interest points in the correspondence between the input I^i and the target I_j^t. The object recognition task is done by assigning the object class of the selected target I_*^t. The pose estimation task is done by outputting the selected homography matrix $\hat{\mathbf{H}}_*^i$ as the relative pose change from the selected target I_*^t to the input I^i.

In the inference process, we directly use our deep segmentation network module s() of Sect. 2.3 trained with no cost of mask image supervision and can perform the segmentation task efficiently. The segmentation network module s() predicts the input mask $\hat{I}_m^i$ of the input I^i using the feature p(I^i) extracted in the 2D image registration module r() after the recognition module performs the object recognition and pose estimation tasks.

3 Experiments

3.1 Dataset

We evaluated the segmentation accuracy, recognition accuracy, and pose estimation error of our network on a dataset mixed with three popular datasets for the picking process scenario; YCB dataset [3], APC dataset [12], and ARC dataset [2]. We used 17 rectangular objects and 10 planar objects: six rectangular objects and four planar objects in YCB dataset as shown in Fig. 5(a), six rectangular objects and one planar object in APC dataset as shown in Fig. 5(b)

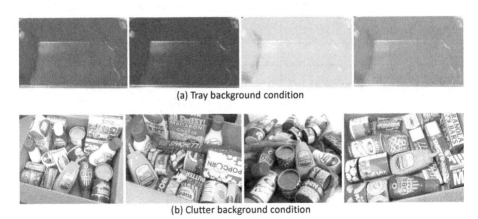

(a) Tray background condition

(b) Clutter background condition

Fig. 6. Examples of the background condition used in our experiments.

and five rectangular objects and five planar objects in ARC dataset as shown in Fig. 5(c). Each object in these datasets consisted of a 3D mesh model and a texture map.

We generated the query I^q by applying 3D rendering with three degrees of freedom (3-DOF) rotation, translation, and scaling to the objects randomly. The 3-DOF rotation angles were sampled in the range of $[-30, 30]$ degrees. The translation parameters were sampled in the range of $[-150, 150]$ pixels. And, the scale parameters were sampled in the range of $[0.8, 1.2]$.

We used two different background conditions: tray background as shown in Fig. 6(a) and clutter background as shown in Fig. 6(b). In the tray background condition, we used red, blue, yellow, and green trays. In the clutter background condition, we randomly placed 28 objects in Household Objects for Pose Estimation (HOPE) datasets.[1] Note that the objects contained in HOPE dataset were completely different from the objects in the datasets of Fig. 5. We show examples of the query I^q in the tray background condition of Fig. 7(a) and the clutter background condition of Fig. 7(b).

We acquired the target I^t using the manner described in Sect. 2.2. We used 30,000 pairs of the query I^q and the target I^t for the training process. We also used 3,000 inputs I^i for the inference process. Note that we completely separated the pose parameters of the inputs I^i from those of the training image pairs $\langle I^q, I^t \rangle$. For the inference process, the set of target images T included all canonical planes of the 27 objects contained in the dataset of Fig. 5. The number of images contained in T was 122, i.e., $17 \times 6 + 10 \times 2$, because a rectangular object contains six canonical planes and a planar object contains two canonical planes. The size of each image was fixed to 600×600 pixels. In the 2D image registration module r(), we used the size of the input images at 600×600 pixels. In the deep segmentation network module s(), we resize the input images to 100×100 pixels.

---

[1] https://github.com/swtyree/hope-dataset.

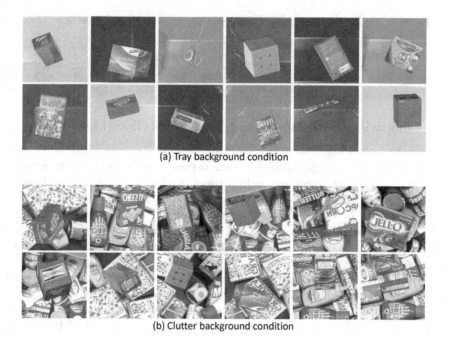

(a) Tray background condition

(b) Clutter background condition

Fig. 7. Examples of the query I^q used in our experiments.

3.2 Implementation and Performance Metrics

The encoder layer e() of the deep segmentation network module s() consisted of one pooling layer and four convolutional layers. The merging layer m() consisted of one upsampling layer for the features p(I^q) extracted in the 2D image registration module r(), one concatenate layer, and one convolutional layer for dimensionality reduction. The decoder layer d() consisted of two deconvolutional layers, one convolutional layer, and one upsampling layer. We simply used the pre-trained SuperPoint [6] + SuperGlue [14] network that are officially available. We set the hyperparameters of SuperPoint and SuperGlue to default provided values. We trained our network using stochastic gradient descent with a learning rate of 10 and a momentum parameter of 0.9 for 100 epochs.

We used the following three metrics for performance evaluation. The intersection over union (IoU) between the predicted mask image and the ground truth mask image was used to evaluate the segmentation accuracy. The correct match rate was used to evaluate the recognition accuracy. The Frobenius norm of the difference between the estimated homography matrix and the ground truth homography matrix was used to evaluate the pose estimation error. Note that we computed the pose estimation error only when the object class of the input I^i is the same as that of the target I^t_* selected by the recognition module. We used the average performance over the three runs, each with different training-testing splits.

Table 1. Performance of our network and SuperPoint [6] + SuperGlue [14].

	Seg. Acc.		Rec. Acc.		Pose Err.	
	Tray	Clutter	Tray	Clutter	Tray	Clutter
SuperPoint + SuperGlue	n/a	n/a	0.81 ± 0.01	0.75 ± 0.01	0.09 ± 0.01	0.22 ± 0.01
Ours	$\mathbf{0.82 \pm 0.01}$	$\mathbf{0.75 \pm 0.01}$	0.81 ± 0.01	0.75 ± 0.01	0.09 ± 0.01	0.22 ± 0.01

3.3 Comparison with SuperPoint [6] + SuperGlue [14]

We first evaluated the effectiveness of our network by comparing with original SuperPoint [6] + SuperGlue [14]. Our network performs the segmentation, object recognition, and pose estimation tasks, while the original SuperPoint + SuperGlue performs only the object recognition and pose estimation tasks. The results are shown in Table 1. The recognition accuracy and pose estimation error were consistent between the original and our network because we used the same SuperPoint + SuperGlue network. We confirmed that our network could perform the segmentation task in addition to the object recognition and pose estimation tasks by introducing the weakly supervised deep segmentation network module s() into the framework of the 2D image registration.

We show qualitative results of the deep segmentation network module s() in Fig. 8 of the tray background condition, and those in Fig. 9 of the clutter background condition. In each row of these figures (from left to right), we show the input I^i for the inference process, the segmentation region masked by the input mask $\hat{I}_m^i$ of s(), the transformation region converted by the homography matrix $\hat{H}_*^i$ of the recognition module, and the target I_*^t of the recognition module. Note that we replaced pixel values of the background region from 0 to 255 in these figures. When generating the transformation region, we used the inverse matrix of $\hat{H}_*^i$. We see that the deep segmentation network module s() accurately works because the appearances of the object between the transformation region and the target I_*^t are similar.

3.4 Comparison with Existing Segmentation Networks

To analyze the effectiveness of the deep segmentation network module s(), we compare our network with fully and weakly supervised segmentation networks. As fully supervised segmentation networks, we used Feature Pyramid Network (FPN) [9], DeepLabv3+ [4], and Unet++ [17]. As weakly supervised segmentation networks, we used Pixel-level Semantic Affinity (PSA) [1], Self-supervised Equivariant Attention Mechanism (SEAM) [16], and Puzzle-CAM [8]. Note that the existing segmentation networks do not consider performing the pose estimation task, and PSA does not even consider performing the object recognition task. We applied fine-tuning to the pre-trained networks of existing segmentation techniques. We used the default provided hyper-parameters. The results are shown in Table 2. Our network performs inferior to any fully supervised segmentation networks in both segmentation accuracy and recognition accuracy. In contrast, our network outperforms all weakly supervised segmentation networks in both segmentation accuracy and recognition accuracy. Furthermore,

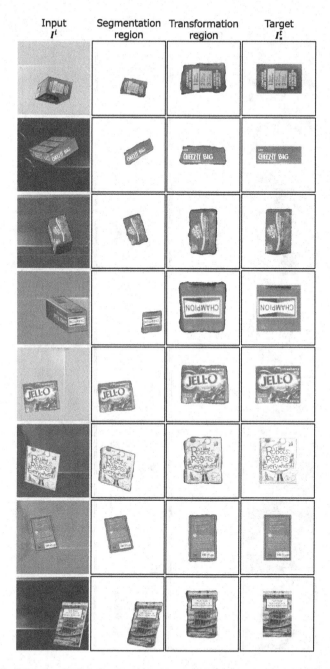

Fig. 8. Qualitative results of the deep segmentation network module s() in tray background condition. We see that the appearance of the transformation region is similar to that of the target I_*^t.

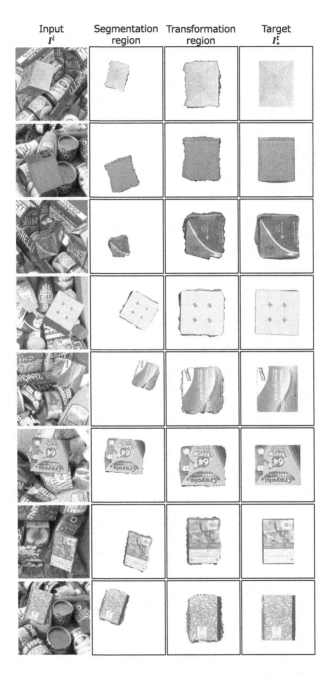

Fig. 9. Qualitative results of the deep segmentation network module s() in clutter background condition. We see that the appearance of the transformation region is similar to that of the target I_*^t.

our network was the only one that was able to obtain pose estimation outputs. We believe that our deep segmentation network module is advantageous for not requiring mask image supervision.

Table 2. Performance of our network and existing segmentation networks.

	Mask supervision	Seg. Acc.		Rec. Acc.		Pose Err.	
		Tray	Clutter	Tray	Clutter	Tray	Clutter
FPN [9]	w/	0.98 ± 0.01	0.98 ± 0.01	0.99 ± 0.01	0.99 ± 0.01	n/a	n/a
DeepLabv3+ [4]	w/	0.98 ± 0.01	0.98 ± 0.02	0.99 ± 0.01	0.99 ± 0.01	n/a	n/a
Unet++ [17]	w/	0.99 ± 0.02	0.99 ± 0.01	0.99 ± 0.01	0.99 ± 0.01	n/a	n/a
PSA [1]	w/o	0.46 ± 0.01	0.34 ± 0.05	-	-	n/a	n/a
SEAM [16]	w/o	0.16 ± 0.04	0.18 ± 0.01	0.64 ± 0.08	0.56 ± 0.07	n/a	n/a
Puzzle-CAM [8]	w/o	0.33 ± 0.07	0.06 ± 0.02	0.45 ± 0.04	0.15 ± 0.09	n/a	n/a
Ours	w/o	$\mathbf{0.82 \pm 0.01}$	$\mathbf{0.75 \pm 0.01}$	$\mathbf{0.81 \pm 0.01}$	$\mathbf{0.75 \pm 0.01}$	$\mathbf{0.09 \pm 0.01}$	$\mathbf{0.22 \pm 0.01}$

Table 3. Performance of our network with and without features $p(I^q)$ extracted in the 2D image registration module r().

	Seg. Acc.		Rec. Acc.		Pose Err.	
	Tray	Clutter	Tray	Clutter	Tray	Clutter
Ours (w/o $p(I^q)$)	0.80 ± 0.02	0.74 ± 0.01	0.81 ± 0.01	0.75 ± 0.01	0.09 ± 0.01	0.22 ± 0.01
Ours (w/ $p(I^q)$)	$\mathbf{0.82 \pm 0.01}$	$\mathbf{0.75 \pm 0.01}$	0.81 ± 0.01	0.75 ± 0.01	0.09 ± 0.01	0.22 ± 0.01

3.5 Performance Without Features Extracted in 2D Image Registration Module

As described in Sect. 2.1, our network uses the features $p(I^q)$ extracted in the 2D image registration module r() to help the segmentation task by combining $p(I^q)$ with the features $e(I^q)$ in the merging layer m(). To analyze the impact of the features $p(I^q)$, we evaluated the performance of our network without the use of $p(I^q)$. The results are shown in Table 3. Comparing our network with and without $p(I^q)$, the segmentation accuracy of our network with it was slightly better. We consider that the use of $p(I^q)$ with $e(I^q)$ has a little bit impact on the performance of our network.

3.6 Comparison with the Other 2D Image Registration Technique

We evaluated the performance of our network using ORB [13] instead of Super-Point [6] in the 2D image registration module r(). Our network used RANSAC [7] instead of SuperGlue to search the correspondences of local descriptors between the interest points. Because ORB extracts local descriptors not using deep neural networks, we did not use the features $p(I^q)$ for ORB. We used the default provided hyperparameters for ORB. The results are shown in Table 4. We confirmed that our network using SuperPoint is superior to that using ORB in terms of the segmentation accuracy, recognition accuracy, and pose estimation error. We consider that SuperPoint is better than ORB for introducing our segmentation network module into the framework of the 2D image registration.

Table 4. Comparison with the other 2D image registration technique.

	Seg. Acc.		Rec. Acc.		Pose Err.	
	Tray	Clutter	Tray	Clutter	Tray	Clutter
Ours (ORB [13])	0.68 ± 0.01	0.57 ± 0.01	0.56 ± 0.01	0.35 ± 0.01	1.35 ± 0.01	2.90 ± 0.01
Ours (SuperPoint [6])	$\mathbf{0.82 \pm 0.01}$	$\mathbf{0.75 \pm 0.01}$	$\mathbf{0.81 \pm 0.01}$	$\mathbf{0.75 \pm 0.01}$	$\mathbf{0.09 \pm 0.01}$	$\mathbf{0.22 \pm 0.01}$

4   Conclusions

We proposed a deep segmentation network module without mask image supervision, which is easily attached to the framework of the 2D image registration. For this purpose, we trained the segmentation network module with the help of 2D image registration between the query and target images belonging to the same canonical plane. We demonstrated that our network accurately performs the segmentation, not requiring the cost of mask image supervision. In future work, we expand to evaluate the performance of our network on datasets of objects with various shapes. We intend to develop a network for handling more complex transformations than homography transformation. We would like to thank Mr. Tokachi SHIRAHATA for his cooperation in our experiments.

References

1. Ahn, J., Kwak, S.: Learning pixel-level semantic affinity with image-level supervision for weakly supervised semantic segmentation. In: Proceedings of IEEE/CVF Conference on Computer Vision and Pattern Recognition (CVPR), pp. 4981–4990 (2018). https://doi.org/10.1109/CVPR.2018.00523
2. Araki, R., Yamashita, T., Fujiyoshi, H.: ARC2017 RGB-D dataset for object detection and segmentation. In: Proceedings of Late Breaking Results Poster on International Conference on Robotics and Automation (ICRA) (2018). https://doi.org/10.48550/arXiv.1810.00818
3. Calli, B., Singh, A., Walsman, A., Srinivasa, S., Abbeel, P., Dollar, A.M.: The YCB object and model set: Towards common benchmarks for manipulation research. In: Proceedings of International Conference on Advanced Robotics (ICAR), pp. 510–517 (2015). https://doi.org/10.1109/ICAR.2015.7251504
4. Chen, L.C., Zhu, Y., Papandreou, G., Schroff, F., Adam, H.: Encoder-decoder with atrous separable convolution for semantic image segmentation. In: Proceedings of the European Conference on Computer Vision (ECCV), pp. 801–818 (2018). https://doi.org/10.1007/978-3-030-01234-2_49
5. Correll, N., et al.: Analysis and observations from the first Amazon picking challenge. IEEE Trans. Autom. Sci. Eng. (T-ASE). **15**, 172–188 (2018). https://doi.org/10.1109/TASE.2016.2600527
6. DeTone, D., Malisiewicz, T., Rabinovich, A.: Superpoint: self-supervised interest point detection and description. In: Proceedings of CVPR Workshop on Deep Learning for Visual SLAM, pp. 337–33712 (2018). https://doi.org/10.1109/CVPRW.2018.00060
7. Fischler, M.A., Bolles, R.C.: Random sample consensus: a paradigm for model fitting with applications to image analysis and automated cartography. Commun. ACM **24**(6), 381–395 (1981). https://doi.org/10.1145/358669.358692

8. Jo, S., Yu, I.J.: Puzzle-cam: Improved localization via matching partial and full features. In: Proceedings of International Conference on Image Processing (ICIP) (2021). https://doi.org/10.48550/arXiv.2101.11253

9. Kirillov, A., He, K., Girshick, R., Dollar, P.: A unified architecture for instance and semantic segmentation. http://presentations.cocodataset.org/COCO17-Stuff-FAIR.pdf

10. Leitner, J., et al.: The ACRV picking benchmark: a robotic shelf picking benchmark to foster reproducible research. In: Proceedings of IEEE International Conference on Robotics and Automation (ICRA), pp. 4705–4712 (2017). https://doi.org/10.1109/ICRA.2017.7989545

11. Lowe, D.: Distinctive image features from scale-invariant keypoints. Int. J. Comput. Vision **60**, 91–110 (2004). https://doi.org/10.1023/B:VISI.0000029664.99615.94

12. Rennie, C., Shome, R., Bekris, K.E., Souza, A.F.D.: A dataset for improved RGBD-based object detection and pose estimation for warehouse pick-and-place. IEEE Robot. Autom. Lett. **1**, 1179–1185 (2016). https://doi.org/10.1109/LRA.2016.2532924

13. Rublee, E., Rabaud, V., Konolige, K., Bradski, G.: Orb: An efficient alternative to sift or surf. In: Proceedings of 2011 International Conference on Computer Vision (ICCV), pp. 2564–2571 (2011). https://doi.org/10.1109/ICCV.2011.6126544

14. Sarlin, P.E., DeTone, D., Malisiewicz, T., Rabinovich, A.: Superglue: Learning feature matching with graph neural networks. In: Proceedings of the IEEE/CVF Conference on Computer Vision and Pattern Recognition (CVPR), pp. 4938–4947, June 2020. https://doi.org/10.1109/CVPR42600.2020.00499

15. Ueno, K., Irie, G., Nishiyama, M., Iwai, Y.: Weakly supervised triplet learning of canonical plane transformation for joint object recognition and pose estimation. In: Proceedings of International Conference on Image Processing (ICIP), pp. 2476–2480 (2019). https://doi.org/10.1109/ICIP.2019.8803383

16. Wang, Y., Zhang, J., Kan, M., Shan, S., Chen, X.: Self-supervised equivariant attention mechanism for weakly supervised semantic segmentation. In: Proceedings of the IEEE Conference on Computer Vision and Pattern Recognition (CVPR), pp. 12275–12284 (2020). https://doi.org/10.1109/CVPR42600.2020.01229

17. Zhou, Z., Rahman Siddiquee, M.M., Tajbakhsh, N., Liang, J.: UNet++: a nested u-net architecture for medical image segmentation. In: Proceedings of Deep Learning in Medical Image Analysis and Multimodal Learning for Clinical Decision Support (DLMIA), pp. 3–11 (2018). https://doi.org/10.1007/978-3-030-00889-5_1

Lightweight Encoder-Decoder Architecture for Foot Ulcer Segmentation

Shahzad Ali[1]📷, Arif Mahmood[2]📷, and Soon Ki Jung[1(✉)]📷

[1] School of Computer Science and Engineering, Kyungpook National University (KNU), Daegu, South Korea
{shazadali,skjung}@knu.ac.kr
[2] Department of Computer Science, Information Technology University (ITU), Lahore, Pakistan
arif.mahmood@itu.edu.pk

Abstract. Continuous monitoring of foot ulcer healing is needed to ensure the efficacy of a given treatment and to avoid any possibility of deterioration. Foot ulcer segmentation is an essential step in wound diagnosis. We developed a model that is similar in spirit to the well-established encoder-decoder and residual convolution neural networks. Our model includes a residual connection along with a channel and spatial attention integrated within each convolution block. A simple patch-based approach for model training, test time augmentations, and majority voting on the obtained predictions resulted in superior performance. Our model did not leverage any readily available backbone architecture, pre-training on a similar external dataset, or any of the transfer learning techniques. The total number of network parameters being around 5 million made it a significantly lightweight model as compared with the available state-of-the-art models used for the foot ulcer segmentation task. Our experiments presented results at the patch-level and image-level. Applied on publicly available Foot Ulcer Segmentation (FUSeg) Challenge dataset from MICCAI 2021, our model achieved state-of-the-art image-level performance of 88.22% in terms of Dice similarity score and ranked second in the official challenge leaderboard. We also showed an extremely simple solution that could be compared against the more advanced architectures.

Keywords: Medical image segmentation · Foot ulcer segmentation · Attention mechanism · Encoder-decoder architecture

1 Introduction

Diabetes is a lifelong condition, and a diabetic person is at lifetime risk for developing foot ulcer wounds, which severely affects the life quality. Getting an infection further complicates the situation and may lead to limb amputations and even death. Such diabetic foot ulcer wounds need to be examined regularly,

K. Sumi et al. (Eds.): IW-FCV 2022, CCIS 1578, pp. 242–253, 2022.
https://doi.org/10.1007/978-3-031-06381-7_17

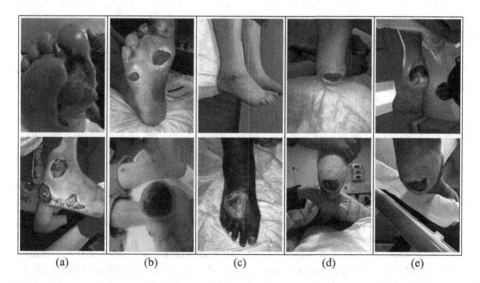

Fig. 1. Typical challenging cases from the Foot Ulcer Segmentation (FUSeg) Challenge dataset: (a) heterogeneous wound shapes and their random positions, (b) color variations of wounds, (c) changes in skin tone, (d) background clutter, and (e) change in viewpoints. These images are cropped, and padding is stripped off for better display. (Color figure online)

by the healthcare professionals, for diagnosis and prognosis, including assessing current condition, devising a treatment plan, and estimation of complete recovery accordingly.

Innovations in technology have resulted in better sensors and storage media thus, paving the way for advanced clinical procedures. The use of cameras and smartphones is getting common to obtain images of ulcer wounds each time a patient comes for an examination. The foot ulcer analysis is a lengthy process beginning from the visual inspection of wounds to determining their class type, severity, and growth over time by comparing past images side by side. Such subjective measures may cause human errors resulting, even with the utmost care, in an additional variability in enormously gathered data and hours of work in producing annotations. By utilizing artificial intelligence (AI) algorithms in general and deep learning (DL) techniques in particular, a vast amount of medical data is possible to process and analyze faster, accurately, and affordably. These algorithms are helping the healthcare industry to administer improved medical procedures, rapid healing, save huge expenses, and boost patient satisfaction. The segmentation is an essential step in a foot ulcer analysis pipeline. Having a reliable and efficient wound segmentation model could better aid in the evaluation of the condition, analysis, and deciding an optimal treatment procedure.

The goal of foot ulcer wound segmentation is to label every pixel in an image either as wound *(foreground)* or everything else *(background)*. There are several challenges in performing foot ulcer segmentation (as shown in Fig. 1) like heterogeneity in wound shape and color, skin color, different viewpoints, background clutter, lighting conditions, and capturing devices.

In this study, we propose an end-to-end lightweight deep neural network to perform foot ulcer wound segmentation which is robust to the challenges and generalizes well across the dataset without requiring any user interaction. Our model is inspired by the U-Net [16] and ResNet [9] and includes the key features of both models. Each residual block in the proposed model has group convolution layers [12] to keep the number of learnable parameters low. In addition, a residual connection, channel attention, and spatial attention are also integrated within each convolution block to highlight the relevant features and identify the most suitable channels to improve the prediction accuracy. The following are the main contributions of this study:

- We propose an end-to-end lightweight model for the foot ulcer wound segmentation primarily utilizing group convolutions.
- Channel and spatial attention layers are combined with the residual connection within each block to form new *residual attention* (ResAttn) block. There is no need to use standalone attention blocks resulting only in an increase in total trainable parameters and having a significant toll on overall model training time.
- We use test time augmentations (TTA) with the majority voting technique to get better segmentation results.
- Experimental evaluation on publicly available Foot Ulcer Segmentation (FUSeg) dataset shows superior results. Our method stood second when compared with the top methods from the FUSeg Challenge leaderboard[1].

The remainder of this paper is organized as follows. In Sect. 2, we provide an overview of the related work on the segmentation problem and attention techniques. Section 3 describes our proposed model and experimental setup. Section 4 presents the experimental details, results, and a brief discussion. Finally, the conclusion is given in Sect. 5.

2   Related Work

2.1   Classical Segmentation Methods

Several probabilistic and image processing methods, machine learning, and deep learning techniques fall under this category. Edge detection, clustering, adaptive thresholding, K-means, and region-growing algorithms are a few well-known image processing methods used for segmentation [2]. These methods being not data hungry are fast, and most struggle to generate a reliable outcome for unseen data and thus fail to generalize their performance. Earlier machine learning algorithms typically made the best use of hand-crafted features based on image gradients, colors, or textures for segmentation. Such algorithms include classifiers such as multi-layer perceptron (MLP), decision trees, support vector machine (SVM) [20].

---

[1] (https://uwm-bigdata.github.io/wound-segmentation) last accessed on Jan. 6, 2022.

2.2   Deep Learning-Based Segmentation Methods

Convolution neural networks (CNNs) have been successfully used for biomedical segmentation tasks such as segmenting tumors from breast, liver, and lungs using MRI and CT scans, nuclei segmentation in histological images [1,4], skin lesion, polyp, and wound segmentation in RGB images [8,13,18]. Deep learning-based approaches have outperformed other approaches for foot ulcer segmentation [4] since they are good to learn hidden patterns and generalize well for new data. Some well-known CNN-based architectures such as *Fully Convolutional Neural Network* (FCN), *U-Net, Mask-RCNN,* and lightweight mobile architecture like *EfficientNet* [8,13,16] are utilized to perform wound segmentation in various studies [5,18].

2.3   Attention Mechanisms

These mechanisms allow a vision model to pay better attention to the salient features or regions in the input feature maps. This concept is closely related to image filtering in computer vision and computer graphics to reduce the noise and extract useful image structures. Bahdanau et al. [2] made the very first successful attempt to include the attention mechanism for an automated natural language translation task. *Residual Attention Network* proposed by Wang et al. [21] used non-local self-attention to capture long-range pixel relationships. Hu et al. [11] used global average pooling operations to emphasize the most contributing channels in their proposed *Squeeze-and-Excitation* (SE) blocks. Several other efforts have been made to incorporate spatial attention. Woo et al. [22] made a notable effort with the *Convolutional Block Attention Module* (CBAM). It consisted of the channel and spatial attention in a sequential fashion which led to significant improvement in the model representation power. Wu et al. [23] proposed an *Adaptive Dual Attention Module* (ADAM) that captured multi-scale features for recognizing skin lesion boundaries.

3   Proposed Method

3.1   Model Overview

Our proposed model derives its key strength from the U-Net and ResNet architectures. We extended a U-shape model with the *residual attention* (ResAttn) blocks. In each ResAttn block, convolution layers with variable receptive fields combined with channel and spatial attention better emphasize the contribution of meaningful features at different scales. Figure 2 shows the proposed architecture having two branches for image encoding and decoding purposes. Each branch contains a series of ResAttn blocks either with max-pooling or transpose convolution layers. Given an input image, feature extraction is performed during downsampling (encoding), followed by the reconstruction branch to upscale the feature maps (decoding) back to the input size. A series of transpose convolution layers upscales the element-wise summation of the feature maps. These feature

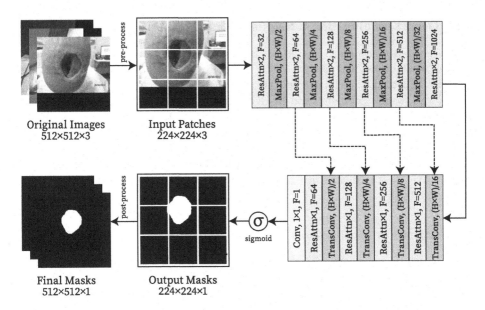

Fig. 2. The proposed foot ulcer segmentation model is a U-shape model with redesigned convolution blocks as *ResAttn* blocks. Final activation is sigmoid (σ), used instances of ResAttn are given in every block name (e.g., "ResAttn×2" means two block), F indicates the number of output feature maps, and dotted lines represent a skip connection between encoding and decoding blocks.

maps come from the previous block and skip connections and thus have the same spatial size. The last ResAttn block outputs 64 channels that are reduced to 1 by a 1×1 convolution layer. Finally, a sigmoid function scales the dynamic range to $[0, 1]$ interval.

We carefully considered the impact of design choices. The *point kernel convolutions* were preferred inside the ResAttn blocks since they require fewer training parameters than a convolution with a 3×3 or higher kernel. Our model initially produces 32 feature maps for each input RGB patch rather than 64 in the case of a standard U-Net. Since these feature maps grew twice in number by each encoding block, we saved a large amount of memory. Likewise, we found the *group convolutions* extremely useful in remarkably reducing network parameters. The total trainable parameters of our model went down to 17% as of its vanilla counterpart. We also observed that setting the value of *groups* parameter to a multiple of 32 was sufficient for producing quality segmentation results.

3.2 Loss Function

In the training process, we used a linear combination of binary cross entropy loss $\mathcal{L}_{bce}$ and dice similarity loss $\mathcal{L}_{dice}$. The total segmentation loss $\mathcal{L}_{seg}$ was calculated as:

$$\mathcal{L}_{seg} = \lambda_1 \mathcal{L}_{bce} + \lambda_2 \mathcal{L}_{dice}, \tag{1}$$

$$\mathcal{L}_{dice} = 1 - 2 \frac{\sum_i g_i p_i}{\sum_i g_i \sum_i p_i}, \tag{2}$$

$$\mathcal{L}_{bce} = - \sum_i \left(g_i \ln\left(p_i\right) + (1 - g_i) \ln\left(1 - p_i\right) \right), \tag{3}$$

where g is the ground truth binary mask, p is the model prediction, λ_1 and λ_2 in Eq. 1 are weighing parameters which were set to 1. The segmentation loss $\mathcal{L}_{seg}$ well trained our model and produced satisfactory segmentation performance.

3.3   Residual Attention Block

Each ResAttn block has three convolution layers with kernel sizes of 1×1, 3×3, and 1×1, respectively, along the main path. The fourth convolution layer with a 1×1 kernel serves as a *residual connection* only when the number of input channels (F_{in}) is not equal to the number of output channels (F_{out}). All convolution layers are followed by the activation and batch norm layers. The total number of network parameters was reduced by choosing small and fixed-size kernels. Such small sized kernels reduce the effective receptive field resulting in the loss of spatial information. Furthermore, every pixel within a receptive field does not contribute equally to the output [14]. This constraint can be alleviated by utilizing an attention mechanism to capture the global context information

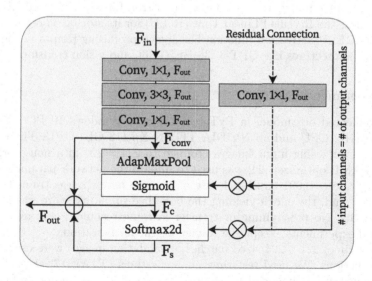

Fig. 3. Residual attention (ResAttn) block in our lightweight model. Each convolution layer produces the same number of output feature maps (F_{out}). As long as the input and output channels are the same (i.e., $F_{in} = F_{out}$), the block input serves as a residual connection; otherwise, the dotted path is used. All convolution operations are followed by the batch norm and activation layers.

and improve the representation capability of extracted features. The spatio-channel attention as shown in Fig. 3 remarkably increased the ability of model to pay attention to the meaningful task related information.

- **Channel Attention:** The channel attention vector $F_c \in \mathcal{R}^{(C \times 1 \times 1)}$ was obtained by squeezing the spatial dimension of an input feature map. We used adaptive max-pooling followed by a sigmoid function to get the probability estimate of the distinctiveness of each feature.
- **Spatial Attention:** Unlike most spatial attention mechanisms proposed previously, we found that a 2D softmax over features to each spatial location was enough to yield a spatial map $F_s \in \mathcal{R}^{(1 \times H \times W)}$. It attended the meaningful regions within the patches.

Both attention maps were multiplied with the residual connection. It is either the block input or 1×1 convolution of the block input when the number of input channels were different from the number of output channels. Then their element wise summation with the output was obtained from the $conv - bn - gelu$ path. These operations can be expressed as Eq. (4) whereas the detailed scheme is given in Fig. 3.

$$F_{out} = F_{conv} + \alpha F_c + \beta F_s, \tag{4}$$

where F_{conv} is the output from the series of $conv - bn - gelu$, F_c is the channel attention, F_s is the spatial attention, and the two learnable weights are denoted as α and β. In our experiments, Gaussian Error Linear Units (GELU) were preferred over the Rectified Linear Unit (ReLU) for its stochastic regularization effect [10]. GELU activation function has shown promising results in the state-of-the-art architectures like GPT-3 [3], BERT [6], and vision transformers [7].

3.4   Experimental Setup

We implemented our model in PyTorch [15] on a Windows 10 PC having an 8-core 3.6 GHz CPU and an NVIDIA TITAN Xp (12 GB) GPU. The training was carried out using input images cropped to 224×224 in a non-overlapped fashion. LAMB optimizer [24] was used to update the network parameters with a learning rate of 0.001 and batch size of 16. The network was trained for 100 epochs only and, the epoch yielding the best dice similarity score was included in the results. No pre-training or transfer learning technique was used in any performed experiments except the Xavier weight initialization.

At test time, 224×224 sized patches of validation images were used to generate predictions. We used test time augmentations (TTA) [17] at patch-level. Such augmentations included horizontal/vertical flips and random rotation by the multiple of 90°. We did not use multi crops at test time because the quality gain was negligible over the increase in computation time. The majority voting technique was used to decide the label at the pixel level.

4   Experiments

4.1   Dataset

This dataset was released for the *Foot Ulcer Segmentation Challenge* at the International Conference on Medical Image Computing and Computer Assisted Intervention (MICCAI) in 2021 [19]. It is an extended version of the chronic wound dataset and has 810 training, 200 validation, and 200 test images. The size of images was kept fixed at 512×512 pixels by applying zero-padding either at the left side or bottom of the image. The ground truth masks for the test images were held private by the organizers for the final evaluation of challenge participants so we evaluated the model performance for validation images only. We employed online data augmentation transformations including horizontal/vertical flips, multiple random rotate by $90°$, and random resized crops with high probability ($p \sim 1.0$). Other augmentations of significantly low probability ($p \sim 0.3$) included randomly setting HSV colors, random affine transformations, median blur, and Gaussian noise.

4.2   Evaluation Metrics

The quality of predicted segmentation masks was evaluated comprehensively against the ground truth using five different measures such as Dice similarity index (DSC), Jaccard similarity index (JSI), sensitivity (SE), specificity (SP), precision (PR), which are defined as:

$$DSC = \frac{2TP}{2TP + FP + FN}, \tag{5}$$

$$JSI = \frac{TP}{TP + FP + FN}, \tag{6}$$

$$SE = \frac{TP}{TP + FN}, \tag{7}$$

$$SP = \frac{TN}{TN + FP}, \text{ and} \tag{8}$$

$$PR = \frac{TP}{TP + FP}, \tag{9}$$

where TP, FN, TN, and FP represent the number of true positive, false negative, true negative, and false positive respectively. The output values of all these measures range from 0 to 1, and a high score is desired. Before evaluating the model performance, all obtained predictions were first binarized using a threshold value of 0.5.

4.3   Comparison with Baseline Model

We evaluated all model predictions obtained for the validation data on both patch-level and image-level for a fair comparison with other methods. A standard

---

250   S. Ali et al.

Table 1. Architecture and performance comparison (in terms of %) between at the patch level. The best results shown in bold.

Model	Param(M)↓	GFLOPS↓	DSC↑	JSI↑	SE↑	SP↑	PR↑
U-Net (vanilla)	31.03	30.80	89.74	81.39	89.01	**99.73**	**90.48**
Proposed method	**5.17**	**4.9**	**91.18**	**83.79**	**92.99**	99.69	89.44

U-Net was trained from scratch, keeping the training configuration and augmentation transformations close to the original paper [16], gave the best dice score of 89.74% as compared to 91.18% achieved by our lightweight architecture as shown in Table 1. The total number of parameters and the total number of floating-point operations per second (FLOPS) were significantly reduced to 16% of the vanilla U-Net model. The first column in Table 1 has the total network parameters in millions, the second column is for *giga-floating-point operations per second* (GLOPS), and the rest of the columns present the performance metrics given in Sect. 4.2.

Some example of patches extracted from the validation dataset images are shown in Fig. 4. The predicted segmentation results were almost identical to the ground truth masks. In some cases, as in Fig. 4(c) and (d), the model showed sensitivity to fresh wounds since they were high in color contrast in comparison to their surroundings. Figure 4(a) represents a case where the model exhibited

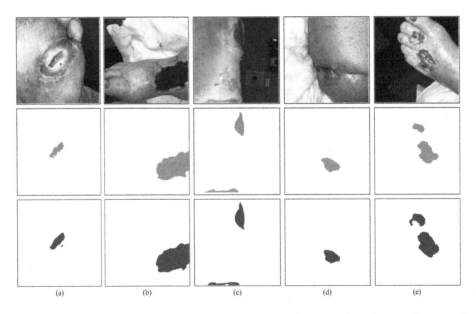

Fig. 4. Example patches from the images of FUSeg validation data (*top row*), ground truth masks in red color (*middle row*), and segmentation prediction obtained from the proposed model in green color (*last row*). (Color figure online)

Table 2. The leaderboard of MICCAI 2021 Foot Ulcer Segmentation (FUSeg) Challenge. Our proposed method achieved the second-best place.

#	Team	Model	DSC↑
1	Amirreza Mahbod, Rupert Ecker, Isabella Ellinger (Medical University of Vienna, TissueGnostics GmbH)	U-Net+LinkNet	0.8880
	Proposed method	**U-Net with residual attention blocks**	**0.8822**
2	Yichen Zhang (Huazhong University of Science and Technology)	U-Net with HarDNet68 as encoder backbone	0.8757
3	Bruno Oliveira (University of Minho)	–	0.8706
4	Adrian Galdran (University of Bournemouth)	Stacked U-Nets	0.8691
5	Jianyuan Hong, Haili Ye, Feihong Huang, Dahan Wang (Xiamen University of Technology)	–	0.8627
6	Abdul Qayyum, Moona Mazher, Abdesslam Benzinou, Fabrice Meriaudeau (University of Bourgogne Franche-Comt)	–	0.8229
7	Hongtao Zhu (Shanghai University)	U-Net with ASPP	0.8213
8	Hung Yeh (National United University)		0.8188

poor performance in capturing the fine-grained details potentially due to the extremely low number of learnable parameters.

4.4 Comparison with Challenge Records

For image-level evaluations, all 224×224 patch-level predictions were unfolded to recover the original image of size 512×512. The statistical results of our method for the validation images are given as Table 2 in comparison with the participating teams in the challenge. Our method ranked second on the leaderboard and successfully competed with other wider and deeper architectures. These models often utilized pre-trained backbone in a U-shape architecture along with extensive ensemble approaches.

5 Conclusion

The use of deep learning methods for automated foot ulcer segmentation is the best solution to the laborious annotation task and analysis process. We proposed using ResAttn block based on the residual connection, spatial attention, and channel attention. Our lightweight architecture, with ResAttn blocks, outperformed several recent state-of-the-art architectures at the leaderboard of the Foot Ulcer Segmentation Challenge from MICCAI 2021. In addition, this study offers an alternative perspective by showing how minor yet highly valuable design choices can lead to excellent results when using a simple network architecture.

Acknowledgment. This study was supported by the BK21 FOUR project (AI-driven Convergence Software Education Research Program) funded by the Ministry of Education, School of Computer Science and Engineering, Kyungpook National University, Korea (4199990214394).

References

1. Kumar, N., et al.: A multi-organ nucleus segmentation challenge. IEEE Trans. Med. Imaging **39**(5), 1380–1391 (2020). https://doi.org/10.1109/TMI.2019.2947628

2. Bahdanau, D., Cho, K.H., Bengio, Y.: Neural machine translation by jointly learning to align and translate. In: 3rd International Conference on Learning Representations, ICLR 2015 - Conference Track Proceedings, September 2014. https://arxiv.org/abs/1409.0473v7

3. Brown, T.B., et al.: Language models are few-shot learners. Adv. Neural Inf. Process. Syst. **33**, 1877–1901 (2020). https://proceedings.neurips.cc/paper/2020/file/1457c0d6bfcb4967418bfb8ac142f64a-Paper.pdf

4. Caicedo, J.C., et al.: Nucleus segmentation across imaging experiments: the 2018 data science bowl. Nat. Methods **16**(12), 1247–1253 (2019). https://doi.org/10.1038/s41592-019-0612-7

5. Chino, D.Y., Scabora, L.C., Cazzolato, M.T., Jorge, A.E., Traina, C., Traina, A.J.: Segmenting skin ulcers and measuring the wound area using deep convolutional networks. Comput. Methods Programs Biomed. 105376. https://doi.org/10.1016/j.cmpb.2020.105376

6. Devlin, J., Chang, M.W., Lee, K., Toutanova, K.: BERT: pre-training of deep bidirectional transformers for language understanding. In: NAACL HLT 2019 - 2019 Conference of the North American Chapter of the Association for Computational Linguistics: Human Language Technologies - Proceedings of the Conference, vol. 1, pp. 4171–4186, October 2019. https://arxiv.org/abs/1810.04805v2

7. Dosovitskiy, A., et al.: An Image is Worth 16×16 Words: Transformers for Image Recognition at Scale, October 2020. https://arxiv.org/abs/2010.11929v2

8. He, K., Gkioxari, G., Dollár, P., Girshick, R.: Mask R-CNN. IEEE Trans. Pattern Anal. Mach. Intell. **42**(2), 386–397 (2020). https://doi.org/10.1109/TPAMI.2018.2844175

9. He, K., Zhang, X., Ren, S., Sun, J.: Deep residual learning for image recognition. In: Proceedings of the IEEE Conference on Computer Vision and Pattern Recognition, pp. 770–778 (2016). http://image-net.org/challenges/LSVRC/2015/

10. Hendrycks, D., Gimpel, K.: Gaussian Error Linear Units (GELUs). arXiv preprint arXiv:1606.08415, June 2016. https://arxiv.org/abs/1606.08415v4

11. Hu, J., Shen, L., Sun, G.: Squeeze-and-excitation networks. In: Proceedings of the IEEE Conference on Computer Vision and Pattern Recognition, pp. 7132–7141 (2018). http://image-net.org/challenges/LSVRC/2017/results

12. Krizhevsky, A., Sutskever, I., Hinton, G.E.: ImageNet classification with deep convolutional neural networks. Commun. ACM (6), 84–90. https://doi.org/10.1145/3065386

13. Long, J., Shelhamer, E., Darrell, T.: Fully convolutional networks for semantic segmentation. In: Proceedings of the IEEE Computer Society Conference on Computer Vision and Pattern Recognition, issue number 4, pp. 3431–3440. https://doi.org/10.1109/CVPR.2015.7298965

14. Luo, W., Li, Y., Urtasun, R., Zemel, R.: Understanding the effective receptive field in deep convolutional neural networks. In: Advances in Neural Information Processing Systems (Nips), pp. 4905–4913 (2016). https://arxiv.org/abs/1701.04128

15. Paszke, A., et al.: PyTorch: an imperative style, high-performance deep learning library. In: Wallach, H., Larochelle, H., Beygelzimer, A., d'Alché-Buc, F., Fox, E., Garnett, R. (eds.) Advances in Neural Information Processing Systems. Curran Associates Inc. https://proceedings.neurips.cc/paper/2019/file/bdbca288fee7f92f2bfa9f7012727740-Paper.pdf

16. Ronneberger, O., Fischer, P., Brox, T.: U-Net: convolutional networks for biomedical image segmentation. In: Navab, N., Hornegger, J., Wells, W.M., Frangi, A.F. (eds.) MICCAI 2015, Part III. LNCS, vol. 9351, pp. 234–241. Springer, Cham (2015). https://doi.org/10.1007/978-3-319-24574-4_28

17. Simonyan, K., Zisserman, A.: Very deep convolutional networks for large-scale image recognition. In: 3rd International Conference on Learning Representations, ICLR 2015 - Conference Track Proceedings

18. Wang, C., et al.: Fully automatic wound segmentation with deep convolutional neural networks. Sci. Rep. (1), 21897. https://doi.org/10.1038/s41598-020-78799-w

19. Wang, C., et al.: FUSeg: The Foot Ulcer Segmentation Challenge. arXiv preprint arXiv:2201.00414, January 2022. https://arxiv.org/abs/2201.00414

20. Wang, L., Pedersen, P.C., Agu, E., Strong, D.M., Tulu, B.: Area determination of diabetic foot ulcer images using a cascaded two-stage SVM-based classification. IEEE Trans. Biomed. Eng. **64**(9), 2098–2109 (2017). https://doi.org/10.1109/TBME.2016.2632522

21. Wang, X., Girshick, R., Gupta, A., He, K.: Non-local neural networks. In: Proceedings of the IEEE Conference on Computer Vision and Pattern Recognition, pp. 7794–7803 (2018). https://openaccess.thecvf.com/content_cvpr_2018/html/Wang_Non-Local_Neural_Networks_CVPR_2018_paper.html

22. Woo, S., Park, J., Lee, J.-Y., Kweon, I.S.: CBAM: convolutional block attention module. In: Ferrari, V., Hebert, M., Sminchisescu, C., Weiss, Y. (eds.) ECCV 2018, Part VII. LNCS, vol. 11211, pp. 3–19. Springer, Cham (2018). https://doi.org/10.1007/978-3-030-01234-2_1

23. Wu, H., Pan, J., Li, Z., Wen, Z., Qin, J.: Automated skin lesion segmentation via an adaptive dual attention module. IEEE Trans. Med. Imaging (1), 357–370. https://doi.org/10.1109/TMI.2020.3027341

24. You, Y., Li, J., et al.: Large Batch Optimization for Deep Learning: Training BERT in 76 minutes. arXiv preprint arXiv:1904.00962, April 2019. https://arxiv.org/abs/1904.00962v5

Recognition/Generation

Implementation of Digital Transformation for Korean Traditional Heritage

Jae-Ho Lee(✉), Hye-Bin Lee, Hee-Kwon Kim, and Chan-Woo Park

Creative Content Research Division, Electronics and Telecommunications Research Institute,
Daejeon, Korea
{jhlee3,lhb32096,hkkim79,gamer}@etri.re.kr

Abstract. In this paper, we introduce technologies for transforming Korean traditional heritage into digital assets and applying them to various platforms. To transform low resolution and distorted historic images to high-resolution usable digital assets, we have trained deep learning models accustomed to analyzing traditional heritages. We have also established steps and specifications for acquiring high-quality 2D/3D models of traditional heritage for the generation of digital assets. Korean natural language processing and object detection models for analyzing relics tagged with historic information were also implemented for extracting relations and creating an intelligent search system. With the attained digital assets, a web-based intelligent database system was built regarding of an intuitive UI that allows museum curators to easily upload and retrieve the assets needed. Arranging and presenting the attained 3D digital heritage through VR/AR/WEB platforms were achieved through adequate transformation of data formats. By demonstrating and storing traditional relics thorough digital platforms, we expect further development of Korean traditional heritage preservation and education.

Keywords: Digital traditional heritage · Digital transformation · 2D/3D traditional heritage

1 Introduction

Over the past few years, the need for bringing traditional heritage to digital based platforms has been increasing. Presenting relics through digital platforms is not only an effective tool for education and research but also brings huge convenience in the management of cultural assets. For this reason, this research aims to convert Korean traditional heritages into refined digital assets, as well as providing adequate platforms for managing and presenting them.

In this paper, we introduce the process of attaining digital cultural heritage combined with the newest AI technology, for it has shown great level of development in their performance and output throughout recent years [1–4]. It will be used for transforming old and damaged image data into high resolution recognizable image and videos. High-quality digital cultural heritage asset acquisition technology is also involved, which will provide a safe systematic environment for acquiring cultural heritage data.

© The Author(s), under exclusive license to Springer Nature Switzerland AG 2022
K. Sumi et al. (Eds.): IW-FCV 2022, CCIS 1578, pp. 257–270, 2022.
https://doi.org/10.1007/978-3-031-06381-7_18

Also, through the attained cultural heritage datasets, we have tagged its historic information to derive useful keywords and create a historic knowledge graphs. Name Entity Recognition (NER) technology and language models accustomed to Korean syntax analyzation were applied. Object detection in traditional paintings were also implemented in this section, allowing more assets to be tagged and analyzed.

Building an Intelligent Curation Platform was subsequently required due to the effective use of attained traditional heritage and to effectively deal with existing vast amount of cultural heritage data. The platform allows elastic search for user convenience and automates the creation of diverse relation graphs between different cultural heritages. It also provides an exhibition visualization program, which offers curators to easily simulate the arrangement and placement of objects. The assets in the curation database aim to be readily used for implementing immersive interactive contents for future VR/AR exhibitions.

The paper is organized as follows. Section 2 introduces the process of attaining high resolution 2D/3D objects and implementing text analysis for intelligent search and detection systems of cultural heritage based on Artificial Intelligence technologies. Section 3 provides an overview of the Intelligent curation Platform, and how it leads to creating immersive cultural contents. Finally, Sect. 4 concludes the research and suggests future research directions.

2   Attaining High-Quality Digital Heritage

Since there were no adequate guidelines or practical standards for digital data acquisition of Korean Traditional Heritage, many of the preserved photographic films or video assets have faded in color or distorted through time. Before transferring into digital platforms, pre-processing in both past and newly acquired data were necessary for future use.

2.1   Enhancement of Existing Data

Image Enhancement. Old photos and videos of Korean traditional relics attained in the past decades lacked many qualities for analyzing and were poor in preserving the original information. Technology for enhancing imagery was necessary for retrieving meaningful information.

Color Enhancement and Noise Reduction. By applying computer vision algorithms of color enhancement, we have developed a Palette-based Re-colorization technique that divides the image into uniform additive mixing layers by RGBXY space. It can adjust the weighted value of the layers, which corresponds to the palette colors it refers to. Light enhancement technology based on the LIME algorithm was also applied. Unlike the Retinex Theory, which estimates both reflection factor and lighting factor, the LIME algorithm downsizes the space needed for the solution, and only tracks the lighting factor to reduce the amount of computation. To enhance the accuracy, we have used augmented Lagrangian Multiplier to correctly refine the Illumination map, and it has led to improvement in illumination quality.

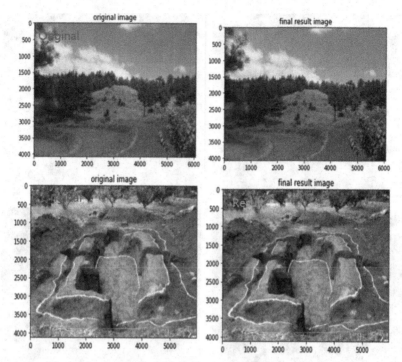

Fig. 1. The Re-colorization and Deblurring results

However, images enhanced by LIME algorithm tend to acquire noise, so we applied the BM3D algorithm in the last step for noise elimination. The results are shown in Fig. 1.

With the original image, it was hard to distinguish subtle details in the dark areas. By applying the LIME algorithm and BM3D algorithm, the results showed increased illumination and clearness in the dark parts, which allowed unseen objects to be more recognizable.

Deblurring. The deblurring mechanism for old traditional heritage image/videos focuses mainly in out of focus blur. It involves sharpening of blurry images, and quality enhancement by Guided Filter optimization. This process can be implemented in three steps, Blur map Generation, Image Deblurring with L1-2 Optimization, and Scale Se-lection. By the calculated local contrast and with guided filter, it proceeds the L1-2 optimization to produce several de-blurred images and by counting all the blur scales of each pixel, we choose the optimal deblurred output. The result images show sharpened edges and offers a clearer vision than the original input image (Fig. 2).

Super Resolution with CNN. Scratched, unclear, or partly lost historic images can be restored through Super Resolution technology, which is an image processing technology that converts low-resolution image into a high-resolution image. There are many preceding researches regarding of super-resolution technology using deep learning such as SRCNN (Super-Resolution Convolutional Neural Network) [5], VDSR (Accurate

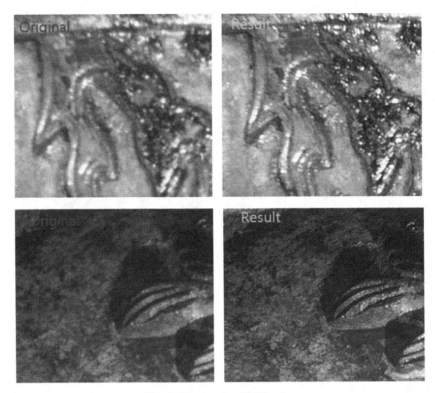

Fig. 2. The result of Deblurring

Image Super-Resolution Using Very Deep Convolutional Networks) [6], ESPCN (Efficient Sub-Pixel Convolutional Neural Network) [7], SRResnet [8], EDSR (Enhanced Deep Residual Networks for Single Image Super-Resolution) [9], and RCAN (Residual Channel Attention Networks) [10], but we propose a model inspired by RCAN that will be specialized for extracting characteristics from cultural heritage image.

Training with Paired Data. We have created a set of paired data that consists of original clean image and artificially degraded image involving scratches and noises. By training with the paired image inputs, the goal is to produce an enhanced output image from the degradations.

The paired model architecture is based on Operation-wise Attention Network (OWAN). It consists of 1 Feature extraction block, 5 operation-wise attention layer, and 1 output layer with 64 channels. The learning rate was set to 0.001, and an Adam optimizer with $\beta_1 = 0.5$, $\beta_2 = 0.999$. DIV2K dataset applied with low-quality generation code weas used as the dataset (Patch size: 64×64, batch size: 8).

Training with Unpaired Data. This training process is for converting old traditional Heritage videos into videos with modern color and contrast. We have proposed and Image translation model with the Laplacian pyramid (Fig. 3), which Inputs the old

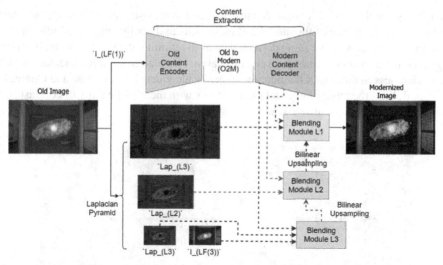

Fig. 3. Proposed network architecture with unpaired data

image and outputs a new image. It was also trained in the reverse direction, by setting the input as the new image and output with the old image.

The encoder and decoder are made of 3 Residual Blocks, and the input domain and output domain are trained with different encoder and decoder. The Latent Translation Module is made of 2 Residual Blocks, Input to Target (I2T), Target to Input (T2I), and two translation modules were trained (Fig. 4).

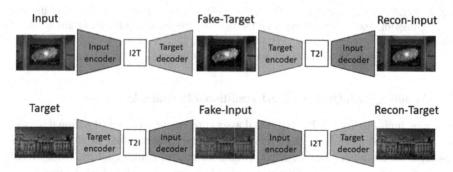

Fig. 4. Training strategy for unpaired model

The Cycle Loss and the Self Reconstruction Loss is calculated as the following:

$$L\_cycle = |Input - Recon\_Input| + |Target - Recon\_Target|$$
$$L\_reconstruction = |Input - Self\_Recon\_Input| + |Target - Self\_Recon\_Target|$$

Results. Since the model was not constructed as a supervised learning model and has no GT, the performance of the model had to be measured not by numeric results, but by qualitive analysis. With the same domain data as the training data, the outputs showed a higher contrast and chromatic features, elimination of sepia-red color pig-mentation, and more clearness in the object boundaries. In grayscale videos, the contrast and clearness increased. With the input of new datasets, outputs with increased quality of contrast and chromatic features were also acknowledgeable (Fig. 5).

Fig. 5. Results of super resolution. The left two pictures are the input and output of the same training domain, and the two pictures on the right are the input and output of a new training domain.

2.2 Attaining High Quality 2D/3D Traditional Heritage Assets

Attaining high-quality 2D/3D traditional assets are crucial in terms of national heritage preservation and creating immersive VR/AR digital content-based exhibitions. In this research, we establish a standardized process for attaining high-quality 2D/3D Korean traditional heritage assets and develop technology for assembling high volume GIGA pixel image data and processing 3D polygon assets.

Acquisition of 2D/3D Heritage and Data Processing. We have established a standard acquisition environment and guidelines for attaining 2D/3D imagery and panoramic multi-image restoring technology. Lighting, distance, equipment specification, NPP (Non-parallax point) settings, data quality enhancement (lens test by 800 mm, 1200 mm), number of cuts were measured and determined in this process (Fig. 6).

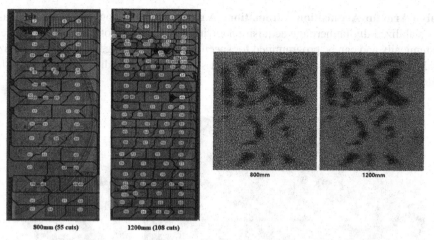

Fig. 6. An example of lens test for data quality enhancement

We have also executed a comparison between 3D data acquired with structured light scanner and multi-view camera, for its accuracy in polygon and point cloud generation. Along with the modeling accuracy, texture mapping qualities were also compared between the two methods (Fig. 7).

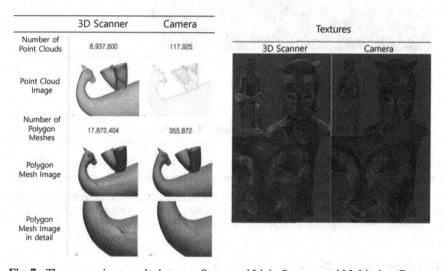

Fig. 7. The comparison results between Structured Light Scanner and Multi-view Camera

Processing Data and Adjustment Technology. Research for texture mapping and polygon modeling was done with the attained 3D datasets. Multi-perspective panoramic image arrangement, texture projection UV remapping, substance painter texture compensation process were the stages for modeling the final 3D object.

Robot Arm for Acquisition Automation. A robot arm technology was used for a safe and stabilized digital heritage acquisition environment. The robot's arm elevates itself systemically and can be programmed for specific positioning (Fig. 8). We input the size of the relic we want to attain, and the robot sets its moving radius depending on the following value.

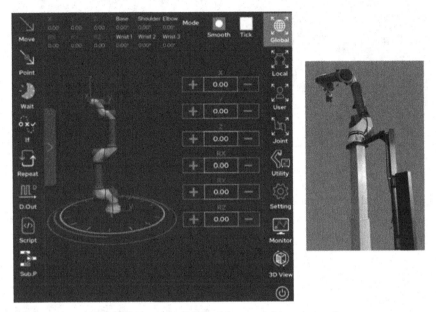

Fig. 8. Robot arm designed for acquisition automation

3   Building an Intelligent Curation Platform

By applying the newest deep learning language models for analyzing Korean semantic segments and object detection in traditional paintings, we have created an intuitive and user-friendly platform for the search and presentation of Korean traditional digital heritage. Also, using the attained 2D/3D traditional assets, we seek the optimal display in virtual museums and web contents.

3.1   Tagging Information and Analyzation

Implementing NER (Named Entity Recognition). For implementing meaning based intelligent search and extracting relation models with traditional heritages, we have collaborated with researchers majoring in Korean History for segment tagging and analysis process. Large-capacity of corpus datasets were retrieved from Korean National e-Museums. By tagging nouns regarding historic features and defining simple relation of each asset, we intended to not only allow intelligent search, but also to apply deep learning technology for automating the recognition and analyzation of future digital heritage inputs.

NER (Named Entity Recognition) is a technology for extracting individual names, such as person names (PS), place names (LC), and organization names (OG) of the input. There are many existing Korean natural language processing models, but in this research, we have used KoBERT and HanBERT, and the RoBERTa [11] model and the Korean language model of ELECTRA [12]. The overall training process for e-museum NER is illustrated in Fig. 9.

Given the input as a text format, the optimized NER language model for analyzing Korean traditional heritage asset creates a sub-word from the dataset and extracts the final keyword.

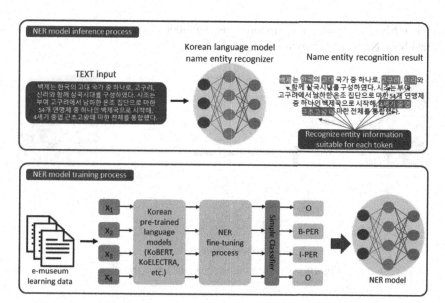

Fig. 9. NER model inference and the training process of Korean historic texts and assets

Results. Here we show the training conditions and the result of each language model (Table 1). We have set different values of training rate for figuring out the optimal condition for traditional asset entity recognition. F1-score evaluation was implemented for calculating the ability of each model, giving the average accuracy of 84.55%.

Object Detection in Traditional Paintings. Recent object detection technologies have shown great ability in detecting objects and producing the desired output. However, since traditional paintings distinguish significantly from natural images, new datasets for training and detection were necessary. Experts with great understanding in Korean traditional paintings worked together as the annotators through image tagging process in creating datasets. We have created a network model for effectively detecting objects in Korean traditional paintings and heritages and automized the training process (Fig. 11).

Table 1. Training conditions and F1-score of each model

Training elements	value	Model	F1-score
Training epoch	10	KoBERT	84.13%
Learning rate	{3e-5, 4e-5, 1e-4}	HanBERT	**84.51%**
Learning seed	5 random seeds	KoELECTRA	83.59%
Weight decay	0.01	RoBERTa	83.51%
Train batch size	256		
Test batch size	128		
GPU	RTX A6000 * 1		

Faster R-CNN object detector and Pytorch based mmdetection package was applied with the Backbone Network of ResNext101_64_FPN (Fig. 10).

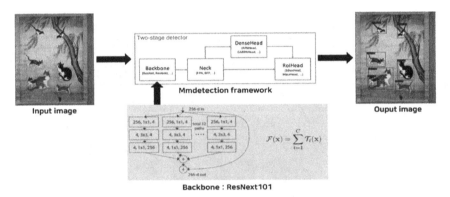

Fig. 10. Overview of the object detection model

Results. For the detection of person in Korean traditional paintings, we have organized three different datasets for training and evaluation, which the first group of all paintings, second with paintings consisting of 5 or less people, and the last group only containing portraits. The evaluation results were, with the IoU value of 0.5, the highest mAP for each group were 41.7%, 77.9%, and 95.3%. And for the detection of animals, for the 12 classified groups, it marked mAP of 64.0%.

With the inference results of the test-set images, the below figure displays the confusion matrix which contains the classification accuracy of the created object detection model. In classifying 11 different groups, it has shown total accuracy of 0.933, precision of 0.861 and recall value of 0.976.

3.2 A Web-based Intuitive Platform

A web-based intelligent curating platform with easy to use and upload facilities were necessary. Elastic search for user convenience, launching the digital asset viewer, seeing

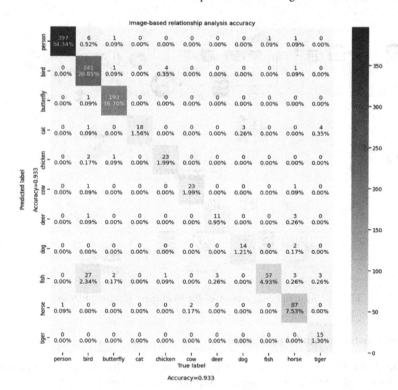

Fig. 11. The Confusion Matrix of person-animal classification in Korean traditional paintings

through keywords and creating knowledge graphs were all implemented in this process [13].

Design of the Intelligent Curation Platform. In the newly constructed Intelligent Cultural Heritage Platform [14], specific assets can be grouped as project units, and by this categorization they can be easily used as organizing new exhibitions considering various topics and themes.

Loading specific modules and creating new projects are all within the server system. Figure 12 shows the configuration of the Intelligent Curation Platform. The asset information data are shared through the database and by separating the role user and administrator, important assets can be safely managed.

Virtual simulation of exhibitions is also possible. The preview feature allows seeing digital traditional heritage assets in detail before the real exhibition. With the intuitive UI and user manuals which museum curators can have easy access in using the system.

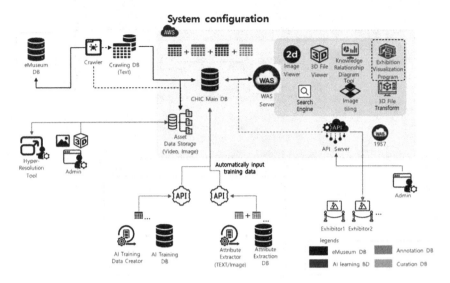

Fig. 12. System configuration of the Intelligent Curation Platform

3.3 Demonstration and Application

With the attained 2D/3D digital heritage data that are readily for use in various platforms, we can now apply the assets for digital exhibition and display (Fig. 13).

Contents for Virtual Museum. For creating virtual museum platforms, preceding research on the existing virtual museums were conducted to create immersive and comfortable formation of the virtual space. Our virtual museum aims to offer individualized curation service with original interaction methods, and transportation between locations.

To accomplish further interactive user experience, tracking and detecting specific user behavior were also implemented in the application. Users can interact with assets in the virtual platform and perform small tasks within the system.

Web Content Demonstration. The web-based e-museum offers users and curators multimedia references for seeing and studying traditional heritage relics.

The Web 3D viewer was developed using Three.js modules. Uploading 3D assets to the web viewer required several steps of file conversion, for 3D files had to be provided as formats accessible in programs such as Unreal, Unity and other DCC tools. The refined 3D object then transforms into various file formats for easy upload and modifications in the web environment.

Fig. 13. Demonstration in VR/WEB platforms

4   Conclusion

Establishing standards for attaining and processing digital cultural heritage assets is now an inevitable process for the preservation of traditional heritage and the changing paradigm of museum exhibitions. Especially in Korea, as this research was the first actual attempt for transferring Korean traditional heritage assets into digital platforms, considerable amount of preliminary research and preparation work had to be done in analyzing the historical assets.

We have developed a customized image enhancement method for old relic photographs and 2D/3D data acquisition technology for Korean traditional heritage using the latest deep learning models. All of this process will help analyze and extract meaningful information regarding of Korean national history.

The digitally transformed Korean traditional assets were also made to be applicable in the VR/AR and web platforms for display, and bring convenience for both users and professional curators in browsing the assets. These digitally preserved data will pass on for future research and education in Korean History.

For future research directions, we aim to develop a more sophisticated asset knowledge linking system with the obtained Korean heritage NER results. Also, more of immersive AR/VR contents with various interactions are to be developed using the 3D digital heritage assets.

Acknowledgment. This research is supported by Ministry of Culture, Sports and Tourism and Korea Creative Content Agency (Project Number: R2020040045).

References

1. Vo, N., et al.: Composing text and image for image retrieval – an empirical odyssey. IEEE Conference on Computer Vision and Pattern Recognition (CVPR), pp. 6439–6448. California, America, (2019)
2. Teichmann, M., et al.: Detect-to-retrieve: efficient regional aggregation for image search. IEEE Conference on Computer Vision and Pattern Recognition (CVPR), pp. 5109–5118. California, America, (2019)
3. Dai, T., et al.: Second-order attention network for single image super-resolution. In: IEEE Conference on Computer Vision and Pattern Recognition (CVPR), pp. 11065–11074. California, America, (2019)

4. Lim, B., et al.: Enhanced deep residual networks for single image super-resolution. In: NTIRE 2017 Workshop. pp.136–144. Hawaii, America, (2017)
5. Dong, C., Loy, C.C., He, K., Tang, X.: Learning a deep convolutional network for image super-resolution. In: Fleet, D., Pajdla, T., Schiele, B., Tuytelaars, T. (eds.) ECCV 2014. LNCS, vol. 8692, pp. 184–199. Springer, Cham (2014). https://doi.org/10.1007/978-3-319-10593-2_13
6. Kim, J., Lee, J.K., Lee, K.M.: Accurate image super-resolution using very deep convolutional networks. In: IEEE Conference on Computer Vision and Pattern Recognition, pp. 1646–1654 (2016)
7. Shi, W., et al.: Real-time single image and video super resolution using an efficient sub-pixel convolutional neural network. In: IEEE Conference on Computer Vision and Pattern Recognition (CVPR), pp. 1874–1883 (2016)
8. Ledig, C., et al.: Photo-realistic single image super-resolution using a generative adversarial network. arXiv:1609.04802 (2016)
9. Lim, B., Son, S., Kim, H., Nah, S., Lee, K.M.: Enhanced deep residual networks for single image super-resolution. In: CVPRW (2017)
10. Zhang, Y., Li, K., Li, K., Wang, L., Zhong, B., Fu, Y.: Image super resolution using very deep residual channel attention networks. In: ECCV (2018)
11. Nie, B., Ding, R., Xie, P., Huang, F., Qian, C., Si, L.: Knowledge aware named entity recognition with alleviating heterogeneity. AAAI Conf. Artif. Intell. **35**(15), 13595–13603 (2021)
12. Tran, Q., MacKinlay, A., Yepes, A.J.: Named entity recognition with stack residual ISTM and trainable bias decoding. arXiv:1706.07598 (2017)
13. Lee, J.-H., Kim, H.-K., Park, C.-W.: Studies on intelligent curation for the Korean traditional cultural heritage. In: ICAIIC (2022)
14. Lee, J.-H., Kim, H.-K., Park, C.-W.: CHIC: cultural heritage intelligent curation platform In: ICEIC (2021)

Facial Mask Region Completion Using StyleGAN2 with a Substitute Face of the Same Person

Hiroaki Koike and Norihiko Kawai$^{(\boxtimes)}$

Faculty of Information Science and Technology, Osaka Institute of Technology,
1-79-1 Kitayama, Hirakata, Osaka 573-0196, Japan
norihiko.kawai@oit.ac.jp

Abstract. In recent years, there has been a worldwide outbreak of coronaviruses, and people are wearing facial masks more and more often. In many cases, people wear masks even when taking photos of themselves, and when photos with the lower half of the face hidden are uploaded to web pages or social networking sites, it is difficult to convey the attractiveness of the photographed persons. In this study, we propose a method to complete the masked region in a face using StyleGAN2, a kind of Generative Adversarial Networks (GAN). In the proposed method, we prepare an image of the same person who is not wearing a mask, and change the orientation and contour of the face of the person in the image to match those of the target image using StyleGAN2. Then, the image with the changed orientation is combined with the target image in which the person is wearing the mask to produce an image in which the mask region is completed.

Keywords: Image inpainting · Image completion · GAN · Facial mask

1 Introduction

A coronavirus pandemic is sweeping the world, endangering many lives. In order to prevent the spread of the infection, people are asked to refrain from going out unnecessarily and to wear facial masks in public places. As a result, people wear masks even when taking photos of themselves. Therefore, when a photo with the lower half of the face hidden is uploaded to a web page or social networking site, it is difficult to convey the attractiveness of the photographed person. For this reason, if we can generate images with unmasked faces, we can convey the attractiveness of the persons even when taking photos while wearing their masks.

One technique that can be used for this purpose is image inpainting/completion, which has been aimed at plausibly filling in unwanted regions in an image. As image completion approaches, diffusion-based [1,3], patch-based [2,4,6,9,10], and machine learning-based [5,12,13,15] methods have been proposed. Since the diffusion-based methods propagate colors to missing regions, they cannot reproduce texture in the missing regions. The patch-based methods

K. Sumi et al. (Eds.): IW-FCV 2022, CCIS 1578, pp. 271–285, 2022.
https://doi.org/10.1007/978-3-031-06381-7_19

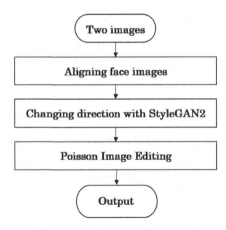

Fig. 1. Flow of the proposed method.

search for similar patterns in the image and synthesizes them in missing regions. However, it cannot synthesize textures that do not exist in other regions in the image. For the application of facial mask area completion, these methods cannot be used because the texture of the nose and mouth cannot be properly reproduced.

On the other hand, the machine learning-based image completion methods using Generative Adversarial Networks (GANs), a type of machine learning, understand the structure of face regions and provide good results for face completion. For example, there are studies that introduced edges [13], segmentation [12], and landmarks [15] to improve the consistency of face structure and texture. In addition, the method in [5] automatically identifies and completes facial mask regions from supervised learning. However, since the nose and mouth are completed depending on the face images used for training, the completed face image does not always have the characteristics of the person.

In this study, we prepare an image of the same person who is not wearing a mask, and change the orientation and contour of the face of the person in the image using StyleGAN2 [7,8]. We also change the face expression according to the user's preference. Then, the image with the changed orientation and contour is combined with the target image in which the person is wearing the mask to produce an image in which the mask region is completed. This approach completes the mouth and nose with the characteristics of the person.

2   Proposed Method

2.1   Overview

The processing procedure of the proposed method is shown in Fig. 1. The proposed method takes two input images, one with a facial mask and the other without a facial mask. Figure 2(a) shows example images wearing a facial mask, and Fig. 2(b) shows an example image of the same person without a facial mask. Next, as a preprocessing step, the faces in the prepared images are aligned so that the parts such as the mouth and nose are in the specified positions. Next, StyleGAN2 is used to estimate the latent variable for the preprocessed image, and generate the image from the estimated latent variable. We then use Style Mixing, one of the features of StyleGAN2, to deform the face of the unmasked image to match the orientation of the face wearing the mask. According to the user's preference, the face expression is also changed by inputting another image with a different expression. Finally, by using Poisson Image Editing [14], the image with the changed face orientation is combined with the image of the face wearing the mask to produce an image in which the masked part is completed. The detailed processing of the proposed method is described below.

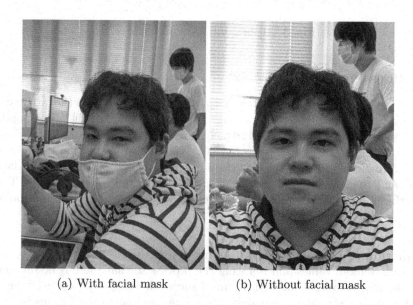

(a) With facial mask   (b) Without facial mask

Fig. 2. Example input images.

2.2   Alignment of Face Images

The StyleGAN2 model used in this study was trained and generated on the FFHQ dataset, which contains a large number of face images, and the landmarks of the faces were aligned to the same position for training. Therefore, if the images are not aligned in the same way before inputting them into StyleGAN2, the quality of image generation will be low. We use Dlib [11], a machine learning library, to detect landmarks on the face and align them. The image is rotated so that the eyes are at the same height, and the center coordinates are obtained from the positions of the eyes and the mouth, and the image is cropped to form a square. Figure 3 shows the aligned images of Fig. 2.

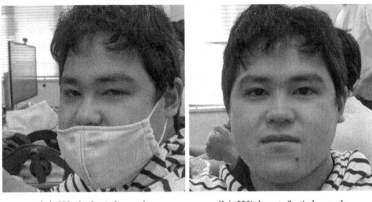

(a) With facial mask   (b) Without facial mask

Fig. 3. Aligned example input images.

2.3   Processing by StyleGAN2

In StyleGAN2, by inputting a latent variable, which is a point in the latent space where various elements of the training data are distributed, the corresponding image is generated. In order to edit a face image using StyleGAN2, the face image to be edited must be generated by StyleGAN2. To do this, we first estimate the latent variable of an image that is close to the prepared image from the latent space, and then generate an image using the estimated latent variable. Then, we perform Style Mixing on the generated image to change the orientation and contour of the face.

Estimation of Latent Variable. Estimation of the latent variable is done by inputting random values and iterating the process so that there is no difference from the image to be estimated. Figure 4 shows the images generated from the latent variable estimated by searching for images close to the images in Fig. 3 300 times each. It should be noted that StyleGAN2 is trained on face images without facial masks. Therefore, even if we input images with facial masks such as Fig. 3(a), face images with masks removed are outputted as shown in Fig. 4(a).

Orientation and Contour Change by Style Mixing. StyleGAN2 is a neural network that generates images by gradually increasing the resolution from 4×4 images to 1024×1024 images. In this process, latent variables are input as style information to generate images for different resolutions, and each resolution has a different effect. StyleGAN2 allows different latent variables to be input at different resolutions, and by inputting two latent variables at different resolutions, it is possible to generate an image that mixes the features of the two images. Specifically, we mainly control the orientation and contour of the face in the low resolutions, and the hair and skin color in the high resolutions.

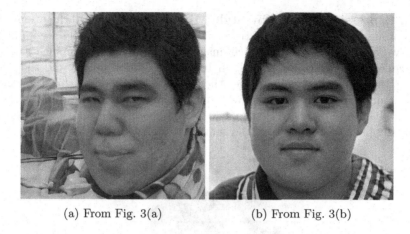

(a) From Fig. 3(a)   (b) From Fig. 3(b)

Fig. 4. Images generated from the estimated latent variable.

In this study, since we want to change the orientation of the face in Fig. 4(b) to match Fig. 4(a), we input the latent variable that generates Fig. 4(a) when generating images with low resolutions such as 4×4 and 8×8 resolutions, and the latent variable that generates Fig. 4(b) when generating images with the other resolutions. This reflects the features in Fig. 4(b) in the generation of the face orientation and contour. The output result from the two latent variables is shown in Fig. 5. The masked region in Fig. 3(a) are completed using this result.

Fig. 5. Result of style mixing using Fig. 4.

Facial Expression Change by Style Mixing. In addition to the orientation and contour, we can also change the facial expression. Specifically, we input the latent variable for generating a face image with some expression such as Fig. 6 with smile when generating a medium 16×16 resolution image, and the latent variable that generates Fig. 5 for the other resolutions. By doing this, the feature of the mouth is reflected, and the face shown in Fig. 5 becomes a smile as shown in Fig. 7. It should be noted that images with different facial expressions do not necessarily have to be images of the same person.

Fig. 6. Smile face.

Fig. 7. Result of style mixing using Figs. 4 and 6.

2.4 Completion with Poisson Image Editing

When Fig. 5 is simply merged with the mask in Fig. 3(a), the different color tones of the images make the boundary of the merged region clear and unnatural. Therefore, we use Poisson image editing to create a seamless image composition.

In Poisson image editing, the pixel values after composition are calculated to minimize the squared error of the gradient between the destination image and the source image. Concretely, f_p is obtained such that the cost function E shown in Eq. (1) is minimized.

$$E = \sum_{(p,q)\in N} ((f_p - f_q) - (g_p - g_q))^2, \tag{1}$$

where f is the pixel value of the destination image, g is the pixel value of the source image, p is the pixel of interest, and q is its neighboring pixel. By doing this, the color tone of the composite region is made to resemble the destination image, and the texture is made to resemble the source image.

Figure 8 shows the results of combining the images of Figs. 5 and 7 into Fig. 3(a) by Poisson image editing for the specified mask area shown in Fig. 8(c). As shown in the figure, the color tones are corrected to match the destination image.

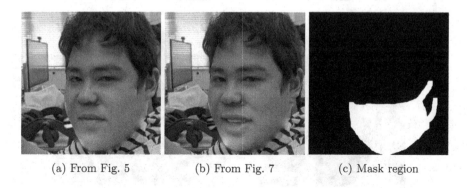

   (a) From Fig. 5   (b) From Fig. 7   (c) Mask region

Fig. 8. Results of Poisson image editing.

3 Experiments

To demonstrate the effectiveness of the proposed method, we prepared face images of persons wearing a mask and frontal images of the same persons as shown in Fig. 9. In this study, we conducted two types of experiments. In the first experiment, we checked the results of completing the mask regions and compared them with the actual face images with the mask removed. In the second experiment, we estimated latent variables in the images showing various expressions and verified the effect of facial expression changes using them.

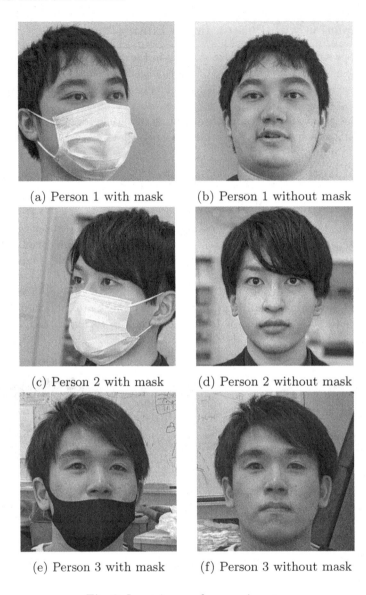

(a) Person 1 with mask   (b) Person 1 without mask

(c) Person 2 with mask   (d) Person 2 without mask

(e) Person 3 with mask   (f) Person 3 without mask

Fig. 9. Input images for experiments.

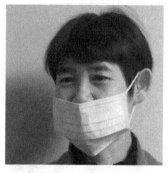

(g) Person 4 with mask   (h) Person 4 without mask

Fig. 9. (*continued*)

3.1 Experiment 1

Figure 10 shows the completion results of the mask regions in Fig. 9 and the actual face image at that angle. The experimental results show that the orientations and contours of the faces are properly modified in all the images. In the case of Persons 1, 2, and 3, the color tones of the faces are properly adjusted by Poisson image editing, and the boundary between the completed area of the facial mask region and the other region in the face is not noticeable. On the other hand, if the quality of the prepared image is poor, as in the image of Person 4, the boundary between the area where the mask is completed and the original image is noticeable.

Next, we compare the completion result of mask regions with the images in which the persons actually took off the facial masks. In the case of Person 1, the shape of the mouth, cheek bulge, and beard as shown in Fig. 9(b) are reflected in Fig. 10(a). However, features of moles were not represented when projecting the real image into the latent space and the moles disappeared. In the case of Person 3, the texture of the skin is reflected, and there are no major differences when compared to the actual person.

In the case of Person 2, the noses and mouths are misaligned in Figs. 10(c) compared to Fig. 10(d), indicating that the parts are synthesized on the front side of the face, rather than the positions of the parts corresponding to the orientation of the actual face. This is because most of the nose in Fig. 9(c) is hidden by a facial mask, making it difficult for StyleGAN2 to estimate the orientation of the face. In fact, in the training of StyleGAN2, there are not many images in which the faces are largely turned sideways. Therefore, when the latent variables are estimated and the face images are created, the orientation of the nose is different from the actual one as shown in Fig. 11.

Another difference is that the completion images in Fig. 10 appears to have slightly longer chins than the actual images. The reason for this is that when the latent variable corresponding to the image with the facial mask is worn is found in the latent space, the image generated from the latent variable tends to

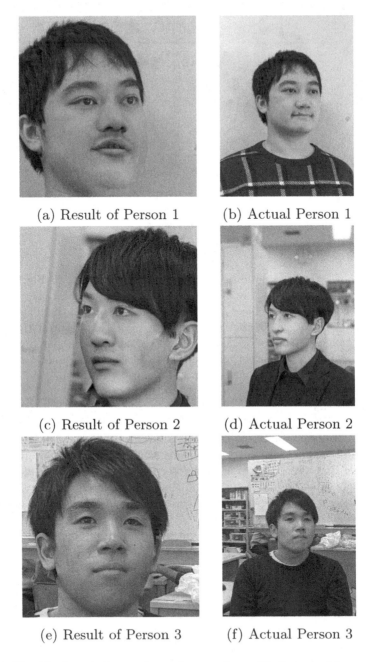

(a) Result of Person 1   (b) Actual Person 1

(c) Result of Person 2   (d) Actual Person 2

(e) Result of Person 3   (f) Actual Person 3

Fig. 10. Completion results and comparison with the actual faces.

(g) Result of Person 4   (h) Actual Person 4

Fig. 10. (*continued*)

have a wider and longer chin due to the puffiness of the facial mask. In style mixing, not only the orientation of the face but also the contour of the face is affected, resulting in the generation of a completion result with a long chin. An improvement would be to use some kind of image inpainting to complete the mask area in advance, and then use that image for style mixing.

3.2 Experiment 2

In this experiment, we examine the effect of facial expression change. Figure 12 shows images representing various facial expressions used for expression change. Figure 13 shows the completion results using the latent variables estimated from these images with various expression for Figs. 10(a) and (e), which were relatively successfully completed in Experiment 1.

The results of the experiment show that the mouths of both Persons 1 and 3 changed significantly in response to the expressions of happiness, surprise, and disgust, and that the mouth of Person 1, whose mouth was originally slightly open, closed in response to sadness. The vertical and horizontal openings for happiness, sadness, surprise, and disgust were reflected, but subtle changes such as the lowering of the corners of the mouth in Fig. 12(b), which was used for the sadness image, were not. In general, not only changes in the mouth but also changes in the eyes can be combined to recognize the entire facial expression. However, since this study focuses on complementing the facial mask region, we believe that the two types of facial expressions, happiness and surprise, which can be easily recognized by changes in the opening and closing of the mouth alone, are practical based on the above results.

Fig. 11. Image generated from Fig. 9(c) by estimating its latent variable.

(a) Happiness   (b) Sadness

(c) Surprise   (d) Disgust

Fig. 12. Various expressions.

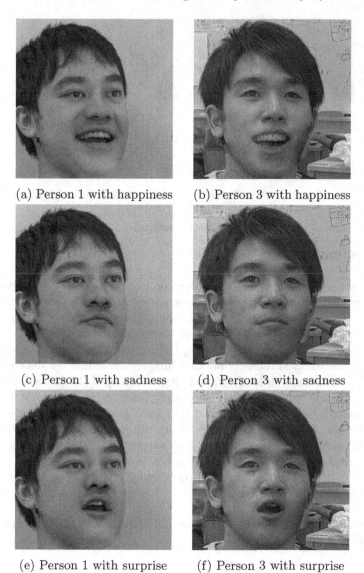

(a) Person 1 with happiness   (b) Person 3 with happiness

(c) Person 1 with sadness   (d) Person 3 with sadness

(e) Person 1 with surprise   (f) Person 3 with surprise

Fig. 13. Input images for experiments.

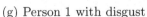

(g) Person 1 with disgust   (h) Person 3 with disgust

Fig. 13. (*continued*)

4 Conclusion

In this study, we proposed a mask region completion method using StyleGAN2 and another substitute image of the same person without a facial mask. In the proposed method, successful completion was achieved by correcting the orientation and contour of the face without a facial mask using StyleGAN2, correcting its color tones and synthesizing it using Poisson image editing. In addition, by estimating the latent variable of another image with a different expression and introducing it in the middle of style mixing, we changed the face expression.

In experiments, we showed that the completion with the features of the person can be achieved, but we also confirmed that small features such as moles are lost due to the low accuracy of latent variable estimation. As for the changes in facial expressions, we confirmed that the changes were reflected in the vertical and horizontal changes of the mouth, but not in the detailed features.

Future work includes the introduction of image inpainting to further improve orientations and contours.

Acknowledgements. This work was supported by JSPS KAKENHI Grant Numbers JP18H03273, JP18H04116, JP21H03483.

References

1. Ballester, C., Bertalmío, M., Caselles, V., Sapiro, G., Verdera, J.: Filling-in by joint interpolation of vector fields and gray levels. IEEE Trans. Image Process. **10**(8), 1200–1211 (2001)
2. Barnes, C., Shechtman, E., Finkelstein, A., Goldman, D.B.: Patchmatch: a randomized correspondence algorithm for structural image editing. ACM Trans. Graph. **28**, 24:1–24:11 (2009)
3. Bertalmío, M., Sapiro, G., Caselles, V., Ballester, C.: Image inpainting. In: Proceedings of SIGGRAPH, pp. 417–424 (2000)
4. Criminisi, A., Pérez, P., Toyama, K.: Region filling and object removal by exemplar-based image inpainting. IEEE Trans. Image Process. **13**(9), 1200–1212 (2004)

5. Din, N.U., Javed, K., Bae, S., Yi, J.: A novel GAN-based network for unmasking of masked face. IEEE Access **8**, 44276–44287 (2020)
6. Efros, A.A., Leung, T.K.: Texture synthesis by non-parametric sampling. In: Proceedings of IEEE International Conference on Computer Vision, vol. 2, pp. 1033–1038 (1999)
7. Karras, T., Laine, S., Aila, T.: A style-based generator architecture for generative adversarial networks. In: Proceedings of IEEE Conference on Computer Vision and Pattern Recognition, pp. 4401–4410 (2019)
8. Karras, T., Laine, S., Aittala, M., Hellsten, J., Lehtinen, J., Aila, T.: Analyzing and improving the image quality of StyleGAN. In: Proceedings of IEEE Conference on Computer Vision and Pattern Recognition, pp. 8110–8119 (2020)
9. Kawai, N., Sato, T., Yokoya, N.: Image inpainting considering brightness change and spatial locality of textures and its evaluation. In: Proceedings of Pacific-Rim Symposium on Image and Video Technology, pp. 271–282 (2009)
10. Kawai, N., Yokoya, N.: Image inpainting considering symmetric patterns. In: Proceedings of IAPR International Conference on Pattern Recognition, pp. 2744–2747 (2012)
11. King, D.E.: Dlib-ml: a machine learning toolkit. J. Mach. Learn. Res. **10**, 1755–1758 (2009)
12. Li, Y., Liu, S., Yang, J., Yang, M.H.: Generative face completion, pp. 5892–5900 (2017)
13. Nazeri, K., Ng, E., Joseph, T., Qureshi, F.Z., Ebrahimi, M.: EdgeConnect: Structure guided image inpainting using edge prediction, pp. 3265–3274 (2019)
14. Pérez, P., Gangnet, M., Blake, A.: Poisson image editing. ACM Trans. Graph. **22**(3), 313–318 (2003)
15. Yang, Y., Guo, X.: Generative landmark guided face inpainting. In: Proceedings of Chinese Conference on Pattern Recognition and Computer Vision, pp. 14–26 (2020)

Generation of Omnidirectional Image Without Photographer

Ryusei Noda and Norihiko Kawai[✉][iD]

Faculty of Information Science and Technology, Osaka Institute of Technology,
1-79-1 Kitayama, Hirakata, Osaka 573-0196, Japan
norihiko.kawai@oit.ac.jp

Abstract. In order to create a virtual reality (VR) space using omnidirectional images, it is desirable to use images without the photographer's inclusion. In this study, we propose a method to generate an omnidirectional image without the photographer's inclusion by using multiple images taken by an omnidirectional camera. In the proposed method, the photographer rotates around the omnidirectional camera and takes several images. Next, we perform feature point matching on the omnidirectional images and unify the appearance of all the images by using the amount of translation calculated from the matching. Finally, the images are combined with graph cut and Poisson image editing to produce an omnidirectional panoramic image without the photographer in it.

Keywords: Omnidirectional image · Photographer removal · Graph cut

1 Introduction

With the widespread use of omnidirectional cameras, more and more people use them in various situations. The size of the omnidirectional camera is getting smaller, and now it can fit in one hand. Therefore, it is easy to take a panoramic image by holding an omnidirectional camera in one's hand. The omnidirectional panoramic images taken by such an omnidirectional camera are used in the construction of VR spaces for the purpose of virtual experience of remote areas such as Google Street View and real estate previews on the Internet. However, when taking an omnidirectional image while holding the camera in one's hand, the photographer appears in a large part of the image, and the background is partially obscured. For this reason, it is preferable to remove moving objects such as the photographer for the above purpose.

One solution to this problem is to set up an omnidirectional camera on a tripod and capture images remotely. However, this method cannot be used over water or on uneven terrain. In addition, even if a tripod is used, the tripod appear in the image. Although inpainting methods for static images [3,9,12,15] may be able to remove the tripod and the photographer from the image, it requires a lot of effort to specify the target area manually, and the inpainted result may be different from the actual background.

In contrast to this, methods have been proposed to display the actual background in the area of the unneeded objects to be removed by taking multiple images and videos of the actual background and combining them. For example, Cohen [2] proposed a method to generate a background-only image by using a video taken with a fixed camera as input and selecting and copying a frame without moving objects for each pixel. However, since a fixed camera is assumed, alignment between frames is not necessary. Different methods are to use optical flow to align its background and restore the background by copying pixel values from other frames [10,14]. However, since optical flow is used, they assume that the camera movement between frames is not too large.

On the other hand, object removal for omnidirectional images captured by an omnidirectional camera has also been studied. The method in [5] removes humans by transforming perspective projection images obtained from omnidirectional images taken at different points by homography and combining them. Since this method uses only a homography transformation for alignment between images, misalignment occurs if the background is not flat. The method in [8] performs structure-from-motion [13] and multi-view stereo [7] on omnidirectional images captured while moving, and the estimated camera pose and background shapes are used to align the images and restore the background of moving objects. As described above, the conventional research assumes the input of omnidirectional images captured with different positions.

In this study, we propose a method to generate an omnidirectional image with the photographer in the image removed without using any equipment such as a tripod. The photographer with an omnidirectional camera takes several pictures while rotating around the omnidirectional camera so that the camera position do not change. The method generates an omnidirectional image without a photographer by aligning the images using feature matching and automatically selecting an appropriate input image without a photographer for each pixel.

2 Proposed Method

2.1 Overview

In the proposed method, (1) we first input multiple omnidirectional images taken by the photographer while rotating around an omnidirectional camera. In this study, we assume that the same object is at approximately the same height in each omnidirectional image because the omnidirectional images are generated using the direction of gravity obtained from the accelerometer in the camera. (2) Harris corner detection is performed for each input image. Patches are set up around the feature points detected by Harris corner detection, and the most similar patches are matched by calculating the sum of squared differences (SSD) of pixel values between the patches in the two images. The horizontal translation between the omnidirectional images is calculated by RANSAC and the least-squares method. (3) The appearance of each input image is unified using the calculated amount of horizontal translation. (4) The appropriate image without the photographer is selected for each pixel by graph cut. Finally, (5) the pixel values are synthesized from the selected images with Poisson image editing to produce an omnidirectional image without the photographer. In the following, steps (2) through (5) are described in detail.

2.2   Calculation of Translation

Each input image is converted to grayscale and Harris corner detection [6] is performed. In Harris corner detection, pixels where large changes in pixel values are observed are detected, and these are used as feature points. Figure 1 shows an image in which feature points were extracted by Harris corner detection.

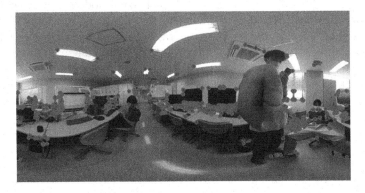

Fig. 1. Example image in which feature points are extracted by Harris corner detection.

Next, the sum of squared differences (SSD) of pixel values is used to correspond the feature points between each input image. Specifically, the method calculates the SSD between the patches centered on the feature points in one of the input images and the patches centered on the feature points in each of the other input images, and finds the feature points with the smallest SSD for each feature point, and corresponds them.

As mentioned above, in each omnidirectional image, this study uses the assumption that the same object is at approximately the same height due to the camera function that outputs omnidirectional images using the direction of gravity of the camera. Therefore, when calculating the SSD between a target feature point and other feature points, the SSD is calculated only for those feature points whose Y-coordinate values of other feature points are within a certain range of the Y-coordinate values of the target feature point. This reduces the computation time and the occurrence of erroneous correspondences.

Next, we calculate the amount of horizontal translation using RANSAC and the least-squares method. RANSAC (Random Sample Consensus) [4] is a robust estimation method that considers the possibility that a given observation contains outliers and aims to eliminate their effects. In this study, we randomly

extract a certain pair of corresponding points from the pairs of corresponding points determined by SSD. We count the number of pairs of corresponding
points whose amounts of translations are within a certain range compared to
the amount of translation between the selected corresponding points. This process is repeated to determine the pair of corresponding points with the highest
number of counts. The corresponding points whose amounts of translations are
not within the range compared to the amount of translation of the determined
pair are excluded as outliers. After the outliers are removed, the least-squares
method is used to find the average of the translations of all the remaining pairs
and calculate the amount of translation between the two images. Note that all
translations are calculated in the plus direction since the image we are dealing
with here is an omnidirectional image, that is, the leftmost pixel is connected to
the rightmost pixel.

2.3   Unifying the Appearance of Multiple Images

The input images other than the reference one are shifted in the X-axis direction by the amount of translation calculated above. This process makes the
X-coordinates of the same object in the background of all the input images
equal, and the appearance is unified. Figure 2(a) shows a reference image and
2(b) shows one of the other images. Figure 2(c) shows the image after translating
Fig. 2(b) so that its appearance becomes Fig. 2(a). As can be seen from Figs. 2(a)
and 2(c), background objects other than the photographer have approximately
the same X-coordinates.

2.4   Image Composition by Image Selection

An appropriate image for each pixel is selected from a set of images with unified appearance by energy minimization using graph cut algorithm [1], and the
images are combined with Poisson image editing [11] to produce an omnidirectional panoramic image without a photographer. Energy function E is defined
as follows:

$$E = \lambda \sum_{u \in A} E_1(f_u) + \frac{\kappa}{2} \sum_{(u,v) \in N} E_2(f_u, f_v), \tag{1}$$

where f_u and f_v are image indices for pixel u and v, respectively. The pixel colors
of the image indices are modified and synthesized to produce the final result. A is
a set of all pixels in the omnidirectional image, and N is a set of pairs of adjacent
pixels in the omnidirectional image. In this study, the leftmost and rightmost
pixels in an omnidirectional image are also considered as a neighboring pair. λ
and κ are weights to balance the two terms.

The first energy E_1 is a data term, which is based on the plausibility of the
background, and defined as follows:

$$E(f_u) = ||\mathbf{I}_{f_u}(u) - \mathbf{M}(u)||, \tag{2}$$

(a) Reference image

(b) Other image

(c) Translated image

Fig. 2. Unifying the appearance by horizontal translation.

where $\mathbf{I}_{f_u}(u)$ is the vector of RGB colors of pixel u in image f_u. $\mathbf{M}(u)$ is the vector of RGB colors of pixel u in the smoothed median image that is generated by calculating the median value of all the unified images for each pixel and smoothing the values by a moving average filter. Here, the median is calculated independently for RGB. In the median image, non-photographer colors are selected with high probability. Therefore, by minimizing this energy, the resulting image is similar to the median image, producing an image without a photographer.

The second energy E_2 is a smoothness term and defined as follows:

$$E_2(f_u, f_v) = ||\mathbf{I}_{f_u}(u) - \mathbf{I}_{f_v}(u)|| + ||\mathbf{I}_{f_u}(v) - \mathbf{I}_{f_v}(v)|| \tag{3}$$

This term prevents from frequently changing image indices between adjacent pixels. Even when the source image indices are different between neighboring pixels, the indices are switched where the difference in pixel values between the source images is small. This makes the border where the indices are different between adjacent pixels less noticeable.

The overall energy E is minimized by graph cut, but this time the number of image indices is larger than 2. For this reason, we use the α-β swap algorithm. Specifically, we extract two indices and use graph cut to swap the two indices. This is done for all pairs of indices. This process is done until there are no more index swaps, or until a certain number of swaps are repeated.

Finally, an omnidirectional panoramic image without the photographer is generated by combining the pixel values from the image for each pixel selected by graph cut with Poisson image editing, which makes the color difference less noticeable at the boundary where the image indices switch.

3   Experiments

To demonstrate the effectiveness of the proposed method, experiments were conducted in three different scenes. We used an omnidirectional camera RICOH THETA Z1 for input, which outputs an omnidirectional image in which the direction of gravity is the downward direction of the image, although the specific algorithm has not been disclosed. The resolution of the omnidirectional images was resized to 1024×512 pixels for the experiments, and three input images were used in each scene. The patch size for SSD calculation was set to 21×21 pixels. The weights of the graph cuts were changed for each scene in the experiment. We also compared the results with the median images. In the following, we describe the experimental results for each scene in detail.

3.1   Scene A: Indoor Scene

Figure 3 shows the input images in scene A. This figure shows that the photographer is at approximately the same position in the image, but the background has shifted to the side. The top left image in Fig. 3 was used as a reference, and the other two images were horizontally translated as shown in Fig. 4. As shown in the figure, background objects other than the photographer have approximately the same x-coordinates.

Fig. 3. Scene A: three input images.

Fig. 4. Scene A: translated input images.

The median image of the three translated input images is shown in Fig. 5. From the figure, we can confirm that the photographer has disappeared, but the image is produced with a blurred texture in the vertical direction. We assume that the original input images were generated by detecting the direction of gravity using an acceleration sensor, but errors in the direction caused by the movement of the hand holding the camera may have resulted in a shift in the vertical texture. As a result, vertical texture blurring occurs when images are merged using the simple median.

Next, we show the results of graph cut in the proposed method. The parameter λ in the graph cut was fixed to 100, and we output the results with three different types of κ. Figure 6 shows the resulting images by just copying the pixel values that were selected by graph cut with each value of kappa and the corresponding images showing the indices of the source images.

Fig. 5. Scene A: median image of three translated input images.

When the value of κ is small, the resulting image is close to the Median image, and vertical blurring can be often seen. We can also confirm that the indices of the images are frequently changed. When κ is 100, the image indices are less interchangeable, and the same indices are clustered in large regions. As a result, blurring of the image in the vertical direction is almost completely eliminated. However, the fluorescent light in the upper right corner and the unnatural skin tone in the middle left corner remain. When κ is 500, an omnidirectional image without the photographer is generated with almost no discomfort in any of the regions. However, with a simple copy of the images, we can observe the edge caused by the difference in color at the floor and ceiling.

Figure 7 shows the final result of the proposed method by applying Poisson image editing to Fig. 6(c). As shown in the figure, even at the boundary where the image indices switch, the edges caused by the difference in colors are no longer noticeable, indicating that the image without the photographer has been successfully created.

3.2   Scene B: Outdoor Scene

We conducted experiments in an outdoor scene as scene B. Figure 8 shows the input images in scene B. In this scene, a high building and some trees are captured. These input images were horizontally translated with the left top image in Fig. 8 as a reference.

The median image of the three translated input images is shown in Fig. 9. Also in this scene, the image has blurred textures in the vertical direction.

Figure 10 shows the result of the proposed method with $\kappa = 500$. In this scene, we were able to generate an omnidirectional image completely without the photographer. However, the shadow of the photographer remained unnaturally on the right side of the composite image. A closer look at this region in the three input images shows that, in the first image it is the photographer's region, in the second image it is this shadow region, and in the third image it is the actual background that is not the shadow of the photographer. Because of the three

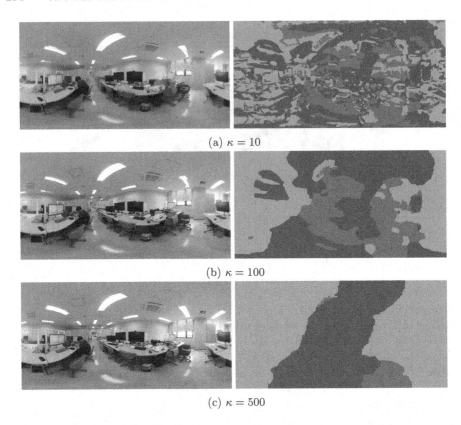

(a) $\kappa = 10$

(b) $\kappa = 100$

(c) $\kappa = 500$

Fig. 6. Scene A: results of graph cut. The left images are resulting ones and the right images indicate the image indices of the source images.

Fig. 7. Scene A: result of the proposed method.

different textures, the actual background was not properly selected in this case. We can also see that in this scene an edge is created at the boundary where the index of the image in the sky region switches, due to the different brightness

Fig. 8. Scene B: three input images.

Fig. 9. Scene B: median image of three translated input images.

of the sky. Figure 11 shows the result after applying Poisson image editing to Fig. 10. The boundary edges in the sky regions were made less noticeable.

3.3   Scene C: Narrow Indoor Scene

We conducted experiments in another indoor scene as scene C. Figure 12 shows the input images in scene C. These images were taken in an elevator, which is a fairly narrow space. There is a mirror in the elevator. These input images were horizontally translated with the left top image in Fig. 12 as a reference.

Fig. 10. Scene B: results of graph cut with $\kappa = 500$. The left image is resulting ones and the right images indicate the image indices of the source images.

Fig. 11. Scene B: result of the proposed method.

The median image of the three translated input images is shown in Fig. 13. The image also has blurred textures in the vertical direction, and unnatural color tones appear in some regions.

Figure 14 shows the result of graph cut with $\kappa = 300$. In this scene, we were also able to generate an omnidirectional image completely without the photographer. However, a vertical texture shift can be observed at the boundary where the image indices switch. As mentioned when showing the median image in scene A, there are vertical shifts in the input images. Especially in a narrow space where the distance between the camera and the object is close, a small error in the direction of gravity can lead to a large shift in the image. In addition, the photographer is reflected in the mirror area. Similar to scene B, in the first image, the region is the one where the photographer is in the mirror, in the second image it is the photographer's region, and in the third image it is the actual background. Therefore, the actual background was not properly selected in this case. Figure 15 shows the final result of the proposed method with Poisson image editing. Although Poisson image editing has made the boundary less noticeable, it is still difficult to compensate for the vertical shift.

Fig. 12. Scene C: three input images.

Fig. 13. Scene C: median image of three translated input images.

3.4   Discussion

Vertical Misalignment. Since the input images have vertical misalignment, this misalignment causes a fatal degradation of the quality of the image by the simple median. On the other hand, the proposed method was able to generate an omnidirectional image without the photographer with little noticeable misalignment by selecting an appropriate image index by energy minimization even when there was some vertical misalignment. However, in a narrow space where the object to be photographed is close to the camera, we confirmed that the vertical misalignment still has a significant impact on the quality of the generated image.

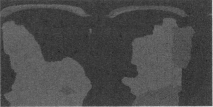

Fig. 14. Scene C: results of graph cut with $\kappa = 300$. The left image is resulting ones and the right images indicate the image indices of the source images.

Fig. 15. Scene C: result of the proposed method.

Number of Input Images. A prerequisite for the proposed method to work well is that the median image should have approximately the value of the actual background. Although the experiments were conducted with three input images, when there are cast shadows from a strong light source or reflections in a mirror, all three images may have different textures in a certain region. In such cases, an appropriate median image is not created, resulting in an unnatural texture being generated in the resulting image. Therefore, in some scenes, more than three images are needed to obtain successful results.

4   Conclusion

In this study, we proposed a method to generate an omnidirectional panoramic image without the photographer in it by using multiple images taken by an omnidirectional camera. In the proposed method, captured images are matched by feature point matching. Then, the amount of horizontal translation calculated from the feature point matching is used to unify the appearance of all the omnidirectional images. Finally, we combine these images by image selection through energy minimization by graph cut algorithm and Poisson image editing to generate an omnidirectional image without the photographer in it.

As future work, it is necessary to correct the vertical misalignment before integrating the images. In addition, although the experiment was conducted with three images, we found that three images were not enough in environments with shadows and reflections. Therefore, it is necessary to conduct experiments using more images.

Acknowledgements. This work was supported by JSPS KAKENHI Grant Numbers JP18H03273, JP18H04116, JP21H03483.

References

1. Boykov, Y., Kolmogorov, V.: An experimental comparison of min-cut/max-flow algorithms for energy minimizaiton in vision. IEEE Trans. Pattern Anal. Mach. Intell. **26**(9), 1124–1137 (2004)
2. Cohen, S.: Background estimation as a labeling problem. In: IEEE International Conference on Computer Vision, pp. 1034–1041 (2018)
3. Criminisi, A., Perez, P., Toyama, K.: Region filling and object removal by exemplar based image inpainting. IEEE Trans. Image Process. **13**(9), 1200–1212 (2004)
4. Fischler, M.A., Bolles, R.C., Bae, S., Yi, J.: Random sample consensus: a paradigm for model fitting with applications to image analysis and automated cartography. Commun. ACM **24**(6), 381–395 (1981)
5. Flores, A., Belongie, S.: Removing pedestrians from google street view images. In: International Workshop on Mobile Vision, pp. 53–58 (2010)
6. Harris, C., Stephens, M.: A combined corner and edge detector. In: Proceedings of Alvey Vision Conference, pp. 147–151 (1988)
7. Jancosek, M., Pajdla, T.: Multi-view reconstruction preserving weakly-supported surfaces. In: IEEE Conference on Computer Vision and Pattern Recognition, pp. 3121–3128 (2011)
8. Kawai, N., Inoue, N., Sato, T., Okura, F., Nakashima, Y., Yokoya, N.: Background estimation for a single omnidirectional image sequence captured with a moving camera. IPSJ Trans. Comput. Vison App. **6**, 68–72 (2014)
9. Kawai, N., Yokoya, N.: Image inpainting considering symmetric patterns. In: IAPR International Conference on Pattern Recognition, pp. 2744–2747 (2012)
10. Le, T.T., Almansa, A., Gousseau, Y., Masnou, S.: Object removal from complex videos using a few annotations. Comput. Visual Med. **5**(3), 267–291 (2019). https://doi.org/10.1007/s41095-019-0145-0
11. Pérez, P., Gangnet, M., Blake, A.: Poisson image editing. ACM Trans. Graph. **22**(3), 313–318 (2003)
12. Telea, A.: An image inpainting technique based on the fast marching method. J. Graph. Tools **9**(1), 23–24 (2004)
13. Wu, C.: VisualSFM: a visual structure from motion system. http://ccwu.me/vsfm/
14. Xu, R., Li, X., Zhou, B., Loy, C.C.: Deep flow-guided video inpainting. In: IEEE Conference on Computer Vision and Pattern Recognition (2019)
15. Yu, J., Lin, Z., Yang, J., Shen, X., Lu, X., Huang, T.S.: Generative image inpainting with contextual attention. In: IEEE Conference on Computer Vision and Pattern Recognition, pp. 5505–5514 (2018)

Optimization of Re-ranking Based on k-Reciprocal for Vehicle Re-identification

Simin Liu[1]([✉])[iD], Yuta Konishi[2][iD], Junichi Miyao[2][iD], and Takio Kurita[2][iD]

[1] Department of Information Engineering, Hiroshima University, Hiroshima, Japan
`liusimin1102@gmail.com`
[2] Graduate School of Advanced Science and Engineering, Hiroshima University, Hiroshima, Japan
{`m213834,miyao,tkurita`}`@hiroshima-u.ac.jp`

Abstract. This paper proposes a re-ranking method for vehicle re-identification based on k-reciprocal Encoding. In recent years, with the development and popularization of deep learning, vehicle re-identification has made great progress and excellent performance. The re-ranking method applied to re-identification has been widely adopted and recognized. However, the existing re-ranking methods still have room to be optimized. The existing k-reciprocal encoding based re-ranking method considers that if the k-nearest neighbor (k-nn) of a gallery image includes the probe image, it is more likely to be a positive matching result, and we called these gallery images are the k-reciprocal nearest neighbors (k-rnn) of the probe image. By encoding its k-rnn into a single vector to calculate the k-reciprocal features, and use this vector to re-ranking by the Jaccard distance. The final distance is calculated as a combination of the original distance and the Jaccard distance. Our idea is that when k-rnn are encoded as a single vector, the k-rnn with a higher-ranking should be given a higher weight, and the k-rnn with a lower-ranking should be given a lower weight. This method will make matching results that are more likely to be a positive result get a higher ranking. In this paper, we use the above idea to assign weights to k-rnn to re-ranking the results of re-ID.

Keywords: Vehicle re-identification · Re-ranking · k-reciprocal encoding

1 Introduction

With the development of intelligent transportation and the popularization of cameras, the demand for vehicle tracking and recognition technology is also increasing. Vehicle re-identification (re-id), as an important task of identifying vehicles, refers to the retrieval of all the images of the target vehicle captured by other cameras in a collection of a large number of vehicle images captured

K. Sumi et al. (Eds.): IW-FCV 2022, CCIS 1578, pp. 300–311, 2022.
https://doi.org/10.1007/978-3-031-06381-7_21

by multiple cameras as shown in Fig. 1. Vehicle re-identification has a great significance for traffic surveillance and intelligence applications and has recently attracted more attention from academia and industry.

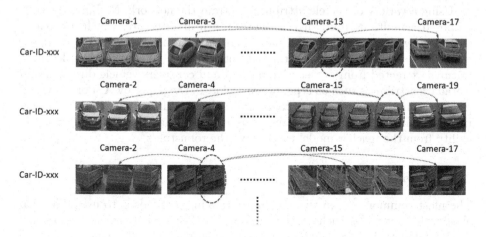

Fig. 1. Explanation of the vehicle re-identification task.

The difficulty of vehicle re-identification is to distinguish the difference between similar vehicles, and to identify the same vehicle shot from different angles. If we only use the models to extract features to retrieve the targets, it's difficult to obtain high accuracy. Therefore, in vehicle re-identification, not only relying on the models to extract features but the re-ranking method is also used as an effective method to improved the results obtained by the models.

In this paper, to solve these problems, we propose a re-ranking method that does not require the use of other information sources, which performs better than the existing re-ranking methods.

2   Related Works

In the field of re-identification, person re-identification has made a lot of progress and developed many novel methods. In recent years, with the improvement of deep neural networks and the development of image recognition technology, researchers' attention has gradually turned to more challenging vehicle re-identification tasks.

2.1   Vehicle Re-identification

X. Liu et al. [9] proposed a deep relative distance learning (DRDL) method, which uses a two-branch deep convolutional network to project the original vehicle image into Euclidean space, and calculates the similarity using the distance in the space ranking. Y. Shen et al. [19] proposed a two-stage Siamese-CNN + Path LSTM framework, which generates candidate spatio-temporal paths through a chain MRF model with deep learning potential function. The candidate paths and paired queries are used to generate similarities score.

Using a variety of vehicle attributes to train the network, N. Jiang et al. [6] proposed a multi-attribute-driven multi-branch architecture, which uses three branch networks to extract color, model, and appearance features. T.-W. Huang et al. [5] proposed a perceptual time attention model which uses deep learning features extracted from consecutive frames, and considers vehicle direction and metadata attributes such as type, brand, color. In the paper by A. Porrello et al. [17], a training strategy of viewpoint knowledge distillation (VKD) is designed. In this framework, the student model is used to learn the feature extraction ability from the teacher model to improve the robustness.

2.2   Re-ranking

The most common way in the existing re-ranking methods is to use additional attributes of vehicles such as the temporal and spatial information attached to the data set. The re-ranking strategy in the paper by N. Jiang et al. [6] is to introduce the temporal-spatial relationship between vehicles from multiple cameras to construct similar appearance sets. The Jacobian distance between these similar appearance sets is used to re-rank. P. Moral [16] introduced the post-processing steps of vehicle trajectory information.

These methods all rely on hand-crafted features. The other approach is to use the correlation between pictures for re-ranking. Z. Zhong et al. [22] proposed a k-reciprocal encoding method to re-rank the re-ID results. The idea behind this approach is that it is more likely to be a true match if a gallery image is similar to the probe in the k-reciprocal nearest neighbors. F. Wu et al. [21] proposed an improved re-ranking method based on Jaccard distance and k-reciprocal nearest neighbor to optimize the initial ranking list.

3   Proposed Method

3.1   Baseline Model

The k-reciprocal encoding re-ranking method proposed by Z. Zhong et al. [22] base on the similarity with the k-reciprocal nearest neighbors. However, this method will produce poor re-ranking results if there are more mismatches in the initial ranking because it heavily relies on the relationship between the results of k-nearest neighbors. This means that the accuracy of the initial ranking is very important. Therefore, we used the strong baseline (BoT-BS) proposed by H. Luo et al. [13,14] as the baseline model in this paper. Unlike the method of splicing multiple local features to achieve high accuracy, BoT-BS only uses a global feature and a large number of tricks to achieve good performance. Some settings of BOT-BS have been modified in order to further improve performance in the paper by S. He et al. [4]. The output function is followed by the BNNeck structure, which divides the ID loss (cross-entropy loss) and triplet loss into two different embedding spaces. Also, the central loss is removed because it will not greatly improve retrieval performance while increasing computing resources. The detailed experimental settings will be explained in detail in the experimental chapter. The framework of the baseline model is shown in Fig. 2.

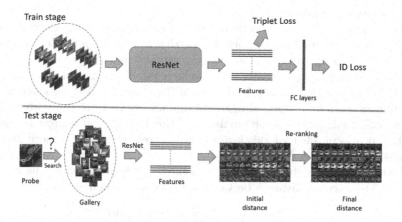

Fig. 2. The framework of the proposed method.

3.2 k-reciprocal Encoding

Following the previous works [18] and [22], we input a probe image p to the trained model and obtain k-nearest neighbors in the gallery. The k-nearest neighbors are denoted as $N(p, k)$ and defined as

$$N(p, k) = \{g_1, g_2, ..., g_k\}, \quad |N(p, k)| = k, \tag{1}$$

where $|.|$ denotes the number of the search results in the set. Then we select elements in $N(p, k)$ to calculate its k-nearest neighbors in both probe data set and gallery data set. If the k-nearest neighbors of $N(p, k)$ contain the initial query image probe p, in other words, if they are in each other's k-nearest neighbors, these images are considered to have higher similarity and reliability. They are called k-reciprocal nearest neighbors (k-rnn) $R(p, k)$ of p. Then the k-rnn $R(p, k)$ can be defined as

$$R(p, k) = \{g_i | (g_i \in N(p, k)) \wedge (p \in N(g_i, k))\}. \tag{2}$$

It is known that the k-nearest neighbors of the initial ranking may include a lot of noise. But the k-reciprocal nearest neighbors are more likely to be a positive match result than the k-nearest neighbors. By relying on the credibility of k-reciprocal nearest neighbors, the possibility of the positive match to the probe p will be improved by constructing a more robust set $R^*(p, k)$ [22]

$$R^*(p, k) \leftarrow R(p, k) \cup R(q, \frac{1}{2}k)$$

$$s.t. \quad |R(p, k) \cap R(q, \frac{1}{2}k)| \geqslant \frac{2}{3}|R(q, \frac{1}{2}k)|, \quad \forall q \in R(p, k)$$

(3)

where q represents the sample in $R(p, k)$.

According to the above conditions, the half of the k-reciprocal nearest neighbors of each q in $R(p, k)$ are combined with $R(p, k)$ into $R^*(p, k)$. It is expected that the set $R^*(p, k)$ contains more positive samples and is more closely related to probe p. Namely, its credibility will also increase. Therefore, in this paper, we used $R^*(p, k)$ as context knowledge for the next re-ranking. As mentioned above, if the images in the k-reciprocal nearest neighbors $R^*(p, k)$ of the probe p have more identical images, then the reliability of this k-reciprocal nearest neighbors is higher. It also means that this k-reciprocal nearest neighbors is more likely to be a positive match result.

Then we can calculate the similarity of the two images based on the Jaccard distance. The Jaccard distance between the p with g_i is defined as

$$d_J(p, g_i) = 1 - \frac{|R^*(p, k) \cap R^*(g_i, k)|}{|R^*(p, k) \cup R^*(g_i, k)|}.$$

(4)

In order to shorten the time to calculate the intersection and union in Jaccard distance, the k-nearest neighbors are encoded into a simpler and equivalent vector [1]. This encoding can greatly reduce the computational complexity while maintaining the original structure of k-nearest neighbors.

According to the above inference, the higher rank in k-nearest neighbors of the probe p should be more representative and more likely to be positive matching results. So the higher rank search results of probe p should be assigned a higher weight. Therefore, all neighbors are weighted according to the original distance between the probe p and its neighbors. Thus the k-reciprocal nearest neighbors are encoded as a vector $V_p = [V_{p,g_1}, V_{p,g_2}, ..., V_{p,g_N}]$, where V_{p,g_i} function is defined as

$$V_{p,gi} = \begin{cases} e^{-d(p,g_i)} & \text{if } g_i \in R^*(p, k) \\ 0 & otherwise, \end{cases}$$

(5)

where $d(p, g_i)$ represents Mahalanobis distance between the probe p and the image g_i.

Based on the above notations, we can rewrite the Jaccard distance d_J of Eq. 4 as

$$d_J(p, g_i) = 1 - \frac{\sum_{j=1}^{N} \min(V_{p,g_j}, V_{g_i,g_j})}{\sum_{j=1}^{N} \max(V_{p,g_j}, V_{g_i,g_j})}.$$

(6)

When considering the final ranking, only consider the original distance or only consider the Jaccard distance will cause a big deviation. Therefore, the final distance is defined as the combination of the original distance and the Jaccard distance as

$$d^*(p, g_i) = (1 - \lambda)d_J(p, g_i) + \lambda d(p, g_i). \tag{7}$$

In Eq. 7, $\lambda \in [0, 1]$ is an adjustment parameter. When $\lambda = 0$, it corresponds to considering only the Jaccard distance, and when $\lambda = 1$, it corresponds to considering only the original Mahalanobis distance. The setting of λ remains the same as the baseline.

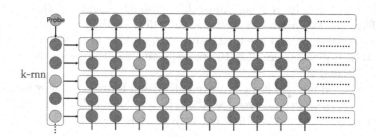

Fig. 3. The blue circle in the picture represents the probe, the green circle represents positive matching, and the red circle represents negative matching. The leftmost column is the probe and the k-reciprocal nearest neighbors of the probe. Starting from the second row on the right are the k-nearest neighbors of the sample on the left. The first row on the right represents the result of local query expansion. (Color figure online)

3.3   Local Query Expansion with Weight

According to the viewpoint in [22], it can be inferred that the k-reciprocal nearest neighbors of the probe image p should have a higher correlation with the probe image p. Therefore, the k-reciprocal nearest neighbors of the probe p are used to implement local query expansion. In Fig. 3, at the first, we use the target probe image p and obtain the k-nearest neighbors of the corresponding k-reciprocal nearest neighbors in the gallery. Then, the local query expansion defined as

$$V_p = \frac{1}{|N(p, k)|} \sum_{g_i \in N(p,k)} V_{g_i}. \tag{8}$$

Finally, we re-rank the k-nearest neighbors of the probe using the results of the local query expansion.

By this operation, we can obtain the features V_p of k-nearest neighbors by using information of the k-reciprocal nearest neighbors of the probe p. as a result of the local query expansion, the k-reciprocal nearest neighbors of the probe p is used to combine and generate the feature V_p of k-nearest neighbors. However, it is not considered that the k-reciprocal nearest neighbors with higher rankings have higher similarity with probe image p in Eq. 8. In order to take advantage of this fact in the definition of the feature, two types of weighted methods depending on the rank are introduced in the the definition of the local query expansion of Eq. 8. They are defined as

$$V_p = \frac{1}{|N(p,k)|} \sum_{g_i \in N(p,k)} (V_{g_i} * e^{-\frac{i}{k*\sigma}}) \qquad (9)$$

and

$$V_p = \frac{1}{|N(p,k)|} \sum_{g_i \in N(p,k)} (V_{g_i} * \frac{\sigma}{i+1}). \qquad (10)$$

In Eq. 9 and Eq. 10, σ is an adjustable parameter, and i is the rank of the query. Through the improved formula, the effect of different rankings on the local query expansion and the final result of re-ranking is considered more comprehensively. Equation 9 and Eq. 10 are respectively our proposed method 1 and proposed method 2.

Our proposed method is an improved algorithm for re-ranking, which adjusts the weight ratio between targets, so there is no additional computational step, and the processing speed is consistent with the baseline.

4   Experiment

4.1   Evaluation Metric

In this experiment, we use the mean average precision (mAP), rank1 and rank5 in the cumulative match curve (CMC) to evaluate the accuracy of re-identification. At the first, we define the average precision (AP) as

$$AP(p) = \frac{1}{N_{gt}(p)} \sum_{k=1}^{n} P(k) * \delta_k \qquad (11)$$

The AP represents the re-identification retrieval accuracy of a single probe p, where k represents the number of rank in the rank list, n represents the total number of vehicles that need to be retrieved, and N_{gt} represents the total number of correct matches corresponding target vehicle in the gallery set. Also, $p(k)$ denotes the precision at cut-off k, and δ_k represents whether the k-th image in the rank list is correctly matched, if it is a correct match, the value is 1, otherwise, the value is 0. Then we can define the overall re-identification retrieval accuracy mAP as

$$mAP = \frac{1}{Q} \sum_{p}^{Q} AP(p), \qquad (12)$$

where Q represents the number of all images in the query set.

However, only relying on mAP to evaluate the accuracy of re-identification is incomplete. It is necessary to use the CMC curve together to evaluate the accuracy. The CMC curve represents the probability of a positive match among the first n retrieved results. Regardless of how many matches are actually occured in the data set, CMC only counts the first match start from the top of the rank list. Compare with the mAP, the CMC curve is a fine-grained measurement that shows the variation of accuracy with grade. The CMC curve is a good complementary measure of the mAP. The calculation method of CMC is given as

$$cmc@k = \frac{1}{Q}\sum_{p}^{Q} f(p,k),\qquad(13)$$

where $f(p,k)$ is a detection tool, which starts from the highest rank of the rank list. If a positive sample appears in rank k for the first time, the values after k and k are both equal to 1, the previous values are all equal to 0.

4.2 Data Sets and Implementation Details

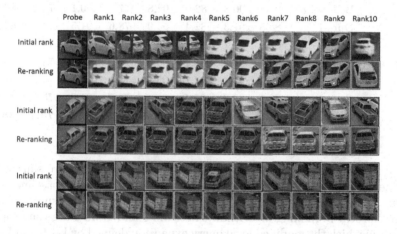

Fig. 4. Comparison of visualization results of baseline model (BoT-BS) and proposed method on veri-776. The green box represents the positive matching result, and the red box represents the negative matching result. (Color figure online)

The effecitiveness of the proposed method is evaluated by using VeRi-776 [10] and VehicleID [9] data sets. VeRi-776 data set contains images of 776 vehicles captured by 20 fixed cameras. The data set is divided into a training set (37,781 images, 576 IDs), a test set (11,579 images, 200 IDs), and a gallery set (1,678 images, 200 IDs). VehicleID data set is a larger and more challenging data set than VeRi-776. It contains 26,267 vehicles (221,763 images in total) with their respective identification tags. The training set contains 13,134 vehicles. However, in this paper, we use a test set composed of 800, 1600 and 2400 vehicles divided into the data set to test the performance of the re-ranking method (Fig. 4).

We adopt ResNet50 and ResNet101 as the backbone model in our experiments. The input images are resized to 320 × 320. In the train stage, the batch size is set to 48 (6 IDs, 8 for each ID). We totally train the model 80 epochs with SGD optimizer. The initial learning rate starts from 0.001, and linearly increases to 0.01 in 10 epochs, and then at the 40th and 70th epoch, the learning rate is reduced to 0.1 times the previous. And σ in Eq. 9 and Eq. 10 are set to 3.

4.3   Experiments on VeRi-776 and VehicleID

We evaluated the proposed method on the VeRi-776 and VehicleID data set.

Table 1. Results on VeRi-776 and VehicleID data set.

| Method | | VeRi-776 | | VehicleID | | | | | |
| | | | | Small | | Medium | | Large | |
		mAP	rank1	rank1	rank5	rank1	rank5	rank1	rank5
ResNet50	BoT-BS	80.8	95.9	80.2	93.9	76.8	90.7	74.0	87.3
	BoT-BS-RR	88.8	96.8	82.0	94.8	77.3	90.1	73.8	86.3
	Ours-1	88.5	97.3	82.4	94.9	78.6	91.5	74.5	88.1
	Ours-2	89.0	97.1	82.1	95.1	78.8	91.9	74.8	88.2
ResNet101	BoT-BS	82.1	96.2	81.4	95.3	77.9	90.8	74.5	88.3
	BoT-BS-RR	**89.2**	97.1	82.1	95.8	78.0	91.1	74.2	87.3
	Ours-1	89.1	97.2	**82.8**	**95.9**	78.8	91.9	75.0	88.2
	Ours-2	**89.2**	**97.7**	**82.8**	**95.9**	**78.9**	**92.1**	**75.1**	**88.8**

The results of the experiments on VeRi-776 and VehicleID are summarized in Table 1. In this table, BoT-BS represents the result of the baseline model without re-ranking, and BoT-BS-RR represents the result of using the original k-reciprocal re-ranking algorithm. The Ours-1 and Ours-2 are the proposed methods in which the modified local query expansion defined by Eq. 9 and Eq. 10.

It can be found that in the VeRi-776 data set, the results of our proposed method 1 are relatively close to BoT-BS-RR, and the proposed method 2 is slightly higher than BoT-BS-RR. But in the VehicleID dataset, the overall performance of our proposed methods 1 and 2 are better than BoT-BS-RR. Especially in the large test set of VehicleID, the performance of BoT-BS-RR is even worse than BoT-BS. But, our proposed methods are still effective in improving the accuracy.

However, the performance of the proposed method and the baseline on mAP is similar. I think this is related to the calculation method of mAP. The proposed method can only improve the retrieval accuracy of high rankings, but cannot improve the overall retrieval accuracy. Therefore, they show the same performance in the value of mAP.

Table 2. Comparison with state-of-the-art approaches on VeRi-776 data set.

Method	Year	mAP	rank1
FACT [10]	2016	19.92	59.65
FACT + Plate-SNN + STR [12]	2016	27.77	61.44
Siamese-CNN+Path-LSTM [19]	2017	58.27	83.49
RAM [11]	2018	61.50	88.60
GAN+LSRO+re-ranking [20]	2018	64.78	88.62
JDRN+re-ranking [8]	2019	73.10	–
Part-regularized Near-duplicate [3]	2019	74.30	94.30
PVEN [15]	2020	79.50	95.60
BoT-BS	2020	82.10	96.20
BoT-BS-RR	2020	**89.20**	97.10
Ours-1	2021	89.10	97.20
Ours-2	2021	**89.20**	**97.70**

Table 3. Comparison with state-of-the-art approaches on VehicleID data set.

Method	Small		Medium		Large	
	rank1	rank5	rank1	rank5	rank1	rank5
DJDL [7]	72.3	85.7	70.8	81.8	68.0	78.9
RAM [11]	75.2	91.5	72.3	87.0	67.7	84.5
VAMI [23]	63.1	83.3	52.9	75.1	47.3	70.3
PRN [2]	78.9	94.8	74.9	92.0	71.6	88.5
BoT-BS	81.4	95.3	77.9	90.8	74.5	88.3
BoT-BS-RR	82.1	95.8	78.0	91.1	74.2	87.3
Ours-1	**82.8**	**95.9**	78.8	91.9	75.0	88.2
Ours-2	**82.8**	**95.9**	**78.9**	**92.1**	**75.1**	**88.8**

Table 2 and Table 3 show the comparison results with other methods in VeRi-776 and VehicleID dataset. It can be noticed that the proposed method provides better performance and increases reliability and accuracy on the basis of the original algorithm.

5 Conclusion

In this paper, we propose new re-ranking methods in which weighting ratios are introduced in the local query expansion in the task of vehicle re-ID. These weights can make matching results that are more likely to be positive results get a higher ranking. Through the experiments on the VeRi-776 data set and the VehicleID data set, it is shown that the proposed methods give better performance than previous methods. These results show the importance of high-ranking matches in the re-ranking.

However, we think the proposed methods do not make full use of spatial information. This paper only used the ranking, but the corresponding spatial distance is not used. No experimental data are given to prove whether the use of spatial distance for weight distribution, or whether the combination of the two will produce better performance. In addition, except for the proposed weight ratio formula, whether to use other functions for weight ratio distribution will be more appropriate. Evaluation experiments for these tasks are future work.

References

1. Bai, S., Bai, X.: Sparse contextual activation for efficient visual re-ranking. IEEE Trans. Image Process. **25**(3), 1056–1069 (2016). https://doi.org/10.1109/TIP.2016.2514498
2. Chen, H., Lagadec, B., Bremond, F.: Partition and reunion: a two-branch neural network for vehicle re-identification. In: Proceedings of the IEEE/CVF Conference on Computer Vision and Pattern Recognition (CVPR) Workshops, June 2019
3. He, B., Li, J., Zhao, Y., Tian, Y.: Part-regularized near-duplicate vehicle re-identification. In: Proceedings of the IEEE/CVF Conference on Computer Vision and Pattern Recognition (CVPR), June 2019
4. He, S., et al.: Multi-domain learning and identity mining for vehicle re-identification (2020)
5. Huang, T.W., Cai, J., Yang, H., Hsu, H.M., Hwang, J.N.: Multi-view vehicle re-identification using temporal attention model and metadata re-ranking. In: Proceedings of the IEEE/CVF Conference on Computer Vision and Pattern Recognition (CVPR) Workshops, June 2019
6. Jiang, N., Xu, Y., Zhou, Z., Wu, W.: Multi-attribute driven vehicle re-identification with spatial-temporal re-ranking. In: 2018 25th IEEE International Conference on Image Processing (ICIP), pp. 858–862 (2018). https://doi.org/10.1109/ICIP.2018.8451776
7. Li, Y., Li, Y., Yan, H., Liu, J.: Deep joint discriminative learning for vehicle re-identification and retrieval. In: 2017 IEEE International Conference on Image Processing (ICIP), pp. 395–399 (2017). https://doi.org/10.1109/ICIP.2017.8296310
8. Liu, C.T., et al.: Supervised joint domain learning for vehicle re-identification. In: Proceedings of the IEEE/CVF Conference on Computer Vision and Pattern Recognition (CVPR) Workshops, June 2019
9. Liu, H., Tian, Y., Wang, Y., Pang, L., Huang, T.: Deep relative distance learning: tell the difference between similar vehicles. In: Proceedings of the IEEE Conference on Computer Vision and Pattern Recognition, pp. 2167–2175 (2016)
10. Liu, X., Liu, W., Ma, H., Fu, H.: Large-scale vehicle re-identification in urban surveillance videos. In: 2016 IEEE International Conference on Multimedia and Expo (ICME), pp. 1–6 (2016). https://doi.org/10.1109/ICME.2016.7553002
11. Liu, X., Zhang, S., Huang, Q., Gao, W.: RAM: A region-aware deep model for vehicle re-identification (2018)
12. Liu, X., Liu, W., Mei, T., Ma, H.: A deep learning-based approach to progressive vehicle re-identification for urban surveillance. In: Leibe, B., Matas, J., Sebe, N., Welling, M. (eds.) ECCV 2016, Part II. LNCS, vol. 9906, pp. 869–884. Springer, Cham (2016). https://doi.org/10.1007/978-3-319-46475-6_53

13. Luo, H., et al.: A strong baseline and batch normalization neck for deep person re-identification. IEEE Trans. Multimedia (2019). https://doi.org/10.1109/TMM.2019.2958756

14. Luo, H., Gu, Y., Liao, X., Lai, S., Jiang, W.: Bag of tricks and a strong baseline for deep person re-identification. In: The IEEE Conference on Computer Vision and Pattern Recognition (CVPR) Workshops, June 2019

15. Meng, D., et al.: Parsing-based view-aware embedding network for vehicle re-identification. In: Proceedings of the IEEE/CVF Conference on Computer Vision and Pattern Recognition (CVPR), June 2020

16. Moral, P., Garcia-Martin, A., Martinez, J.M.: Vehicle re-identification in multi-camera scenarios based on ensembling deep learning features. In: Proceedings of the IEEE/CVF Conference on Computer Vision and Pattern Recognition (CVPR) Workshops June 2020

17. Porrello, A., Bergamini, L., Calderara, S.: Robust re-identification by multiple views knowledge distillation. In: Vedaldi, A., Bischof, H., Brox, T., Frahm, J.-M. (eds.) ECCV 2020, Part X. LNCS, vol. 12355, pp. 93–110. Springer, Cham (2020). https://doi.org/10.1007/978-3-030-58607-2_6

18. Qin, D., Gammeter, S., Bossard, L., Quack, T., van Gool, L.: Hello neighbor: accurate object retrieval with k-reciprocal nearest neighbors. In: CVPR 2011, pp. 777–784 (2011). https://doi.org/10.1109/CVPR.2011.5995373

19. Shen, Y., Xiao, T., Li, H., Yi, S., Wang, X.: Learning deep neural networks for vehicle re-id with visual-spatio-temporal path proposals (2017)

20. Wu, F., Yan, S., Smith, J.S., Zhang, B.: Joint semi-supervised learning and re-ranking for vehicle re-identification. In: 2018 24th International Conference on Pattern Recognition (ICPR), pp. 278–283 (2018). https://doi.org/10.1109/ICPR.2018.8545584

21. Wu, F., Yan, S., Smith, J.S., Zhang, B.: Vehicle re-identification in still images: application of semi-supervised learning and re-ranking. Signal Processing: Image Communication **76**, 261 – 271 (2019). https://doi.org/10.1016/j.image.2019.04.021, http://www.sciencedirect.com/science/article/pii/S0923596518305800

22. Zhong, Z., Zheng, L., Cao, D., Li, S.: Re-ranking person re-identification with k-reciprocal encoding (2017)

23. Zhou, Y., Shao, L.: Viewpoint-aware attentive multi-view inference for vehicle re-identification. In: Proceedings of the IEEE Conference on Computer Vision and Pattern Recognition (CVPR), June 2018

Sequence Recognition of Indoor Tennis Actions Using Transfer Learning and Long Short-Term Memory

Anik Sen[1,2], Syed Md. Minhaz Hossain[1,2],
Russo Mohammad Ashraf Uddin[3], Kaushik Deb[1(✉)],
and Kang-Hyun Jo[3]

[1] Department of Computer Science and Engineering, Chittagong University of Engineering and Technology (CUET), Chattogram 4349, Bangladesh
debkaushik99@cuet.ac.bd
[2] Department of Computer Science and Engineering, Premier University, Chattogram 4000, Bangladesh
[3] Department of Electrical, Electronic and Computer Engineering, University of Ulsan, Ulsan, South Korea
acejo@ulsan.ac.kr

Abstract. Recognizing tennis actions during a practice session can be widely used as the coaching assistant. Accurate classification of actions is tricky, with a massive similarity among different actions. Hybrid deep neural networks composed of Convolutional Neural Network (CNN) and Recurrent Neural Network (RNN) such as Long Short-term Memory (LSTM) are widely employed while dealing with spatial and temporal features. We leverage transfer learning as the spatial feature extractor, allowing weights extracted by training over a massive dataset. Transfer learning from three pre–trained models such as InceptionResNetV2, ResNet152V2, and Xception are utilized in this work. Two approaches are exercised to determine the best one: (a) developing a single hybrid CNN–LSTM model and (b) passing extracted CNN features to a single LSTM-based model. Experimental results prove the effectiveness of the latter approach for recognizing indoor tennis actions. The publicly available THETIS dataset is employed for all the evaluations and approaches, which contains 12 different tennis actions performed in indoor practice sessions. The Xception–based model outperforms other models by attaining 75% accuracy.

Keywords: Convolutional neural network · Long Short-term Memory · Indoor tennis actions · Transfer learning

1 Introduction

The development of various technologies and the use of numerous devices such as computers, mobile, and IoT devices switch people's way of perception around the world. In many cases, the 4th industrial revolution paves the way for replacing workers with robots for various applications. As robots or other devices perceive the information around their environment, it is necessary to recognize human actions. There is an opportunity for human action recognition in sports. In most cases, analysis of different actions helps to analyze the matches by generating a summary of sport tactics [5]. Another application of action recognition in sports is to analyze the training phases of players for increasing the performance of individuals [19].

In some cases, it is pretty challenging to afford a trainer for analyzing each tactic of players due to financial concerns. Therefore, an automated sports training summary is a solution. It can work as an alternative to a coach and help the athletes get better performance without the assistance of others. Moreover, accurate recognition of tennis actions during practice sessions helps generate a summary - how many shots an athlete has practiced during a practice session. Deep learning algorithms are widely incorporated to solve problems such as recognizing actions by automating the feature extraction process and modeling the temporal dependency. However, these algorithms require massive samples to drive the best network weights. Therefore, transfer learning from the pre–trained models assists in utilizing network weights that are already derived after training a massive volume of samples. Moreover, we can overlook the manual feature extraction such as detecting athletes, explicit pose estimation, etc.

A large number of videos on sports such as UCF-sport [24] and Sports-1M [13] provides the opportunity to perform numerous intelligent methods for analyzing the actions of sports. However, datasets are limited to only inter-class sports actions in most cases. It is pretty challenging to explore distinct sport in depth using these datasets.

Moreover, computational intelligence methods such as Fuzzy systems in [4,16] are applied for the sports training session. The evolution of machine learning approaches, such as Support Vector Machine (SVM), K-nearest Neighbour (K-NN), Random Forest (RF), Logistic Regression (LR), Decision Tree (DT), etc. opens a path for planning, realization, control, and evaluation in sports training [2,11,12,21]. However, Artificial Neural Network (ANN) in [3,12,20] are also performed to evaluate the human actions in sports sessions. In recent years, as deep learning techniques have become popular for their deep and complex features, Long Short-term Memory (LSTM) is further performed to evaluate the human actions in sports sessions [1,5,15]. In addition, most of the works in the sports training session are performed for soccer, weight lifting, and running [19]. As fewer works are done in tennis action classification, there is an opportunity to extend the latest trends.

The contributions of our work are listed below:

(i) Develop a model that distinguishes 12 different indoor tennis actions during the practice session.
(ii) Evaluate model performance for 2 approaches: (i) single hybrid CNN–LSTM and (ii) passing CNN extracted features to a single model.

(iii) Evaluate the performance of 3 pre–trained model features focusing on less trainable parameters.

The rest of the paper is organized as follows. Section 2 discusses the related works as literature review; workflow and proposed model for indoor tennis practice session is presented in Sect. 3; experimental results and observations are illustrated in Sect. 4; and finally, the paper is concluded in Sect. 5.

2   Literature Review

Numerous intelligent methods are utilized for automated sports training [19]. Authors in [4] executed a fuzzy technique for scheduling training sessions for a tennis coach. The fuzzy approach is also performed in [16] for cricket coach for suggesting the best strokes. It was also reasonable for bowling and fielding coaches.

The evolution of machine learning approaches, such as Support Vector Machine (SVM), K-nearest Neighbour (K-NN), Random Forest, Logistic Regression (LR), Decision Tree (DT), etc. open a path planning, realization, control, and evaluation in sports training [2,11,12,21]. Acikmese et al. [2] proposed a system for recognizing basketball training tactics automatically using motion sensors. It was helpful for sport gesture recognition and achieved 99.5% accuracy for SVM. In [11], K-NN and RF are applied for classifying basketball actions using a wearable wristwatch. Among them, RF achieved better accuracy of 95%.

The authors in [12] proposed the models those estimated the recovery time of an injured player in soccer using SVM, Gaussian process, and ANN. However, no model performed accurately enough to express. Rossi et al. [21] applied a decision tree for estimating injuries by using training load and physical ability. It also generated a set of rules for professional soccer players.

In recent years, Artificial Neural Network (ANN) in [3,12,20] and Deep Learning techniques such as LSTM [1,5,15,22,23] are performed to evaluate the human actions in sports sessions. Authors in [1] proposed a coaching system for a cyclist using LSTM. In [5], authors proposed a deep historical LSTM for tennis action recognition and achieved the highest accuracy of 95%. The drawback of this work is the lack of real-time scenarios due to detection time and lack of tuning with other deep learning based algorithms except for LSTM.

Lim et al. [15] proposed LSTM based coaching method using practice session data perceived from inertial movement sensor. In [17], the authors proposed an LSTM based action recognition model in tennis. This model classified similar classes effectively, and it was 81.23%–88.16% accurate.

Authors in [22], proposed a deep learning based technique comprising two models: Convolutional Neural Network (CNN) and Gated Recurrent Unit (GRU). Initially, spatial features have been extracted using VGG16 and then temporal dependencies are extracted using GRU. This work categorized 10 different actions in soccer and achieved on an average 94% accuracy.

In [23], a deep learning based technique is proposed comprising two models: Convolutional Neural Network (CNN) and Gated Recurrent Unit (GRU).

Initially, spatial features have been extracted using VGG16 and then temporal dependencies are extracted using GRU. This work categorized 10 different shots in cricket and achieved on an average 86% accuracy. Further investigations have been done by freezing except the last 4 layers and 8 layers, and achieved 93% accuracy in both cases.

3   Workflow and Proposed Architecture

This section highlights the steps for building and evaluating indoor tennis action classification models. Two different approaches to developing models are highlighted. Dataset splitting, data pre–processing, spatial features extraction using transfer learning from pre–trained models, feature vector formation, network design using LSTM, and softmax layer; all steps are briefly described in this section. This section mentions all the specifications and hyperparameters of our proposed architecture.

The process begins by splitting the samples of the whole THETIS dataset [8]. Randomly 80% samples were placed in the training set, and 20% samples acted as the test set.

Then the pre–trained models, which were already trained over the ImageNet dataset [7], were loaded. We utilized transfer learning from the pre–trained models such as Xception [6], ResNet152V2 [9], InceptionResNetV2 [25]. All the fully–connected layers were dropped as the input shape for the models was considered as 180 × 180 pixels. Pre–processing was applied to both the training and test samples so that the Float32 formatted pixel values ranged from 0 to 1. All the remaining layers of the pre–trained models were disallowed to update weights during the backpropagation.

We then conducted 2 experiments based on the Xception model. Two approaches were followed: (i) by using a single hybrid model of pre-trained CNN–LSTM model (ii) by extracting features using pre–trained model, formatting data, and then passing the data to LSTM [10].

In the first approach, the RGB frame values are extracted from each video sample. The output shape for both the training set and test set becomes *(Samples, Frames, Width, Height, Channels)*. Pre–trained Xception model and LSTM were used jointly to design the single hybrid network. All the Xception model layers were disallowed to update weights during backpropagation.

In the second approach, the Xception model was used to extract the spatial features from the sampled video frames. The final CNN block of the Xception model has 2048 feature maps having 6×6 dimension. Thus, the shape becomes *(Samples, 15, 6, 6, 2048)*, where *Samples* symbolizes the value of training samples and test samples, respectively. For this approach, the first layer of the network is a LSTM layer, which requires the input shape to be *(Samples, Time Steps, Units)*. To accommodate this input shape, we reshaped the extracted features vectors for both training set and test to have the similar shape compatible to LSTM layer.

We noticed a huge accuracy variation between the two approaches with the initial observations, and the latter approach was superior to the former. So, for all the further experiments, second approach was utilized.

We considered 180 × 180 pixels RGB frames, and 15 frames were randomly sampled from each video. As the main tennis action can occur in any part of the video, we considered frames from all through the video samples. Features were extracted using the pre-trained models for each RGB frame. The output shape for the InceptionResNetV2 was reshaped to be *(Samples, 15, 24576)*, as shown in Table 2. For ResNet152V2 and Xception, the shape was reshaped as *(Samples, 15, 73728)*. The value of *Samples* was the value similar to the training samples and test samples. After 80%–20% dataset split, the *Samples* value was 1584 for the training set and 396 for the test set.

LSTM was introduced as the first layer of our proposed network, which takes 15 as the timestep value. LSTM can deal with the vanishing gradient problem of vanilla recurrent network [18]. After manual hyperparameter tuning, we used 256 hidden units in the LSTM layer. Unlike vanilla RNN, LSTM is capable of modeling larger sequence. To maintain the regularization, 10% dropout rate was set, which prevented the model from overfitting the training data. Later, 64 hidden units were used in the fully–connected layer, where ReLU was used as the activation function.

Finally, the softmax activation layer was used to measure the probability distribution of 12 different indoor tennis actions. The probability values add up to 1 for the 12 tennis actions. Adam optimizer [14] with 0.00001 learning rate was used. We used categorical cross_entropy as the loss function. The network was fed with 1 sample at a time.

The workflow of the proposed approach for recognizing 12 different tennis actions during practice sessions is portrayed in Fig 1. For the overall process, second approach is followed by placing LSTM as the first layer and passing reshaped input data to this LSTM layer.

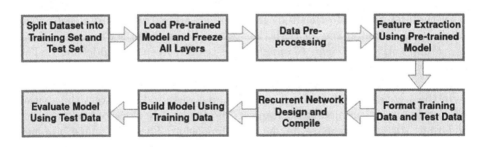

Fig. 1. Working flow of the proposed method for indoor tennis action recognition.

The summary of the proposed models is tabulated in Table 1. All the models has LSTM as the first layer. The specification of layers, output shape, and parameters for each layer are highlighted in the table.

Table 1. Summary of the proposed models using CNN features and LSTM–based model for indoor tennis action recognition.

	Layer	Output shape	Param #
InceptionResNetV2	LSTM	(None, 256)	25428992
	Dense	(None, 64)	16448
	Dense	(None, 12)	780
ResNet152V2	LSTM	(None, 256)	75760640
	Dense	(None, 64)	16448
	Dense	(None, 12)	780
Xception	LSTM	(None, 256)	75760640
	Dense	(None, 64)	16448
	Dense	(None, 12)	780

4   Results and Observation

In this section, we have outlined the system configurations. Various accuracy measures such as precision, recall, f1–score of the best model are highlighted. For further analysis of the best model, the confusion matrix, classification report, and performance graphs are analyzed. The confusion matrix represents how much a model is confused about other classes.

4.1   System Configuration

Keras framework was used for API usage. We used Python 3.7 version, and the Sklearn package was utilized to generate various reports and matrices. All the experiments were conducted in a system of AMD Ryzen 7 processor, 32 GB RAM, Nvidia RTX 2060 Super with 8 GB GPU, 240 GB SSD storage, and 1 TB HDD storage.

4.2   Performance Analysis of Combined Xception–LSTM Model

To measure the performance of the combined Xception–LSTM model, we observed the accuracy curve and loss curve against each epoch, as shown in Fig 2. The performance is recorded for only 50 epochs. From the accuracy performance, it was evident that training accuracy is increasing while there is no significant improvement in the test accuracy. After 50 epochs, the highest accuracy on the test was recorded to be 12.37%, and for the training set up to 50 epochs, it was 52.40%. The loss performance graph also indicates something worse scenario. Up to 50 epochs, training loss decreases while there is no notable improvement in the test loss. The performance graph indicates the poor performance of the single hybrid CNN–LSTM architecture approach.

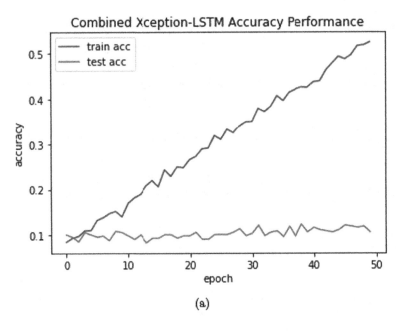

(a)

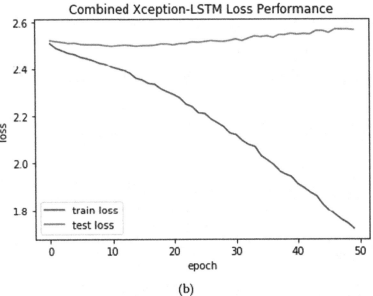

(b)

Fig. 2. Combined Xception–LSTM performance curves: (a) Training Accuracy and Test Accuracy, (b) Training Loss and Test Loss.

4.3   Results of Pre-trained CNN Features and LSTM

Subsection 4.2 illustrated the worst performance of a single hybrid CNN–LSTM model. Therefore, we are accustomed to the second approach, i.e., extracting spatial features using pre-trained models and then passing the extracted features to a single LSTM–based model. We set the value of 256 as the hidden units in the LSTM layer. Hyperbolic tangent (tanh) function was used as the activation function. For the recurrent step, sigmoid activation function was initialized. InceptionResNetV2 recorded the lowest accuracy, i.e., 66% average precision, 65.83% average recall, and 65.58% average f1–score among ResNet152V2 and Xception. ResNet152V2 recorded 70.75% average precision, 70.58% average recall, and 70.17% average f1–score on the test set. However, pre-trained model, Xception, which was developed on the concept of depthwise separable convolution, attained the best performance for the THETIS dataset by attaining a 75.25% average precision, 75.50% average recall, and 75.25% average f1–score.

Table 2. Results of various proposed hybrid LSTM-based models using CNN features.

Pre-trained model	Input feature shape	LSTM hidden units	Average precision (%)	Average recall (%)	Average F1-score (%)
InceptionResNet152V2	(Samples, 15, 24576)	256	66.00	65.83	65.58
ResNet152V2	(Samples, 15, 73728)	256	70.75	70.58	70.17
Xception	(Samples, 15, 73728)	**256**	**75.25**	**75.50**	**75.25**

4.4   Results of the Best Model

From the previous Subsect. 4.3, the results for the 3 pre-trained models and LSTM were outlined, which proved the superiority of Xception from the remaining 2 transfer learning models. In this section, some results of the best model are depicted.

Figure 3 summarizes the confusion matrix for the best model, which demonstrates how much the model is confused among different tennis actions.

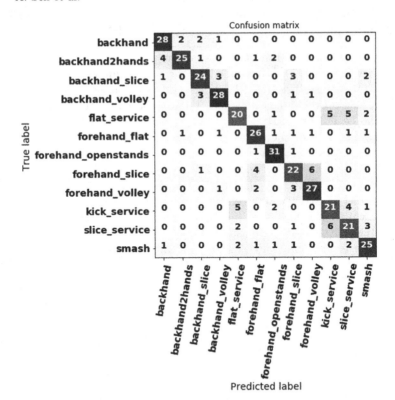

Fig. 3. Confusion matrix for Xception features and LSTM–based model for indoor tennis action recognition.

From the figure, it is apparent that the model is highly confused around similar tennis actions. 5 *flat service* actions were misclassified as *kick service* and *slice service*, respectively. Similarly, 6 actual actions of *slice service* were wrongly predicted as *kick service*, 3 actions as *smash*, and 2 actions as *flat service*. The model functioned better for the category *Forehand Openstands* and successfully classified the highest 31 out of 33 samples.

The classification report is depicted in Table 3. Each category in the test set contains 33 samples; therefore, the support value for all the action categories is 33. *Backhand to Hands* recorded the highest precision of 89% as only 3 samples of other actions were classified as *Backhand to Hands*. *Slice Service* has the lowest precision of 64% as a total of 12 samples of different actions were misclassified as *Slice Service*.

Flat Service has the lowest recall value of 61% as the highest 13 samples were misclassified as other tennis actions. As the f1–score accuracy measure combines both the precision and recall, we finally considered the f1–score for measuring the model performance-the f1–score value for the best Xception features based LSTM model was reported to be 75.25%.

Table 3. Classification report for the Xception features and LSTM–based model.

	Precision	Recall	f1-score	Support
backhand	0.82	0.85	0.84	33
backhand2hands	0.89	0.76	0.82	33
backhand_slice	0.77	0.73	0.75	33
backhand_volley	0.82	0.85	0.84	33
flat_service	0.69	0.61	0.65	33
forehand_flat	0.74	0.79	0.76	33
forehand_openstands	0.82	0.94	0.87	33
forehand_slice	0.67	0.67	0.67	33
forehand_volley	0.77	0.82	0.79	33
kick_service	0.66	0.64	0.65	33
slice_service	0.64	0.64	0.64	33
smash	0.74	0.76	0.75	33

The performance curve for both the accuracy and loss for 300 epochs is depicted in Fig 4. We previously mentioned using a 10% dropout rate to prevent the model from overfitting the training data. As the THETIS dataset comprises samples of identical tennis actions, the model recorded 75.25% test accuracy while the training accuracy was 100%. The loss curve symbolizes that after 200 epochs, the test loss is no more lowering, and there is a certain gap maintained between the training loss and the test loss.

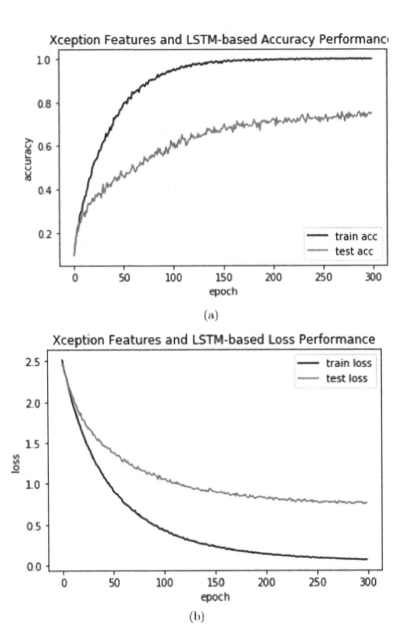

(a)

(b)

Fig. 4. Xception features and LSTM-based model performance curves: (a) Training Accuracy and Test Accuracy, (b) Training Loss and Test Loss.

5 Conclusion

In this work, we designed a hybrid deep neural network and investigated the performance in recognizing twelve different indoor tennis actions from the publicly available THETIS dataset. We conducted experiments by utilizing two approaches (i) using a single hybrid CNN–LSTM model and (ii) passing CNN features to a separate LSTM model. The THETIS dataset is contesting due to its tremendous similarities between tennis actions. Experimental results verified the superiority of using a separate LSTM approach over the single hybrid model approach to classifying 12 different indoor tennis actions. Pre-trained CNN models, namely InceptionResNetV2, ResNet152V2, and Xception, were applied to extract the spatial features from input video frames. These models were considered on account of their less trainable parameters. LSTM with input features from Xception recorded comparatively better accuracy than other pre-trained models by registering 75% accuracy. Due to the black-box nature of neural network, it is difficult to conclude a decision about why a particular model performed better than others. However, deep learning models generally attain better accuracy for the different problem domains than traditional machine learning models. More efforts are still to be made to improve accuracy using less trainable parameters. Moreover, the performance of designing a custom network can be measured to check if the accuracy can be improved compared to the transfer learning approaches for this dataset.

References

1. Silacci, A., Khaled, O.A., Mugellini, E., Caon, M.: Designing an e-coach to tailor training plans for road cyclists. In: Ahram, T., Karwowski, W., Pickl, S., Taiar, R. (eds.) IHSED 2019. AISC, vol. 1026, pp. 671–677. Springer, Cham (2020). https://doi.org/10.1007/978-3-030-27928-8_102

2. Acikmese, Y., Ustundag, B.C., Golubovic, E.: Towards an artificial training expert system for basketball. In: 2017 10th International Conference on Electrical and Electronics Engineering (ELECO), pp. 1300–1304 (2017)

3. Apostolou, K., Tjortjis, C.: Sports analytics algorithms for performance prediction. In: 2019 10th International Conference on Information, Intelligence, Systems and Applications (IISA), pp. 1–4. IEEE (2019)

4. Bačić, B.: Bridging the gap between biomechanics and artificial intelligence. In: XXIV International Symposium on Biomechanics in Sports - ISBS 2006, pp. 371–374 (2006)

5. Cai, J., Hu, J., Tang, X., Hung, T.Y., Tan, Y.P.: Deep historical long short-term memory network for action recognition. Neurocomputing 407, 428–438 (2020)

6. Chollet, F.: Xception: deep learning with depthwise separable convolutions. In: Proceedings of the IEEE Conference on Computer Vision and Pattern Recognition (CVPR) (2017)

7. Deng, J., Dong, W., Socher, R., Li, L.J., Li, K., Fei-Fei, L.: ImageNet: a large-scale hierarchical image database. In: 2009 IEEE Conference on Computer Vision and Pattern Recognition, pp. 248–255. IEEE (2009)

8. Gourgari, S., Goudelis, G., Karpouzis, K., Kollias, S.: Thetis: three dimensional tennis shots a human action dataset. In: Proceedings of the IEEE Conference on Computer Vision and Pattern Recognition Workshops, pp. 676–681 (2013)

9. He, K., Zhang, X., Ren, S., Sun, J.: Identity mappings in deep residual networks. In: Leibe, B., Matas, J., Sebe, N., Welling, M. (eds.) ECCV 2016. LNCS, vol. 9908, pp. 630–645. Springer, Cham (2016). https://doi.org/10.1007/978-3-319-46493-0_38

10. Hochreiter, S., Schmidhuber, J.: Long short-term memory. Neural Comput. **9**(8), 1735–1780 (1997)

11. Hölzemann, A., Van Laerhoven, K.: Using wrist-worn activity recognition for basketball game analysis. In: Proceedings of the 5th International Workshop on Sensor-based Activity Recognition and Interaction, pp. 1–6 (2018)

12. Kampakis, S.: Comparison of machine learning methods for predicting the recovery time of professional football players after an undiagnosed injury. In: MLSA@PKDD/ECML, pp. 58–68 (2013)

13. Karpathy, A., Toderici, G., Shetty, S., Leung, T., Sukthankar, R., Fei-Fei, L.: Large-scale video classification with convolutional neural networks. In: Proceedings of the IEEE Conference on Computer Vision and Pattern Recognition, pp. 1725–1732 (2014)

14. Kingma, D.P., Ba, J.: Adam: a method for stochastic optimization. arXiv:1412.6980 (2014)

15. Lim, S.M., Oh, H.C., Kim, J., Lee, J., Park, J.: LSTM-guided coaching assistant for table tennis practice. Sensors **18**(12) (2018)

16. Mandot, C., Chawla, R.: Artificial intelligence based integrated cricket coach. In: Unnikrishnan, S., Surve, S., Bhoir, D. (eds.) ICAC3 2013. CCIS, vol. 361, pp. 227–236. Springer, Heidelberg (2013). https://doi.org/10.1007/978-3-642-36321-4_21

17. Mora, S.V., Knottenbelt, W.J.: Deep learning for domain-specific action recognition in tennis. In: 2017 IEEE Conference on Computer Vision and Pattern Recognition Workshops (CVPRW), pp. 170–178 (2017)

18. Pascanu, R., Mikolov, T., Bengio, Y.: On the difficulty of training recurrent neural networks. In: International Conference on Machine Learning, pp. 1310–1318. PMLR (2013)

19. Rajšp, A., Fister, I.: A systematic literature review of intelligent data analysis methods for smart sport training. Appl. Sci. **10**(9), 3013 (2020)

20. Rao, V., Shrivastava, A.: Team strategizing using a machine learning approach. In: 2017 International Conference on Inventive Computing and Informatics (ICICI), pp. 1032–1035 (2017)

21. Rossi, A., Pappalardo, L., Cintia, P., Iaia, F., Fernández, J., Medina, D.: Effective injury forecasting in soccer with GPS training data and machine learning. PLOS ONE **13**, e0201264 (2018). https://doi.org/10.1371/journal.pone.0201264

22. Sen, A., Deb, K.: Categorization of actions in soccer videos using a combination of transfer learning and gated recurrent unit. ICT Express **8**(1), 65–71 (2022)

23. Sen, A., Kaushik, D., Dhar, P., Koshiba, T.: Cricshotclassify: an approach to classifying batting shots from cricket videos using a convolutional neural network and gated recurrent unit. Sensors **21**, 2846 (2021)

24. Soomro, K., Zamir, A.R.: Action recognition in realistic sports videos. In: Moeslund, T.B., Thomas, G., Hilton, A. (eds.) Computer Vision in Sports. ACVPR, pp. 181–208. Springer, Cham (2014). https://doi.org/10.1007/978-3-319-09396-3_9

25. Szegedy, C., Ioffe, S., Vanhoucke, V., Alemi, A.A.: Inception-v4, inception-resnet and the impact of residual connections on learning. In: Thirty-first AAAI Conference on Artificial Intelligence (2017)

Multi-region Based Radial GCN Algorithm for Human Action Recognition

Han-Byul Jang and Chil-Woo Lee[✉]

Chonnam National University, Yongbong-ro 77, Buk-gu, Gwangju, Republic of Korea
leecw@chonnam.ac.kr

Abstract. Action recognition is to classify the spatio-temporal changes of the human body as a qualitative pattern, so an efficient representation method that can reflect the structural characteristics of the human body is required. There-fore, in deep learning-based action recognition, graph convolutional network (GCN) algorithms with skeleton data as input were mainly used. However, these methods are difficult to use in the real situation without first obtaining accurate skeleton data. In this paper, we propose a multi-region based radial graph convolutional network (MRGCN) capable of end-to-end action recognition using only optical flow and gradient of the image. This method uses the optical flow and gradient as an oriented histogram, compresses it into a 6-dimensional feature vector, and uses it as an input to the network. Since the network that learns this feature vector has a radial hierarchical structure, it can learn the structural deformation of the human body. As a result of applying a performance experiment on 30 actions, MRGCN obtained Top-1 accuracy of 84.78%, which is higher than that of the existing GCN-based action recognition method. These results show that MRGCN is a high-performance action recognition algorithm suitable for using in the field of surveillance systems where skeleton data can-not be used.

Keywords: Human action recognition · Graph convolutional network · Optical flow · Image gradient · Radial GCN

1 Introduction

Action recognition is to classify human movements into predefined motion patterns in the spatio-temporal domain. Therefore, the input data must include temporal and spatial information at the same time. In addition, a structural representation method that can express the unique hierarchical characteristics of the three-dimensional structure of the human body must be used.

Skeleton data is a record of the joint coordinates of a moving person and has the advantage of being able to express action very quantitatively, so it is frequently used as input data in action recognition. Especially, most of the GCN-based action recognition studies that are receiving attention recently use skeleton data as input data. ST-GCN [1], the first GCN-based action recognition research, recognized actions using a graph structure that mimics the joint structure of the human body as shown in Fig. 1. Since

© The Author(s), under exclusive license to Springer Nature Switzerland AG 2022
K. Sumi et al. (Eds.): IW-FCV 2022, CCIS 1578, pp. 325–342, 2022.
https://doi.org/10.1007/978-3-031-06381-7_23

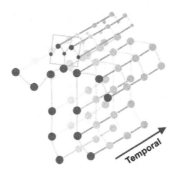

Fig. 1. The graph of ST-GCN (The source is [1]).

this method can express well the contextual dependence of actions arising from the hierarchical structure of the human body, a remarkably improved recognition rate can be obtained compared to the previous method.

However, the problem with action recognition based on skeleton data is that, paradoxically, it is difficult to acquire accurate skeleton data in an actual application environment. Skeleton data can only be obtained by using a special device such as Kinect or using extra software such as OPENPOSE. If we use an expensive additional device, we can obtain quantitative and accurate skeleton data. However, at the same time, there is a constraint that an environment in which this device can be used must be considered. In other words, in most cases, it is difficult to control the environment of an application system that requires action recognition such as CCTV to acquire input data.

Unlike using special equipment, software such as OPENPOSE estimates the joint coordinates of a person from the input RGB image through various calculations. Since these methods estimate 3D information from 2D images, it is generally difficult to obtain accurate joint coordinates. In addition, when deep learning is applied for accurate estimation, an additional computational process is required. Also, since accurate skeleton data can be obtained only when an image suitable for processing is input, it is difficult to obtain accurate skeleton data in real environment. Most of the currently serviced surveillance systems use only a video camera as an input device, so it is difficult to apply an action recognition algorithm using skeleton data as an input in the real world.

In this paper, we propose MRGCN (multi-region based radial graph convolutional network), an action recognition algorithm that can be used efficiently in a surveillance system where it is difficult to acquire skeleton data. The first feature of the MRGCN algorithm is that it uses optical flow and image gradient information as input data instead of skeleton data. For the algorithm, we first assumed that action could be expressed through the combination of 'motion and poses with a special meaning'. Therefore, optical flow that can express motion information well and image gradient that can express pose (shape) information well are selected as input data, and a method of combining the two information was taken. Input data is obtained from a region of motion (RoM) that is a rectangular data acquisition region defined in an image and is input to each node of the graph structure. RoMs that provide input information are arranged to overlap each other (ORoM: overlapped region of motion) to obtain a more robust recognition result. In addition, the input data is reduced to 6-dimensional feature information, enabling faster and more effective neural net-work learning.

The second characteristic of MRGCN is that we developed a graph structure suitable for the input data and applied it to the GCN learning model. MRGCN can obtain high-performance action recognition results by analyzing the characteristics of input data, designing the graph connection structure and the location and size of ORoM suitable for the characteristics, and reflecting it in the GCN model. The MRGCN algorithm has been improved through the previous papers [2, 3], and [4], and this paper describes the completed algorithm by synthesizing the partial proposals in the previous papers. The previous paper [1] dealt with the first implementation of the structure of the MRGCN algorithm, [2] proposed a method for reducing the size of the input data, and [3] described the improvement method in the data acquisition area. This paper corrects the experimental errors of previous papers and further describes the experiments of real-time system. Also, the structure of the comprehensive algorithm is explained more clearly.

The structure of this paper is as follows. First, in Sect. 2, we look at related studies in the field of action recognition. Section 3 describes the MRGCN algorithm in detail. After explaining the results of comparative experiments with ST-GCN in Sect. 4, the conclusion is drawn in Sect. 5.

2 Related Studies

In the past, the study of action recognition mainly used pattern recognition methods, but now the deep learning method is the mainstream among them. In particular, recently methods using the GCN model are receiving a lot of attention because they show a high recognition rate. In the past pattern recognition method, first, the action data was transformed into a more suitable form for recognition, and then the type of action was determined by applying the pattern recognition technique to the transformed action data. At this time, the most important point is how to express the temporal and spatial deformation of the human body in an efficient way. In order to find a vector space that can express action more efficiently, various calculation methods, mathematical expression techniques, and researchers' intuition were applied. [5] proposed a method for recognizing action by converting skeleton data into curves on a mathematical space called 'Lie group' and then using the vector of the curve as an input to the SVM for an example of past action recognition research. [6] processes the skeleton data to obtain a covariance matrix of joint positions according to time, and then recognizes the action by using the covariance matrix as a descriptor of the action.

In recent years, most of the action recognition research has been conducted using deep learning. The deep learning technique has the advantage of being able to find minute features of input data that are difficult to find out with the existing pattern recognition method by training the artificial neural network. Actional data is composite and complex data that deals with changes in space and time. The detailed analysis method using deep learning is very suitable for action recognition because it matches the characteristics of these actional data well. [7] also shows action recognition using deep learning methods. In this study, a convolutional neural network (CNN) model is trained by re-expressing the skeleton data as a two-dimensional map-image. [8] uses a spatiotemporal long short-term memory (LSTM) neural network model to which the search tree structure is applied.

[9] divides the human body into five large parts and generates and uses input data of a recurrent neural network (RNN) model for each part.

An action recognition method that has recently received attention is to use a GCN model. GCN can apply convolution only when nodes are connected by reflecting the connection structure of the graph in the learning process. In other words, GCN can define contextual features existing in data as a graph structure and reflect them in learning. ST-GCN [1], which used GCN for action recognition for the first time, obtained dramatically improved results by using a graph connected to the shape of a human body. ST-GCN connects nodes in the same way as the human body's connection structure, and temporally nodes of the same joint are continuously connected along the data frame. In other words, good results were obtained because the context of the action occurrence created by human movement could be reflected in the neural network.

[10] is an example of a study using a more improved GCN method. In this study, after dividing the human body into four large parts, the method of constructing GCN for data of each part is used. [11] uses both the human body shape graph and the additional graph according to the characteristics of the action. [12] optimizes the strength of graph connections using the graph regression based GCN (GR-GCN) algorithm, which obtains an optimized graph using Chebyshev approximation which is a field of mathematics about approximating functions with simpler functions and regression analysis. However, it is difficult to find cases that fundamentally deviate from the graph structure of the human body used in [1] in current GCN-based studies. This is because it is difficult to design a graph structure that better expresses the context of action in skeleton data.

Although the MRGCN in this paper is an action recognition algorithm using the GCN model, it has similarities to the previously applied research methods in that the algorithm re-expresses data to better recognize the action. In addition, because new input data is used instead of skeleton data, it has the characteristic of artificially designing and using a new graph structure, unlike existing GCN-based studies.

3 MRGCN Algorithm

3.1 Input Data Generation Procedure

For the MRGCN algorithm proposed in this paper, we assume that action can be expressed through *combination of special motions and poses*. Therefore, optical flow that can represent movement well and image gradient that can represent pose-that is, the shape of a person well was selected as input data. In addition, since optical flow and image gradient have a polar coordinate format that has magnitude and direction components in common, they also have the advantage of being applicable to the same calculating process.

One input vector of MRGCN is generated for each node of the graph, and a data acquisition area for generating one vector is defined as a region of motion (RoM). As shown in Fig. 2, RoM is a rectangular area defined to have an appropriate location and size according to the characteristics of the node. In order to prevent unnecessary data acquisition, RoM is placed in a partial area that separates only the person portion from the image, called the 'person area'. As shown in Fig. 3, the person area is obtained by first finding the human head and then expanding the head to a size that can cover the entire body. As for the method of finding a human head, it is okay to use a suitable method among various recognition techniques. However, when RoMs are placed in contact with each other in a grid-like manner in MRGCN, information located at the boundary between RoMs is inputted only to one node to which it belongs. But, information on the boundary is natural only when it can affect all nearby nodes. Therefore, ORoM (Overlapped RoM) is used so that information can be spread to neighboring nodes by extending the RoM area as shown in Fig. 4.

Fig. 2. Example deployment of 4 RoMs (portrait is taken from NTU RGB+D data set [13]).

Fig. 3. The 'person area' obtained based on the position of the head.

The optical flow and image gradient acquired in RoM are converted into histograms using a histogram of gradient (HoG) algorithm. At this time, a histogram of 32 dimensions, 16 dimensions for each optical flow and image gradient, is generated using a bin of $22.5°$, and the obtained histogram data is called a histogram of flow and gradient (HoFG). Also, optical flow and image gradient are acquired using different sampling methods. Optical flow is obtained only from pixels with strong curve characteristics, and image gradient is obtained from all pixels in RoM. The reason why the sampling method is different is to remove a lot of noise information generated in the optical flow. Finally, since the histogram uses a different sampling method, normalization is applied by dividing by the number of samples taken as in Eq. 1.

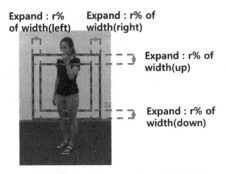

Fig. 4. Extend the length and width of RoM by r% so that the RoMs in contact overlap each other.

$$Normalized\ HoFG_i = \frac{Histogram\ value\ of\ bin_i}{Sampling\ counts} \tag{1}$$

The obtained 32-dimensional histogram can be directly used as an input to the neural network, but the histogram is reduced to 6-dimensional data for faster processing. The reduced input data is three-dimensional for each optical flow and image gradient, and its components are the three features of *HoFG Code, mean,* and *deviation.*

The first element, *HoFG Code,* is information indicating the distribution shape of the histogram. To calculate the *HoFG Code,* first define a bin having a larger value than the surrounding bin as a mode bin as shown in Fig. 5, and then arrange the modes in the order of the mode value. The sorted order is called *order* and has a range from 1 to k. That is, *order = 1* means the bin with the largest value. Apply *order* to Eq. 2 to calculate the *Mode(order)* value. At this time, the bin index of the equation has 16 kinds of values from 0 to 15, and if the *order* of the mode histogram does not exist, the *Mode (order)* value is set to 0. Finally, the *HoFG Code* is calculated by applying the *Mode (order)* value to Eq. 3. In this case, *k* in the formula means the range of order, and *C* is a constant for calculation. For the value of *C,* a number greater than 17 can be used, which is larger than the dimension of the histogram, but in this paper, 20 is used for convenience.

As shown in Fig. 6, the distribution of the histogram can be expressed through the *HoFG Code* values. However, *HoFG Code* does not have information related to the size of the histogram value. Therefore, the second and third factors, *mean* and *deviation,* are used. The *mean* and *deviation* can be obtained by calculating the arithmetic mean and standard deviation of the histogram.

$$Mode(order) = \begin{cases} (bin\ index\ i) + 1 : if\ the\ bin\ is\ mode \\ 0 : otherwise \end{cases} \tag{2}$$

$$HoFG\ Code = \sum_{order=1}^{k} Mode(order) * C^{k-order} \tag{3}$$

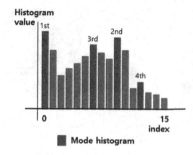

Fig. 5. Mode position with a larger value than the surrounding histogram.

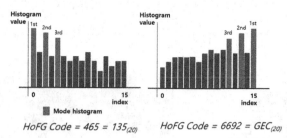

Fig. 6. The difference between HoFG Code values according to the distribution shape of the histogram.

3.2 Design of Graph Structure

Since MRGCN uses new input data instead of skeleton data, it is necessary to develop and use a new graph structure suitable for the data. In addition, to design a graph effectively, design principles and units for graph construction are defined and used. First, the principles for designing graphs mimic how humans use different perspectives to solve problems. Just as a person analyzes a problem by dividing it into a whole and a partial perspective, MRGCN uses a method of systematically connecting nodes of large RoM and small RoM. At this time, to facilitate systematic configuration, nodes and RoM are defined using a layer structure. Next, since designing the entire graph right away is too complicated, an intermediate unit for graph construction called 'graph-unit' is defined. As shown in Fig. 7, 'graph-unit' has two types: 'single-graph-unit' and 'multi-graph-unit'. A 'single-graph-unit' corresponds to one node, whereas a 'multi-graph-unit' is corresponds composed of five nodes of partial areas (All: A, Left: L, Right: R, Up: U, Down: D) and has predefined internal connections. In other words, 'multi-graph-unit' is a systematic pre-connection of information from different perspectives.

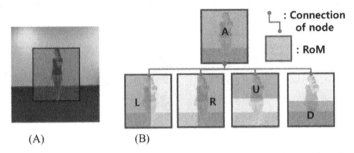

Fig. 7. Graph-unit: (A) Single-graph-unit, (B) Multi-graph-unit. Single-graph-unit corresponds to one graph node, and multi-graph-unit corresponds 5 single-graph-units: all (A), left (L), right (R), top (U), bottom (D). Also, multi-graph-unit has internal graph connection.

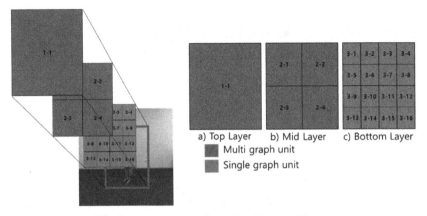

Fig. 8. Arrangement of graph units using 3 layers

A layer structure is used to systematically configure the nodes of the graph and the region of RoM. As shown in Fig. 8, 'graph-units' are arranged in a three-level layer structure at the top, mid, and bottom. At this time, 'multi-graph-unit' is placed on the top and mid layers and 'single-graph-unit' is placed on the bottom layer. When such an arrangement method is used, the total number of nodes according to the number of layers is shown in Table 1 below. As shown in Table 1, the one-two layers structures have too few nodes constructing a graph of suitable size to analyze action, and the four layers or more layers structures have too many nodes. Because it is appropriate to use 41 nodes to analyze the action by dividing RoM meaningfully according to the size of the human body. Therefore, it is most efficient to take a three-layers structure for analysis of action.

Table 1. Number of nodes and evaluation according to the number of layers

Layer	Node	Evaluation
1	5	Too few nodes
2	9	Fewer nodes
3	41	Suitable
4	169	Too many Nodes

The 'multi-graph-unit' has predefined internal connections. Therefore, defining graph connections between layers completes all spatial graph construction. The graph connection between layers uses the method of connecting nodes with overlapping RoMs as shown in Fig. 9. At this time, 'multi-graph-unit' divides all area (A) node and partial (L, R, U, D) node into upper node and lower node, respectively, and connects the lower nodes of the upper layer and the upper nodes of the lower layer with each other. Also, as shown in Fig. 10, MRGCN uses a method in which the nodes of the front and rear frames are sequentially connected in time. This method is the same as the method of constructing the temporal graph connection in ST-GCN [1] and 180 frames are connected sequentially.

The top view of the entire graph connection is shown in Fig. 11. In the figure, this algorithm is named multi-region based radial GCN because the nodes are arranged radially along the layers. Also, the flow chart of the entire MRGCN algorithm is shown in Fig. 12. The algorithm first pre-processes the input image and then separates the 'person area'. After generating input data in the separated person area, it is applied to the neural network. At the last stage of the neural network, it passes through an action classifier and outputs the final action recognition result.

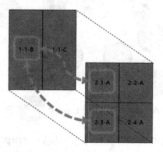

Fig. 9. Connection nodes method between layers: connect nodes that are in contact between layers (connect 1-1-B to 2-1-A and 2-3-A).

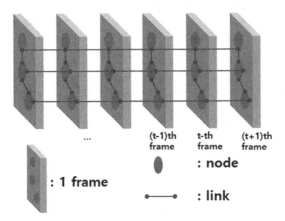

Fig. 10. Temporal connection method of graph nodes: connect the nodes of consecutive frames in sequence.

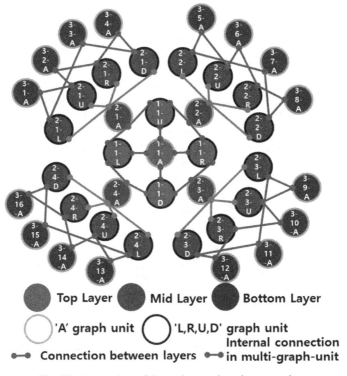

Fig. 11. A top view of the entire graph node connection.

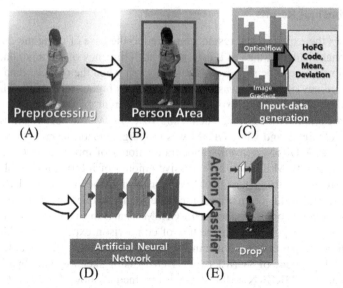

Fig. 12. Flowchart of overall algorithm. (A) Preprocessing input image, (B) Separation of people area, (C) Generation of input data, (D) GCN stages and (E) Action classification.

4 Experiment

4.1 Experimental Environment and Structure of Neural Network

The performance of MRGCN is verified through comparative experiments with ST-GCN [1]. ST-GCN is a representative GCN-based action recognition algorithm and uses skeleton data. Therefore, it can be a good comparison target with MRGCN using new input data which is a GCN-based action recognition algorithm. The training and evaluation experiments of the network were conducted using a computer with a Ryzen 3700 CPU and an Nvidia 3060 GPU. Also, as shown in Tables 2 and 3 below, two experimental data sets were created by selecting actions from the NTU RGB+D data set [13]. Experimental data set 1 contains 10 actions and aims to quickly test the effectiveness of the compressed data dimension and the effectiveness of ORoM. Data set 2 contains 30 actions and aims to evaluate the overall performance of the algorithm.

The structure of the MRGCN neural network used in the experiment is shown in Fig. 13. As shown in the figure, MRGCN has a 9-level GCN neural network. A normalization layer is placed in front of the GCN neural network to apply the data to the learning process. The 1st–3rd GCN layers have an output channel size of 64. The 4th–6th GCN layer has an output channel size of 123, and the 7th–9th layer has an output channel size of 256. Also, the GCN layers use padding to prevent dimensionality reduction due to convolution, the Resnet mechanism is used, and a dropout of 0.5 probability is applied at each GCN layer. In the final action classification step, after obtaining a one-dimensional vector through global average pooling, the result is output through a fully convolutional network layer. Also, this neural network structure is set identically to ST-GCN for fair comparison.

4.2 Experimental Results

Table 4 shows the experimental results compared to the case of using the non-reduced 32-dimensional histogram data as it is to verify the efficiency of the input data reduced to 6 dimensions. As can be seen from the table, even when the reduced data was used, the Top-1 accuracy of 94.17% was obtained, which is higher than that of the original data. In addition, the results of experiments with different overlapping rates of ORoM are shown in Table 5. At this time, when using 10% ORoM, the best Top-1 accuracy of 94.28% was obtained, and when ORoM was too large, performance deteriorated. The reason is that 10% ORoM delivers a moderate amount of information to neighboring nodes, but larger ORoM delivers an excessive amount of information. Tables 6 and 7 show the confusion matrix when ORoM is not used and when the optimal 10% is used. By comparing the confusion matrices, it can be found that actions that are difficult to recognize are better recognized when using ORoM. That is, by using ORoM, more robust recognition becomes possible. The results of comparison experiments with ST-GCN using Experiment data set 2 are shown in Table 9 below. As shown in the table, MRGCN obtained Top-1 accuracy of 84.78% over ST-GCN using skeleton data. In addition, the confusion matrix of MRGCN and ST-GCN is obtained as shown in Tables 6 and 8.

Table 2. Actions in experimental data set 1

No.	Action	No.	Action
1	Eat meal	6	Stand up
2	Drop	7	Hand waving
3	Pick up	8	Kicking something
4	Throw	9	Jump up
5	Sit down	10	Staggering

Table 3. Actions in experimental data set 2

No.	Action	No.	Action
1	Drink water	16	Put on a shoe
2	Eat meal	17	Take off a shoe
3	Brush teeth	18	Put on glasses
4	Brush hair	19	Take off glasses
5	Drop	20	Put on a hat/cap
6	Pick up	21	Take off a hat/cap
7	Throw	22	Cheer up

(*continued*)

Table 3. (*continued*)

No.	Action	No.	Action
8	Sit down	23	Hand waving
9	Stand up	24	Kicking something
10	Clapping	25	Reach into pocket
11	Reading	26	Hopping
12	Writing	27	Jump up
13	Tear up paper	28	Phone call
14	Put on jacket	29	Play with phone/tablet
15	Take off jacket	30	staggering

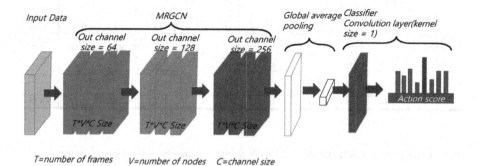

Fig. 13. MRGCN neural network schematic.

Comparing these confusion matrices reveals different types of action that the two algorithms do not recognize well. The reason is analyzed to be because the parts with advantages and disadvantages differ according to the characteristics of the data.

Table 4. Experimental results according to data dimension using dataset 1

Data type	Top-1 accuracy	Top-5 accuracy
Uncompressed 32 dimensional data	93.88%	99.78%
Reduced 6 dimensional data	94.17%	99.74%

Table 5. Experimental result according to ORoM using dataset 1

Overlap rate (%)	Top-1 accuracy	Top-5 accuracy
No overlapped	94.17%	99.74%
10%	94.28%	100%
20%	92.60%	99.78%
30%	92.62%	99.89%

Table 6. Confusion matrix of MRGCN without overlap using dataset 1

		Actions									
		1	2	3	4	5	6	7	8	9	10
Actions	1	95.26	2.92	0	0.73	0	0	0.73	0.36	0	0
	2	3.27	88.36	0	1.82	2.55	0.73	0	3.27	0	0
	3	0	0	98.18	0	0	1.45	0.36	0	0	0
	4	1.82	0.36	2.18	82.91	0.73	0.36	7.64	2.55	0.36	1.09
	5	0	0.37	0.37	0	94.14	0.37	0	1.83	0	2.93
	6	0	0	0	0.37	0	98.17	0	0.73	0.73	0
	7	1.82	0	0	0	0	0	98.18	0	0	0
	8	0	0.73	0.36	0	0.36	1.09	0	94.89	1.82	0.73
	9	0	0	0	0	0.36	1.81	0	0	97.83	0
	10	0.36	0	0	0	0	0	0	5.8	0	93.84

Table 7. Confusion matrix of MRGCN using 10% overlap ORoM using dataset 1

		Actions									
		1	2	3	4	5	6	7	8	9	10
Actions	1	93.43	4.74	0	1.09	0	0	0.73	0	0	0
	2	2.91	90.91	0	1.82	2.55	0	0	1.82	0	0
	3	0	0	99.64	0	0	0.36	0	0	0	0
	4	1.82	0.73	1.82	83.64	0.36	0	9.82	0.36	0	1.45
	5	0	0.73	0	0.37	97.44	0	0	0.73	0	0.73
	6	0	0	1.47	0.73	0.73	95.6	0.37	0.37	0.37	0.37
	7	2.55	0.36	0	0	0	0	97.08	0	0	0
	8	0	3.28	0	1.09	0.36	0	0	93.07	0.73	1.46
	9	0	0	0	0.36	0	0	0	0	99.64	0
	10	1.09	0	0.72	0	1.81	0.36	0	3.62	0	92.39

Table 8. Confusion matrix of ST-GCN using dataset 1

		Actions									
		1	2	3	4	5	6	7	8	9	10
Actions	1	84.36	8.36	0	1.82	0	0	5.45	0	0	0
	2	1.09	92	0	0.73	1.82	0	1.09	2.55	0	0.73
	3	0	0	98.91	0	0.73	0	0	0	0	0.36
	4	3.64	0	2.18	84.36	0	0	8.36	1.45	0	0
	5	0.37	0	0.73	0	98.17	0.37	0.37	0	0	0
	6	0	0	0.37	0.73	0	98.17	0.37	0.37	0	0
	7	3.65	3.65	0	0.36	0	0	92.34	0	0	0
	8	0	1.81	0	2.54	0	0.36	0	92.03	2.17	1.09
	9	0	0	0.72	0	0	0	0	0	99.28	0
	10	0	0.36	1.45	0	1.09	0	0	3.99	0	93.12

Table 9. Experimental results using data set 2

Algorithm	Top-1 accuracy	Top-5 accuracy
ST-GCN	84.05%	97.93%
MRGCN	84.78%	98.13%

4.3 The Experiment of Real-Time Action Recognition System

When action recognition is applied in actual environment, it should be possible to recognize natural human actions. However, since humans perform various types of actions in a row, it is necessary to implement a real-time system that can recognize actions that occur continuously. However, since the current MRGCN algorithm is being tested according to the prepared data set, it is not suitable for implementing effective real-time recognition. Here, the implementation of the prototype real-time action recognition system will be described prior to the implementation of the accomplished real-time system.

Since an experiment using a data set is conducted in such a way that one result is obtained for one data, data of a long frame sequence is used. However, real-time action recognition cannot use long sequences because it requires an immediate analysis of the circumstances in which the action occurs. In addition, the experiment using a data set selects the action with the highest output score of the action classifier as the result, but in a real-time system, it is necessary to withhold outputting the result according to the recognition status of other actions, even if it is the highest-scoring action. For example, if it is ambiguous to output a certain result, it is necessary to output the 'None' status as the result.

Therefore, the real-time system uses a shorter input sequence and determines the result of action recognition by re-judging the output score of the action classifier as Eq. 4. In this case, $actionscore_{max}$ means the highest action score, and $action_{maxscore}$ means the action with that score. If the highest score is greater than the $score_{minimum}$ and the standard deviation of scores is greater than the $STD_{minimum}$, the highest-scoring action is output as a result, and if the condition is not satisfied, the result is determined as 'None'. The following Fig. 14 shows the process of recognizing the action, 'hand waving' through the real-time camera image. As shown in the figure, it can be seen that more definite results are being output when the action becomes more clear.

$$action\ result = \begin{cases} action_{maxscore}: \ if\ (actionscore_{max} > score_{minimum})and \\ \qquad\qquad (STD_{scores} > STD_{minimum}) \\ \qquad None: \ otherwise \end{cases} \qquad (4)$$

Real-time action recognition experiment generates significantly more errors than experiment using data sets. The reason is that MRGCN algorithm is optimized for the data set and does not perform well in a function suitable for a real-time system. To compensate for this, it is necessary to improve the algorithm so that consistent data can be acquired even when the input device changes, and the context of actions can be naturally grasped using a shorter data sequence. In addition, a more complete real-time system can be realized only when it is developed to better understand the change in the actional state and use the information of surrounding objects additionally.

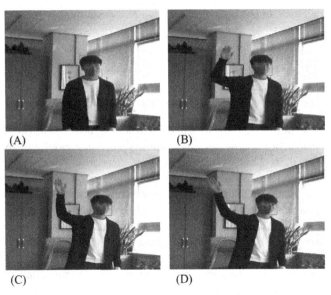

(A)   (B)

(C)   (D)

Fig. 14. Real-time recognition of 'hand waving'. (A) First image: recognized 'None', (B) Second image: recognized 'None', (C) Third image: recognized 'Hand waving' with score 22 and (D) Fourth image: recognized 'Hand waving' with score 40.

5 Conclusion

Skeleton data has the advantage of intuitively expressing the context of action, so it is frequently used as general input data in GCN-based action recognition research. However, since obtaining accurate skeleton data requires the use of separate equipment or software, it is not suitable in an actual environment using a simple input device such as

CCTV. In particular, it was difficult to obtain accurate skeleton data in a field with a bad data acquisition environment such as a surveillance system, so the existing GCN-based action recognition methods could not be applied. To complement this, this study proposes MRGCN, an action recognition algorithm that can be used in surveillance systems. MRGCN enables end-to-end recognition because it uses optical flow and image gradient information that can be acquired through CCTV, which is commonly used in surveillance systems, as input data instead of skeleton data. In addition, it has the characteristic of constructing GCN by artificially designing a graph suitable for the characteristics of new input data. The MRGCN algorithm realizes more effective learning by reducing the input data from a 32-dimensional size to a 6-dimensional size and obtains a more robust recognition result by arranging the data acquisition areas to overlap each other.

As a result of performing a comparative experiment on 30 actions, MRGCN obtained Top-1 accuracy of 84.78%, which is higher than the result of the method using the skeleton data. It shows that MRGCN is an algorithm that can achieve high-performance action recognition without using any secondary processed data like skeleton data. Therefore, MRGCN can be a good alternative in fields where it is difficult to use skeleton data, such as an intelligent surveillance system. Since the surveillance system can prevent fatal events such as violence, accidents, and terrorism using action recognition, the high value of MRGCN is clear.

However, the current MRGCN has a limitation in that it only analyzes human motions. Actual human actions often use tools and are closely related to the actions of other people around them. Therefore, there is a need to develop an algorithm to comprehensively interpret action-related objects such as tools and other action information around them. In addition, it is necessary to implement a natural real-time action recognition system. A real-time system is an essential element for the application of action recognition. In order to expand the application field of MRGCN and develop more natural automation services, the MRGCN algorithm should be improved to be suitable for real-time action recognition.

Acknowledgments. This research is supported by Ministry of Culture, Sports, and Tourism (MCST) and Korea Creative Content Agency (KOCCA) in the Culture Technology (CT) Research & Development Program (R2020060002) 2020.

References

1. Yan, S., Xiong, Y., Lin, D.: Spatial temporal graph convolutional networks for skeleton-based action recognition. In: Thirty-Second AAAI Conference on Artificial Intelligence, pp. 7444–7452 (2018)
2. Jang, H.-B., Kim, D.J., Lee, C.W.: Human action recognition based on ST-GCN using optical flow and image gradient. In: The 9th International Conference on Smart Media and Applications, pp. 255–260 (2020)
3. Jang, H.-B., Lee, C.-W.: ST-GCN based human action recognition with abstracted three features of optical flow and image gradient. In: Jeong, H., Sumi, K. (eds.) IW-FCV 2021. CCIS, vol. 1405, pp. 203–217. Springer, Cham (2021). https://doi.org/10.1007/978-3-030-81638-4_17

4. Jang, H.-B., Lee, C.W.: A human action recognition based on MRGCN using overlapped data acquisition regions. In: The 10th International Conference on Smart Media and Applications, pp. 10–15 (2021)
5. Raviteja, V., Arrate, F., Chellappa, R.: Human action recognition by representing 3d skeletons as points in a lie group. In: Proceedings of the IEEE Conference on Computer Vision and Pattern Recognition (2014)
6. Mohamed, E.H., et al.: Human action recognition using a temporal hierarchy of covariance descriptors on 3D joint locations. In: Twenty-Third International Joint Conference on Artificial Intelligence, pp. 2466–2472 (2013)
7. Li, C., et al.: Skeleton-based action recognition using LSTM and CNN. In: 2017 IEEE International Conference on Multimedia and Expo Workshops (ICMEW), pp. 585–590. IEEE (2017)
8. Liu, J., Shahroudy, A., Dong, X., Wang, G.: Spatio-temporal LSTM with trust gates for 3D human action recognition. In: Leibe, B., Matas, J., Sebe, N., Welling, M. (eds.) ECCV 2016. LNCS, vol. 9907, pp. 816–833. Springer, Cham (2016). https://doi.org/10.1007/978-3-319-46487-9_50
9. Du, Y., Wang, W., Wang, L.: Hierarchical recurrent neural network for skeleton based action recognition. In: Proceedings of the IEEE Conference on Computer Vision and Pattern Recognition, pp. 1110–1118 (2015)
10. Kalpit, T., Narayanan, P.J.: Part-based graph convolutional network for action recognition. arXiv:1809.04983 (2018)
11. Li, M., et al.: Actional-structural graph convolutional networks for skeleton-based action recognition. In: Proceedings of the IEEE/CVF Conference on Computer Vision and Pattern Recognition, pp. 3590–3598 (2019)
12. Gao, X., et al.: Optimized skeleton-based action recognition via sparsified graph regression. In: Proceedings of the 27th ACM International Conference on Multimedia, pp. 601–610 (2019)
13. Amir, S., et al.: NTU RGB+D: A large scale dataset for 3D human activity analysis. Proceedings of the IEEE Conference on Computer Vision and Pattern Recognition, pp. 1010–1019 (2016)

Impression Estimation Model of 3D Objects Using Multi-View Convolutional Neural Network

Keisuke Sakashita[1], Kensuke Tobitani[2] ⓘ, Koichi Taguchi[3], Manabu Hashimoto[3] ⓘ, Iori Tani[4] ⓘ, Sho Hashimoto[5], Kenji Katahira[6] ⓘ, and Noriko Nagata[1(✉)] ⓘ

[1] Kwansei Gakuin University, 2-1 Gakuen, Sanda-shi 669-1337, Hyogo, Japan
nagata@kwansei.ac.jp
[2] University of Nagasaki, 1-1-1 Manabino, Nagayo-cho, Nishi-Sonogi-gun, Nagasaki 851-2195, Japan
[3] Chukyo University, 101-2 Yagoto Honmachi, Showa-ku, Nagoya-shi 466-8666, Aichi, Japan
[4] Kobe University, 1-1 Rokkodai-cho, Nada-ku, Kobe-shi 657-0013, Hyogo, Japan
[5] Seinan Gakuin University, 6-2-92 Nishijin, Sawara-ku, Fukuoka 814-8511, Japan
[6] Waseda University, 1-104 Totsukamachi, Shinjuku-ku, Tokyo 169-8050, Japan

Abstract. The ultimate goal of this study is to provide intuitive design support for 3D objects. As a first attempt, we propose a method for estimating impressions of common 3D objects with various characteristics. Although many studies have been conducted to estimate objects' aesthetics, not enough research has been conducted to estimate the various impressions of objects necessary for design support. The data set of human impressions of 3D objects is constructed based on psychological methods. To account for the variability in people's ratings, the distribution of ratings is represented by a histogram. By learning the distribution of impression ratings, with the estimation model, we can realize an impression estimation model with high estimation accuracy. In the accuracy validation experiment, the proposed method's estimated results (estimated impression distribution) showed a moderate to high positive correlation with the distribution of human impressions. In addition, we confirmed that the proposed method has greater estimation accuracy than previous studies and that it captures the tendency for variation in people's impression evaluations (the global tendency of impression distribution). Furthermore, visual confirmation of the relationship between the estimation results of the constructed impression estimation model and 3D objects suggests that the proposed method is capable of identifying the main physical features associated with impression words, confirming the proposed method's validity.

Keywords: DNN · Impression estimation model · Multi-viewpoint images · Kansei · Aesthetic concepts

1 Introduction

Since the fourth industrial revolution, the rapid development of 3D printer technology and the spread of 3D model databases have created an environment for outputting a

K. Sumi et al. (Eds.): IW-FCV 2022, CCIS 1578, pp. 343–355, 2022.
https://doi.org/10.1007/978-3-031-06381-7_24

variety of 3D modeling objects. These changes in the environment provide a wide range of users with opportunities for personal manufacturing activities. However, there are challenges in the spread of personal manufacturing activities because many users do not have specialized knowledge or skills in manufacturing. Even if users have latent needs for design, it is not easy to reflect them in the form of an object. To provide a wide range of users with opportunities for manufacturing activities in the future, it is necessary to support users so that they can engage in manufacturing intuitively and easily. As one such support, a design support system that searches for and recommends 3D objects based on words that express sensory impressions (e.g., "gay," "hard-looking," etc.) is considered effective because impression words are intuitive and sensory to the user and easily express the user's latent needs. To realize these design support systems, it is necessary to map the relationship between 3D objects' physical features and the impressions the objects evoke. Recently, many studies have been conducted on estimating objects' aesthetics, but these studies have dealt with preferences and feelings toward objects, and not enough research has been conducted on estimating the impressions of objects.

The ultimate goal of this study is to provide intuitive design support for 3D objects, and as a first attempt, we propose a method for estimating the impression of a 3D object. Here, the impression of a 3D object is only based on shape and does not take into account other factors, such as texture or color. For estimation, we use a multi-view convolutional neural network (MVCNN), which takes as input a set of images rendered from multiple viewpoints of a 3D object. The data set of people's impressions of 3D objects is created based on psychological methods. To account for the variation in people's ratings, the distribution of ratings is represented by a histogram. By learning the distribution of ratings, the impression estimation model can achieve an estimation model that has a high correlation with the human impression ratings. Finally, we confirm this study's effectiveness by conducting experiments to verify the proposed method's accuracy.

2   Previous Research

Examples of research utilizing impressions of objects include retrieval technologies that use words expressing impressions (hereafter referred to as "impression words") as queries [1–4]. All of these techniques are realized using the relationship between the object's physical characteristics and the impressions it evokes. Research on such impression estimation has been conducted mainly on two-dimensional images, but there are some reported cases of its application with 3D objects [5, 6]. However, these studies used geometrically simple 3D objects, and no systematic results have been reported on the impression evaluation of general 3D objects with various features.

On the other hand, research has been actively conducted to model human sensibilities toward objects, such as preferences, aesthetic scores, and aesthetic values, using deep-learning techniques [7–9]. However, in many fields, such as psychology, design, and Kansei engineering, it is assumed that a clear distinction is made between the evaluator's emotional response to an object, such as aesthetics, and the properties of the object itself [10]. For example, aesthetic evaluations such as "beautiful" and "preference" are mediated by more emotional reactions in the processing of information about the object's specific properties, such as "gay" and "hard-looking." These properties of objects are called aesthetic concepts [11–13]. In an intuitive design support system, the grasp of aesthetic concepts is indispensable for design creation using the object's properties as a query. Only in a few studies have researchers used deep-learning techniques to model aesthetic concepts. In this study, we define an aesthetic concept as an impression and propose a method for estimating the impression of a 3D object by modeling the relationship between its physical features and the impression of it using deep-learning techniques.

Estimating impressions from 3D objects can be described as a recognition problem based on classification and regression, in which the objective variable is the impression evaluation value and the explanatory variable is the physical-feature value of the 3D object. Although research on 3D-object recognition was initially focused on the design of 3D features [14], recently, end-to-end learning and recognition methods using deep neural networks (DNNs) have become mainstream. Recognition methods based on this DNN can be roughly classified as RGBD-based [15, 16], Point Cloud-based [17, 18], Voxel-based [19, 20], and multi-view-based [21, 22]. Currently, multi-view-based methods are considered more accurate than others in large-scale 3D-object recognition [23]. Studies of aesthetic estimation of 3D objects using MVCNN [21], a multi-view-based method [9], have been reported. However, there have been no reports on impression estimation of 3D objects. Therefore, we propose constructing an impression estimation model for 3D objects.

In addition, for the selection of impression words to be used in the construction of the impression estimation model, it is necessary to select impressions that are necessary and sufficient for intuitive design support. We have conducted impression evaluation experiments using various abstract shapes based on psychological methods and clarified the structure of impression evaluation that can be common to various 3D shapes [10, 24]. In this study, too, the quantification of impressions of 3D objects is based on psychological methods and takes into account the structure of people's evaluations of 3D objects. This effort yields valid impression evaluation data. Furthermore, by using a multi-view-based DNN, this data set is trained in an end-to-end manner to achieve impression estimation of various 3D objects. The estimation model is constructed using 3D-model data sets of multiple object categories with human impression evaluation data, and we will determine whether the MVCNN, which has shown high-quality performance in the 3D-object recognition task, is also effective in the 3D-object impression estimation task.

3   Modeling the Relationships Between Visual Impressions and Physical Characteristics

In this study, we propose an impression estimation method for 3D objects using a multi-view convolutional neural network (MVCNN) [21]. Figure 1 shows the proposed method's basic design. First, we conduct impression evaluation experiments on 3D objects to quantify the impressions 3D objects evokes. We use the resulting impression distribution as a supervisory signal for the model. The distribution of impressions includes the variability of evaluations caused by differences in individuals' sensory evaluation tendencies. Next, we create a multi-view image of a 3D object rendered from multiple viewpoints and used it as an input signal for the model. Finally, we use a MVCNN to model the relationship between the aforementioned input signal and the supervisory signal to achieve impression estimation of the 3D object. The above basic design enables us to verify the task of impression estimation of 3D objects using MVCNN.

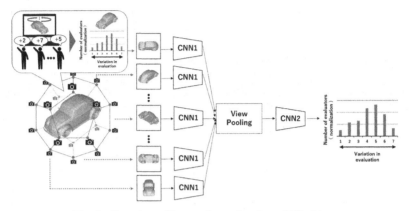

Fig. 1. Overview of impression estimation of 3D objects

4 Building an Impression Estimation Model

4.1 Data Set

In this section, we show how to create the dataset needed to build the impression estimation model.

Collection and Selection of 3D Model Data. We collected and selected 3D model data. To ensure the diversity and comprehensiveness of shape expressions, we collected 3D models from ShapeNet [23], ModelNet40 [25], and CG DATA BANK [26], which are large-scale databases of 3D models. As a result, we collected 3D model data from the Car (632 models), Vase (575 models), and Chair categories (985 models).

Rendering a 3D Model Data for Multi-viewpoints Images and Stimulus Presentation Video. We used the 3D model to create experimental stimuli. There are two types of experimental stimuli: multi-view images used as input signal for the estimation model and images for impression evaluation experiments. We used the experimental images to present to the subjects when they evaluated the impressions the 3D model evokes. The common pre-processing for creating both experimental stimuli is shown below. First, we obtained each 3D model's size, and we standardized their sizes among the models by scale conversion based on the values. Next, we used the local reference frame (LRF) to unify the 3D models' postures. We describe the rendering method below. We used Phong's reflection model for rendering. We rendered the multi-view image from each vertex of the dodecahedron in the direction of the center of gravity of the 3D model encapsulated in the dodecahedron. In this way, we created a set of 20 multi-view images. To render the experimental images, we set the camera position at 18° vertical to the ground to capture the 3D model rotating in the horizontal direction.

Assigning Impression Evaluation Values. To quantify the impressions of 3D objects, we conducted impression evaluation experiments using the semantic differential method (SD) based on the findings of previous studies [24]. We used three adjective pairs, "soft-hard," "gay-sober," and "stable-stable," as evaluation words. We selected these adjective pairs based on the findings of a previous study [24] that the three factors (evaluation, activity, and potency) [27] that frequently appear in SD studies also constitute the main criteria for impressions of 3D shapes. In the evaluation of impressions, we presented the images for the aforementioned impression evaluation experiment, and we evaluated the impressions from various directions comprehensively. As a result of the experiment, we obtained 7 levels (-3 to $+3$) of impression evaluation values for the three adjective pairs. Next, we numerically assigned the seven ratings (-3 to $+3$) to class labels from 1 to 7, and we used the discrete probability distributions as the impression distributions in the 3D model. Because the number of raters differed among the samples, we normalized the impression distribution by the number of raters in each sample. We used the normalized impression distribution as the supervisory signal for the estimation model. Table 1 shows the specification of the created data set.

In this study, we conducted the impression evaluation experiment by crowdsourcing, so the evaluation data was cleaned from the content and response time of the subjects. We describe the cleaning procedure below. (1) We designated experimental participants who could not successfully complete the evaluation due to malfunction of the response system or network conditions as unevaluated respondents and eliminated all of their evaluation data. (2) We checked experimental participants who answered 0 (middle of the 7-point scale: neither) to one or more models, and considered insincere respondents, and all of their evaluation data were eliminated. (3) We checked the distribution of the insincere respondents' response time, and we designated the experimental participants who finished their responses in 156 s or less, which was the most frequent value, as short-time respondents and eliminated all of their evaluation data. As a result, of the 6101 total respondents, 388 were unevaluated respondents, 628 were dishonest respondents, and 307 were short-time respondents, so the final number of valid respondents was 4778.

Table 1. Data set specifications

3D object category	Car Vase Chair
Number of sample	632 575 985
Database	ShapeNet, ModelNet40, CG DATA BANK
Number of evaluations per model	20-40 people
Experiment participants	Men and women (ages 20-60)
Presentation format of the 3D model	Model rotation video
Evaluated word	3 adjective pairs
Rating scale	7-step SD

Table 2. Detail of DNN architecture

Layer		Input size	Output size	Kernel	Stride
CNN1	conv1	227 × 227 × 3	55 × 55 × 96	11 × 11	4
	maxpool1	55 × 55 × 96	27 × 27 × 96	3 × 3	2
	conv2	27 × 27 × 96	27 × 27 × 256	5 × 5	1
	maxpool2	27 × 27 × 256	13 × 13 × 256	3 × 3	2
	conv3	13 × 13 × 256	13 × 13 × 384	3 × 3	1
	conv4	13 × 13 × 384	13 × 13 × 384	3 × 3	1
	conv5	13 × 13 × 384	13 × 13 × 256	3 × 3	1
	maxpool3	13 × 13 × 256	6 × 6 × 2526	3 × 3	2
View pooling		20 × 9216	9216	–	–
CNN2	fc1	9216	4608	–	–
	fc2	4608	4608	–	–
	fc3	4608	7	–	–

4.2 Training

In this study, we used a 3D model database (632 car categories, 575 vase categories, and 985 chair categories) with the impression distribution shown in Sect. 4.1 for model training and evaluation. We constructed the model using a total of nine combinations of object categories and adjective pairs. For cross-validation, we divided the data set into train, validation, and test (8:1:1) and adopted a 9-fold cross-validation.

Next, we describe the structure of the DNNs we used in the model (Table 2). The structure of the CNN1 layer is based on AlexNet. The CNN1 layer shares the weights in the CNN to be optimized with each viewpoint. The view-pooling layer smooths the image features of each viewpoint output from the CNN1 layer into one dimension, combines them in the row direction, and extracts the values of the viewpoint with the largest value one column at a time. In other words, the view-pooling layer is responsible for selecting the viewpoints that are effective for impression estimation. The activation function for the output layer is the softmax function. We used Adam as the optimization algorithm for training. To avoid the gradient vanishing problem that is a concern in DNNs, we used rectified linear units as the activation function. The loss function is the cross-entropy error. We set the learning rate to 0.001, the number of epochs to 300 for the Car and Vase category and 200 for the Chair category.

5   Results and Discussions

To verify the proposed method's effectiveness, we conducted a validation experiment using several comparison methods, 3D ShapeNets [19], a Voxel-based method, and single-view CNN (SVCNN), which inputs a single-view image to the proposed method.

We used correlation coefficients and mean squared errors as evaluation measures of estimation accuracy. We calculated the correlation coefficient by converting the distribution of human impressions and the estimation results (estimated impression distribution) into expected values. We calculated the mean squared error from the sum of the errors of each class in the human impression distribution and the estimated impression distribution.

Table 3. Average of Correlation coefficient (LCC) and Mean squared error (MSE)

Car

Method	Input Format	soft-hard		gay-sober		stable-unstable	
Index	-	LCC	MSE	LCC	MSE	LCC	MSE
3D ShapeNets	voxel	-0.10	0.06	0.07	0.09	0.01	0.07
SVCNN	single-image	0.54	0.05	0.72	0.05	0.21	0.05
MVCNN	multi-image	0.60	0.05	0.78	0.05	0.31	0.05

Vase

Method	Input Format	soft-hard		gay-sober		stable-unstable	
Index	-	LCC	MSE	LCC	MSE	LCC	MSE
3D ShapeNets	voxel	0.01	0.08	0.07	0.09	-0.06	0.14
SVCNN	single-image	0.32	0.05	0.48	0.05	0.65	0.06
MVCNN	multi-image	0.46	0.04	0.54	0.04	0.74	0.05

Chair

Method	Input Format	soft-hard		gay-sober		stable-unstable	
Index	-	LCC	MSE	LCC	MSE	LCC	MSE
3D ShapeNets	voxel	0.10	0.08	-0.28	0.11	0.16	0.09
SVCNN	single-image	0.58	0.05	0.59	0.05	0.62	0.05
MVCNN	multi-image	0.60	0.05	0.60	0.05	0.62	0.05

5.1 Overall Performance

Table 3 shows the average of the correlation coefficients and mean squared errors obtained in each verification. Table 3 shows that the proposed method showed a strong positive correlation in two of the nine conditions and a moderate positive correlation in six conditions. We thus confirmed the proposed method's practical effectiveness.

Next, we confirm the superiority of the proposed method over the comparison methods. The estimation accuracy of the proposed method is much better than that of 3D ShapeNets. In the comparison between the proposed method and SVCNN, we confirmed that the accuracy of the proposed method is higher than that of SVCNN, although the improvement is not as high as that of 3D ShapeNets. In particular, the correlation coefficients of the proposed method improved by about 0.1, compared to SVCNN in the "soft-hard" condition of the Vase category. In the next section, we will discuss the comparison of methods and object categories.

5.2 Comparison of the Proposed Method with Each Comparison Method

To compare the methods' accuracy, we conducted a multiple comparison test using the Dunnett method with the proposed method (MVCNN) as the control group and each compared method as the treatment group. The alternative hypothesis is $\mu c > \mu i$ (μc: mean value of the correlation coefficient or mean square error of the control group, μi: mean value of the correlation coefficient or mean square error of the treatment group).

First, we compare MVCNN to 3D ShapeNets. The results of the significance test between the proposed method (MVCNN) and 3D ShapeNets showed that both indices were significantly different ($p < 0.05$) in 9 out of 9 conditions. This result can be attributed to the fact that MVCNN's input signal has a higher resolution than that of 3D ShapeNets. On the other hand, 3D ShapeNets is a method that shows a high recognition rate of about 77% in the 3D object recognition task [19]. When we applied this method to the impression estimation task, the estimation accuracy decreased significantly. This result suggests that the impression estimation task requires a higher-resolution representation of the object shape than the 3D object recognition task.

Next, we compare the MVCNN and the SVCNN. The results of the significance test between the proposed method (MVCNN) and SVCNN differed in the evaluation indices. The correlation coefficient showed a significant difference ($p < 0.05$) in five conditions. In contrast, the mean squared error was not significantly different in all nine conditions. These results can be attributed to the different nature of the two evaluation indices. In this study, we calculated the correlation coefficient from the expected value of the separation probability distribution. Because the expected value is weighted by the probability of belonging to each class in the impression distribution, it is more suitable for evaluating the global trend of the distribution than the mean square error. The fact that the proposed method showed significant differences only in the correlation coefficient indicates that the proposed method captures the global tendency of the impression distribution, i.e., the tendency of the variation of people's impression evaluation, better than SVCNN. In other words, we suggest that the proposed method captures the tendency of the variability of human impression evaluation better by using the shape information from multiple viewpoints rather than from a single viewpoint.

5.3 Comparison of Impression Estimates for Each Object Category

We focus on three object categories. In all object categories, the estimation accuracy of the proposed method is better than that of SVCNN. However, there are some conditions where the effect of using MVCNN is stronger and some conditions where it is weaker, depending on the inherent properties and structures related to the shapes of the object categories. Specifically, the estimation accuracy of the Car category and the Vase category tends to be improved by using MVCNN, while the accuracy of the Chair category remains unchanged. From these results, we can confirm that the proposed method is superior to SVCNN, especially in the object category condition where the appearance and impression of the shape changes depending on the viewpoint. We believe that quantifying the impressions of 3D objects for each viewpoint and learning the distribution of impressions will be effective in improving the estimation accuracy. Furthermore, the introduction of an EMD-based loss function can be used to improve the accuracy [8].

5.4   Relationship Between Estimated Evaluation Value and 3D Models

In this section, we will visually check the relationship between the model's estimation results and the 3D object's shape. We assigned estimated evaluation values to the data for test and converted them to expected values. For each combination of object category and evaluation term, we adopted the model with the highest accuracy in the cross-validation for estimation. For each object category, we sorted the expected values in descending order and identified the top and bottom 15 samples. Figure 2, 3, and 4 show the results.

From the results in Fig. 2, we can see that the impression estimation model we have developed is mainly based on the "soft-hard" condition of the Car category in terms of shapes such as corners, straight lines, curves, and curved surfaces; the "gay-sober" condition in terms of shapes such as overlapping surfaces and edges; the "stable-unstable" condition was mainly characterized by characteristics such as height and length. Next, with the results in Fig. 3, we confirmed that the "soft-hard" condition of the Vase category was characterized mainly by the shapes of corners, straight lines, curves, and curved surfaces and that the "gay-sober" condition was characterized mainly by the shapes of overlapping surfaces and edges. Finally, from the results in Fig. 4, we confirmed that

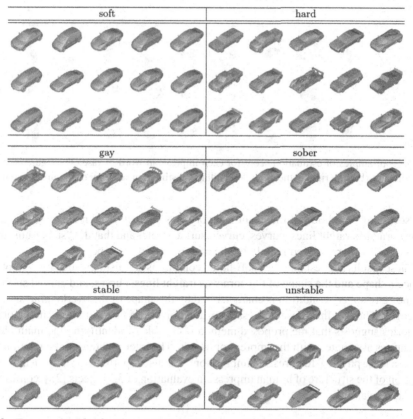

Fig. 2. Top samples of estimation score for each impression word in car. The figure is sorted from top left to bottom right in the order descending of estimation score for each impression word.

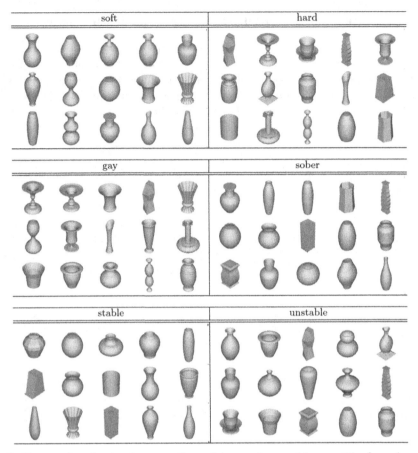

Fig. 3. Top samples of estimation score for each impression word in vase. The figure is sorted from top left to bottom right in the order descending of estimation score for each impression word.

the "soft-hard" condition of the Chair category was characterized mainly by the shape of the corners, straight lines, curves, curved surfaces, etc. and that the "stable-unstable" condition was characterized mainly by the bottom surface's shape.

These results suggest that the "soft-hard" conditions are distinguished by the bottom surface's shape and the shape of the corners, straight lines, curves, and curved surfaces, and the "gay-sober" condition is characterized by the shape of the overlapping surfaces and edges. The fact that these impression evaluation criteria are common among object categories suggests that the proposed method is capable of identifying the main physical features associated with the impression words. The interpretation of the relationship between these physical features and impressions was also reported in a study on the quantification of the structure of human impression evaluation of 3D objects [28], confirming our claim's validity.

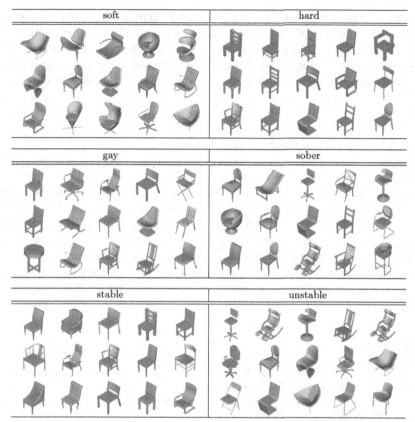

Fig. 4. Top samples of estimation score for each impression word in chair. The figure is sorted from top left to bottom right in the order descending of estimation score for each impression word.

On the other hand, some conditions made it difficult to interpret the relationship between impressions and shape, such as Chair's "gay-sober" and Vase's "stable-unstable" conditions. For such conditions, it is considered possible to capture the relationship visually between shape and impression by using visualization techniques such as Grad-Cam [29], which can explain CNN's decision criteria.

6 Conclusion

The ultimate goal of this study was to provide intuitive design support for 3D objects, and as a first attempt, we proposed an impression estimation method for 3D objects. We used a multi-view convolutional neural network to estimate impressions of various 3D objects. For training and evaluation of the estimation model, we used 3D model data, to which we added impression evaluation data. To ensure the validity of the impression evaluation data, quantification of the impressions evoked by the 3D objects was based on psychological methods.

In the validation experiments, we estimated the impression distributions of three adjective pairs ("soft-hard," "gay-sober" and "stable-unstable") for three object categories (Car, Vase, and Chair). The estimation results of the estimation model and the distribution of human impressions showed more than moderate positive correlations in eight out of nine conditions, confirming the proposed method's practical effectiveness. In addition, in the verification of the accuracy by the correlation coefficient, we confirmed that the proposed method has greater estimation accuracy than the comparative method and captures the global tendency of the impression distribution, that is, the tendency of the variation of the human impression evaluation.

In addition, we used the impression estimation model trained by the proposed method to check the relationship visually between the estimation results and 3D objects. As a result, we confirmed that the "soft-hard" condition was associated with shapes such as corners, straight lines, curves, and curved surfaces and that the "gay-sober" condition was associated with shapes such as overlapping surfaces and edges. The fact that these relationships are common among object categories suggests that the proposed method is capable of interpreting the physical features associated with the impression words.

For future work, we need to visualize the basis of judgment for impression estimation toward the ultimate goal of this research, which is to support intuitive design of 3D objects.

References

1. Kurita, T., Kato, T., Fukuda, I., Sakakura, A.: Sense retrieval on a image database of full color paintings. IPSJ J. **33**(11), 1373–1383 (1992)
2. Ogino, A., Kato, T.: Kansei system modeling: design method for Kansei retrieval systems. IPSJ J. **47**(SIG4(TOD29)), 28–39 (2006)
3. Ota, S., Takenouchi, H., Tokumaru, M.: Kansei retrieval of clothing using features extracted by deep neural network. Trans. Japan Soc. Kansei Eng. **16**(3), 227–283 (2017)
4. Chen, Y., Huang, X., Chen, D., Han, X.: Generic and specific impressions estimation and their application to kansei-based clothing fabric image retrieval. Int. J. Pattern Recognit. Artif. Intell. **32**(10), 1854024 (2018)
5. Mukae, A., Kato, T.: Modeling visual impression on shapes and material textures of 3D objects. IPSJ J. **47**(SIG8(TOD30)), 134–146 (2006)
6. Lee, W., Luo, M.R., Ou, L.: Assessing the affective feelings of two- and three-dimensional objects. Color. Res. Appl. **34**(1), 75–83 (2009)
7. Wang, L., Wang, X., Yamasaki, T., Aizawa, K.: Aspect-ratio-preserving multipatch image aesthetics score prediction. In: 2019 IEEE/CVF Conference on Computer Vision and Pattern Recognition Workshops (CVPRW), pp. 1833–1842. IEEE, Long Beach (2019)
8. Talebi, H., Milanfar, P.: NIMA: Neural Image Assessment. IEEE Trans. Image Process. **27**(8), 3998–4011 (2018)
9. Dev, K., Lau, M.: Learning perceptual aesthetics of 3-D shapes from multiple views. IEEE Comput. Graphics Appl. **42**(1), 20–31 (2022)
10. Katahira, K., Muto, K., Hashimoto, S., Tobitani, K., Nagata, N.: The hierachical approach to semantic differential method - the equivocality of evaluation factor in the EPA structure -. Trans. Japan Soc. Kansei Eng. **17**(4), 453–463 (2018)
11. Sibley, F.: Aesthetic concepts. Philosop. Rev. **68**(4), 421–450 (1959)
12. Back, J., Jr., Kahol, K., Tripathi, P., Kuchi, P., Panchanathan, S.: Indexing natural images for retrieval based on kansei factors. Hum. Vis. Electron. Imag. IX **5292**, 363–375 (2004)

13. Chen, Y., Chen, D., Han, X., Huang, X.: Generic and specific impression estimation of clothing fabric images based on machine learning. In: 2015 12th International Conference on Fuzzy Systems and Knowledge Discovery (FSKD), pp. 1753–1757. IEEE, Zhangjiajie (2015)

14. Hashimoto, M., Akizuki, S., Takei, S.: A survey and technology trends of 3D features for object recognition. Electron. Commun. Japan **100**(11), 31–42 (2017)

15. Lai, K., Bo, L., Ren, X., Fox, D.: Sparse distance learning for object recognition combining RGB and depth information. In: 2011 IEEE International Conference on Robotics and Automation, pp. 4007–4013. IEEE, Shanghai (2011)

16. Song, X., Herranz, L., Jiang, S.: Depth cnns for RGB-D scene recognition: Learning from scratch better than transferring from RGB-CNNs. In: Thirty-first AAAI Conference on Artificial Intelligence, vol. 28, Issue 2, pp. 4271–4277. San Francisco (2017)

17. Li, J., Chen, B.M., Lee, G.H.: SO-Net: Self-organizing network for point cloud analysis. In: 2018 IEEE/CVF Conference on Computer Vision and Pattern Recognition, pp. 9397–9406. IEEE, Salt Lake (2018)

18. Deng, H., Birdal, T., Ilic, S.: PPFNet: Global context aware local features for robust 3d point matching. In: 2018 IEEE/CVF Conference on Computer Vision and Pattern Recognition, pp. 195–205. IEEE, Salt Lake (2018)

19. Wu, Z., Shuran, S., Khosla, A., Yu, F., Zhang, L., Tang, X., Xiao, J.: 3D ShapeNets: a deep representation for volumetric shapes. In: 2015 IEEE Conference on Computer Vision and Pattern Recognition (CVPR), pp. 1912–1920. IEEE, Boston (2015)

20. Sedaghat, N., Zolfaghari, M., Amiri, E., Brox, T.: Orientation-boosted voxel nets for 3D object recognition. arXiv:1604.03351 (2017)

21. Su, H., Maji, S., Kalogerakis, E., Learned-Miller, E.: Multi-view convolutional neural networks for 3D shape recognition. In: 2015 IEEE International Conference on Computer Vision (ICCV), pp. 945–953. IEEE, Santiago (2015)

22. Kanezaki, A., Matsushita, Y., Nishida, Y.: RotationNet: joint object categorization and pose estimation using multiviews from unsupervised viewpoints. In: 2018 IEEE/CVF Conference on Computer Vision and Pattern Recognition, pp. 5010–5019. IEEE, Salt Lake City (2018)

23. Large-scale 3D shape retrieval from ShapeNet Core55 Homepage. https://shapenet.cs.stanford.edu/shrec17/

24. Katahira, K., et al.: Major factor in kansei evaluation of 3D objects. Trans. Japan Soc. Kansei Eng. **15**(4), 563–570 (2016)

25. Modelnet40 Homepage. https://modelnet.cs.princeton.edu/

26. Cgdata bank Homepage. https://cgdatabank.com/

27. Osgood, C., Suci, G., Tannenbaum, P.: The Measurement of Meaning. University of Illinois Press (1957)

28. Miyai, S., Katahira, K., Sugimoto, M., Nagata, N., Nikata, K., Kawasaki, K.: Hierarchical structuring of the impressions of 3D shapes targeting for art and non-art university students. In: Stephanidis, C. (ed.) HCII 2019. CCIS, vol. 1032, pp. 385–393. Springer, Cham (2019). https://doi.org/10.1007/978-3-030-23522-2_50

29. Selvaraju, R.R., Das, A., Vedantam, R.: Grad-CAM: why did you say that? arXiv:1611.07450 (2016)

Author Index

Printed in the United States
by Baker & Taylor Publisher Services

Printed in the United States
by Baker & Taylor Publisher Services